# I Am
# My Father's
# Child

*In HIS Presence I Am Free*

# ANTOINETTE PENICK

**DLG Publishing**

DLG Publishing

ISBN: 978-0-578-15659-0

PRINTED IN THE UNITED STATES OF AMERICA

*DJ and Dominique, You were my reasons for living*
*when I could see no other.*

*~~~~ Sugga Mama Loves You*

# My Praise

*J*esus is my Lord and Savior. God is my all and all. No man shall come before Him and no other God shall receive my Praise for there is only one. To God be the Glory. I will Honor and Praise You all the days of my life. You have given me the Victory. Lord I Thank You.

*L*ove, Grace, and Mercy from You, showered over me as I went through my trials and my tribulations. When my pain was so deep that no words would come from my mouth only uttered moans, You heard and understood me. When my face was washed with tears, You comforted me. And it was You Lord that shields me when the enemy thought he had me. Lord I Thank You.

*W*hen my mind and flesh were weak, You were patient with me Lord. You never left me or forsake me. Who am I but a mere vessel? I am honored that You choose me. I raise my hands and voice to sing Hallelujah so that my praise can be heard from the Heavens. I am not ashamed to say that I never could have or would have made it without you Lord. I Thank You.

# Contents

**My Own
Beginning......
Part III**

# In the Beginning

# PART I

# Chapter 1

**FEAR WAS INTRODUCED** to me at a very young age and unfortunately it would affect a great deal of my life. I can only assume that fear became a part of my daily life because it was thought of as a way of getting respect. Day to day I lived in fear. Surviving one day only to wake up having to survive the next wasn't of much comfort to me. Dealing with Fear would become something normal for me. I came to learn how to endure its physical pain, but mentally I was no match. There would be nowhere to hide. No matter how much I would wish for its demolishment it seemed indestructible. In my innocence I was nice to Fear thinking that it would deter Fear from its evil ways. I learned that Fear had no conscience. One particular night Fear would place me at Death's door, but Faith would be there to answer it instead.

Somehow, knowing the damage Fear caused and created it was still allowed to stay and dwell. I could never understand why it wasn't made to leave. Even though I never saw Fear rise up against anyone besides myself, I could only guess that it had other ways of having power over others. But a part of me would never accept that as a reason for someone not protecting what belonged to them. The love, trust, and security that a child comes to expect from its mother would forever be lost for me with every new man that entered into my mother's life. Some say you can never miss what you never had. But you can when you know it should have been there.

Years would pass before I found the strength inside of me to confront Fear. Nervously, but yet strong I stared Fear in the eyes and without saying a word I told Fear that I had had enough. Fear had taken so much from me; I could not allow it to take anymore. One day Fear would disappear out of my sight but not out of my life. Even long after its reign, I was still reminded of its power. Unfortunately, where Fear left off another force would step in and take its place causing other uneasy situations in my life. And still there was no protection from it. Now in my early teens, yet again I find myself searching for strength within to stand up to this Thief only to tell him no more would he take what was not given, offered or gifted unto him.

One thing that I had to learn if I was going to survive this was, even though I could not control my circumstances I could not allow my circumstances to control me.

Because of the many trials and tribulations that I have been through in my life, I am reminded of a greater power; GOD. He made me the person that I am. His hands formed me. I am here because God's plan allows me to be here at this time in life to fulfill His purpose. I know that I am not here by chance but by God's Favor. It wasn't until I realized who I belonged to that I understood my purpose in life. And when I looked back over my life, God let no weapon that was formed against me to prosper. Because I Am...My Father's Child.

<hr>

I guess that I should start from the beginning so you can understand my story. Up state Detroit, Michigan in the early 70's is where my story starts and my roots lay. The earliest time that I can remember, I guess I was about five years old. That would put me in the year 1976. It was my mama, older sister who was seven and myself living at my grandparent's house; my mama's parents. My grandparents had a big house. That's because they had a big family, nine children all together; four boys and five girls. In this two story house, there were two bedrooms up stairs where the girls sleep and three more down stairs where the boys slept. Pleaded fabric shutter doors in the upstairs hallway were easy to spot at the top of the stairs. They lead into the apartment that Granddaddy had made from the attic. It had a big living room. I remember sitting on the white linoleum floor watching cartoons while mama braided my hair. The bedroom had enough room to fit a queen bed and a set of bunk beds and that's where we all slept. I got the feeling that it had been home for us for a while.

The house was always busy with everyone running around doing whatever it was that they had to do that day. But one day, it was a little bit busier than most. We were all upstairs when all of a sudden we heard some yelling coming from downstairs. We jumped up and raced downstairs to see what all the commotion was about. I saw my grandma standing in the middle of the living room looking out the window. I looked over at the front door as it stood wide open. I could see Granddaddy outside throwing water on my mama's mustard color mustang. It had mysteriously caught on fire while everyone was in the house. Ignoring granddaddy's instructions to stay in the house; mama ran outside to help granddaddy throw more water on the car in hopes to put the fire out. But no matter how much water they threw on the car the fire keep coming. In her concern grandma kept yelling out the front door for them to get away from the car before it blew up. Realizing that they were going to need some more help, grandma finally called the fire department. Sis and I couldn't believe what was going on. The fire grew stronger and after a while all we could do was stand back and let the fire have its way. Several minutes went by before the fire department came and finally put the fire out. I just remember thinking how dead the car looked. There was nothing left but a black frame of a car with smoke rising from it sitting there on two round spheres that use to be tires.

Everyone was talking back and forth to each other. In all the excitement I could have sworn I heard my grandma say that my mama's boyfriend might have had set the car on fire. My grandma wasn't much for words but when she did speak, she spoke the truth. But I thought to myself; that's not nice, my daddy wouldn't do something like that. In her truth grandma wasn't talking about my daddy but indeed my mother's boyfriend. Mama's boyfriend, who was grandma talking about? I never saw any man around besides granddaddy and my uncles.

I would later learn that my daddy died when I was only one and a half years old and that it was shortly after his death that we came to live with my grandparents. Sadden by the fact that I would never get to meet my father, my whole outlook on life would change. For a long period of time I would be left to carry a sense of lost and emptiness because my mother never spoke of my father while we were young. I never went to visit a grave site or seen pictures of my father while I was young either. I soon came too realized as a child there are a lot of things that you don't understand or know and that is something adults come to depend on.

In the early fall of that same year my mama brought home a baby boy. She named him Willie after his father. At my young age, I didn't know where he came from. I didn't remember mama walking around the house with a big belly or anyone talk of a baby coming. I just remembering mama taking this baby out of his carrier so she could give him a bath and telling me that it was my baby brother. I didn't think much of him. I just wondered; where was his daddy at? It wouldn't be long before I would know the answer to that.

Late one night, I awoke and to my surprise I was on the floor at the foot of my mama's bed. I didn't notice if my sister was next to me but if she wasn't, she had to have been somewhere nearby. The first thought that came to mind was why I even was on the floor and not in my bed; I had never slept on the floor before. The room was quiet and the only light was that from the moon that shined in through the bedroom window above my mama's bed. Not hearing or seeing anything, I decided to check and see if mama was in her bed since I wasn't in mine. I slowly got up on my knees and peaked over the foot rail of the big bed. To my surprise, there they all were positioned in the bed like they were the royal court. The king sat in the middle big and tall; Big Willie we would come to call him. To his left lay his queen; my mama. And on his right arm rested his new born prince: my little brother. I felt like me and my sister had become ladies in waiting. Big Willie said nothing just greeted me with a mean stare. I looked over at mama who was woke but I could tell that she had no intention of moving from beside this man. Only a sheet would cover their naked bodies. "Lay back down and go back to sleep," my mother told me. She sounded different. Something in her voice wasn't right. I laid back down wondering if it was because of Big Willie that she sounded so different. What kind of power did he have over her? Unfortunately I would learn soon enough of this power first hand.

Still living with my grandparents, mama now had three mouths to feed and no man around. After that night of seeing my little brother's father, I didn't see him around at all. I don't think granddaddy liked him too much; Grandma neither for that matter.

Days turned into months and life went on as usual. One day mama got us all dressed up to go take a family portrait; father's not included. I think my baby brother was about nine months or a year old around this time because he was able to sit up on his own and he had two little teeth. Mama had me and my older sister Sis dressed in our yellow cotton turtle necks and brown pants. She put our hair in three pretty pony tails. Still to this day when I look at that picture of the four of us, the smiles on our young faces seem to say that we were happy. But there was no smile on my mother's face. It seems as if she tried to force a smile but it just wouldn't come through. Her eyes seemed to be filled with sadness. It always made me wonder what demons she was fighting. It may sound crazy but that picture is the only proof that I have that at one point and time I did have some happiness in my childhood even if it was for only a short period of time.

# Chapter 2

**AS I AWOKE** one morning to my surprise I wasn't at my grandparents' house anymore in our upstairs apartment, but we were in a new house. We must have moved in the middle of the night while I was sleep. It seemed like we had moved so far away from my grandparents but we were only four blocks down the road on the opposite side of the street. I was happy to know that if I stood in front of the new house on the sidewalk that I could look down the street and see grandma if she was standing on the sidewalk in front of her house. We were now living in a small white house on the corner with a fenced in yard.

I shared a room with my Sis. I never got to see much of my sister during the day since she was in school and I wasn't. Only when it was time to go to bed did I see my sister and my baby brother; who still remained a stranger to me for the most part. It seemed like we were always separated from each other even though we all lived in the same house. I did stay in my room a lot since there was no one to play with. My brother's father Big Willie was living with us now. We never called him daddy, not that I would have anyway. But the house felt weird, not like at my grandparents' where it was happy. Here everything felt serious. Some days we all seemed like a family and other days we seemed like strangers and then there were days when all hell would break out. On good days music was always being played around the house and Big Willie would usually have some of his friends over. I never saw my aunts or uncles come to our house to visit, which I thought was very strange since they were such a tight family. Mama never had any of her friends over either which I thought was even stranger.

During the spring mama and Big Willie had this big painting party at the new house. Music was blasting, smoke was floating, and glasses were filled with beer or your liquor of choice. Everyone was laughing, talking, dancing and having a good old time. That must have been some good stuff that they were smoking because Big Willie painted this big pink tree on the wall. It looked to be like a family tree. The party went on until the painting was done three days later.

For the next couple of months things were good. We would take evening walks down to my grandparents' house to visit but Big Willie never came with us. As we would walk down the block neighbors had their screen doors and windows open enjoying the night air and listening to Lou Rawls new single "You'll never find" in that deep voice of his. You could hear another neighbor playing "Me and Mrs. Jones" by Billy Peter. I so enjoyed our evening walks. I would have preferred to spend my days at my grandparents' house instead of stuck in my room all day.

Usually when mama would go to the store, it would be just her and I, while Big Willie stayed behind at home with my brother, but this particular day Big Willie came along with us. Sis was at school and I guess my mama had dropped my little brother off at grandma's house because he wasn't in the car with us.

Big Willie was driving and I was sitting in the back seat of the car. "Do you know your ABC's" he asked me. He had this crazy grin on his face. "Yes." I answered, not thinking anything of it. Mama sat in the passenger seat not saying a word looking out the window. "Say them", he demanded. I started saying the alphabet starting with A and ending in Z and I stopped. "Say them again", he ordered me. So I started over again, put I was puzzled by his request when I knew I had said them all the first time. Maybe he didn't hear a letter and so he thought I must didn't know my alphabet. A through Z I repeated and stopped. I said them a little slower this time. I had been watching Sesame Street every morning singing along with them, so when I got to L M N O P the first time I might have ran them all together. I didn't know what he thought he heard me say, but the look on his face let me know that he didn't like it.

Big Willie suddenly stopped the car in the middle of the street. "Get out the car", he told my mama. She just turned and looked at him with a puzzled look on her face. "Get out the damn car", he yelled. The roar of his voice was something I had never heard before. He startled mama so that she jumped in her seat and all she could do was stare at him in disbelief.

I guess mama wasn't moving fast enough for him. Big Willie reached across her lap, grabbed the door handle and flung the door open. "Get out the goddamn car I said." Big Willie made himself very clear. "What are you doing?" mama asked him. I wanted to know too. Big Willie didn't say another word; he just pushed my mama out of the car leaving her standing in the middle of the street. He reached back over and slammed the car door shut. I became so scared and I began to wonder to myself why she was letting this man push her around. Was she going to do anything, like jump back in the car and yell back at him? At that very moment I declared that this man was crazy. I wanted to get out of the car myself but I couldn't without passing by him. I just looked at my mama as she stood hopelessly in the middle of the street. I'm glad no cars were coming; she might have gotten hit by one.

"Get up here", Big Willie said as he turned away from the steering wheel to look at me as I continued to stay in the back seat. He looked bigger than normal to me for some reason. I quickly got up front and sat down where my mama once sat. Instantly he reached across and locked the car door. I think that's when mama finally realized that he was actually going to leave her in the middle of the street. Mama ran up to my side of the car grabbing the door handle trying to open it. "Unlock the door, unlock the door," she yelled as she beat on the window as if she knew what was about to happen next.

I was scared, my head felt like a ping pong ball at the heat of the game. Right, left, right, left; looking at Big Willie who was yelling at me to say the alphabet over and over again and looking at mama who was yelling and beating on the window for me to unlock the car door. Which one do I listen to? I had to make the right choice and quickly. Here I was six years old making life or death decisions for myself. Sitting in the car with Big Willie there was nothing that stood in the way of him grabbing me by the neck and shaking the alphabet out of me. And mama on the other hand had to fight a locked door in order to save my neck. With no chance of her getting through that locked door, I decided to save my own neck and say the alphabet.

"No, start over" Big Willie said hitting the steering wheel with his fist. The next thing I knew, the car started moving; slow at first than it picked up speed. Being careful not to stop saying the alphabet, I looked out the window and all I could see was mama running beside the car yelling for this crazy man to stop the car. I just knew someone in another car that would pass by would see what was going on and stop to help. But there was no such person.

He started driving faster and faster. Mama was no match for the speed of the car. He turned at a corner and then another corner. After a while, I couldn't see mama any more. Big Willie started to laugh, it became like a game to him. He made sharp turns when he approached the corners making me fall up against the car door. Is he going to kill me, I thought to myself. Why didn't mama stand in front of the car so he couldn't drive off? Never mind she probably knew he would be crazy enough to run her over and kept going. Several times he drove around the block while yelling at me and me saying my ABC's. I could always tell when he made a complete circle because there mama would be standing on the sidewalk in the same spot yelling at Big Willie to stop the car and to let me out. The first three times, he never stopped. He would just speed up and start laughing. I guess about the fifth trip around mama started running after the car again. She knew he wasn't going to stop or come to his senses and let me out of the car. But again she disappeared. Even though Big Willie had me trapped in the car that wasn't my biggest fear; it was the thought of me coming around that corner and not seeing my mama standing there on the sidewalk.

I said my alphabet several more times, but Big Willie was still not satisfied with that. "You're going to learn your ABC's." he would say whenever I finished. I don't know who he was listening to but it was obvious that he wasn't listening to me. If this was his way of teaching me something no thanks, I'll learn on my own.

Suddenly the car came to a stop exactly where this whole thing began. Mama ran up to the car on my side crying and screaming, "Let her out of the car, now." I guess by this time Big Willie grew tired of his little game, he gave me a smirk, reached over and unlocked the car door and let me out. Mama grabbed me by the hand and we just started running. I could hear the car following behind us. We never looked back and mama didn't stop running until we reached the police station.

Mama was out of breath but that didn't stop her from trying to explain to the officer behind the big desk what had just taken place in the past thirty minutes. "He kidnapped my daughter." She was finally able to blurt out. "Who kidnapped your daughter ma'am?" The officer asked.

"My boyfriend did." Mama said catching her breath between words. "How?" the officer asked as he looked over at me with a puzzled look on his face as if to say; if this is the child you speak of how can she be kidnapped when she stands right here before us. "He kicked me out of the car and took her. He went driving around the block several times and would not let her out of the car." She went on to explain. "Do you want to press charges?" he asked. There was no answer. "Is the child hurt?" he wanted to know. Mama looked down at me as I stood by her side. Hope of doing the right thing seemed to leave her. "No, she's not hurt and no I don't want to press any charges." She dropped her head and said.

Looking at mama, now I have the puzzled look on my face. You mean to tell me after all that screaming and yelling, crying, and running after the car trying to get me out a locked car cause this crazy man done pulled off leaving you standing in the middle of the street while he plays once, twice, eight times let's go around the block with me scared to death in the car she's not going to press charges. Here's her chance to do something and yet she does nothing.

"Well ma'am", the officer began to say. "You have her back and she's not harmed and you don't want to press charges, my hands are tied." Mama grabbed me by the hand and we walked out of the police station. At the moment I truly believed that Big Willie had some kind of strong control over my mother. Was she blinded by love for him I wondered. Why wasn't the love for her child stronger?

As we walked out of the police station, there was Big Willie parked waiting on us. I looked up at mama then back at the police station building; she still had enough time to change her mind before we got to the car. I wanted to run back in and tell the officer yes we wanted to press charges so he would take Big Willie away, but we never stop walking towards the car and mama never looked back. "Come on and get in the car." He said in his normal voice as if what had happened just thirty minutes ago didn't. If I wasn't convinced before I was definitely convinced now; this man is crazy or on something.

Mama continued walking to the car like she was a zombie or in a trance. I just knew we weren't getting back in the car with that fool. I couldn't have been more wrong. The next thing I knew, Mama was grabbing the handle and opening the car door.

I looked up at mama looking for some type of sign that she had changed her mind, but there was none. Reluctantly I crawled in the back seat of the car as Big Willie held the passenger sit forward. He was trying to act like a gentleman, like in the old movies when the man held the car door for the lady to get in first. But it was too late, he wasn't fooling me. Mama got in the car and closed the door. Big Willie didn't drive off right away. We all just sat there for a moment and didn't say a word. To be honest I was enjoying the quietness. "I'm sorry," Big Willie finally said. More like crazy if you ask me. I was watching him in disbelieve. I didn't hear mama say anything. Then again I guess she must have said something because the car started up and we were on our way.

Needless to say, we never made it to the store. Big Willie dropped me and mama off in front of my grandparents' house. He drove off before we could even make it to the front porch. As soon as I got out the car; I ran to the front door, yanked it open and ran straight to grandma. I fell into her arms hugging her so tight. I had never been so happy to see her in my life. She didn't ask any questions, she just hugged me back. I knew then that I was safe.

You know the weird thing though, Big Willie never asked me to say the alphabet again after that day or anything else for that matter. But he had frightened me so bad with learning the alphabet, that when mama started teaching me my time-tables; I made sure I knew them inside and out. Mama had written them all out on a piece of paper for me. A list of the one's through six's was on the front. Seven's through twelve's were on the back. That paper stayed glued to my hand. I may have even slept with it under my pillow once or twice. Ironically Big Willie never asked me to say them either. And I never heard mama raise her voice at Big Willie ever again about anything.

After the kidnapping incident; mama thought it best that I go stay at my grandparents for a little while. I really didn't mind the visit. At my grandparents' things were so peaceful. Granddad worked during the week and after grandma got everyone off to school; in between her cleaning we would watch her morning game shows, afternoon talk shows, soap operas, and my afternoon cartoons while she got dinner started. On the weekend granddaddy was always fixing things around the house and working on the family station wagon in the garage.

The best part of my grandparents' house was the backyard. I loved running around in the green grass and in between the clean sheets that grandma had hung out on the clothes line to dry. But after a month or so, I ended back at home with mama and Big Willie. There was still no sign of my little brother and older sister.

Things were quiet when I first returned home. To me Big Willie's mood and actions were always clear that he was there for one reason and one reason only; his son. He never took on the role as a father to me and my sister because that wasn't part of his plan. It seemed he would tolerate us because we were there and breathing. But he never acknowledged us as part of this union with him and my mother. In his eyes there was only the three of them. I always felt that my mother knew how Big Willie felt about me and my sister because she always would make sure we were out of sight, out of mind.

I tried not to do anything to make any waves. I felt tense and I was always second guessing myself before I did anything; wondering if this was the way Big Willie would do it. I figured if I did it the way he would he would have no reason to yell at me. When I made my bed in the morning I made sure it was perfect. When I played with my toys I made sure I played quietly and in a small space in my bedroom. Whenever we ate I made sure never to ask for seconds no matter how hungry I was because of how little was put on my plate. I did any and everything not to draw attention to myself and to stay out of Big Willie's way.

Mid-day mama had to go to the store and to my surprise she didn't take me with her. It might've had something to do with me getting a case of the sticky fingers the last time she took me to the store with her. I don't know what came over me. We were standing in line getting ready to check out and there was all that candy just staring back at me on the candy rack. I thought I could help myself to one but mama told me otherwise. So now I'm being left behind with Big Willie who was also watching my baby brother. I guess since everything had been going okay; meaning no crazy outrageous incidents and he had been acting normal, that I would be fine at home with him. I did ask if I could go but mama only told me no and ensured me that she would be right back.

I stood at the front gate and watched as mama got into the yellow cab and drove off. The sky was gray and the wind was blowing, it looked as if it was about to storm. Feeling that I had a better chance surviving the storm than one of Big Willie's outbreaks; I stayed outside and played in the front yard. I was hoping that he wouldn't call me to come into the house.

After a long while later the yellow cab returned with mama in it.

She got out while trying to balance three or four bags in one hand and the biggest purple ball I had ever seen in my life in the other. It had to have been as big as the moon. The wind wasn't of much help; it lifted the huge ball right out her hands. Mama managed to take a couple of steps so to catch up with it before it went too far down the street. She giggled at her efforts after she got the ball back in her hand. I must say that was the first time in a long time that I heard my mama laugh or even seen her smile. I ran out of the yard to help her with the big purple ball. Yeah, it was as big as the moon. "Who is this for?" I asked mama. "It's for you silly."

I never remember mama buying any gifts before. She must have felt bad about what had happened a couple of months ago. But this would be the first of things that mama would buy to make up for Big Willie. It really didn't matter to me why mama bought the big purple ball that was as big as the moon but as I played with it in the front yard I was just glad that the yellow cab brought mama back home.

Many times I would walk down the street to my grandparents' house to spend the day. On my way back home something caught my attention. I passed by a little green and white house and a little girl sat on the steps. I had never seen her before. I noticed she had something on her arms; some type of padding. It started at her wrist and went all the way up to her shoulders. From afar I could see that she had some type of design that covered one whole side of her face. She waved at me and I waved back as I walked by. The further I made it down the street I would turn around to see if she was still sitting on the steps; she was.

A couple days later on my usual route to my grandparents I came pass the green and white house again. And there she was sitting on the steps this time she waved at me and smiled. As I was waving back her mom came outside to give her something to drink. The little girl looked so lonely to me. I knew how she felt. "Can she come to my house and play?" I asked her mom. "She's not well enough to leave the house. I need to keep a close eye on her until she's better," she went on to explain to me. I just dropped my head with disappointment. "But you can come back and play with her here." The little girl sitting on the front steps looked up at me and we both smiled. "Okay than, I'll be back tomorrow." I ran home to tell mama about the little girl who lived down the street in the green and white house.

It didn't matter to me that her face looked different or that she wore these weird things on her arms. I just knew she felt like me, lonely and needed someone to play with like I did. Mama didn't seem to have time for me anymore. She had a one year old baby and her new man to take care of. I've seemed to have lost my place on her list of things to do. I no longer feel important to her anymore. I just felt like she was always sending me away even if it was to my grandmas.

The next day instead of walking to grandma's house I ran to the little green and white house. There she was like she had been many days before sitting on the steps but today she had a big smile and waving happily waiting on me. She was shy at first she would always try to hide the side of her face that had the design on it from me. After a week of playing together, I learned her name was Cindy. Cindy would become my very first and best friend. I didn't mind that she couldn't leave off the steps and that she couldn't leave out her yard. I would bring my baby dolls over to Cindy's house so we could play because she didn't have any toys.

Cindy had the prettiest smile. I would always try not to be rude and stare at the design on her face but I became curious about it. "Cindy, what happened to your face and why do you wear those things on your arms?" I asked carefully. I hope I didn't hurt her feelings by asking. "My old house caught on fire and I was in it." She told me. "It burnt my face and arms real bad. I can't leave off the steps because my mom is scared that I might fall and hurt myself. She doesn't let me have friends because she doesn't want them to tease me because of how I look." Cindy went on to explain. After that day we never talked about the design on her face and the things she wore on her arms ever again. One thing I did notice about Cindy was that her daddy wasn't around either. I wondered if he died in the fire. It was just her and her mom. I think that's was another reason why we connected; we both had experienced lost at a very early age.

Every day I found myself playing at Cindy's house, I was so happy. Days turned into weeks and weeks turned into months. Except for one day on my way to Cindy's house the closer I got couldn't see if she was sitting on the steps. I made it to the fence at her house but Cindy wasn't sitting in her normal place. Maybe she was waiting in the house for me today; maybe we were going to play inside today. I went to knock on the door but there was no answer. It was a sad day. I went back home walking ever so slowly. Where was Cindy? Where was my friend? The next day I went to Cindy's house again. She wasn't sitting on the steps. I didn't bother to stop; I just ran my hands along the top of the fence as I passed it on my way to grandma's house. I didn't see Cindy for a whole week after that. Had I done something? I decided on my way home that I would stop by Cindy's house.

I knocked on the door; Cindy's mom came to the door. "Is Cindy home" I asked. "Yes baby, but she is sick. Come back next week hopefully she will feel better enough so you two can play." How could she be sick? I thought to myself. "Okay then, tell her I stopped by and that I hope she gets better soon."

"Okay, I will." Cindy's mom quickly closed the door as if she was in a rush to get back to whatever she was doing before I stopped by. I guess she had to get back to Cindy. Panic set in as I walked back home. I didn't want Cindy to be sick. There was nothing wrong with Cindy the last time I saw her. Maybe her mom didn't want us to play together anymore. No, that couldn't be it, Cindy's mom was nice. If Cindy doesn't get better that means I have to go back to being by myself again. I don't want to be by myself.

It seemed as if that was the longest week of my life. I couldn't wait until the week was over so I could be able to play with my best friend. I was tired of playing by myself. I had no one to talk to but my baby dolls who didn't talk back.

Early that Saturday morning I darted out the house and ran down the street to Cindy's. It seemed the closer I got to the green and white house the faster I ran. I couldn't wait to see Cindy. I could see someone sitting on the steps. I lit up like a firecracker. By the time I got to the fence, I was out of breath. I could only smile and wave at Cindy who seemed just as happy to see me. She slowly motioned for me to come sit next to her. We acted like we hadn't seen each other in years. I could tell by the way she was moving slowly that I couldn't hug her, I might have hurt her. So instead we just sat and laughed and told it each other about all the things that had happened in the three weeks that we were apart.

Suddenly something came over me. I had missed Cindy so much that I became mad remembering the times that I was alone because she was sick. I wanted her to feel as hurt as I did those days that I didn't get to play with her and not knowing whether I would ever see her again. I turned to Cindy and said "you're ugly." Cindy looked at me confused,

"What did you say?" Cindy asked as she stops combing the baby doll's hair that she was happily playing with. "You're ugly and I hate you." I repeated. I could feel the hatred coming out of my body. "That's not nice." Cindy cried. "So what, I hate you." I really didn't hate Cindy, I was just mad that the pass three weeks I missed my friend. It wasn't fun being alone. I looked at Cindy; her eyes were full of tears. Cindy got up from the stairs, threw down her baby doll and ran in the house crying. I didn't care; Cindy shouldn't have gotten sick and left me by myself for so long.

Cindy's mom came to the door, "go home." She said in a soft voice. I slowly got up from the steps, picked up the baby dolls that Cindy and I had been playing with and walked out of the yard. When I got to the fence I looked back hoping to see my friend standing there on the steps and ask me to come back and play with her, that way I could tell my best friend that I was sorry and really didn't mean what I had said. But Cindy wasn't there.

At that very moment I knew I had just lost my best friend in the whole world. That was the very first time that I was ever mean to someone and I vowed that it would be my last. I had confused myself with the feeling of abandonment from mama at home whom I never saw anymore and her betrayal of loving a man more than protecting me; with Cindy being sick thinking she had done the same to me. But Cindy didn't abandoned or betray me; she just got sick.

No matter how many times I passed by the little green and white house on my way to grandma's; I never saw the little girl with the pretty smile and the design on her face sitting on the steps again.

# Chapter 3

**IT HAD BEEN** a long day and mama was getting everyone settled down and ready for bed, all while being careful to keep us quiet and out of Big Willie's sight as usual. She tucked me and my sister into our bunk-bed, we said our good nights and mama turned off the lights and pulled the door to being carefully not to close it completely. The bathroom light across the hall was still on so that was used as our little night light. I was all settled in bed wearing my powder blue two piece pajamas when all of a sudden, I had to go to the bathroom. Mama had hurried us into bed that she forgot to let us go to the bathroom.

I whispered to my sister who lay in the top bunk that I had to pee. She laid still and quiet at first as if she didn't hear me but I know she did because I kicked her bed where I knew her butt was and suddenly her hand came hanging down from on the side of her bed. That was her sign to me to stop kicking her bed. We had to learn early how to communicate with each other without saying a word. You see, my sister was the quiet one of the two of us. She would avoid anything if it was going to cause trouble. She didn't want to make the mistake of Big Willie walking down the hall and so happen to hear her talking when he was probably told that we were sleep. She hesitated for a while but then when she knew the coast was clear she finally got up the courage and whispered for me to go to the bathroom. I could hear the caution in her voice but I had to pee.

I slowly got out the bed and tip-toed to the bedroom door. I peeked out and looked down the hall. Just so happened mama was walking down the hall in my direction. "What are you doing out of bed?" mama asked me. "I got to pee." Mama walked me to the bathroom. As I sat on the toilet in relief, I heard the doorbell rang. Mama told me to finish up and when I did to wipe off, flush the toilet and go and get back in the bed. I told mama okay and she left out the bathroom to go and answer the door. I sat there for another minute or two after she left.

When I was finished, I did what mama told me to do. I even took the time to wash my hands. I stepped one foot out of the bathroom and ran straight into Big Willie. I panic and froze with fear, where was mama? She should have come back by now from answering the door. But she wasn't and I knew it was too late. "What are you doing out of bed?" Big Willie asked me. "I had to go to the bathroom." I explained. "You better not be lying. When I come back I'm going to check the toilet." First of all when have I ever lied to him, I barely speak to him. And the last time anyone checked my toilet water, I was potty training and since then I've learned how to flush.

Panic and fear set in even more because I knew that when he would go check the toilet that there would be nothing to see because I had already flushed the toilet. I already knew that I was going to get in trouble, I just didn't know to what extent. Big Willie continued down the hall to the living room. I guess he heard the doorbell too. All I could do was make my way to back to my bedroom. I thought about going back to the bathroom to see if I had any more pee left in me, but I already knew that I didn't so there was no use in wasting time.

When I got back to the room, my sister was sleep; I think. I put the door back like mama had it and I crawled back into bed. The bathroom light was still shining into the bedroom. I would watch for Big Willie's shadow to pass by our door as he went to the bathroom to check the toilet, but he never did. The room was so quiet. Sometime had gone by so I thought Big Willie had forgotten about the bathroom incident. He didn't.

Mama later came in the bedroom and told me that Big Willie wanted to see me in the living room. I didn't see mama anymore that night. I walked down the hallway to the living room. Normally the hallway seemed so long, but for some reason tonight it was short. One lamp was on and music was playing. There was a gentleman sitting in the chair who I had never seen before. He must have been the one ringing the doorbell. Big Willie was standing in the middle of the living room. In one hand he held the iron and in the other hand held its cord.

The gentlemen who sat in the chair said nothing. My first thought was that Big Willie was going to plug up the iron and burn me with it. I couldn't see him beating me with the iron. I had only known for people to use the iron for one thing anyway and was to iron clothes. My second thought was where was my mama? And that I knew Big Willie wasn't going to burn me in front of this man.

"What were you doing out of bed?" Big Willie asked me again. I just looked over at the stranger who was still sitting in the chair hoping that he would say something, but he said nothing. "I had to go to the bathroom," I explained to Big Willie again. "Mama took me." I said in hopes that he would know that I wasn't playing around when I should have been in bed. "Go sit on the couch" he said. So many thoughts ran through my young mind. Was he going to burn my hands, maybe even my arms? Will I have to wear those things that Cindy wore? Maybe he was going to burn my face. What was Big Willie going to do to me?

I slowly walked over to the couch and sat down in the middle of it. I looked over at the stranger sitting in the chair once again, and again he said nothing. I looked at Big Willie who was now standing directly in front of me. Big Willie wouldn't dare hit me in front of this man; he was just trying to scare me, right? I sat on the couch not knowing my fate. I just knew my mama would walk into the living room any minute now and stop all of this. She never came because she wasn't there.

Big Willie had talked mama into going to get something to eat for him and his friend. He was such a manipulator. I can only assume that he knew that he had to come up with something to get mama out of the house once he knew what he was going to do. Big Willie raised his hand over his head while holding the extension cord of the iron in it.

I heard a gentle voice in my head that was not mine or anyone's in that room say; "cover your face and put your head down in your lap". Without hesitation, I did what the voice said. Though I wouldn't be able to recall the actual severe beating and pain of that night myself; I can only believe that I had heard the voice of an angel.

I don't remember walking back to my bedroom, so I don't know how I got back in my bed. I would later learn that Big Willie had beaten me until I had passed out. He would be the one to carry me back into my room and put me to bed. When mama returned from her run, she had no idea what had taken place. Big Willie told her to go to the room and check on me. He must have gotten scared thinking that maybe he had gone too far and may have even killed me.

Not thinking anything of his request, mama just stuck her head in the room from the bedroom door using the bathroom light that was still on across the hall. From what she could tell, I was fast asleep and doing just fine. Mama went back to Big Willie and told him that I was asleep and doing just fine. He knew better, for he knew what he had done. He grabbed her tightly by the arm and nearly drags her back down the hall back to my bedroom. He turned on the bedroom light and shoved mama into the room. "Check her again." He ordered.

Mama was horrified by what she saw. What the dark had hidden from her, the light now revealed. There laid what she just knew was my lifeless body all beaten and bloody. Mama said she panic and tried to clean up the mess that Big Willie had made. Once she realized that I wasn't dead but just had passed out, she removed my pajama top and started to clean my wounds. I was told that she laid me on my stomach so that I would rest as comfortably as circumstances would allow.

Not being able to recall any of what happened the night before, the next morning was like any other morning. I got out of bed and I didn't see my sister; which I thought was odd. She must have left for school early. I went to wash my face and brush my teeth. The house seemed awfully quiet for some strange reason. I made my way back to my bedroom. I made my bed and changed out of my pajamas. I put on my brown pants and went in search for my yellow and brown turtle-neck shirt. After looking through my drawers, there it lay in my bottom drawer all neatly folded.

I went to put my shirt over my head, but for some strange reason I couldn't raise my arms up pass my shoulders. I thought that I was do-ing something wrong. This is the same way that I put on my shirt every morning I had never had trouble before. Did someone develop a new way to put on shirts and forget to tell me? I tried putting on my shirt again, but every time I got ready to raise my arms pass my shoulders they would stop. I examined my favorite turtleneck shirt to see if maybe something was attached to it that was keeping me from putting in on. But there was nothing there that I could see. I didn't want to try again by myself, so I went looking for help with my turtleneck.

Making it to the living room I found Big Willie sitting in a chair smoking a cigarette. He looked like he was thinking about something. Not hearing or seeing anyone else, Big Willie would have to do; I couldn't walk around all day without a shirt on. "Willie, I can't put my shirt on." I told him as I handed him my shirt. He didn't take it. "I know," he said as he put out his cigarette. I looked at him totally puzzled. How did he know I couldn't put on my shirt? Oh wait, I know somebody told him and he was going to wait until this morning to tell me. I get it now. "Willie I can't put my shirt on," I told him the second time so that he would show me the new way. But again he didn't take the shirt from me. He just passed by me as I stood in the middle of the living room and walked towards the kitchen. "Oh, don't worry about that now," he said "just come and eat you some breakfast." He said in a nice voice. There was a bowl and a box of TRIX cereal which was my favorite, sitting on the breakfast table. I had a seat and Big Willie poured me a bowl and some milk. When I was at grandma's house, she use to leave the cereal box out so I could look at all the cartoons and games on the cereal box, but when I was back at home Big Willie never let us leave the box out on the table. But this morning he did. "Your mama will help you with your shirt when she comes back." Big Willie said as he went and sat back down in the chair in the living room and lit another cigarette.

Where was mama at anyway? I thought to myself. It was awfully early for her to have left to go to the store. Maybe she took my sister to school, but it was still too early for that too. Eating my cereal and enjoying the cartoons on the box got my mind off where my mama could have gone.

I was done eating my cereal and about to drink my milk from the bowl when all of a sudden the front door flew open and scared the crap out of me. Four police officers charged into the house and went straight for Big Willie who had jumped up out of his chair. The police were pointing their guns at him and yelling for him to get down on the floor. I dropped my bowl on the table, what in the world was going on? They all wrestled Big Willie down to the floor and put handcuffs on him. Where is my mama? The next thing I know people with big cameras and big bright lights and funny looking microphones were coming through the door. There was still no sign of my mama. It was so loud in the house. Everyone was talking and yelling, taking pictures and asking Big Willie questions as the police took him out the house. Still scared as crap and not knowing what is really going on, I was still sitting at the breakfast table when mama finally came in the house with a nurse who was all dressed in white walking behind her. I grabbed my shirt and ran to her. "Mama, I can't put on my shirt, Big Willie said that you would help me when you got here." Mama just looked down at me at first and smiled softly, not saying a word. She looked worried about something. The nurse then came over to me and she also softly smiled, she turned me around so to take a look at my back as though something was on it. "Don't worry; you're going to be okay." I wasn't worried and what was she talking about. I just wanted my shirt on. "Mama, I need my shirt on." The nurse took the shirt out of my hand and gently put it on for me. "You're going to take a little ride with me okay," the nurse told me. I looked over at mama who was now holding my coat in her hand. "Are you coming too mama?" I asked my mama. It had been a lot going on this morning and I wasn't about to just leave with this stranger. "Yes baby," mama said. "I'm coming with you."

The nurse led me outside to a hospital red and white station wagon that was waiting for us. I kept looking back to make sure that mama was close behind me. "Mama, where are we going?" I asked "its okay baby. We're just going for a ride." Mama and the nurse just kept walking never saying a word to each other. An ambulance was also parked along the street in front of the house. The crowd of people with the cameras had surrounded the police car, but I could still see Big Willie who sat in the back seat.

We all climbed into the back seat of the station wagon. I sat in the middle between mama and the nurse. The nurse told the driver to take us to the hospital. "Everything is going to be okay." The nurse assured me again. Still being confused on why the nurse kept saying that and all that had happened that morning, I turned to mama and asked why we were going to the hospital. Mama didn't say a word; she just pulled me close to her and hugged me oh so gently. She never let me out of her arms the whole ride. The nurse gave me two little white pills and told me to swallow them. I looked up at mama and she nodded her head for me to do so. Minutes later I became very sleepy and fell asleep in my mother's arms.

When I awoke I was in a hospital bed and dresses in hospital pajamas. There were so many pillows piled up behind me so I couldn't lay down. Mama and my aunt Nancy were sitting next to my bed in chairs. I remember looking around the room and seeing another bed but it was empty. The big window allowed me to see the beautiful blue sky and white fluffy clouds. No one had told me yet why I was in the hospital.

Mama was looking very sad and so was my aunt Nancy. They weren't talking much at all. Was I dying and didn't know it.

A new nurse came in the room and told mama that it was time for my bath. My mama kissed me on my forehead. "We won't be here when you get back from your bath baby," mama began to tell me. "But we will be back before you go to bed tonight." Mama and my aunt started to walk out of the room. "Do I have to stay here?" I asked. "Yes baby, until you get better." she said. Get better, what did she mean by that? What was wrong with me? Mama and my aunt left out the room. "You ready for your bath?' the nurse asked. At this point I guess that I really didn't have a choice. The nurse helped me out of bed and into a wheelchair.

I was wheeled to a room where there were about ten large tin buckets that were the size of tubs. She took me over to one that already had water in it. I wasn't comfortable with this stranger giving me a bath. My mama was the only one who gave me a bath, that's if I didn't give myself one. That's if you call playing in the water; a bath. But the nurse took her time and she was oh so careful when removing my gown. The nurse slowly eased me into the tin tub full of water and I sat down. So far so good everything was. She never made any sudden moves that would make me nervous. As I sat in the warm water she pulled up a short stool up next to the tub so she could have a seat at my level. First she just took a wash cloth and soaked it with the warm water and placed it on my arms. Every now and then she would squeeze the wash cloth so the water would come out and run down my arm. "How are you feeling today?" She asked me. "Okay." I answered wondering why she asked me that. "What happened today?" the nurse asked. "Nothing." I told her. I figured if she needed to know my mama would have told her. I was still confused myself about this morning's events.

The nurse then added soap to the wash cloth and began to wash my arms being careful not to lift them too high. "What's your name?" she asked. She was starting to get on my nerves with all these questions, but I answered them anyway. I told her my name thinking her questions would stop. "What happened to your back?" the nurse asked as she washed around my neck. "Nothing" and I really did mean nothing. There was nothing wrong with my back that I knew of. It was my arms that were the problem, I couldn't get them to lift pass my shoulders. Maybe that's why I was in the hospital, because of my arms. I was puzzled by her questions yet again. "Baby, you can tell me what happened." I looked at the nurse, what on earth was she talking about? There was nothing wrong with my back. The look on her face said otherwise. "Nothing," I repeated. The nurse began to rinse the soap out of the wash cloth. She then filled the cloth with water. Careful not to rub my back with the wash cloth, she let the water fall from it onto my bare back. I let out a scream so loud, I know my daddy heard his little baby girl.

What was wrong with my back was now what I wanted to know. What happened to me that has caused all this pain? It was like someone had set my flesh on fire. I continued to scream; I couldn't stop nor did the pain. I started to cry. "I'm so sorry." The nurse began to say, "It'll all be over in a minute. I have to clean your wounds so they don't get infected." Clean my wounds, what wounds? What is she talking about? Through my tears, I could see the pain on her face. "Who did this to you?" There could only be one answer, but through my screaming and crying I couldn't tell her that Big Willie did this to me.

Was that why I couldn't put my shirt on this morning? Is that why the police busted in our house arrested Big Willie this morning? All those people were in our house. Is that why I couldn't raise my arms this morning? Is that why I was brought to the hospital? What exactly had Big Willie done to me and why hadn't mama said anything to me? I later learned that mama had snuck out the house early that morning while Big Willie was still asleep and called the police to have him arrested. That's why she wasn't home when I woke up.

My bath didn't last much longer but my pain did. "Okay baby, we're all done now." I was still crying as the nurse helped me out of the tub. I couldn't stand straight up. My posture was that of an eighty year old woman. It hurt to even breathe. The nurse gently dried me off. I could feel the towel touch on certain areas of my back where she could dry me off without disturbing the wounds on my back. I knew she didn't want to cause me anymore pain. By now I had stop screaming and only tears ran down my face. I felt very weak. I slowly got dressed. Getting back in the wheelchair was the worst. I couldn't sit all the way back and I wanted nothing to touch me. I was frozen with pain and shocked by the reality of what Big Willie had done to me and that now I was away from my family in the hospital. Everyone around me seemed to be sick. No one looked happy and now after my bath neither was I.

We arrived back to my room and as the nurse wheeled me in. There next to my bed on the table was a cup of water and a smaller plastic cup with two small white pills it in. The nurse handed me the small plastic cup and told me to take the pills, which it would help with the pain. I did like I was told and handed her back the cup. "Good girl." I knew my stay here was going to be very long. I looked at my bed with all its pillows piled high; I knew why they were there now. I couldn't lay flat on my back. I couldn't put any pressure on my back. "Do you want to see?" asked the nurse. I just looked at her wondering if she was trying to show me my back to be spiteful or she wanted to show me my back because she thought I had the right to know what was done to me. "Do you want to see your back?" she asked me again. I didn't know if I should wait for mama to come back and do this with her or not. I wanted to see for myself what had caused me to scream and cry the way that I did. "There's a mirror over there if you want to see." The nurse pointed to a tall mirror on the wall across the room by the empty bed. I looked over at the mirror afraid of what it might show me, but I needed to know. I looked back at the nurse hoping she had changed her mind thinking it wasn't a good idea for me to look. But instead she would help me out of my wheelchair and lead me to the direction of the mirror.

Slowly I made it to the mirror. I stood in the mirror and I was able to bring forth a smile to myself because front the front everything looked normal. I waited a little while starring at myself before turning around so I could see myself from the back. My gown was tied closed at the top so at first glance I couldn't see anything. I reached around to untie my gown, stood on my tippy-toes and slowly stretched my wings out like I was an airplane. That made my open up so I could see my back. What I saw my eyes could not understand. I starred at my back for what seemed like eternity. Tears started rolling down my face for I knew that I would be scared for life. My back looked like the surface of the moon. There was a lot of my skin that was missing leaving behind nothing to cover the exposed white meat of my back. Big Willie had beaten me like I was a disobedient slave and he was my owner.

Oh my God, did I deserve this just for having to go to the bathroom. I could only imagine what would have happened if I had wet the bed. I probably would have lost a limb. I put my arms down and looked over at the nurse who was making my bed comfortable as possible for me. She looked up at me with sorrow in her eyes as if I were her own. I had no words. I did know where to begin so this could all make sense to me. My opinion of Big Willie now was that he was a viscous and evil man, just plan evil. I hoped that I would never have to see him another day of my life. I knew that my mama was going to kick his butt out the house after what he had done to her child.

The nurse motioned for me to come to her. "You're going to be okay baby. We're going to take good care of you. We'll get you all healed up and all better so you can get back home with your family." But all I could think to myself as I remember what I saw in the mirror was; if this happened to me at home where I'm supposed to be safe than home is the last place I want to be.

"Who did that to you" she asked "Big Willie" I told her with my eyes full of tears as I looked at the bed of pillows wondering if I would have to sleep like that for the rest of my life.(Many years later I would see a movie called *The Elephant Man*. I instantly understood his pain.) "Is Big Willie your father?" Shaking my head I answered, "No." Oh how I missed my own at that moment. My father would have never done anything like this to his little girl, I thought to myself. What had I done to make Big Willie hate me so much, was all I wanted to understood? "No, Big Willie is not my father. He is my mother's boyfriend and they have a baby boy together." I answered. "Why did he do this to you," The nurse took one last look at my back before closing my gown and tying it back. "Because I went to the bathroom," I told her. She just looked at me with such sorrow. "Well, let's get you into bed." My tears hadn't stopped, just slowed down as I crawled up into bed. "You can't lay down on your back so just sit up and rest against the pillows." She explained to me. I tried but it was so impossible to do. "Don't cry baby." She wiped away my tears but more followed. She pulled up a chair and turned on the television and watched morning cartoons with me.

After a couple of cartoons I began to get sleepy; just then my mother and another one of my aunts walked in my hospital room. I wasn't expecting here back until later close to my bedtime like she had told me. The nurse stood up to acknowledge my mother's presence in the room. She proceeded to the door but turned to look back at me. She nodded her head and gave me a smile, and then she was gone.

"What's wrong baby." Mama asked. I couldn't bring myself to say a word. I was surprised to see her; I didn't think I would see her until bedtime. I wasn't sure if I was happy to see her or not. What's wrong?!!!!

Does she not realize that she's visiting her child in a hospital? Did she forget about all that happen this morning? I guess the police bust down everybody door every morning at breakfast. I could only think how she could have let him do this to me. She knew how crazy that man was. She saw my back, how did she think I felt? My aunt just stood back. She was there to support my mother but her face was full of pain as she looked at me. I could tell she wanted to say something but she didn't want to upset my mother. No one wanted to talk about the reason why I was there so, we all just watched cartoons.

"Time to order lunch." Someone said from the doorway of my hospital room. "Hi sweetie", the young lady said walking to my bedside with her writing pad in hand. "Here's a menu, you can have anything you want," she handed me "just tell me what you want to eat for lunch." I looked over the list of many choices that I could pick from. "Oh, baked potatoes. I never had a baked potato before. This would be a perfect time to have one." I told the lady. Mama and my aunt Earlene were busy talking amongst themselves. The young lady waited patiently as I made my choices. I added green beans, meatloaf, applesauce, and some juice. "Lunch will be ready by twelve, I'll be back then. She took up the menu and left the room.

I thought this would be a good time for mama to talk to me about my back and what happened last night and this morning since it would be an hour before lunch was ready. But mama said nothing to me and continued her small talk with my aunt. I started to wonder if she even cared. Was she only here so no one would think that she was a bad mom? Not once has she asked me how I was feeling or that she was sorry that this happened. Or that she would make sure that Big Willie never has a chance to hurt me again. Nothing, she said none of this to me. I watched television without saying a word and after a while I just tuned out its sound and everything around me. Maybe if I tuned everything out it would go away, including my pain.

Just like she promised, she was back at twelve with lunch. "Lunchtime." She said pulling a table tray up to my bed and sitting my lunch on it. "Are you ready to eat?" she asked. I was excited because I would be able to eat a baked potato for the first time. She lifted the lid that covered my food. I looked over at my baked potato and I started screaming and crying. "Take it away, take it away, please; take it away." There was a scary face on the skin of the potato. It looked evil and mean. It was as if it was looking straight at me and laughing making fun of me. I became so afraid. "Take it away." I repeated. "What sweetie what," I have confused the lady. My screaming had caused my mother and aunt to stop talking. "What's wrong with you girl?," my mother asked. The tone of her voice made me think that I was bothering her while she was in the middle of something important.

"The potato has an evil face on it." I said pointing at the potato. Everyone looked at the potato on my plate, but no one saw what I saw. I think it was only meant for me to see it. No one saw the evil face on the potato. "Oh girl there's nothing wrong with that potato," mama said. My aunt just looked at the potato and then looked back at me. "No, no" I said and started screaming even more because when I looked back down at the potato and the face was still there. I wasn't crazy, I know what I saw. "Take it away please, take it away." I begged the lady since obviously mama wasn't going to even though she saw how frighten I was. "Okay baby, you don't have to eat the potato. I'll take it away." The young lady said. She seemed so concerned about what I thought I saw. She grabbed a napkin and threw it over the potato so I couldn't see its evil face anymore and removed it from my plate. I had never seen anything like that before. Its face was so scary.

"Okay, now you can eat the rest of you lunch, the mean potato is gone. I'll be back to pick up your food tray later." And with that she left the room. Mama looked at me and starting laughing, "Girl you're crazy." How dare she laugh at me? My aunt Earlene continued to sit in silence as she looked at my mother shocked by her response. I know what I saw. There was an evil face on that potato. From that day forward, I would resent my mother.

My stay at the hospital was very long, like I knew it would be. Days turned into weeks and weeks turned into months. Mama's schedule visit was twice a day. She always brought one of my aunts with her to see me; I guess my sister couldn't come. Mama still never spoke of what happened that night to me my entire stay in the hospital. But there was no need; I had figured it all out.

My nights were short and my days were long. Some days I just wanted to sleep because the pain was so terrible, it was too much to bare. My bath time was the worst. At times it was like electric shocks were going across my back. Nurses were always in my room. If they weren't giving me medicine every couple of hours for the pain, they were there to put medicine on my back. They still had to give me baths and help me in and out the bed when I had to go to the bathroom. It would be a while before I would be able to lift my arms pass my shoulders. And one by one the pillows would go away. For a long time I was kept in my room away from the other children in the hospital and the other bed in my room stayed empty.

One thing I did like about the hospital was that every night the ice cream cart would come by just before it was time to go to bed. When I first arrived at the hospital I would be sleep by the time the ice cream cart would come to my room because of all the medicine I was on. So the ice cream cart lady would just leave a cup of sprite on my night table and in the morning I would drink it. Still till this day, I love the taste of stale sprite.

# Chapter 4

**AFTER SOME TIME,** I was finally well enough to join the other children in the hospital. "Good morning sweetie." My nurse had come in earlier than usual one morning to wake me. "Are you ready for breakfast?" she asked. She had a wheelchair sitting next to my bed. I had always eaten breakfast in my room so I didn't know what the wheelchair was for. I only used the wheelchair when I was going for a bath and that was always after breakfast. I looked at the wheelchair, "what's the chair for?" I asked. The doctor wants you to eat breakfast with the other children this morning in the breakfast room. He thinks you're well enough to be around other children now. I wasn't allowed to walk around the hospital so I never saw any other children. Every now and then one would pass in the hall with a nurse.

My nurse helped me into my wheelchair and I just looked up at her, I really didn't want to go. I never even talked to another child here, now I'm expected to eat with them. I guess the nurse could see the concern on my face. "Don't worry sweetie, you'll be fine." I had become so use to my room, I felt safe there. "Soon as you're finished eating I'll be back to take you for your bath." She explained. Oh please don't do me any favors. She wheeled me to the elevator which took us a couple of floors up.

We arrived to a large room where there happen to be at least ten kids in there. The room was painted in bright colors and the television was playing morning cartoons. There were toys to play with and music nursery rhythms could be heard playing in the room. Still not being allowed to walk, the nurse wheeled me over to a breakfast table. "Today is pancake day." She announced. I just looked around the room at all the kids. Some were rolling on the floor playing, some were yelling and screaming. Others were running around the room throwing balls at each other. "Do you want milk or juice?" she asked. What I wanted was to go back to my room. It was too noisy in here for me and these kids were acting crazy to me. I had lost my appetite. The nurse walked away to get me some pancakes. The kids were still yelling and throwing stuff all over the room. I tried to watch television until my nurse came back but there was no use because I couldn't hear it over all the commotion in the room.

Glancing around the room I was just thinking that it was too early for all this noise. "Here you are sweetie." My nurse had come back with my food. She had bought both milk and juice for me. Many times I wished that she was my mama. She had been taking so good care of me since I had been in the hospital. "I'll be back in a hour." She told me. "Can't you stay here with me." I asked. "You'll be okay. Eat your pancakes, I'll be back soon." She promised. I looked down at my pancakes that sat in front of me. I poured some syrup on them and took a couple of bites. I was ready to go. I said nothing to any of the kids the whole time I sat there.

The longer I sat there the more things seemed so different to me. I could tell something even inside of me had changed. I now knew evil existed and I wanted no part of it. It had taken me away from my family. Evil had caused me pain. And now I was alone. At one point the voice that I had heard that fatal night came to me again. It took me out of my chair and above the room. I could look down and see myself sitting in my wheelchair as the other children played around me. It told me not to be afraid and that I would always rise above my situations. The voice was gone and I was back in my wheelchair. Not being able to watch television, I just stared out the window wishing that I was anywhere but here and wondering what everyone at home was doing.

One by one the kids left the breakfast room as their nurses came to get them. After there were about three of us left in the room, I was finally able to watch cartoons and actually hear them. "It's time for someone's bath." I heard my nurse say. I was glad that she kept her promise and came back. "How were your pancakes?" she asked as she looked at my plate. "They were okay." I said. As we left the breakfast room, I remembered what the voice had told me.

My daily routine continued with my morning bath. "Well, let's go and get you all cleaned up. I think you're going to have company today." The longer I stayed in the hospital, the more tolerable my baths became. The nurses learned how to wash my back so that it wouldn't hurt so much. When I returned to my room, my nurse asked me a question. "Do you want to take a look at your back? It's been healing very well." I hadn't seen my back since the first day that I had come into the hospital. I could only assume that since the pain had not been as bad as it once was that maybe it wouldn't look as bad as it once did. I was excited to see. "Yeah, I want to see." Just then my mama and another one of my aunts entered the room. "Good morning," they said. I was happy to see that my aunt came to visit me. My mother on the other hand could have waited in the car.

"She was just about to take a look at her back," my nurse explained. With the many months that I have stayed in the hospital, I never remember my mother looking at my back to see how or if it was healing well or not. Maybe she didn't want to be reminded of what Big Willie had done to me. Maybe if she didn't look, she could believe it never happened. Maybe if she looked it would make her feel guilty. Maybe one day I would be able to forgive her; maybe.

I walked over to the mirror like I had once did before. I positioned myself in front of the mirror so I could see clearly. I untied my own gown now that I was able to raise my hands pass my shoulders. The whole room became silent and everyone seemed to be holding their breathe; including me. I was hoping to see that everything was back to normal. Time stood still for that very moment. With my back facing the mirror, I took one last look at my nurse, aunt, and my mother who stood over by my bed. I turned and looked in the mirror; I was just as horrified this time as I was the last time that I looked in the mirror.

I looked away with tears in my eyes. I looked back again in the mirror at my reflection and I knew that I would be scarred for life. It no longer looked like the surface of the moon, but like someone had glued eight black charcoals to my back. I looked back to my nurse, the one who I came to trust all this time. "We have to take them off." She walked over to me as I stood frozen in the mirror. "We have to take the scabs off so your wounds can get some air and heal better." She turned me away from the mirror. "Is it going to hurt?" I was so worried. "It may hurt a little, so I will go slowly." She promised. I looked over at my mother, she had nothing to say. Why should this time be any different?

The nurse's hands were cold when they touched my back. She slowly began to peel off one of my scabs, but no matter how slow and careful she was I felt every pull and tare of my skin. I tried to be a big girl and not cry too much. A little a couple of times I found myself swarming. Some of them seem to get stuck to my skin and wouldn't come off so easy. "Ouch," I would say when I felt one completely did come off. "I'm sorry, just a little while longer." One by one she peeled them all off. "See, they're all off now." The nurse showed me her hands. They were now filled with the black charcoal looking scabs that were once on my back.

I wanted to touch them. The nurse took my hand, "it's okay, they can't hurt you, and it's just hard skin like a turtle's shell." She placed on of my fingers on one of the scabs. I only touched it for a second and I snatched my hand back but not before I noticed that it felt like a rock. "This was on my back?" I asked. The nurse just nodded her head yes. I reached out for it again, this time I held it in my hand and turned it over. And indeed it did look like a turtle's shell. I quickly handed it back to the nurse. "We can throw them away now". There sitting next to the bathroom door sat a waste basket. The nurse took my hand in hers, "You ready to get rid of this?" she asked. The scabs made a thumping noise as the hit the bottom of the waste basket. My mother and aunt started clapping. "Good girl. You did very well today. I will let the doctor know"

I would see my doctor sometimes, but not as much as I saw my nurses. When I did see my doctor he would wheel me around the halls and we would just talk about my condition and the other kids that were in the hospital sick like me. So to hear that I had a good day would be pleasing to him.

My nurse knew that I was in some pain as she walked me back over to my bed. "In you go, I'll be back with something for the pain." But before she left she went over to the waste basket and took the bag that had my scabs in it. There was little if any conversation between me and my mother after the nurse left. I didn't care one way or another; I just wanted her to hurry back with my medicine. I always wondered why my mother never had that much to say to me; was it because she didn't know what to say to make the situation better. But did she know by not saying anything only made the situation worst. My little brain could only handle one issue at a time, and right now I just needed to concentrate on getting better. My nurse did return shortly with some medicine like she had promised. Soon after taking it I fell off to sleep leaving my mother and aunt sitting by my bed side talking.

As the weeks passed, I did get better. I was even able to start walking around on my own. A lot of times I was allowed to hang out at the nurses' desk. The phones were always ringing and the bells were always going off on the big switch board that they had to tell them that someone from a room needed them. Sometimes the board was lit up like a Christmas tree, that meant that they were real busy and I would have to go back to my room.

I even spent a birthday in the hospital. My doctor bought me a big bag of candy for my birthday so he and I walked around and was handing it out to all the kids there were sick in their rooms. I think all that walking was a bit much for me and my doctor could tell. He picked me up to carry back to my room. The closer that I got to my room the sleeper I got. Just then my mother came around the corner; she had arrived for her daily visit. "Oh doctor, she's a big girl, don't carry her." Mama took me from my doctor's arms. She struggled to get me back to my room. I don't know why she didn't just let my doctor finish carrying me to my room and she could have just followed us. I don't think my size had anything to do with it. I think my mother could tell that I was getting very attached to the nurses and my doctor at the hospital. And I don't think that she liked the idea of that at all.

For some strange reason my mother came by herself that day. She got me all settled in bed and then see pulled out a whole bunch of things out of her bag that she had brought with her. There were Color books and crayons along with some other toys. A Tom and Jerry color book caught my attention first; they were my favorite cartoon ever. Pinocchio and Bozo the clown coloring books were there too. I was excited about getting the gifts but I knew there was a reason behind them. My mother had never celebrated my birthday before now. But surprising this was the most that my mother and I had spoken since I had been in the hospital. I colored in my new coloring books for a while before drifting off to sleep.

# Chapter 5

**I MUST HAVE** been out for a while because when I woke up there were voices in the room that I didn't recognized. My mother and now my aunt were sitting by my bed and they weren't talking; their soap operas were on. I looked over to the other side of the room where the voices were coming from where the empty bed was, but it wasn't empty anymore.

There was another little girl in the room with me. A nurse and her mother were getting her settled into her bed. The first thing that I noticed about the little girl was that she had worn a big fluffy pink bow in her hair. Then I realized that she wore pink pajamas and that she had a pink blanket along with a pink rob.

She seemed the same age as me but she was heavier. I wondered what was wrong with her. She didn't look like anything was wrong with her. But something had to be wrong because she was in the hospital. As usual I sat in my bed watching television as mama and auntie talked among themselves. All I heard from the other side of the room was the little girl whining. She wasn't crying like something was hurting her; but whining for juice, her teddy bear, and her blanket or something. And there her mama was by her bedside like a jumping bean completing her daughters every request to make her comfortable. You could tell that the whining was starting to get on mama nerves because every now and then she and auntie would stop talking and look over to that side of the room.

The whining continued for a while. Her mother tried to calm her down but the little girl insisted to keep whining. At one point to me it seemed she was doing it on purpose just because she knew her mother would do anything for her. Trying to block it out was close to impossible. After sometime mama had had enough, she and auntie left. I wanted to go too because my new roommates was already starting to get on my nerves and it was only her first day.

After thirty minutes of this non-stop whining, I had had enough. I just started to stare at the little girl it seemed she wanted attention so I gave her mine too. Five minutes went by and her mother noticed me starring at her whining spoiled brat of a daughter, so she got up and closed the curtain that divided the room. I couldn't see her anymore but I still could hear her.

As the weeks went on mama started to visit less and less. My new roommate on the other hand seemed too have many visitors every day. I didn't mind, it was just the consent whining. She really did act like a spoiled brat. During her stay at the hospital we never really said that much to each other. I think one day I did offer her one of my coloring books; being careful not to give her my favorite one, Tom and Jerry. I just gave her the one that I didn't care too much for. That turned out to be a quiet day for once. But during her stay it wasn't too many of those that I got to enjoy.

I'm not going to lie, one day I guess I wasn't feeling too good or maybe I was just mad at the fact that no one was coming to see me as much anymore; but I just couldn't take the whining anymore. She had gotten on my last nerve. She was whining about something, to who I don't know. I know she didn't think that I was going to get out my bed and see about her. The nurses didn't even come in as much and check on her for that very reason. Anyway, after fifteen minutes of listening to her whine about her teddy bear; which happened to be at the end of her bed, I just looked over at her and yelled, "could you just please shut up." She just looked at me for a second, and then all of a sudden she started crying and wouldn't stop. I didn't think that I was being mean; I said please.

"What are you crying for?" I asked. "You yelled at me." She said with her pouting bottom lip. "That's because you've been acting like a spoiled brat ever since you got here." What I said that for. She started to cry even more. I just turned up my television and blocked her out. Ten minutes later her mother walks it the room. Concerned as any parent would be (*except mine*) her mother asked what was wrong and hurried to her bedside; what a scene. Through her crying she couldn't talk, so she just pointed in my direction. Her mother turned around and looked at me as if she wanted to say something. Oh great, I didn't want to hear nothing she had to say. I rolled over and looked at the wall and eventually went to sleep. I guess she got the message.

When I woke up from my afternoon nap, to my surprise it was quiet. I looked over to the other bed and it was empty. Did they move her to another room, I wondered. Or did she check out and go home? Either way; she was gone and I was glad. Forty days and forty nights of listening to someone whine was enough to last me a life time.

I guess I stayed another week or two in the hospital. I was starting to feel much better. So much that I was down to one pillow and that was for my head and I was able to lay on my back. "Hey sweetie, it's time to order lunch." My lunch lady had arrived at her normal time. "What are we having today?" she asked. I made sure that I never order another potato since my last incident. You only get once to make a first impression and I was not impressed. I really wasn't too hungry, so I just ordered s sandwich and some tomato soup. She looked over my choice. "Not too hungry today I see." She said. "No" I told her.

For some reason my spirits had been a little gloomy that morning and I didn't know why. Maybe I was just tired of the hospital life since I had been there for so long. I think I was ready to go home.

"Well then, I'll be back in a little while." Cartoons were on and instead of watching them, they were watching me. Lunch lady returned with my food but seeing it in front of me didn't change my appetite. I nibbled at my sandwich, took a couple sips of juice and a couple of spoons of my soup. That was enough for me, I pushed my tray away.

My nurse came in to see me, "have you had your lunch already?" she asked "As much as I'm going to have." I told her. "Well, the doctor wants you to take your medicine early today, so here you go." She handed me my medicine that I would take a night to help me go to sleep. She pushed my lunch tray over by the door and had a seat next to my bed until I fell off to sleep.

When I woke up from my nap, I wasn't in the hospital anymore and I wasn't at home , but instead I was in my youngest aunt bedroom at my grandparents' house. Paul McCartney and the Wings song; Open the Door, was playing on the radio. I looked outside the window by my bed and the sun was very bright. That must have been a double dose of medicine from what I would normally take. I didn't remember leaving the hospital or mama coming to get me. I didn't remember the ride to my grandparents' house either.

There was no sign of my mother in the room. But I shouldn't be surprised by that. Instead I noticed that my young auntie Silvya; who was also young enough to be my older teenage sister was just sitting in her bed staring at me. My auntie was only a kid herself. I noticed though that she was coloring in my favorite coloring book, Tom and Jerry. "No, no don't color in that one." I told her. I went over to her bed and snatched my coloring book out her hand and put it back in my bag of stuff that was sitting at the foot of my bed. "Why not, you have so many others that you can color in." she told me as she snatched the book back and took my bag from me and began to look in it some more. Auntie Silvya was bigger than me and I didn't feel like fighting with her.

I already see that this girl was going to get on my last nerve so I was going to have to handle her in a different way. I noticed that she would only want something if you liked it so, I reversed my books. "But, I like this coloring book the most; you can color in this one." I told her as I handed her my Pinocchio coloring book as she slowly handed me back Tom and Jerry. She was more than happy to take it. She went back over to her bed and starting coloring. Woe that was a close call. I held my favorite coloring book tight to my chest. I laid back down only to drift back off to sleep. Why wasn't I at home with my mother anyway? Why am I at my grandparents' house?

# Chapter 6

**IT WOULD BE** awhile before I would be able to return home to my mother. I later learned that I wasn't allowed to live with her right away. You see, with all of the confusion of that fatal night when my mother saw my limp body laying beaten and bloody in my bed, she panic. She thought she was helping me by cleaning my wounds, but when she cleaned them, she did it with alcohol which made matters worse, because she burnt me. So when CPS (Child Protective Services) did their investigation of that night they assumed that she took part in the abuse. They found my home with her not to be safe and so instead I was signed over temporary custody to my grandparents until CPS felt my home was safe for me again.

I lived at my grandparents for so long, my younger aunts and uncles became more like my brother and sister. My aunt Nancy took on the mother role when grandma wasn't around. Every morning after grandma would get everyone ready and off to school, she would wake me up for breakfast. Biscuits and syrup was my favorite. Sometimes I would get up early enough to see my uncle Nicholas get on his school bus. I loved sitting at the kitchen table with the lime green refrigerator to my back, just enjoying the peaceful mornings. Grandma would be at the sink washing dishes from breakfast that morning

When I was well enough to go back to school, Aunt Nancy would walk me half way to school every morning. One morning I got mobbed by a pack of neighborhood dogs. They were only puppies but it was a lot of them. I didn't want to walk by myself to school anymore after that, so auntie would walk me a little bit further then where the dogs lived, then I would walk the rest of the way to school on my own. In the afternoon after school someone was always waiting to meet me and walk me home.

My mother didn't come and visit me much at my grandparent's house. But, I remember one visit she came, she brought me a gift. She knew how much I loved Wonder Woman so she bought me a Wonder Woman outfit. It was yellow, blue and red with Wonder Woman's face on the front of the shirt. That was the happiest day of my life. Was this her way of telling me that she was sorry, or did she feel guilty about what she let happen to me. Even though I was safe at my with grandma , I still felt miss placed and abandoned by my mother who only lived five minutes away from grandmas. I wanted to be at home with my sister and little brother. The next day I wore my Wonder Woman outfit to school. That's the day I got mobbed by the puppies. I didn't feel so wonderful.

I will never forget the time my sister came to visit. It was a rainy day so we sat out on the front porch. We talked and laughed for a while. At times we whispered to each other as to tell secrets that only we would know. But at times, the rain grabbed my full attention. It seemed to me when it rained the grass got greener and stood up straighter and the trees got taller. Rain water was falling off the side of the house like a slow clear river stream. I thought the rain water was different than any other water. It had to be; it came from heaven.

No longer talking to my sister but in a trance by the rain; I wanted to touch it to see if it made me feel like the trees. I walked over to rain stream and let my hand rest in it. My sister whispered, "I dare you to drink it." I looked back at her. I didn't think it was a bad idea. But one thing I learned was no one asks you to do something for nothing. What did she want in return from me if I drink the water? I declined and went back and sat down. But she only dared me again. She seemed eager for me to do it. And again I declined. But I did want to taste its pureness. The longer I watched the water the more I didn't care what her reason was. "You're going to tell on me." I told her. She said she wouldn't but I didn't believe her.

I had to go back to the rain stream, I had to taste it. "You promise you won't tell on me?" I asked. She nodded in agreement. I slowly walked over to the rain stream and left my cupped hands sit in it so it could fill up. I slowly pulled them to me; being carefully not to spill a drop. I looked in my hand, there was only a little? The water was so clear and it was cold. I took a sip and it was all gone. I dried my hands on my pants and I sat back down with a smile on my face. "How did it taste?" my sister asked. "It was cold," was all I told her. How it made me feel, I kept to myself.

The next thing I know my sister jumped up out her chair, "Oooo, you gonna get in trouble. I'm gonna tell mama." And she ran in the house to tell on me like she promised that she wouldn't do. I was sad; my sister had betrayed me and I knew I was going to get in trouble. I swear you can't trust anybody any more. But never the less, I couldn't wipe the smile off my face for drinking the sweetest and purest water that fell from heaven. She was just mad because I didn't share with her.

My mother came out the house onto the porch scolding me, "Girl, what's wrong with you? Are you thirsty?" Looking at my sister as she passed back by me to go back to her chair, she now had a smile on her face as she sat down. "No." I told my mother. "If you wanted some water, you should have come in the house. That was so stupid of you, that water is nasty." She said that, but the water didn't look nasty, it didn't taste nasty to me. My mother went back in the house. I looked at my sister in disbelief. Grandma came out on the porch a few minutes later; I guess my mother told her what I had done. "Baby, God uses that water to clean things and give things life." She smiled at me and went back in the house. And that's exactly how I felt, like God had cleansed me and given me life. And so I sat there on my grandparent's porch that day smiling as I watched the water fall from heaven and every now and then I would stick my hand out to let a couple of drops dance on my fingertips only to lick them dry once again. I'm not sure but I think I saw my Sis do it once or twice herself.

Holidays came and went and I do believe even a birthday went by and I was still living at my grandparents. On the weekend granddaddy was always in the garage working on the family car. I would ride my red tricycle up and down the drive way. One day my wheel fell off. He would fix it but soon as I would ride it the wheel would fall off again. He would fix it again, but the wheel just wouldn't stay on. Granddaddy wouldn't give up, he tighten up that wheel and dared it to fall off. I rode my tricycle down the drive way and I fell off and cut the inside of my thigh. Grandma had been watching from the kitchen window. She ran outside and picked me up off the ground, "that's enough" she said. Granddaddy did his best to try and fix it but the little red tricycle just didn't want to be fixed. It ended up on the trash pile. I cried and grandma made me feel better by making me my favorite; I loved my peanut butter and syrup sandwiches.

There was never any arguing, yelling or screaming at my grandparents' house; except one terrible morning that I will never forget.

The house seemed different and everyone was quietly shuffling around the house this particular morning. No one would sit still, not even for a moment. Bedroom doors were opening and closing. My aunt and uncles were constantly going in and out of my grandparents' bedroom. This was something that I had never seen before. My oldest two uncles were in the hallway like guards as they paced back and forth in front of the bedroom door.

One of my aunts opens the door to my Aunt Penny's bedroom and I heard a terrible whaling coming from her. She was in deep pain, I could tell. What was wrong? What has happened? Why is auntie sad? The door closed and the house was silent again. One of my uncle's stops pacing for a moment and went back into my grandma's room, leaving my other uncle to pace the hall by himself. I stood at the beginning of the hall, too scared to enter it. Yelling, screaming, and crying were all I heard coming from behind the doors. I could hear my aunt Nancy telling me Aunt Penny that everything was going to be okay. But I could tell my Aunt Nancy's voice that it really wasn't. She was just telling my aunt Penny that in the hopes that she would stop crying and to calm her down before she gave herself a heart attack. I sat on the bottom steps watching as my aunts took turns going back and forth in and out of my Aunt Penny's bedroom and into the bathroom for a wet washcloth. Every time the door would open hers cry and screams were worst.

A week later I sat in the front row of a church. My sister sat to my left and to my right sat Big Willie and he was holding my baby brother in his arms. Next to him sat my mother. My mother was sad and she was crying; she looked tired and very weak. She only had strength enough to hold a tissue that wiped away her tears. We were all dressed in black. In front of me sat a long shinny brown box sitting on a table surrounded by so many beautiful flowers. In it lay my grandmother. Was she taking a nap? Why would everyone be crying just because my grandma was taking a nap? I've seen my grandma take a nap before in her favorite chair while watching television. It didn't make me cry it made me laugh because even when grandma fell asleep in her chair her cheeks were rosy and she looked like she was smiling. But she didn't look like that today. Today her cheeks weren't rosy and she didn't look like she was smiling I saw my grandmother laying there but I only thought she would wake up soon. I looked around at everyone and they were so sad. We were in this big church and it all felt like a dream. I looked back at my grandma and I starred at her for a long time. I figured if she heard everyone crying that she would wake up but she only lay there very still. Now I understood why my auntie' Penny was crying. She couldn't get my grandma to wake up. I will never forget the screaming and crying that filled the halls that day.

Today was a sad day. But I was being a big girl for grandma. I didn't cry. I sat up straight and paid attention as the people in robes sang songs and the big man behind the stand talked loud. I sat hopeless and watched as my aunts and uncles cried wishing that their pain would go away. The impact of my loss began to confront me. My father was already gone and now the only person that I felt safe with is now gone. Who's going to protect me now? Unknown to me, there was another watching over me. He would never leave me nor forsake me, even in my darkest hour.

Weeks went by after that sad day and I was still living at my grandparents. I was still hoping and waiting for grandma to wake up and come home. My daily routine didn't change. My aunts took over what my grandma use to do. One weekend I woke up to some loud noise. There was some music playing downstairs. I could hear my aunts and mama laughing. Had grandma woke up and come back home; I wished to myself. That could only be the reason for what sounded like a celebration downstairs. I hurried up got dressed and ran down stairs so I could give grandma a big hug and tell her how I had been a good girl while she was gone.

I stood at the bottom of the stairs and peeked around the corner into the living room at all the commotion that was going on. My mother and my aunts were dancing, singing, and laughing as they moved my grandma's furniture around into different places. What were they doing? They had no right to change things. Grandma had her house the way she wanted it. They better put that couch back before she gets home. I had never seen anyone clean the house before but grandma. And the furniture had been sitting in the same place for as long as I could remember.

Two chairs with a table and lamp sitting between them sat In front of the big window in the living room. The green couch with the pretty print design sat across from it on the opposite wall, it still had the plastic on it. Grandma always sat in the chair by the big window that sat closest to the door; that was grandma's chair. They had better put my grandma's chair back; who do they think they are?

They continued to go about the house cleaning, changing and moving things around the house. A heavy feeling came over me; I realized that grandma was gone forever and that she wasn't coming back home. I started to cry. I walked over to my mother who was helping move the green couch. Everyone stopped what they were doing. My mother looked down at me. "What's wrong with you?" she asked. "Grandma's dead and she's not coming back." I cried. "Oh girl, go sit down," she said to me sending me away from her as if I was some peasant on the street begging for change. But I did just that, I went back and sat on the bottom of the stairs and I just cried. I secretly told grandma that I missed her and that I will always love her, and that when it was my turn to be a grandma; that I was going to be a good grandma to my grandchildren as she was to me.

I looked down the hall at where grandma's bedroom was. Still crying and getting annoyed by all the laughing my aunts and mother were still doing, I walked to her bedroom door and opened it. The room was quiet. The bed was neatly made, not a wrinkle in it. The walls were painted a soft blue. Picture frames holding moments of life sat on dressers. I had never been in my grandparent's bedroom before, but it was the way that I always thought it would be, a peaceful place. Everything was in its place, it was so nice and clean. But there was no trace of grandma anywhere. I would never see her again, how could this be? I guess I was still hoping when I had opened the door that she would be sitting on the side of her bed. I closed the door behind me and went back to the bottom of stairway and sat down.

I was still crying when my aunt Nancy passed by on her way to the kitchen. She stopped and kissed me on the forehead and whipped my tears away. "Everything is going to be okay." She smiled at me and gave me a hug. I really wanted to believe her. That would be the last time I saw my aunt Nancy.

# Chapter 7

**AFTER A WHILE** staying with my oldest aunt Earline became the new living arrangements for me, my sister, baby brother and my mother sometime after grandma's death. With seven kids and two adults, there wasn't much space but there was a lot of laughter. I kind of didn't mind staying with Aunt Earline; I got to know my cousins very well and we became very close. It was good to see two sisters helping each other out. Family is very important. My cousins' father wasn't around either, I don't know whether men made a pact with each other back in those days; love the ladies, make the babies and shake the stay-bees. I really don't know how long we lived with my aunt Earline, but sometime in the middle of the night, my mother packed us up and we left my aunties' house. I never saw my cousins again.

We were all packed into a car. My mother sat up front in the passenger seat while I crawled in the back seat with my sister. There was already a man who I had never seen before sitting back there. The gentleman politely lifted me up and sat me on his lap so we could all have room and not be mushed up in the back seat. "Don't put her in your lap", I heard a familiar voice say. "She's too old for that; she can sit on her own." The gentleman didn't say a word he just moved over making room for me in the back seat. I looked up at the driver where the voice was coming form and to my surprise, it was Big Willie. Oh my God what was he doing here? I thought after he put me in the hospital that my mother wouldn't want to have anything to do with him, but obviously I was wrong. I should have known that he was still hanging around when I saw him at my grandmother's funeral. What was wrong with her? Was she crazy, we already know Big Willie liked to act crazy? Why was she still even talking to this man? He damn near beat your child to death; do you not remember that. Do you not remember that your child was taken away from you and you turn right around and put me back in the same situation? I began to question her loyalty and love; did she have any for me? Me personally if he had beaten my child causing her to be hospitalized he would have been six feet under or gone down the highway on a one way street. But that's just me and that's the philosophy that I carried with me for when I had kids.

I later learned that Big Willie did go to jail for child abuse. But when grandma died, I guess my mother regained custody of me. I guess I became an orphan for a little while until my mother was clear of any wrong doing. But I think if they knew that Big Willie had been hanging around, she wouldn't have gotten me back. Maybe he had changed or promised my mother that he would never put his hands on me again. Whatever the reason was for him still being around still wasn't good enough for me. I wish my aunt Nancy would have taken custody of me; I would have been a good girl.

We had to stop by grandma's house to pick up some things. We pulled away from the house; I never looked back at grandma's house. We reached our little white house on the corner, but instead of stopping, we passed right by it. I thought we were going home. Where were we going? Where was this man taking us? The whole ride, I could just feel Big Willie watching me through his driver's mirror. We drove all night long.

I awoke the next morning not in the back seat of the car but in bed. I was in a different place. I had a feeling we weren't in Detroit anymore, I was right. I was in a house and when I looked around, I seemed to be the only one in the bedroom. I got dressed quickly and found my way downstairs. The house was quiet and big. When I got downstairs, the first thing I noticed was a huge white fireplace and two very large black velvet canvas painting that hung on each side of the fireplace. One of the paintings was that of a beautiful brown skinned woman who was for the most part naked but tastefully partially covered in certain places. You couldn't help but to admire her beauty, but her nakedness made you blush. And the other painting was of a man and woman embracing each other. Our black is very beautiful but I thought the pictures were a bit much for our young eyes to see every day. You wouldn't have seen anything like that hanging on grandma's wall.

There was furniture in the living room already. To my right was the dining room and there sitting at the table was my Sis and Big Willie who was holding my baby brother on his lap. And of course yet again there was no sign of my mother. I hope nothing happened while I was sleep. I didn't want to star in another episode of lights, camera and action after the police bust down the door. But for the most part everything seemed normal.

Sis was eating her cereal while Big Willie was feeding my little brother. "Come get something to eat." Big Willie said to me as he pulled a chair away from the table for me to sit in. I climbed up into the chair and poured myself a bowl of cereal. I picked the cereal box that had the chocolate cow on the front of it. I went to reach for the gallon of milk which was a little out of reach for me. Big Willie; who saw my dilemma had passed me the milk, but he never took his eyes off me. He was being awfully nice to me this morning. I guess he didn't want another episode of lights, camera, action and jail.

I went to pour some milk over my cereal but it was so heavy I struggled with it. I got some milk in the bowl, but I also spilled a little bit on the table by accident. My heart stopped beating as I looked down at the spilled milk on the table. I looked up at Sis who had seen what had happened. She looked at me for a split second then she lowered her head and looked only into her cereal bowl. I think at that moment she wished she could have dove in the bowl and hid in it.

I looked over at Big Willie who I thought was going to direct me to the kitchen so I could get a dish cloth so I could clean up the spilled milk. That's what my aunt Nancy would have done. Grandma would have just got a paper towel and wiped it up. It was an accident for crying out loud. For some reason the look on his face to do something so simple seemed out of the question for him. "Go stand over by the fireplace," is what he instructed me to do instead. I had no idea what he was about to do. You know how they tell you don't cry over spilled milk, that's because they never spilled milk around Big Willie.

I slowly slid out of my chair and went to stand by the fireplace. Big Willie went over to the cabinet next to the fireplace and pulled out a belt. Not the kind of belt you wear with your pair of pants, but that thick belt you see the body builder muscle men wear around their waist when their lifting weights. Was he really going to hit me with that over some spilled milk? Big Willie walked over to me "face the fireplace and put her hands on the ledge," he told me. There was no sign of emotion on his face. He just had a look of not wanting to repeat himself. But I was more confused. Didn't he learn from the last time when he beat me what happened. I guess that's why he took us away from Detroit, so he could do whatever he wanted to do with us and my mother would have no family to run to and help her.

I tried to brass myself for what was about to happen. He beat me in front of everyone as to make an example out of me. The first three hits with Big Willie's weight belt were the worst. The first hit made a loud whack sound and the impact of it took my breath away. This was not normal. With every hit my knees got weaker. By the third hit, my body went numb. I thought for sure my mother would hear the noise and come out running from wherever she was and stop this, but she never did. For some reason, I didn't cry. Probably because I was so mad. Why does he continue to pick on me? I wasn't a bad child, why me? Why any of us? Two more whacks Big Willie gave me before he put the belt away. He walked back over to the table and began feeding my brother again. I stiffly walked back over to the table and slowly sat down in my chair. Thank God the chair had a cushion on it. No one said a word. I cleaned up the milk that I had spilled. I had lost my appetite but I made myself eat. Tears eventually mixed in with my cereal and milk. I knew if I didn't eat that would have given Big Willie another reason to beat me. He would have said I was wasting food. I looked across the table at Sis but she never looked up from her cereal bowl.

I received many beatings with that weight belt. And for some reason, it seemed like I was the only one. Don't get me wrong I never wanted Sis to get in trouble; I just got tired of getting beat. It seemed like Big Willie was always watching me. As if he was waiting for me to do something wrong. Waiting for me to do anything to give him an excuse to take out that weight belt and beat me. I couldn't think straight anymore. I would do the same thing three or four times to make sure it was right, but it didn't matter. I could do nothing right in his eye. If Big Willie woke up that morning and felt like beating on me, he did. And what I hated the most, my mother was never there to stop him from beating me. I started to think that something was wrong with me; that I was a troubled child. Maybe I was asking for it. Big Willie had no reason not to like me; but he did.

With all the beatings came scars. It was kind of odd to me; my mother wasn't there to stop Big Willie from beating me, but she was always there afterward to cover up my scars. Coco butter became a second skin for me. It worked really well at making all the evidence of Big Willie's beatings go away. But for some reason my mother wouldn't make Big Willie go away. She saw that he as abusing me. I wanted to go back to Detroit to my grandparent's house, but we were so far away. That was a long summer.

The new house became a party house too. Big Willie always had a lot of his friends and their girlfriends over partying and drinking at the house. I wasn't complaining because that kept his mind off of me and for a long while, the beatings stopped. And oh yeah that guy who was in the back seat of the car that night, him and his girlfriend lived with us for a minute too. We hardly saw him because he was always shut up in his room doing adult stuff. Sometimes you could hear it through his bedroom door when you passed through the hall. He was known to us as Uncle Joe. He wasn't such a good uncle.

The holidays were coming up. All the Christmas cartoons and holiday specials were showing on television; *Santa Claus, Rudolph, Frosty the Snowman, T'was the Night Before Christmas, Charlie Brown Christmas*. My mother had put up a Christmas tree and on it she hung a lot of baby candy canes all around. We would always pass by the Christmas tree on the way to the kitchen. We knew to look but to never touch anything. That's how things were run around this house.

We were all upstairs playing in our room when all of a sudden you could hear my mother and Big Willie arguing. Well it was more so Big Willie yelling at my mother about something and then him calling all of us downstairs to the living room. Just the sound of Big Willie's voice at times had me scared to breathe. We always went in birth order; the oldest to the youngest whenever he would call for all of us. Sis first; then me followed by my little brother we all came down stairs. We were like little ducklings that had followed their mother across the road.

When we got downstairs Big Willie was standing by the Christmas tree starring at it. My mother was standing next to him trying to calm him down without success. Uncle Joe and his girlfriend were sitting on the couch. They must have needed to come up for air from all that adult activity. "Come over here," Big Willie yelled. "Who ate the candy canes off the damn Christmas tree?" he demanded to know. "There were twenty four candy canes on this tree now there are only eighteen on here." I thought to myself was he serious. He's screaming and yelling because someone ate some candy canes off the Christmas tree. For once I was proud to know that I wasn't going to get in trouble because I knew this day was coming and I knew not to touch one candy cane off that tree. This man is crazy. This big grown ass man is yelling and screaming about some candy canes missing off the Christmas tree. Isn't that what candy is for; for you to eat it. Uncle Joe and his girlfriend were laughing. I didn't know if they were laughing because they were high; which they usually are. Or if they were laughing at Big Willie because of how stupid he was sounding. Or if they were laughing because they had done something and someone else was going to get in trouble for it while they got away with it.

Sis and I just looked at each other. At first we said nothing, and then Big Willie asked again who ate the candy canes off the Christmas tree. First of all I would like to know who in their right mind goes around and counts candy canes on a Christmas tree every day to make sure there are twenty four. Big Willie's craziness never seems to disappoint me. I had never seen Sis with a candy cane and she had never seen me with a candy cane; so that cleared us so we thought. My little brother was too short to even reach the candy canes on the tree, so that cleared him. So we all just shrugged our shoulders and said that we didn't know who ate the candy off the Christmas tree; that made Big Willie's blood boil. Because he didn't see anyone take the candy off the tree; he really couldn't blame anybody.

Big Willie walked around the tree pointing every place where a candy cane used to hang. The closer he got to the side of the tree where we were standing, we knew not to be in arms reach; at least I did. I knew he would try to snatch me up first and make an example out of me. We all stepped back and let him pass by. My mother stood by not saying another word. "I'm going to beat your ass if you don't tell me?" was it really that serious? Joe and his girlfriend was stilling laugh as if Big Willie had said something funny. Getting a beating by Big Willie was not funny to me. I knew that I didn't eat the candy canes off the tree so I immediately pleaded my case. Not that it ever saved me from a beating before. "Big Willie," I started to say, "I didn't eat any candy off the tree." I could feel the tears starting to build up in my eyes. By this time I was so tired of the whole situation.

Big Willie could have cared less about what I had just said. He started to yell even louder; "I said who ate the damn candy off the tree?" he just starred at all of us with that crazy mad-man look on his face. My mother was still standing there; not saying a word to protect her ducklings. Joe and his girlfriend settled down to a giggle. I wanted to go over there and slap his girlfriend because I really didn't see what was so funny and I didn't appreciate her laughing at us knowing we were about to get the piss beat out of us. But we all still claimed our innocence, "we didn't eat any candy off the tree,: we all said. That still wasn't what Big Willie wanted to hear. "You all get your ass up stairs, now," he yelled pointing in the direction of the stairs. "I'm going to come up there and beat your ass."

I just dropped my head and slowly started walking towards the stairs. We didn't eat any candy off the tree and there was no convincing him of that. Sis was in front of me and she too was headed for the stairs, I guess we were moving too slow because all of a sudden I hear Big Willie running up behind us, " get your ass up stairs now", he yelled. Sis and I took off running up the stairs. Big Willie went to reach for my shirt but he tripped on the bottom step when he lunged for me. I looked back and saw that he was picking himself up off the step. I'm really going to get it now for making him fall.

Even after we made it upstairs and into our room, you could still hear Big Willie fussing about the candy canes that were missing off the tree. All I could think about how bad we were going to get it. We never saw Big Willie for the rest of the day. Just the thought of the bedroom door flying open and Big Willie standing on the other side holding his weight belt in his hand was too much for me to bare. So much that I cried and rocked myself to sleep that night. I vowed that a candy cane would never hang from any Christmas tree that I owned.

Big Willie never came to our room that night. Mama later told us that our so-called Uncle Joe and his high ass girlfriend confessed that they were the ones who ate the candy canes off the Christmas tree. To my surprise we didn't see Uncle Joe anymore.

Christmas morning finally came. But it wasn't like the ones you saw on television where the whole family sat around the Christmas tree and happily opened presents that were wrapped in pretty paper topped with bows. Instead there in three separate piles were unwrapped gifts sitting on the couch. Everything was done in birth order Sis, me, and my little brother. So when mama called us downstairs we already knew which pile to go to. My pile had a beautiful beige teddy bear sitting on top of it. That was a good day.

Just like in my other house back in Detroit my bedroom was where I spent most of my time trying to stay out of harm's way. Here in Akron, Ohio it would be also. But the only difference in this house was that I was finally playing with my sister and little brother. But that was only because we all shared the same room and we all slept in the same big bed together. It seemed like we were always in our room. The only time we came out was to eat and go to the bathroom. But we kept ourselves busy. Sis used to play her records on a little record player that she got that Christmas. Natalie Cole *This Will Be* would be played over and over. That's the only record she had. We didn't mind at all. We learned every word to that and *Our Love*. We were always coloring and playing with our baby dolls. But there was one game that I didn't like to play and that was *house*.

Since it was three of us; Sis would always played the mama, my brother was the youngest so of course he played the baby and she would always make me play the daddy. For some reason *house* became a game that my sister liked to play a lot. The more and more she played the more aggressive she got with the things that she wanted the daddy to do to the mama. I knew that these were only things that real mamas and daddies did to each other. When I would refuse to do certain things that she asked she would get mad at me or promise me that next time when we played *house* that I could be the mama.

I didn't want my sister mad at me, she was like my best friend; my only friend that I had in this whole situation that I started to call my life. I did the things she asked me to do even though I knew they were wrong. Somehow it seemed she got pleasure from me doing those things to her and I didn't understand why. Where did she learn this stuff from? Someone had to have been showing her these things.

One night Sis wanted me to play *house* again. I told her no because I didn't like the things that she was making the daddy do to the mama. We never played *house* again after that. I loved my sister but I hated to think that she had been playing *house* with someone else who was making her do those bad things to them. Her innocence was stolen and I'm afraid she will never get it back.

Over time, we found ourselves moving a lot. There was one huge house that we lived in and it had an attic, basement, and a big back-yard. At one point Big Willie embraced his love for dogs at this house. He had big dogs, small dogs, fat dogs, skinny dogs. Some of the dogs had short hair, long hair even curly hair or some had no hair at all. And he kept them all down stairs in the basement. Those were too many dogs to take out for a walk which he never did; so you could just imagine the mess and the smell in the basement.

One good thing about the dogs is that they were friendly. They never barked at us or even tried to bite us when we would come down to the basement and clean up their mess. I can only imagine the reason for that was that they were glad to see us. They didn't want to scare us away. You can only stand your filth but for so long. I know that I will never forget the smell of week old dog crap and pee for the rest of my life.

One day I was out in the backyard playing and unknowingly to me Big Willie had let one of the smaller dogs out. After about an hour of me being outside playing Big Willie came outside on the upstairs balcony and asked me if I had seen Bailey. Bailey was a small beige curly haired dog. I told Big Willie that I hadn't seen Bailey. "You better find him or I'm going to beat your ass." I thought to myself; The Great One has spoken because that's how he looked standing up there on the balcony. Like he was ruler over the land and his word was bond. And of course I went into panic mode. The beatings had slowed down and I didn't want to awaken them. Lord knows that I didn't want to wake that sleeping giant.

I frantically looked around the whole yard. There was no sign of Bailey anywhere. I started talking to myself. At one point I think I even started praying and pleading for my life. As I walked the yard, I noticed that the gate was open. Maybe Bailey walked out. I ran to the gate which leads right onto the sidewalk just knowing that I would see Bailey walking down the street. I looked left down the sidewalk and then I looked right down the street but there was no Bailey. I started to talk to myself again. Tears started to build up in my eyes as I went back in the back yard. Where was Bailey?

I began to get mad as I looked over the backyard and still didn't see Bailey. Big Willie's words are all that ran through my mind as I looked up at the balcony where he once stood. I could feel the pain of the weight belt going through my body like an electric shock. Something told me to go back to the gate and look down the sidewalk again and so I did. I ran back to the gate and looked down the street. Through my blurred vision I saw Sis walking towards the house with something in her arms.

The closer Sis got to the house I could make out what she was holding, it was Bailey. Sis just doesn't know that she saved my ass. I was so relieved to see Bailey that I ran out and ran down the street to meet them on the sidewalk. "Bailey must have followed me to the store", Sis said. She handed me the dog as if she knew that I had been looking for Bailey. I just smiled. I had never been so happy to see someone in my life. Not even Santa Clause with all his presents could have gotten a smile like that out of me. "Oh thank you so much", I said to Sis.

With Bailey in my arms, I ran back to the house. When I got in the house I could hear Mama and Big Willie in the kitchen where they were painting it a sunflower yellow. I ran in the kitchen. I was so excited I didn't notice that I was standing in a tray of paint as I announced that I had found Bailey. Mama looked up at me from where she was painting the wall, and then she looked down at my feet and started laughing. I looked down at my feet. My blue tennis shoe was covered in sunflower yellow paint. Sis saved my behind from getting a beating for losing Bailey but now I'm going to still get a beating for stepping in the paint making a mess. But to my surprise, Big Willie started to laugh.

"You were so excited about the dog, you done stepped in the paint," mama said as she slowly removed my shoe. "Yeah" I said with a little nervous giggle; still not sure or not whether I was going to get a beating for it. "Here take your shoe outside so it can dry" mama told me. I hopped on one foot all the way to the door to sit my shoe on the porch. I guess after I found Bailey nothing else mattered to Big Willie; his baby was home. From that day forward; Sis and I had each others back.

The dogs weren't the worst thing about the house it was the other four legged creatures; the rats. They were the one thing that I hated about this house. The one thing that I loved about this house was that mama use to always play music when we had our big clean up days which was usually on Saturday.

We would be in the kitchen, Sis washing dishes and me drying them while we boogied to Frankie Beverly. I think that was mama's favorite. I fell in love with music. It became my escape from the real world. A band called *Earth, Wind, and Fire* had a hit out called *Reasons* it rang throughout the whole house over and over. But there was one song that really got my attention; *Always and Forever* by *Heatwave.* That song made me want to fall in love. I didn't know anything about love but I knew I wanted that kind of love that he sung about in that song.

The music kept our mind off cleaning and even made it fun but it didn't keep the rats away. There were way too many and they were way too big. It was hard to ignore them when they were running across your feet in the kitchen. Seeing dead rats caught in traps and just laying right there thrown on top of the trash was a daily sight. Their beady black eyes showed no sign of life. There were even times when we would bait them out. I would stand in the middle of the kitchen and beat on the floor with a wooden bat or broom to draw them from up under the sink. I felt like the Pied Piper. It wasn't too long after that, that I woke up one morning in yet another house. I guess mama got tired of the rats. Since it seemed like they didn't want to move, she did.

In the weeks and months that would follow, we would move so many more times, it started to seem like we were running away from something. The more we moved the more far away Detroit seemed.

# Chapter 8

**IN OUR NEW** place it wasn't as big as the last one but still big enough for us. The only furniture we had was a dining room table. The one good thing about this house was that we had our own beds even though we were still all in the same room. I didn't mind that so much. The one other good thing was Big Willie wasn't there and he wouldn't be around for a while. And for a long while things were nice. Me and Sis had a chance to be little girls for the first time.

With Big Willie being gone, Mama was around her children more. She wasn't isolated in her bedroom like she would have been if Big Willie was around and neither were we. We didn't have a lot but mama did the best she could with what she had. We ate a lot of pinto beans but mama always made sure we had something sweet for dessert. Mama knows she could bake a cake.

Just like grandma's house; this house had a big porch that I loved sitting on while it rained. At this house I even made friends with the little girl next door. The houses sat so close together you didn't have to leave the porch to have a conversation with your neighbor. My new friend taught me the funniest rhythms I had ever heard. My cousins back home had taught me and Sis one called *Rockin Robin*. All four of us would sit in a circle and do pitty-pat as we song the rhythm. But my new friend taught me one called *Miss Mary Mac*. I would sing myself to sleep many a night with that rhythm. My friend taught me and Sis how to play Hop Scotch and Chinese Jump rope and even taught us how to play Jacks. Sis became the queen of Jacks. I guess it helped that she had those long skinny fingers; it helped her pick up way more Jacks than me.

One thing about being here; whatever state we were in was that we were finally stable enough to rest our feet for a minute. I remembered going to school while we were at this house. Again it was around Christmas time and our music class had to put on a play. We had to learn a song called *Up On The House Top*. That is still my favorite Christmas song.

One good thing happened while Big Willie was away, mama joined the church. I really didn't understand all the hoopla at first but the more and more we went I knew that church was the place you wanted to be and it made mama happy. My mother seemed at peace when she joined the church. I think it kept her mind occupied while Big Willie was away. The church was the size of a basement and stayed filled on Sunday morning. We didn't miss a Sunday. On the really hot days the church doors would stay open so air could come in. I remember the older ladies in church clapping, shouting, and dancing as they sung their church songs. The organ played and the drum had a language all its own. Mama kept us in church when Big Willie wasn't around. I use to love to see my mama catch the *Spirit*. Her praise was in her hands. I loved to see my mama clap her hands in church. She had a rhythm and every so often she would sneak in an extra clap which took her praise to another level.

Every Sunday after church we would run over to the corner store and buy penny candy. Grape, chocolate, and banana *now and later* candy became my favorite along with *Boston baked beans* and lemon heads. The Sundays when we got fifty cent were the good Sundays to me.

I remember that mama use to make our church dresses and we would always find the jelly shoes to match. Jelly shoes were fun to wear because they came in so many different colors. The only thing that I didn't like about jelly shoes was when it got hot they seem to melt and stick to your feet and they didn't protect your feet from getting dirt between your toes. It was so funny when you would take off your jellies; the shoe print would still be on your foot. Mama would sew my little brother a new pair of pants and find a matching shirt at the store so we could go to church. Mama with a sewing machine made miracles happen. Girls get dresses made all the time but to see my mother make my little brothers pants to match with a shirt that she bought at the store seemed to be a bit much for me. Every other Sunday or so, I had a new pretty dress for church. Again the signs of us being poor were there and even embarrassing at times but the feeling of being safe and away from Big Willie, I would choose being poor any day. Mama did the most with the little money she had. She would make Sis and my Easter dress so she would have enough money to by us new shoes. I thought that she would buy my little brother a suit but she made that too.

With no or very little money there was no car, so we had to walk everywhere we had to go mostly it was to the laundry mat or the grocery store. Mama had this steel basket cart with wheels and a long handle that she used when we went to the grocery store so we didn't have to carry so many bags. I really didn't mind the walk; it was the early Saturday mornings that I didn't like. Saturday was laundry day so we had to get up real early and get to the laundry mat before all the washer and dryers got taken. After washing and folding clothes; walking was the last thing I wanted to do. The long walks did us some good though. We had time to talk to each other and enjoy it other. Mama seemed fun and seem to have a lot of insight on things. She seemed different when she didn't have a man around to distract her from her children. It was like we were getting to know my mother for the first time. I never remember us being able to spend time or even talk to mama when Big Willie was around. Once a month mama would even take us to see the latest Disney movie that was out; *Pinocchio, Snow White, or Cinderella* followed by a trip to Burger King for something to eat.

My brother was growing up without a father and he was a hand full. Mama had left us home one day while she went to run an errand leaving Sis in charge. He was about five years old I think and he decided to climb up on a small shed roof in the backyard. Sis ended up going after him but not before he saw a dead bird. We thought we swore him to secrecy but that night when mama gave him a bath he went to babbling on about a dead bird he saw and spilled the beans. Mama seemed confused because she that he was talking about something he might have seen on television. But she became curious when he began to describe the dead bird in such detail. After asking Sis what the world my little brother was going on about and Sis explaining my little brothers adventure we ended up going to bed that night without cake for dessert.

Mama would always leave Sis in charge of me and my little brother when she had to leave and go run errands. Some errands seem to take longer than others and mama would be gone for what seemed like forever. But when mama feed us and got us settled down in bed while the sun was still up and strongly stressed for us not to get out of the bed for nothing and she meant nothing, it felt long she was never going to come back. She seemed as if she was rushing to meet with someone. After mama was satisfied that we understood her clearly she left the house. We talked amongst ourselves until we fell asleep.

The next morning when I came down for breakfast, Big Willie was sitting at the table. I hadn't seen him for so long; he looked so different to me. He looked much calmer and nicer. I guess that's what sitting in a jail cell will do to a person. I wished he would go back. We didn't need him here. We had been doing just fine without him. Yes he was nice but I didn't trust him. It wasn't long before he went back to his old ways. The beatings started again for one reason or another. It wasn't long after Big Willie returned, we had moved again. I can never remember the actual moves. I don't remember packing anything or seeing a moving truck in front of our old places. I just know that we always move at night because I'm always waking up the next morning in a new place.

Normally we lived in houses but this time we moved into a duplex apartment building. Four units to each building, we lived in the upstairs apartment. In the apartment you had your main level then you had a door and stairs that lead up to an upstairs attic slash bedroom with its own bathroom with just a sink and toilet. It had a huge clothes closet with a big window that let in a lot of sunshine. I had never seen a closet with a window it in; I thought that was the coolest thing. Not many clothes hung in that closet it seemed like we left with just the clothes on our back. We were poor and we knew it. Of course, our bedroom was where we spent all our time. Our three beds fit in perfectly with plenty of room to spare.

Our days of getting up early on Saturday morning and walking to the laundry mat were over; instead we washed clothes in the downstairs bathroom tub on a scrub board, and I hated it. Mama would fill the tub up with hot water for the white clothes, added the bleach and detergent and let the clothes soak for thirty minutes. Every couple of minutes me or Sis would have to take a stick and go and stur the clothes around in the tub. When mama figured the clothes had soaked enough she then had me and Sis take turns scrubbing them clean on an old scrub board. You know the kind you would see in the hillbillies' bands that they rubbed the spoons against to make a sound. But instead of spoons scrubbing the board; it was our poor little knuckles. The dark clothes were washed in cold water. Yeah, like that was a lot of fun, not! Just imagine washing blue jeans on a scrub board; our knuckles didn't stand a chance. Your knees and back begged for a break. Ringing out all the water out the clothes was a process too. When we were finished; I think we were just as soaked as the clothes that came out the water. Now I knew how people felt when they had to wash their clothes down by the river side oh so long ago. Beating their clothes on the rock to get them clean and then hanging them on a tree branch to dry.

When all the clothes were washed and since we didn't have a dryer; we had to hang the clothes up around the clothes anywhere there was an empty spot. We hung the pants on the top ledge of the door end to end to drip dry onto newspapers that we would slide underneath the doors. All dry all you heard was drip, drip, drip. Sometimes there would be a double drip. We would hang our shirts on hangers and hope that we didn't use up all the doors with the pants. We would take the hangers and hook them along the top of the door ledge but on the back of the door. You couldn't just open the door all the way when you came in the bedroom because the hangers would stick out like elbows.

Mama bought some kind of wooden rack stand that folded open. Across the top were three rows where you could hang things; that's where we hung all the underwear. Then it stood two levels high: that's where we hung all the socks. And on the corners we hung up mama's bras by the strap so they could dry. Thank God she was the only one who wore bras because I don't think that poor stand could have stood any more clothes on it. On laundry day it would look like the house got sick and threw up clothes everywhere. Boy, how I starting to miss getting up early on Saturday mornings walking to the laundry mat.

At some point mama or Big Willie bought and old washing machine and sat it on the back porch since there was nowhere to hook it up in the apartment. The washing machine had to be from the early fifties. I really didn't care how old it was; it got us up off our knees and it was saving our knuckles and back. It sat on four legs, had a big round tub, and above the tub sat two things that looked like rolling pins. When the clothes would finish washing, we would have to feed them through the two rolling pins; that was how you rung them out. Sometimes the jeans would be too thick and it would knock the two rolling pins apart causing it to stop working. We would have to stop; pull the pants back out and start all over until the pants would finally fit through. There was still no dryer; old or new.

At this place we didn't go to church but we were able to rest our feet here for a minute too. Mama made friends with the lady who lived next door with her husband and baby. Mama and her neighbor friend use to sit on the porch and watch us kids while we played in the pile of fall leaves in the yard. I was glad mama finally had someone to talk to.

But it wasn't long before the partying stopped and the beatings started up again. But I can say they started to be far and few between. One morning I was getting ready for school and mama was still in the bed. I know because I had to go in their bedroom and ask her for something, then I left out to go finish getting ready for school. All of a sudden while I was in the bathroom brushing my teeth Big Willie came out of nowhere and punched me in the face. I was stunned, what was that for? I felt like one of those balloon clowns with no feet. You know the kind that when you punch it and it falls back but always comes back standing up straight until you punch it again because it has a round bottom like a ball.

Trying to still regain my senses, I watched as Big Willie walked over to a pile of two by fours that had been left behind from a job that they were working on to repair something in the bathroom; and picked on up and started to approach me with it. "Turn around", he said. I braced myself to the bathroom sink. Big Willie hit me four times on my butt with that two by four. I really didn't feel the hits because I was still stunned from the punch. He acted like it was a bat in his hand and that he was in the major leagues trying to hit a home run. Even when he got finished he threw the two by four down on the floor like a hitter who had gotten struck out at home plate. After that, he just went and got back in the bed like it wasn't nothing. I looked in the mirror and one whole side of my face was swollen. I couldn't go to school looking like this; I thought to myself. Just then my mother's voice came from the bedroom telling me to hurry up and finish getting ready for school before I was late. She never once got out of bed to see what was even taking me so long. I just looked at my face in the mirror and shook my head. There was no use of me going to show her my face; she would just send me to school anyhow. I tried to wash the swelling away with cold water, but it didn't help. Remind me never to go in their bedroom again in the morning and ask them anything. I pulled myself together as best

I could. I cleaned myself up, grabbed my coat and walked to school in disbelief of what had just happened.

On my way to school I couldn't hold my head up. I didn't want anyone to see me like this. I looked down at the pretty white snow that had been shoveled into a pile over against a building. I just wanted to lay down in it and go to sleep; die even. I starred at the snow knowing that if I just could lie there for ten minutes maybe someone would come along and find me in the snow and take me home with them. Oh I forgot; you have to be a baby in a basket for anyone to do that. The sound of a car's horn blowing at me because I was standing to close to the street edge brings me back to my reality, so again my dreams of ever leaving this situation that I call *life* are shattered. I hurried off to school so I wouldn't be late.

All day at school I was so devastated. I became angry and even a little defiant. I'm normally a good student in class who pays attention but today my mind was not my own. Everything the teacher would ask me to do; today I told her no. I was mean to the kids in class. If anyone of them said anything to me, I just told them to shut up and to leave me alone. Not one time did my teacher come to me or pull me to the side to ask me what was wrong. She knew this was not normal behavior for me. What's up with this adult? Do they not notice the signs of a child that is being abused? I knew she saw my face and how swollen it was.

I just couldn't shake the image of the reflection in the mirror of Big Willie hitting me with the two by four earlier that morning. And the thought that my mother never got out her bed let alone come out the bedroom to even check on me. I didn't care anymore about myself; I really wanted to die. I felt that was the only way to stop the pain. That day I wrote my name in big bold stick letters across the top of my paper. I normally have beautiful bubble handwriting. But the bold stick letters reminded me of the two by four Big Willie had hit me with. School was finally over that day and I had nowhere to go but home. I didn't hurry home the same way that I hurried to school that morning, but instead it was the longest and loneliest walk home ever. When I got to the pile of snow that I had seen that morning I still wanted to just lay down and die.

The rest of the week at school was a big blur. I wasn't myself. I could feel anger coming out of me like steam racing out of a tea pot that sitting on the stove. I could feel myself becoming devious and wanting to cause mischief with my feelings. It was if evil was spilling over on me. I didn't want to be nice to anyone anymore; what was the point. No one was being nice to me. Big Willie was being mean to me for no reason. Why did Big Willie hate me so much? Why won't my mother stop him from beating on me? Why can't we leave Big Willie here and go back home to Detroit?

Later on that week my teacher handed me an envelope after school. She had written mama a letter. And I knew all too well what it was about; my behavior. All the way home I starred at the envelope with my mother's name on it that I held so tightly in my hand. Should I give it to her? It could be something bad saying how my strange behavior was disturbing the class and she would like for her to have a talk with me about it. Or maybe it was something good saying that she was concerned about me because she had noticed a change in my behavior and wanted to have a talk with her about it. In one sense I thought the letter was a good thing; that someone finally noticed that something was wrong because my mother acted like she didn't. Maybe I could get some help now and the beatings would stop. The longer I looked at the envelope the more I knew it wasn't a good thing. Mama would probably take the letter the wrong way as me going to school running my mouth about what was going on in our house. And not a way of me crying out for help because I didn't know who I could trust or ask for help. Thinking the worst; I slowly released my grip on the envelope and let the wind take it out of my hand. I watched as it danced towards the sky. But then it danced no more but came to a rest on the very spot where I wished I had laid down on earlier that morning.

The next morning when I returned to school with no letter, nothing was said by my teacher. I figured it must wasn't a big deal after all and she wouldn't know whether I gave it to her or not. But I was so wrong. When school was let out a couple of days later my teacher presented me with another letter but this time with instructions. "Make sure you give this to your mother, she has to sign it and return it to me." This one I had better take home, I told myself; so I did just that. Mama mentioned nothing of the letter that night so I figured that I was all worried for nothing and that I should have just given her the first letter that my teacher had written her.

The next day when I got home from school, mama said she wanted to talk to me. She had ran me a tub of water and told me to sit in it.

she left out the bathroom as I got undressed. I thought it was kind of odd that I was going to take a bath so early in the day. But I just figured mama wanted to spend some quality time with me alone and kill two birds with one stone since her schedule was so tight with having to run the house, take care of my little brother and a man. I figured the letter from my teacher made her realize that all the beatings that I was getting from Big Willie was starting to affect me mentally and that the teacher noticed a change in my attitude in school towards my friends and that my grades were dropping because I couldn't concentrate. That maybe she noticed something had been bothering me. I'm thinking that mama wanted to apologize for everything that had been going on and even to assure me that things would change and get better.

As I sat in the clear tub of water; I noticed that there wasn't a wash cloth or soap so I could take a bath. Mama must have remembered that she forgot to get me a wash cloth too because when she returned she had one in her hand for me. "Mama, I need a wash cloth." I said. "I know, here," she said as she handed me the wash cloth. "Put this in your mouth." I looked at her puzzled but I did what she told me to do. For some reason I was thinking she didn't want any water to get in my mouth for some strange reason. I folded the wash cloth small enough so it would fit in my mouth. After mama had seen that I had the wash cloth secured in my mouth; she brought forth a brown extension cord that she had been hiding behind her back all this time. I couldn't believe what was about to happen.

Mama struck me with the extension cord repeatedly. I began to flop around in that tub like a fish out of water. Water was splashing everywhere. I would go under the water and then back on top. I would move from one end of the tub to another trying to avoid the lashes from the extension cord; but I felt everyone one. Mama was talking to me but I couldn't hear a word over the splashing water and my muffled screams. When I would go under the water I couldn't breathe. The wash cloth was blocking my screams as well as my breath. I just knew that I was going to die. The wash cloth in my mouth had gotten wet. The more I opened my mouth to scream or beg mama to stop the deeper it went into my mouth. I thought that I was going to choke on it. I pushed the wash cloth out of my mouth with my tongue because my hands were too busy trying to block the sting from the extension cord. Between lashes at times I would grab on to the side of the tub and pull myself from up under the water. When I came up for air I let out a scream but mama would not stop hitting me with the extension cord. My body stung all over where mama had hit me. The pain was unbearable. I couldn't believe that my own mother was now part of the abuse. When my beating was finally over just as calmly as she told me to get in the tub; she told me to get out of the tub and get dressed. She walked out of the bathroom without saying another word or looking back.

At that very moment, my mother was dead to me. I knew that I could trust no one; not even my own mother. I knew there was no one to protect me; not even my own mother. I knew there was no one that I could depend on; not even my own mother.

I don't know what was in that letter, but it really didn't matter to me. I was more concerned with the fact that when I looked into my mother's eyes while she was beating me that I saw nothing. Her eyes were black like demons eyes. She was not my mother.

# Chapter 9

**MAMA AND BIG** Willie started to leave us home alone a lot and that left Sis in charge. She was a good babysitter. So good that once mama even went out of town leaving us home for a day or two by ourselves. We never once left out of our bedroom, only Sis and that was when she would go downstairs to get us something to eat. It felt kind of scary knowing we were home alone overnight. They even trusted her to watch the neighbor's baby when they did a double date; I helped her with that one. She couldn't have been more than six months old. Sis didn't know how to take care of a baby.

We had to go over to the neighbor's apartment. It was weird to see how other folks lived. We sat down on the couch and Sis was holding the baby while her mama and my mother instructed Sis what to do in the event that the baby started crying. Sis looked like she was having problems just holding the baby. Sis was skinny and fragile while the baby was pump. She probably felt like a sack of potatoes in Sis's arms. I didn't help that the baby wouldn't hold still.

Everyone had left. They had been gone for at least thirty minutes; the baby started crying and she wouldn't stop. It was like a fire alarm going off. I never heard my brother cry like that. Maybe baby boys cried different from baby girls. I don't know but we needed to get this baby to stop crying right away. Sis remembered the instructions that she was given earlier. She checked the baby's diaper to see if she was wet; she wasn't. So now Sis had to see if the baby was hungry. Sis handed me the baby and asked me to hold her while she went in the kitchen to make a bottle; the baby was still crying. With every minute she was getting louder and louder. A baby will do all of that just because it's hungry or wet. It took all of that.

I held the yelling baby while looking down at her wondering what the heck she was crying for. Then I thought to myself; I'm glad someone else is crying besides me for a change. I didn't know why she was crying. I knew I would cry because I felt pain. And for a moment I wanted someone to feel that same pain. I found myself doing things to the baby to make her cry from pain and not circumstance. Being careful not to let Sis catch me, I quickly would pinch the baby real hard on her thigh several times. The baby only screamed louder. At first I was afraid but then I reached into her diaper and pinched her private. I became ashamed of what I was doing and felt no satisfaction from it. I began to feel sad that I was causing her pain. I looked down at the screaming baby and told her that I was sorry. I began to rock her so to comfort her. Her screams returned to faint cries. Sis finally came back from the kitchen with a bottle of milk. I handed her the baby, "I think she's hungry." I told Sis.

Sis and I would babysit the baby girl once or twice more after that. I would play with her to make her happy. I was more pleased with myself that I was doing a good thing and not causing harm to someone. Eventually the young couple moved out of their apartment. But, it wasn't long after that another couple moved in and they had a little girl my age. Her name was Tee-tee.

At first I liked Tee-tee; she was someone to play with. Jumping and rolling in a pile of Fall leaves was fun. She introduced me to mud pies. I think we even got to spend the night over her house once or twice. But then Tee-tee started to act like she was better than me and my sister. I started to distance myself from her. But when I would, Sis would always ask me to give Tee-tee a second chance. Tee-tee knew that we were poor and every time she got something new she would parade it around in our faces. Like she was poking fun at Sis and I. She knew that we didn't have our real father with us; so she would always go on and on about what her daddy had done for her that day. She was starting to sound like a stuck-up brat to me. She would never share her things with us. She would just make it very clear that she had what we didn't. Just the mention of her name started to annoy me.

One day while I was sitting on the steps outside, Tee-tee came out of her apartment and sat down next to me. I just looked at her and politely slid over. "My daddy brought me this candy bar," she started to say. "Why didn't you stay in the house and eat it," I asked. "Oh, I don't know", she said in her proper white girl voice as she slung back her ponytail like the white girls would do their hair. Was she for real, I thought to myself? She is really going over the top. The Hershey candy bar rested in Tee-tee's lap. She started to open it very slowly. She acted like she was unwrapping a Christmas present that she wasn't supposed to find that was hidden in the back of a closet "Can I have some?" I asked. "No", she said without looking up. I watched as she finishes neatly opening the candy bar. I could see that it was melted and mushed. What did her daddy do, sit on it? I watched as this selfish self-centered brat peeled a corner of the candy bar off its wrapper and put it in her mouth. "I didn't want any of your candy anyway," I told her. "It looks like shit." Tee-tee looked at me with tears in her eyes. I didn't care. By this time Sis came outside and sat on the steps next to Tee-tee. Sis asked Tee-tee what was that she was eating. "Shit", I said. Sis just busted out laughing and Tee-tee ran in the house with her melted candy bar. Sis told me that I shouldn't have said that. But we sat there on the steps and giggled about it anyway. With friends like Tee-tee there was no room for enemies.

Being left home alone a lot had its advantages. We got to stay up late and to watch stuff on television that was only meant for adult viewing. Being left home alone was the only other time we were able to come out from upstairs. It seemed Mama and Big Willie was doing great. We were doing well, because they were gone all the time. Big Willie had even joined a local football league and mama was a cheerleader. The Raiders was the name of the team. The local news even show casted one of their football games and we actually saw Big Willie on television on the ten o'clock news. That was kind of exciting to see. When they got home that night from the game we told them that we had saw them on the news. They didn't believe us at first, until the story just so happened to air again.

Besides the news, there was another show that came on late. Back in the seventies there was a London comedian called Benny Hill and he had a television show. It was strictly adult sexual humor. Definitely not for our young eyes and mind; but we would still sneak to watch it. It was always just us three sitting in front of the television watching this white man with a big belly run around slapping a little bold man upside his head and him chasing after half naked girls trying to pinch their butts or grab their boobs. All while a catchy little music tune played in the background. What made it so funny is when the chasing scenes came on; they would speed up the film making their legs move real real fast. When the show would go off, we would go to bed. We never told our little dirty secret of staying up late and watching Benny Hill. If we told we knew that would be the end of our behinds as we knew it.

There came a time for a while when Big Willie wasn't living with us anymore. Mama had been spending a lot of time with us and we weren't tucked away in our upstairs attic bedroom. Mama would find herself staying up late with us watching television. But like anything all good things must come to an end.

One night mama got a phone call. Mama jumped out her chair, got dressed in a matter of seconds and left. We stayed up for a while waiting for mama to come back but when it got too late we realized she might not be coming back that night, so we put ourselves to bed. Several hours later we were awaken by my mother who had finally returned home. She told us to come down stairs that she had needed to talk to us about something. She started off real slow by saying that she had to tell us something about Big Willie.

"Big Willie shot himself in the head tonight." She began to say. "He was playing Russian Roulette." My mother went on to explain what that was. First I thought why would anyone considered that a game and second why would anyone want to play it. My brother was too young to understand exactly what my mother was saying, but I understood every single word. I got a tingling sensation all over my body. Every bone in my body leaped with joy, but I dared not showed it on the outside. Hurray, he's dead I said to myself. I was so relieved and happy that my misery caused by him was finally over. That bastard got what he deserved. I hope he rots in hell. I stood in front of my mother with a straight face all the while having a celebration in my head. I didn't even care that my brother's father had just died. My brother would be better off without him.

My celebration lasted all of five seconds, "he's not dead." Were the next words that came out of my mother's mouth? Who in the world plays Russian roulette, shoots themselves in the head and lives to tell about it. Big Willie had to be the devil himself or he made a deal with the devil one. Maybe Big Willie knew the devil personally and the devil owed him one. There had to be a logical explanation for this. Why wouldn't he die is what I wanted to know. I got that sickening feeling in my stomach. I felt sorry for me now.

My mother went on to say that Big Willie would be coming home and that she would have to take care of him. A week or two later I remember people from the hospital came to the house to deliver a special bed for Big Willie. They set the bed up in the living room. Before Big Willie came home, mama did a deep cleaning of the house.

Any and everything old had to go. The whole house was bleached down, wiped down and swept. The house was spotless. Not a crumb on the floor. Not a finger print on the wall. The windows were so clean that you didn't even know that they were there. Mama had us around that house like busy bees in honey season. And after all that hard work she didn't even say thank you or give us a treat. I felt like she was being ungrateful and underserving of our help. We knew that we weren't cleaning the house like that for us; it was for him. Why was she keeping him around anyway? Now in my eyes she was going to be looking like a fool waiting on him hand and foot. Now she had to take care of him, why? Why not let him lay there and die. I just wanted us to pack our things and go back to Detroit before he came back home. To me, Big Willie hadn't done anything for her but up root her from her family, beat on and do whatever else he sees fit to do to her two little girls. And all the while, he's moving us from house to house and state to state. We've moved so much, it's hard to keep up with what city or state we're even in. Mama has no friends and we never stay around long enough to move on to the next grade in school.

After all that cleaning we headed to our bedroom to rest. Something was on the floor and it caught my eye. It was a stick. With all that sweeping and mopping; there still remained a stick on the floor. It was just a little twig, nothing serious. I sat down in the middle of the floor and started to break the stick into smaller sticks. I wanted to play with the little sticks that I had made so I was rearranging them in different patterns on the floor. Sis came upstairs and saw what I was doing and ran and told mama. I didn't see what the big deal was but I think Sis thought I was making a mess. She knew she had worked too hard for there to be still sticks on the floor. I guess mama thought the same thing because I could hear her telling Sis that she was going to whoop me. I didn't want another bathtub episode with mama so I quickly picked up my sticks off the floor. It was too late; mama had sent Sis back upstairs to get me. I followed Sis down the stairs and the whole while I could hear mama fussing. For one I couldn't believe that she was going to whoop me over some sticks and second that was nothing for Sis to go tell anyhow. And anyway I picked the sticks up off the floor, so what was the big deal.

It seemed now that Big Willie was gone mama wanted to start beating on me. It was bad enough when he was doing it, now here she go with the foolishness. I really didn't feel like getting whooped for what I felt like was no big deal. I made it to the living room where mama was waiting for me. The more she moved towards me fussing, the more I was backing up towards the front door. As soon as I got close enough, I darted out that front door like fire from a mad dragon's nose.

I startled myself that I even made it out the front door. I looked to my right and looked to my left, and then I looked back at mama. For a split second I wondered whether to run or not and if I did would she chase me and where would I go. I knew if I would've gone back in the house that I was really going to get it. I took off running. I could hear mama and Sis behind me. Mama was calling for me to come back but I wasn't hearing that. I wasn't about to stop now. I was going in and out of sight. I was running between houses when finally I came to a corner store. I ran into the store while Sis and mama were lost somewhere behind me. I couldn't stay in there for too long, the clerk was looking at me funny and I didn't want him to think that I was coming in there to steal. When I thought the coast was clear, I ran back out onto the street. "There she go", I heard Sis yelling. I took off running again. I looked back only to see them coming. I had never been this far away from home so I didn't know where I was going. I became scared. I dipped into an alley. Mama passed by and didn't even see me, for a second I held my breath so she couldn't hear my heavy breathing from me running so. I was tired of running. I came out of the alley and walked home. Mama was on one side of me and Sis was on the other. I felt like a caught runaway slave.

I can't remember if mama whooped me when I got home, I don't think she did. I know she was tired. But she did put me on punishment. I couldn't leave out my attic bedroom for the rest of the summer. That was a long summer.

And when Big Willie did come home from the hospital mama took care of him. The only good thing about being on punishment was that I had company. My little brother and Sis were kept away in our bedroom attic along with me. I guess mama didn't want us to see Big Willie laying in the hospital bed looking helpless hanging on for dear life, or she didn't want us to see him walking around the house with his head all wrapped up looking like a mummy.

After Big Willie's brush with death; it slowed him down and the beatings stopped. My fear of him never went away. I was always looking over my shoulder; being careful not to let my guard down because I never knew if and when he would get the urge to start beating on me again. Even though the beatings had stopped for now; I noticed that I had developed a nervous twitch because my nerves were so bad. My right leg would tremble so badly. I couldn't control it. It became part of my every day body function just like the beat of my heart.

The seasons changed; leaves had changed their colors and fell to the ground. And like any other time when Big Willie would be gone for a while shortly after his return we would move; this time was no different.

# Chapter 10

**SOMEWHERE IN PENNSYLVANIA** I think is where this ship has set port. As usual I'm waking up to a different place from where I had gone to sleep the night before. Come to find out we were at his sister's Kathy's apartment. Ms. Kathy was very nice to us while we lived there. She had a son and daughter of her own. We ended up staying with Ms. Kathy for a little while. I even started going to school while we lived with her. Her son seemed to be much older. He was very mature and independent. He was nice enough to do his mom a favor when she would ask him to walk me to school. Kathy had good kids. Her daughter was nice to us but she was older. It seemed her house ran without any fuss. Everyone knew what they had to do and everyday seemed routine and easy. I never heard Ms. Kathy fussing at her kids; I wish our house was like that. Every morning Ms. Kathy was in the kitchen cooking a small breakfast for everyone. I would sit to the kitchen table and watch.

Things were quiet around Ms. Kathy's house until the weekends would come; that meant party time for the block. The song *We Are Family* was a big hit back in those days. When they would have their parties at Ms. Kathy's place; we would sit on the steps and watch as the adults would dance, smoke and sip out their cups. At least we would watch until they started getting a little wild, then we would just head up stairs for bed. One night at one of the weekend parties an argument broke out and someone broke one of Ms. Kathy's glass candle holders or a mirror that she had hanging on the wall. That was the end of the party and our stay at Ms. Kathy's house. I didn't want to leave, I liked it there.

Like traveling gypsies; we ended up at another one of his sister's place where we also stayed for a while. At least we were still in the same state this time. His sister had two young teenage daughters; Lisa and Chi-Chi were their names. Here it was crowded. A two bedroom with two daughters and a dog already and now your brother, his girlfriend and her three kids have moved in. During the day, all the adults went to work; that included Big Willie and mama. Well maybe they didn't go to work, but they left the house at sunrise. At first when we moved to his second sister's house, Sis and I didn't go to school right away. But we would always be awoken by his nieces' alarm clocks, so we would get up anyway and watch them get ready for school. *Easy Like Sunday Morning* by Lionel Richie would play on the radio a lot.

The weekends seem to be like a scene right from Cinderella; with the four of us home and no adults around either. Lisa and Chi-Chi were like oil and water. Chi-Chi was the baby. She acted like it and everyone treated her like she was a princess. She was spoiled. Lisa on the other hand was not the pretty one of the two and she was treated as such. It was obvious that everyone favored Chi-Chi over Lisa. Chi-Chi whined a lot over everything and got her way. While Lisa on the other hand got in trouble about everything. And in return, Lisa took it out on Sis and me by being mean to us. But in this twist of the story Sis and I was the step daughters living with the evil cousins. When the adults were around Lisa and Chi-Chi would act all nice and innocent. But when no adults were around and they figured no one was looking; their true colors showed. Another change in character that was amazing to me was Big Willie. He acted like a total different person around his family. I knew him as the big bad wolf; that I had come to hate, but around his family he was just the big brother whom everyone loved.

It was summer time now and the adults weren't around much at all Me and Sis got to know Chi-Chi and Lisa a little bit better and after a while they became cool; even likeable to be around. We even started to refer to them as our cousins; never forgetting or replacing them with our cousins back home in Detroit. You know how it is when you first meet people that you don't know; you tend to look at them out the corner of your eye and be a little stand-offish until you get know them better and understand them in their situation.

We didn't go outside much because it was hot and Chi-Chi was the type that if a bug landed on her she would just faint. So that left time for us just to hang around the house and talk. Lisa and Chi-Chi introduced us to new things. Orange jelly was one of them. It was orange jelly, but it had orange peels in it. It was the nastiest thing that I had ever tasted. Had they never heard of grape jelly around this place? I guess not because their mama never bought it. A peanut butter and jelly sandwich on soft bread was the best lunch that a seven year old can have. Not for me peanut butter and orange peel jelly just ruined it for me. One day they tried to convince me and Sis to eat canned dog food. They told us sometimes when they get real hungry they would eat it. I didn't believe that for a second. They were just saying that I see if me and Sis were crazy enough to eat it. I just would look at them crazy. But Chi-Chi would almost have us convince that they really did eat dog food. She would take a fork full and put it to her mouth saying that the dog food was made out of real beef. But she would never put the fork in her mouth. We almost tried it; they were very convincing; until we figured out that they were lying. The thought of eating dog food made me love orange jelly; orange peel and all. I think the heat was starting to get to us.

There was one thing that they did introduce us to that I loved; scratch candy. It looked just like the starch that you baked with. I couldn't get enough of the starch candy. I wanted all the time and when it was gone I looked for more. Does that make me an addict?

With Big Willie having such a huge family, there were many cousins to get to know, but there was one cousin that I didn't care for. All the adults were gone as usual and I was upstairs getting dressed, putting lotion on sitting on the edge of the bed where mama and Big Willie slept. I was watching as my little brother and Sis were playing on the bed when all a sudden I noticed some boy was standing in the doorway. He introduced himself as Lisa and Chi-Chi's cousin. I guess any cousin of theirs is a cousin of ours now. We all stopped what we were doing to say hello. I still had a hand full of lotion so I was trying to hurry up and rub it into my legs so we could all go downstairs together. But it was too late, when I looked back up, Sis and my brother had already left the room and I could hear them downstairs.

"You want me to put some lotion on your other leg for you?" their cousin asked. "No." I said. I didn't know him like that. Anyway I didn't want this stranger touching me; cousin or not. He snatched the lotion bottle out of my other hand. "Lay down on the bed." He said. "No" I said. Who the hell did he think he was telling me what to do; he didn't know me like that. He stood tall but he was very thin. He had to be about fifteen I'm guessing because he didn't have any hair on his face but he didn't look like a little boy either.

I went to get up so that I could leave out of the room but as I stood up off the bed, he pushed me back down. "What are you doing?" I asked. "Get up in the bed and lay down." He said. His voice had changed and the look on his face was letting me know that he wasn't taking no for answer. I had said it twice already and it had no effect on him. I was hoping that Sis would notice that it was taking a long time for me to come downstairs and come and get me so I could eat. Knowing that I was already dressed and that all I had to do was put on some lotion. It doesn't take that long to put lotion on those twigs that we called legs. She never came.

I felt trapped. I knew if I didn't do what he said, that he wouldn't let me out the room. I slowly slid to the head of the bed and laid down. I started to feel sick. He climbed on top of me with this stupid grin on his face. He spread my legs open slightly and began rubbing his private parts against mine. The room started to spin to me and I was feeling dizzy. "Get off me," I told him. He told me to shut up and started moving his private parts back and forth on me faster and faster. He acted like he was enjoying it. It reminded me of when Sis wanted to play house with me. I started to cry but he didn't stop. "Let it work, let it work" he mumbled. Let what work, I thought to myself. This isn't working for me.

Suddenly you heard the voice of an adult downstairs; Lisa and Chi-Chi's mama had returned home. When he heard his aunt's voice; dude jumped up off me so quick. I jumped out the bed and ran for the door so I could run out the room and get away from him; with his nasty self. How do you do things like that to people? Kissing cousins was not something that I was trying to be. I thought they only did stuff like that in the country.

I made a mad dash for the door, but before I could get to the door, he caught me by my arm. "You bet not say nothing" he said as he squeezed my arm so tight hurting me. I snatched myself loose from his strong grip and ran downstairs and acted like everything was normal. What he didn't know was that I wasn't going to tell anyone anyway. It wouldn't matter if I did tell mama. What would she care; she still with the man who beat on me causing me to be hospitalized. I couldn't trust anyone to believe me and I would probably get blamed for it anyway.

His little dirty secret was safe with me. After that day, I never remember seeing him back at his aunt's house again. I still to this day don't know whose child he was.

Summer was over and we were still staying with Lisa and Chi-Chi. Big Willie was gone again but his sister watched after mama and us. It was time to get back to school so mama enrolled us in the school that our cousins were going to. It was a private Catholic school. It started at kindergarten and went all the way up to the twelfth grade. So if you wanted to all you had to do was go to one school for your whole life besides college. There were only four black girls in the whole school and three of us lived in the same house. Lisa didn't go to that school. I guess that could have been part of Chi-Chi's problem too. Hanging around a whole bunch of other people can tend to rub off on you after a while; if you know what I mean. The only other black girl at the school was in second or third grade and her older brother was on the football team and the only black boy in school of at least two hundred students. He wore his gold and burgundy football jacket proudly as he walked the halls.

The most popular kids were the cheerleaders and the football players. The cheerleaders were so pretty with their long blonde hair and their short skirts. And yes what you see on television is true; you always have that one slutty cheerleader. Then you have the captain of the football team who was dating the lead cheerleader. In this case I wouldn't call it dating since they really couldn't tell anyone, but you could tell something was going on between the two. But for some reason after seeing the bad reputation that a cheerleader could get; I still wanted to be a cheerleader. I guess I like all the attention the good cheerleader got when they walked down the hall. Everyone would stop what they were doing in the halls and make a path for them to walk through; like they were goddess or something. I know I was one of them giving the attention. I like the cute uniforms and the jackets, their little white socks and tennis shoes. And the pompoms; you were a real cheerleader when you carried your pompoms and a boy student offers to carry your books. There was power in them pompoms.

It didn't bother me that we were the only black kids there. The other kids treated us normal even though we were not Catholic. Up north you really didn't see color, you just noticed it. I loved going to school there even though we had to walk to school every morning. Private school was expensive so after a while Chi-Chi didn't go to school there anymore either. Seeing how mama was getting a check every month for me and Sis due to our father's death; we continued in the school. Even though me and Sis went to the same school our start time was different, so she would leave for school before me. So I ended up walking to the bus stop by myself. At first sometimes mama would walk me half way in the morning and then meet me in that same spot in the afternoon. Some days I would meet Chi-Chi or Lisa there. Mostly Chi-Chi since I think Lisa went off to college or moved in with her boyfriend. Lisa was glad to be out of her mama's house.

When I got to school all us kids would play in the school yard until the first bell would ring, then we would line up and wait for our teacher to come and get us. I didn't bother to try and make friends; I figured we wouldn't be around here long enough for that.

In Catholic schools the teachers were actually nuns. As I would stand in line waiting to go into the school building, I would always stand in awe and admire the big church next to the school. It was a tall beautiful white catholic church with beautiful colored glass windows. I remember how the blue sky looked even bluer because of the church.

The nuns use to walk us across the street to the church once a month. I had never seen anything so beautiful in my life. The inside of the church was huge. There were hundreds of rows of benches neatly lined up one after another. They faced this big what I called a stage but later learned it was an altar. It had tall big gold candle holders that stood on each side up a table where a big gold goblet sat upon. But the one thing that always held my attention when I would sit in the second row was a statue of the Virgin Mother Mary. She was dressed in a white robe and had a baby blue shawl that rest upon her head and draped over her shoulders and was long enough to touch the ground. She held a baby in her arms; his name was Jesus. Mother Mary was so beautiful to me. The Catholic prayed to the Mother Mary and so did we while we attended school. They also prayed to saints. I never understood why they just didn't pray to God and thank Jesus for dying on the cross for our sins.

They did things different here at the Catholic Church. Here is where I first learned about communion. At first when I would see the kids line up and go up to the man who stood in the front of the church with his nice white robe embroidered in gold and he would place something on their tongue that looked like a white piece of paper that was cut in a circle; I guess my face showed my confusion to my nun who explained to me what was going on. She said that I didn't have to do it if I didn't want to. Thinking that I better talk to mama about this first, I didn't get in line. When we would first enter the church we would dip our one finger in a fountain of water and make the motion of the cross by touching our forehead first then our heart and then right to left our chest. We had to kneel to the Virgin Mary before having a seat. I really did enjoy the peaceful atmosphere at the Catholic Church. One thing they were missing though was the choir at our Baptist Church. The Catholic choir didn't sing like our Baptist choir. Our choir would have you stomping on the devil's head up in church. The Catholic choir sounded more like you were just throwing tissues on the devil's head.

My teachers where real nuns; they lived in the dorms next to the church. They wore their black dresses that cover the top of their shoes when they walked. They even wore their black hair covers and the tail of it would flap in the wind. White collar bands would over their necks, while the long sleeves of their dresses covered their arms. The only flesh they showed were their face and hands. You would never be able to say they tempted the priest.

The nuns taught the students. And they addressed each other as Sister and so did we. There weren't any male teachers at this private school. The nuns were nice for the most part; but you know you always have one out of the bunch that seemed just a little bit off their rocker and that was Sister Carol. Sister Carol was a short, heavy set older lady who walked like a pigeon and wore glasses. She taught math and she was mean as hell; maybe her skirt was too tight. Sister Carol use to yell all the time and when she got really mad, small balls of white spit would form in the corners of her mouth. You were wise not to be standing close to her because she would definitely give you a shower of spit.

Sister Carol love walking around the class room with that yard stick in her hand. Sister Carol use to slam that yard stick down on the desk when she felt like you weren't paying attention. There had been a couple of times when I thought she was going to slam that yard stick down on somebody's head. She had her good days that were far and few between. On those days you could get a smile out of her. Even though she was mean and sometimes seemed a little crazy; you could tell that she cared for her students and she only wanted them to get a good education because she knew how important it was to our future. She would go over a math problem again and again with you one on one until you understood. The bad thing was you had to stand at her desk while she did it. The yard stick sat on the chock board ledge right behind her. I never did decide whether she scared me into learning or I learned because I liked math.

Sister Amy who taught spelling was very nice. I looked forward to our weekly spelling bee. I enjoyed taking our spelling test on Fridays and taking home my paper that was marked with a big 100 percent in red. Sister Amy didn't walk around with a yard stick in her hand and she barely spoke above a whisper.

Along with learning math and how to spell very well, I learned how to do something else very well in Catholic school; how to steal. Lord, please forgive me.

The school would have a fundraiser. They would sell chocolate candy bars that were the length of a dollar for a dollar. They would issue the kids a case of each kind. Thirty candy bars came in a case and the candy came in three favors; plain, with crisps, or almonds. I loved the candy bars with the almonds in them. However many candy bars you sold determined the prize you would get. There was a big prize book that had page after page of things you could win, if you sold enough candy bars. You had to sell a whole lot of candy bars to get the big prizes. If you sold thirty candy bars you would win a cup or something small like that. If you sold three hundred candy bars you could win a shirt. To win a tape player with head phones; you had to sell at least a thousand candy bars. Even if you only sold ten candy bars, you got a pencil. I would flip through the book and just imagine what prizes I would win.

We came home with a case of candy, mama told us to take it back to school. She said that she didn't want to be responsible for the candy or collecting the schools money. All I could do was imagine about the prizes in the book, because mama wouldn't allow us to sell any candy.

On fundraiser day I use to sit back and watch the kids as they came back to the class after going to the office signing for their boxes of candy. The kids would act like it was Christmas; comparing and showing off how many cases they signed for and what kinds they were. They would look through the book too and pick out their prizes that they wanted to win. They didn't have to imagine.

I remember when Chi-Chi and Lisa went to the school they use to sell the candy. Chi-Chi let us taste one of her candy bars that she was selling. I think she paid for it. Mama wouldn't let us sell the candy but she did give us a dollar once to buy one; I was hooked. Around fund-raiser time I barley ate lunch. I would spend my lunch money on candy bars. One day I didn't have any lunch money and mama had packed our lunch. I wanted a candy bar so bad.

Someone in class had their case of candy bars sitting by their desk. Someone else had asked them for a candy bar, so they sat it on their desk until the other person went and got their dollar. I wanted that candy bar. The bell rung for lunch and we had to go. So they candy bar would have to wait. As it was left on the desk I thought of a way that I could get it without getting caught. Everyone scramble for their packed lunches and being clearing their desk so we could all get in line to go to the lunchroom. As everyone was getting up heading for the door, I made sure no one was looking as I grabbed the candy bar off the desk. I walked quickly and put in my desk and walked to get in line. I guess the student forgot something at her desk as she went back to it. She noticed the candy bar was gone.

She told Sister Cindy that the candy bar was missing. Sister Cindy didn't want to accuse anyone of stealing: even though that's what I had done. She asked the whole class to help the girl look for the candy bar. And for the first five minutes, we all did; even I pretended to look for the lost candy bar. But then Sister Cindy became impatient with the search and treated the classroom like a crime scene. She said no one would leave the room until she found the candy bar. She made the remark of not having to make her check everyone's desk, but she would if the candy bar didn't turn up. I had to move the candy out of my desk, or I was going to be in big trouble.

I had to find another hiding spot for it. I couldn't put it in my back-pack, I knew she would check those next if the candy bar didn't turn up. Where was going to hide the candy; I wanted it for myself. I spotted a desk in the back of the classroom that I knew was empty and no one sat there; it had no chair. As I continued to pretend that I was help look-ing for the candy bar I went to my desk and removed it. I made it to the back of the class while no one was looking and placed it in the empty desk. Just like I thought; Sister Cindy started checking backpacks. The search went on and Sister Cindy then announced that we would not be going to lunch until we found the candy bar.

I continued to look for something that I knew that was not lost. The other students started to show their concern of not being able to go to lunch. I didn't want to be the reason for them not eating just because I wanted a stupid candy bar. I decided to be thankful for what I had then for what I didn't have. I pretended to still look for the candy bar. I went to the back of the classroom when no one was looking and took the candy bar from the desk. I held the candy bar high above my head in the air. I called out to Sister Cindy to tell her that I had found the candy bar. I took it to her. She asked me where I had found it; I told her but was careful not to tell how it had got there. Everyone in the class was so happy that the candy bar was found. The girl whose candy bar it belonged to even came to me and told me thank you for finding it. I was ashamed of what I had done.

As I sat at the lunch table I looked down at the lunch that mama had packed. That was the best lunch that I had ever had. When we got back to the classroom Sister Cindy had a reward waiting for me. She gave me a chocolate candy bar with crisps. I took the candy bar and went back to my desk. Everyone watched as I walked back to my desk with the big candy bar. Oh boy, I thought to myself; my very own candy bar. I opened it and broke off a piece and put it in my mouth. I started to chew; something was wrong. I know I was eating chocolate but it didn't taste like it; I tasted nothing. I looked at the candy bar and I knew that I didn't deserve it. I broke it up into several pieces and gave it to the students that were sitting at their desk close to me. Sister Cindy saw what I had done and told me that I didn't have to share. I told her but indeed I did.

# Chapter 11

**THE SCHOOL YEAR** had ended and we finally moved into our own apartment. Big Willie was back and he moved in with us. There was something about this place that made me feel safe. I think it was the thought of it being our own. I had the feeling that this place was going to be our home for a while. We even got a cat. I don't think Big Willie liked the cat as much as he did the dogs. We had to keep the cat tied to the back kitchen door on a long string. I felt bad for the cat because she always got her tail caught in the door when someone would go in or out of it. She would let out the most horrible scream. I didn't blame her; you would too if someone kept slamming your tail in the door. One day she got loose from her string and ran away. I didn't blame her for that either. But I always thought someone felt sorry for her and let her loose so she could run away.

I took a hint from the cat and I too one day freed myself. I don't know; I guess I was about nine or ten years old. I know it was a Saturday because mama would always braid me and Sis's hair early that morning after having to wear the same hair style all week. Mama was getting my little brother dressed; she told me to go downstairs and start taking my hair a loose so she could braid my hair first. I went downstairs to the living room and sat in the chair by the big brown floor model television. No one else was downstairs; so I thought. I was taking my hair down when all of a sudden Big Willie came from the kitchen. Part of me froze in fear and my leg began to shake. I kept my eyes down to the floor as he passed on the side of me, but when he passed by in front of me; I raised my head and my eyes locked with his. He continued to walk while looking back at me and I continued to look at him while I continued to take lose my hair. It was as if time was standing still for me. Time was letting me have this moment. The longer I starred Big Willie in the eye the less human he looked to me. I could not tear myself from staring at him. I had to let him know that I was ready to fight even if it killed me. It was time for his torture to stop. The longer I looked at Big Willie, the stronger I felt inside. Big Willie looked at me never saying a word but never taking his eyes of me as he walked over to the stairs. With every step he took he placed himself further and further away from me. I kept my eyes on Big Willie until he was no longer in my sight.

When Big Willie didn't say anything back to me, I knew that I had won that round. I knew that the shackles and chains that Big Willie had mentally placed on me were slowly losing their grip. He seemed to have weakened over the past year or two. I was ready to battle now that he was on my level. I felt a fire burning inside of me. At that very moment I noticed that my left leg had stopped shaking. The nervous twitch that I had developed was no more. I had starred the devil in the eyes and I had not blinked.

Life went on quietly for a couple of months. I can't say normal because at this age I really don't know what normal is. That summer though there was a neighborhood cheerleading squad that was having tryouts for the local little football league. To my surprise, mama let us go. We use to have to cross along the highway and walk a couple of blocks, but me and Sis never missed a practice. We made the cheerleading team; I think it was one of those deals like if you came to practice every day and paid your fee; you made the team.

I guess this was their first year because we didn't have uniforms. You know like the ones the cheerleader wore at my Catholic school; pleaded shirts that flared up when you made a spin. The tailored sleeveless tops that showed off you shape and the little white shoes and white sock that you had to fold down once to make a cuff. And the pompoms; don't forget the pompoms. Instead, we wore green shorts with white t-shirts that had the teams name on the back of it in green iron on letters. We enjoyed being on the cheerleading team but I only remember us going to one game. I remember that game not because we lost but because to my surprise the boy who had me trapped upstairs in the bedroom at his aunt's house was on the team that I was cheering for. The following summer; for whatever reason mama didn't let us tryout. And wouldn't you know that was the summer they got real uniforms and pompoms. They even got jackets. I use to watch as some of the girls in our complex who had made the cheerleading team that year strut across the highway in their pretty green and white cheerleading outfits. "One day", I would promise to myself. "That's going to be me."

It was a typical Saturday night and that meant party time for the adults and staying up late watching grown folks stuff on television that we know that we're not supposed to; for the kids. Me, Sis, and Little Willie were all sitting downstairs watching television; the big floor model box brown one. Big Willie's two sisters had stop by so they could all get dressed and ready together. It seemed to be a big night. Everyone was acting more excited than normal. You could hear all the ladies laughing and talking upstairs while they were getting ready. Mama came downstairs, she wasn't dressed yet. She went and got a chair from the kitchen table. She sat the chair next to the television and had a seat. Me, Sis, and Little Willie were still sitting on the floor in front of the television. We all looked at each other as we wondered why mama was sitting the chair next to the television and why had she sat down. Mama began to talk to us but I couldn't understand a word she was saying. It wasn't that the television was too loud; it was just that the words coming out of mama's mouth wasn't English or the fact that they were slurred so it didn't sound like English.

Something was wrong and I knew it. While still trying to talk to us; mama closed her eyes. Before she could finish her sentence; her head hit the television like it was a cement brick. She had passed out right there in front of us. I thought she was dead. We just sat there looking at our mother not knowing what to do.

The sound of her head hitting the television was so loud that everyone came running from upstairs to see what the loud thump was. Big Willie's sisters saw my mama passed out. They called her name but she didn't respond. They started screaming for Big Willie to come downstairs. Mama still hadn't moved and neither did we. I didn't want my mother to be dead. My father was already dead and we were so far away from Detroit that would mean that Big Willie would have to take care of us and I definitely didn't want that. My first thought was that Big Willie had given her some bad drugs and that she had overdosed on them.

Big Willie finally made it downstairs. He picked mama up out of the chair and stood her up. He shook her a couple of times. We sat there holding each other hand wishing our mother back to life and not be sure of our own at that point. Big Willie's sister Kathy kept calling my mother's name until she finally got a response from her. Mama let out a little mumble as she opened her eyes. Thank God she was alive. "She's going to be okay." Kathy assured us. She could see the panic on our faces. "She just needs to go lay down." Still mumbling mama walked up stairs with Kathy and Big Willie's help.

It was quiet for a while. I don't think any of us believed what we had just seen. After thirty minutes or so, Big Willie came downstairs and sat down in the chair that still remained next to the television. "Your mother is going to be okay." He told us. I saw the worry on his face and for the first time I saw that he cared. We could only take his word for it and hope so. We felt so helpless.

An hour later mama came downstairs and she was fully dressed and alert as if nothing had happened. They left to go party the night away. After watching *All That Jazz*, starring Ben Verrene on HBO; not something we should have been watching at our age, but who was there to stop us. We put ourselves to bed. We got fussed at the next day by mama because my little brother let the cat out the bag and told my mama we had watched the movie with "all the ladies dancing naked" as he put it. I could have rung his neck.

After a while Big Willie was gone again. The next time I would see Big Willie was when we arrived in New Jersey. That was a long ride. When we arrived; it was at night of course, the first thing in the city I noticed was all the lights and the tall buildings. The traffic was busy and noisy but I guess that was the city life. There was this large water fountain in the middle of the street which made the cars go on either side of it. There was a model using the fountain for her background in her photo-shoot. You know the kind you see in the fancy magazine of the model with her hair and dress gracefully catching the wind. Big lights and fans surrounded the photographer as he snapped away with his camera.

Big Willie was staying with a friend in some apartments near the airport, very near. I remember seeing the lights of the blue lights of the runway. It made it very hard to sleep at night when your room is always lit up in blue bright lights. I would spend hours just looking out the window as the airplanes landed; when I should have been sleeping.

Anyhow, I got the feeling that Big Willie was hiding out. Not that I wanted him to, but why he staying here and not back at home.

Staying in a tall apartment building meant that there was no room to play, so mama would send us across the street to the city park. I was so taken by the beautiful green grass which looked more like a carpet that you just wanted to lay down on and take a nap. And the trees; they were so huge and tall. They gave shade for days. It was hot in Jersey, so a good tree was your best friend. Their branches covered with green leaves stretched for miles. The park was so clean; I could have played out there forever. Our visit was short, so my days at the city park were few. That summer would be the last time that I would ever see Big Willie.

Even though I never saw Big Willie again, I never stopped wondering what on earth a five year old child could have done to make a grown man just want to break the spirit or even try to beat the life out an innocent child. Maybe he saw something in me that scared him. I guess he figured he could beat it out of me. I was going through my own hell not knowing that my sister was enduring hers. But, that's her story to tell.

The summer was over and we returned to the Catholic school for the second year. Mama still didn't allow us to sell candy bars for the fundraiser. But I did win a big prize that year. I got the lead part in our school play as Mother Mary. At first I was shocked that I had even got the part. Were they sure that they wanted a little black girl to play virgin Mother Mary. There were no second thoughts about it for them; they were sure. I was so honored to have the part. I only hoped that I looked as beautiful as she did when I saw her in the church. I was just as proud the day of the play when I looked out into the crowd from the stage and saw my mama. I was sitting center stage as Mother Mary who was surrounded in a circle by many angles. And I really believed that for the past three years that's how my life really was; I was surrounded by many of Gods angels who protected me. I guess it is true what they say how art mimics life.

1979 was coming to an end; *Rapper's Delight* was eating up the radio and disco was no longer. That New Year's Eve was the best ever. It seemed we were all celebrating some that night; especially mama. She took us to the store and told us to get whatever we wanted. Our eyes lit up like the Northern Star as we walked through the store picking out cakes, candy, sodas and chips. At times it seemed like we had grabbed too much; but mama was reassuring when she told us over and over to get whatever we wanted. When we got back home we gathered in mama's bedroom. She dumped the whole bag of goodies in the middle of her bed. I swore it looked like we bought the whole store. We all climbed into mama's bed. We stuffed our mouths with our treats as we counted down the minutes and watched on television as the ball fell to bring in a new year.

# A New Beginning

# PART II

# Chapter 12

**AS THE NEW** Year started and it was just the four of us. Mama did take a lot of Greyhound bus rides to go see Big Willie in jail and a couple of his court appearances. She dragged us along with her. The rides were long so I can only assume he was very far away. One bus trip my little brother got sick in a brown paper bag; thank God he was sitting with mama.

With mama not having a man around for financial support she did the best with what she had and found programs that would help single moms with kids. We were poor but we were clean, clothed, feed and safe. Mama saved money where she could and cut corners to make ends meet, but some things you should never cut. For a long time I didn't know that milk came in a plastic gallon jug. Mama would buy powdered milk. I think one of the neighborhood ladies hipped her on to that. They could have kept that to themselves.

The powdered milk came in a blue box. On the front of the box it showed a nice glass of cold milk being poured. That's how I learned about false advertising. Mama would mix the powdered milk up with water in a pitcher and add sugar to make it taste like regular milk; but it didn't. I don't care how much sugar mama put in the milk it was still nasty. I remember if you didn't mix the milk good, it would have lumps and you would have to strain the milk before you could drink it. The cereal we ate wasn't much better. It came in a big white bag with black letters on it. We always ate the same cereal. I must say that was some good cereal though. We ate a lot of jello too. I could only assume because it was cheap.

Big Willie was pretty much out of mama's life. We hadn't ridden a greyhound to see him in a very long time. With mama having space and time to think, we started going to church a lot. Sunday school, Sunday morning service, Thursday choir practice, Wednesday bible study, Tuesday prayer meeting; we were there. Every time the church doors were open; we were there. When the church traveled; we traveled. I really did enjoy going to church. We meet new people and made new friends; so did mama. Most of the people in the complex went to the same church. We were no longer neighbors; we were family.

I can remember one special church service that we attended. We were at a visiting church and as you know at the end of every sermon there is an altar call. Well, the pastor did just that and so I asked mama if it was okay for me to go up and she said sure. Me and a couple of other kids went up to the altar and got down on our knees. The altar was so pretty; there was a picture of Jesus that was lit up by a big bright spot light. So as we are down on our knees the pastor asked everyone to close their eyes and bow our heads for prayer. I closed my eyes but not completely; I didn't want to take my eyes off Jesus. I was peeping at Jesus as the pastor started to pray. Listening to the pastor; I began to say Amen to whatever he was saying. I called out Jesus name and the next thing I knew something had snatched me off my knees and onto my feet. I didn't hear anything going on around me. I was just jumping up and down and crying. When I came to I was no longer at the altar but instead I was back in the pews with mama standing over me. She was crying and I called out for her asking her what had happened. I could hear one of the church ladies telling mama that I was okay, that I had just been slung into the spirit. And I knew at that very moment that God had introduced himself to me at the age of nine years old and told me that his son's name was Jesus Christ and that he would be my Savior. After that day I loved going to church even more now because I knew that God would be there. That summer we all got baptized at church camp.

Besides church; mama added another activity to our schedule. We joined the 4-H Club. It was kinda like the girl Scotts, but it was for intercity kids; if you know what I mean. Mama became one of the group leaders and so that meant having cooking classes and meetings at our house. We learned a lot of new recipes and crafts to do. A tuna fish sandwich with cheese became one of my favorites. Fried bologna and cheese sandwiches ran a close second. We even learned a lot about nature. Many summer evenings were spent catching fireflies in glass jars. Watching their little butts light up was so amazing and fun.

For once I was starting to feel like I was living a normal life. When it was time for us to go back to school; so did mama. She had enrolled in college. I was so proud of mama. I saw one of her report cards; she was very smart. Mama going to school meant we had to take on a little more responsibilities and that meant putting my little brother on the school bus in the mornings. He was a handful in the morning. Some mornings we had to bribe him just to get him on the bus. His bus would come before ours so that meant we had to be outside early. One morning he almost misses the bus because he couldn't find his shoe. Me and Sis had to run out the house, chase the school bus down and put my brother on it so he could go to school. That was a close one. Just imagining having to explain to mama why we all stayed home from school that day was not a conversation that I wanted to be a part of.

When it was time for mama to graduate from college we didn't get to go to the ceremony but some of the ladies in the church went. Mama had made herself a very beautiful silver dress and a sheer silver jacket to match, and of course you know she had the silver heels to go with it. Mama's fashion sense was always on point. Mama came down the stairs in her outfit and she looked like a million bucks.

Months have passed; even weeks something is strange; something is wrong. Mama and one of the sisters' from the church; who is a very close friend of ours who lives right directly in front of us is arguing. Another week has gone by and now they're not speaking to each other. We still are all going to church together though. But mama has told us that we are not allowed to go over their house anymore.

Mama and the sister from church were at it again. Mama had gone over to her apartment and now they are standing at the front door going at it. I listened in on the argument that had gotten really heated between the two of them. From what I could make out through all the yelling: they were arguing over a man. I knew they weren't arguing over Big Willie because he was in jail. When I was cleaning up the kitchen one night I had found some letters that mama had hidden in her sewing machine drawer that Big Willie had written her from jail. I don't know exactly what he did but according to his letters he would be locked up for a very long time. So, who was this man that mama and her use to be close friend are arguing about? I hadn't seen mama with any man. From what I could get from the conversation, he apparently had been seeing both of them at the same time.

Supposedly this guy they were arguing over had come to visit his sister who lived in the same apartment complex and who only lived one building over from us. Still not having seen anyone, I overheard mama on the phone one night talking to someone and they weren't talking about choir rehearsal. It sounded like the person on the other end of the phone was asking her out. So I assumed it was this mystery guy. She told the guy no that she wouldn't go out with him because she didn't know him that well but that he could come over later that night to see her. I must have asked if they could have sex because I heard mama tell him no but that she would let him feel on her chest. I thought that was so slutty of her. I know she didn't learn that at bible study. But I guess that's what grown folks do.

Knowing what I knew, I couldn't sleep. I wanted to see who this guy was that broke up a good friendship and who was this that mama was inviting into this house. I had to stay wake; so all that night I waited up until I heard voices coming from downstairs. I quietly sat on the stairs out of sight listening and watching as mama and her new friend talked. He was short with a lot of muscles and he looked very young. He wore his hair in an afro. He looked more like he could have been mama's younger brother than her possible new boyfriend.

He and mama talked for a while; I learned his name was Peter and that he lived in Florida. He told mama that he was here visiting his sister. Eventually they moved from the couch; where the conversation started to the floor to get more comfortable. Peter popped the question to mama about what she had promised him earlier on the phone. Mama giggled a little bit and then she started to unbutton her shirt. My virgin eyes had seen enough and I wanted to keep it that way. So before anything got hot and heavy or x rated; I made my way back to my bed. I was so disappointed in mama. I guess I thought it would just be us forever. We were finally happy. Why did mama have to get involved with another man? I fell asleep leaving mama and her new friend downstairs doing adult stuff.

The next morning mama didn't look the same to me anymore. I had seen a totally different side of her that I didn't like. I hope this man was worth all the trouble he had caused. That Sunday mama had sent us to church, but she didn't go. Church was only a block away, so walking to church wasn't a problem. The problem was we never walked to church without mama. When we got to church everyone asked where was our mama, Sis told everyone she was home sick. We only assumed she was sick because she had stayed in her room that morning.

When we got in from church, Peter was there. Yeah, she was sick alright. I just rolled my eyes when I saw Peter. I just couldn't get over how young he looked and how short he was. I think Sis was taller than him and she was a thin twelve. Mama was much taller than him. They looked funny standing next to each other. They looked more like a capital and lower case letter standing next to each other on the alphabetical letter line. She introduced him to us but I wasn't being won over that easy with his big bright smile.

Mama didn't have Peter coming around us a lot but we've been showing up on Sunday morning at church without her a lot. And when we come home from church he's there. I was getting the feeling that he was already there before we would leave for church; we just didn't see him. When members from the church would ask us where mama was, Sis being the oldest would always just say that mama was sick. I knew they knew that we were not telling the truth because no one from the church ever came by to check on her. You know how we church folk go check on the shut in and the sick. And how pastor would go visit and pray for you. And the ladies of the church would cook a weeks' worth of food because if you were sick that meant you weren't cooking; no one came.

Many Sundays had passed and mama never bothered to come to church. I understand missing one Sunday; but now you're missing every Sunday. One Sunday morning as mama was sending us off to church; who by the way didn't look sick to me, Sis decided to voice that she didn't want to go to church. Mama asked her why. Sis said because she got tired of everyone asking us where our mama was and she having to stand there and lie by saying that mama was sick knowing that she wasn't. Mama said that we didn't have to go to church anymore if we didn't want to. But we did want to; we just wanted her to come with us like she always did before this Peter came into the picture.

What I didn't understand was instead of missing church for this man; invite him to come to church. And then what kind of man was he that he couldn't see that he was interfering with you going to church.

But instead you suggest to us not to go back to the church so we don't have to cover for you anymore. Oh no, I'm going to church; Vacation Bible School was coming up too. Needless to say, mama did let us go to Vacation Bible School that summer and I won an award and a prize that summer because I brought my bible every single day. Actually it was mama's bible. I use to love seeing her carry it when walked to church on Sunday morning. She would cradle it in her right arm holding it to her heart. When vacation bible school started, I had asked her if it was okay for me to use it since obviously she wasn't using it anymore.

I remember running home to show mama what I had won. Peter was there in her bedroom lying under the covers. It felt strange to see another man lying in my mama's bed after all this time. I just couldn't believe that he was the reason she stopped going to church. Even when Big Willie was around I never saw them in bed together except the one time when my brother was first born. For a minute I ignored what I saw and focused back on the reason why I came in the room. I showed mama my award and my prize which was a game that named all the books of the bible and some other stuff. Mama said she was very proud of me. Peter looked at my prize and said in a funny way, "oh that's nice". I believe he was poking fun at me. He tossed my prize to the side as if it was a day old newspaper. Still proud; I collected my things and went to my room. What did he know anyway?

We never went back to our church after that summer. I found some more of mama's letters from Big Willie, I guess she had told him about her new boyfriend; Big Willie wasn't liking the idea of that at all. But there really wasn't much that he could do about it being that he was locked up. I just hope mama knew what she was doing. What was she going to do when Big Willie did get out? I guess she knew that she had plenty of time to think about that.

Peter was coming around more but I still had my reservations about him. We finally met his sister. They were brother and sister, but they looked like they were cut from a different cloth; off a whole different spool of thread. She was a bright skinned, extra queen size woman with four kids; three boys and one girl. They were poor and it showed. We weren't rich; but we weren't as bad off as they were. They did things a little bit different at their house then we did at ours. She was a single parent and it seemed to have made her very bitter. Ms. Ernestine was more of a drill sergeant than she was a mother. She was very mean to her kids and she was always yelling at them instead of talking to them. Her kids were so afraid of her. Every time she would say something they would jump and get right to it that very second. She always wore a mean face. I never saw her show her kids any type of loving and caring affection; just an iron fist. She took her frustration out on her kids; always hitting on them. She would be little them and say mean things to them right in front of us. I felt so sad for them.

Her second oldest son Arnold had only one arm; the other arm was cut off at the elbow which really creeped me out. We always made a point not to stare or make it obvious that we were uncomfortable around him but he was always slinging it around in the air so you couldn't help but to look. We could also tell that it was one of his insecurities but he always tried to make light of his difference; he was kind of the clown of the family. They say he lost it because he fell out of a moving car and another car ran over his arm. Her baby boy Marcus was very book smart and very soft spoken. Ernestine had high hopes for him and you could tell that she favored him amongst her kids. He didn't get in trouble a lot if at all.

Her oldest son Simon; she treated like he was the man of the house. He was in charge of taking care of the other kids, the house and even some times Ms. Ernestine herself. If the younger kids were supposed to have done a chore and they didn't do it to her liking; they would get in trouble and so would Simon. It was a sad sight to see. We had responsibilities at our house too; don't get me wrong, but we didn't have to take on all the responsibilities. Every time I would see Simon, he just looked so overwhelmed. Simon took a liking to me, but I didn't like him despite what my mother may have thought. Simon was too flaky for me; it you get my drift. He was always crying. My little brother didn't cry that much.

Oh then there was little Ernestine; we called her because she looked just like her mama. She was the baby of the family. I didn't get along with little Ernestine because she was always acting like she was better than me and Sis but yet she had less than we did. I guess if she pretended that she was better than us than she would believe that she was better than us. Or maybe she wanted what we had and was jealous because she didn't.

With mama pretty much separating us from our old friends; who was everyone from our church; we started being around Ernestine and her kids. I'd rather have watched paint dry on a rainy day than to have hung out with this dysfunctional family of four. Well since we didn't go to our church anymore, Ernestine decided to put her sister-in-law role into action and invite us to hers. I was excited when mama told us that we would be going to church. Maybe they weren't that bad after all. If being friends with Ernestine got mama back into the church; she couldn't have been all that bad.

We drove up to a building which was not a church, so I thought we took the wrong directions to get to church. After seeing Ernestine and Peter get out of their car, I assumed yes; that we were at the right place. As we walked up to the double doors I read the sign saying Kingdom Hall Jehovah Witness Worship Center. When we walked in it looked like the place where all the towns' people would come to have a meeting. At this worship center they didn't read from the bible like we did at our church, but instead from booklets that looked like comic books. Each person would take turns in reading a paragraph as the booklet was passed to them. When the reading was complete they would answer the questions at the back of the booklet by passing the microphone to whoever wanted to answer the question. One thing that didn't sit well with me was they didn't say God or Jesus, they just kept saying Jehovah. I just kept looking around to see if I could get a glimpse of this Jehovah. I had never heard of him before. I looked at mama, but she gave no reaction when they said this Jehovah. She acted like it didn't even bother her.

Also in this hall or worship center there was no singing like it was in our church. No one was praising the Lord and giving him thanks. No one was dancing down the aisles filled with the Holy Ghost. I could tell that this was definitely not the place for me. If mama made us come here, I knew she done fell and bumped her head this time. When whatever you want to call it was over; because it sure wasn't church, I learned that the people weren't called Christians but Jehovah Witnesses. I asked mama what that was. I guess she didn't hear me because she didn't answer me. Or maybe she didn't know herself.

Needless to say we gave it a try. We had study sessions every week at our house with Ernestine and her kids. I couldn't call it bible study; remember there was no bible involved. I did learn new things but it only made me confused of the things that I had learned from my church. But what voice does a ten year old have when your mother is so easily influenced by the people around her. Mama finally did explain to us what a Jehovah Witness was. In her explanation all I heard was that they don't celebrate any holidays of any kind or birthdays. Oh hell no; I wasn't down with that. You mean to tell me no more baby Jesus and presents on Christmas. No more Thanksgiving and Charlie Brown pumpkin patch. No more Easter Sunday with the beautiful colored eggs. No more Halloween and all its candy. No birthday cake. Are you serious; no wonder Ernestine and her kids were so miserable, they didn't have any fun. Not celebrating your birthday; what's the point of getting older than if you can't celebrate that you made it to see one more year. Yeah, being a Jehovah Witness wasn't for me and I guess mama either because after only a couple of times going to the worship center; we didn't go any more and nor did we hold any more book studies.

Mama and Peter were in a serious relationship by this time. He was around now and there was no secret of who he was. In the beginning of their relationship, Peter would spend the night at his sister's house but spend the day at ours but then that changed to; he started being here at night. Peter was nice; sometimes he seemed too nice. It wouldn't be long before his true colors would shine through.

# Chapter 13

**THE LOCAL FAIR** had come to town. Mama and Peter went without us. We were mad that we didn't get to go. We thought that the fair was for kids anyway. Peter has already separated mama from her church and friends now I think he's trying to show her how much fun she could have without her kids. I'm starting to keep a very close eye on Peter.

When we woke up the next morning as we headed in the kitchen for breakfast we notice three large round fair candy suckers nicely displayed on top of the brown floor model television. Cotton candy pink, baby powder blue, and sun kiss yellow; they sat there wrapped in their plastic wrapping paper. We had never seen candy suckers so big up close before. Only on the television with the little girl in the candy shop would you see a sucker that big. So, like the children that we are; our eyes got big with excitement and for me Peter was forgiven for not taking us to the fair because he brought us something back. Anticipation ran through our mind as when was Peter going to come down and tell us to pick a sucker. Was he going to come down early this morning or was he going to wait until the afternoon?

Three kids, three suckers; what would you have thought? We started deciding amongst ourselves which sucker that we would choose. Of course my brother being the boy would get the blue. I wanted the pink one but so did Sis. She didn't think that yellow was girly enough. We went back and forth. I would give in and just take the yellow for the heck of it just because I wanted a sucker. But then I would change my mind because I really wanted the pink one. So we decided whoever got what would just give the other half of theirs. We went back and forth for about thirty minutes trying to make a final decision. We touched the suckers to see if they were even real or just an illusion. After realizing the suckers were real; we made our way to the kitchen for breakfast.

Every time we passed by the television that day we checked on the suckers to make sure that they were still there. They were still there but no one had asked us to choose one. Three days had gone by and not a word by anyone about the three big fair candy suckers that sat on the television on display. Mama didn't even say anything about them. The fourth morning when we came downstairs for breakfast; the suckers were gone; Where did they go? We looked at each other in disbelieve. We had been made fools of by Peter. He knew what he was doing by placing the candy out for us to see. He knew that we would think that they were for us. The suckers were never for us. Oh I see he got jokes. He likes playing mind games. Who's the sucker now?

Every time any of us would go in the freezer for anything, there would be the three candy suckers. With every day that went by pieces of the candy would be broken off and none was ever offered to us by Peter. How could mama just walk around the house knowing too that there were three suckers placed on the television and nothing was offered to us? Peter could have just left the candy at his sister's place in her freezer if he wasn't going to give us any. Why not just get one sucker? Why buy three suckers any way and then put them out on display. Peter knew that we were going to think that the suckers were for us. I bet he was somewhere watching us and getting his laugh in while we were picking out "our" sucker.

The suckers in the freezer got smaller and smaller with every day that went by. I wonder if Little Willie or Sis ever got a piece of candy; I know I did. With the candy situation I learned then that Peter was sneaky and that I couldn't trust him.

After long, Peter went back home to Florida and mama now has really be-friended Ernestine after some time. I didn't care much for her or her Klan. We were all civil to each other despite our differences. But there were times when I thought that we were spending too much time with them. Mama and Ernestine got together and thought that it would be a wonderful idea to take a road trip down to Florida. Two adults; women at that, seven kids backed in the back seat of car with no air conditioner and a whole in the back floor board was a great idea. Yeah, right? It took us three days to get there. We were stopping at every other rest stop it seemed like to me. Ernestine had cooked some fried chicken and made some sandwiches. She said the chicken tasted like KFC; she lied. It tasted like some cold chicken that was cooked in some old grease. But to look at her eat only made me lose my appetite.

On the ride down, Ernestine made sure to keep me and Simon separated. I didn't want him; believe that. He sat by one door and I sat by the other door and everyone else sat in between. I was so glad to get out of that car. One more day of driving and we finally made it to Florida.

The Florida that I saw was not the same Florida that they show on television. But I did understand why they called it the sunshine state. It was so hot; you thought that you were standing next to the sun. I saw many houses that were no bigger than a backyard tool shed. The houses sat on five triangle shaped bricks; one for each corner and one in the middle. You could see right underneath the house. You could crawl from one end to the other with no problem. With no cement flat foundation for the house to sit on; just five small triangle shaped bricks, I would often wonder how on earth anyone walked around in the house without falling through the floor. There were no sidewalks for you to walk on, just the red clay roads. You had to share the road with the cars and pray that you didn't get hit by one. It was like we stepped back in time; in slavery time.

Kids were running around outside playing with no shoes on their feet. And I don't know when the last time they took a bath but by the looks of their clothes, it hadn't been all week if you ask me. And all you saw from miles on miles were endless rows of orange trees. I had never seen so many trees in my life. I didn't know Florida was the main state for growing oranges. I believe it was more trees in the state of Florida than there were people. Our visit was short and I was glad. I was ready to get back home to the sidewalks and paved roads. You can definitely tell the difference from city people and country folks.

Christmas was good for us that year. I remember my brother getting a huge bag of green toy soldiers. Me and Sis played hours with him as he made different battle fields and declared war. Mama declared her own little war later that week when she found me and Simon behind the fence. Mama thought me and Simon had been kissing but we weren't. We were just talking like I told mama. Simon did lean in for a kiss but I told him no. Mama went to go and get Ernestine and told her she had found us behind the fence. Ernestine didn't believe Simon when he told her that we weren't kissing. She beat him down to the ground right in front of me and mama. I was horrified. She beat him down like he had stolen something from her. I think mama felt bad for Simon too, so she started yelling at me if front of them. I was afraid that mama didn't want Simon to feel left out so I thought she was going to start beating on me the same way, but she didn't. Mama just put me on punishment; she felt obligated to do something after the beat down Simon had gotten. I could only imagine what they would have done if we had actually kissed. I think we would have been attending Simon's funeral.

At times it seemed to me that whomever mama was around at the time she would be influence by them and pick up some of their habits. Mama had a few more nickels than Ernestine; so we could afford to do things that they couldn't. But Ernestine would always try to convince mama that the poor way was the better way. One day all us kids were hanging out and mama had bought us some food back from Burger King, well we didn't want to be rude and eat in from of them, so we told them that we would be out to play after we finished eating. I guess Ernestine's Klan had ran home and asked her to buy them some from Burger King too because when we finished eating and went over to their house, she had done cooked them some burgers and bought some buns with the seeds on top from the grocery store.

They all were sitting on the back porch as she sat in a chair and handed them a burger from a plate that Simon had brought from out of the house. "See", Ernestine said to us. "You don't have to spend all that money on that dumb food. I cooked us some burgers and they taste just as good and I didn't spend half the money that your mama spent." Ernestine took a bite of her burger and as the mayonnaise oozed out of the side of her mouth I became sick. I made a vow to myself to never eat anything out her house. I looked back at mama who had walked over to Ernestine's to return a bowl she had borrowed. "Yeah, you right. I'm going to try that next time." Mama said. All I could think to myself was; you better not, do you see how nasty that looks? Putting hamburgers on a grill for a family cookout was ideal. But to try and duplicate a Burger King hamburger because you can't afford to go; was a joke.

Ernestine made another suggestion to mama which I ended up living with for the rest of my life. We were out playing on the playground. We were all taking turns on the swing and doing little tricks. Sometimes we would go as high as we could then jump from the swing. Other times we would stand up in the swing to see how high we could get it to go. Everyone had gone and it was my turn next again and I wanted to make sure I could get it the highest than the last time that I did it. I grabbed the chains of the swing on each side and jumped so I could stand up in its seat. My foot hit the back of the swing and flipped the seat up and when I landed, I landed on the ground flat on my face. I jumped up off the ground in so much pain. Blood was just streaming from my mouth. Sis started yelling that I had busted my lip open and that it was hanging. I went to touch it but she told me not to because there was so much blood. I panic when I saw my lip just dangling there from my face. Sis yelled for me to hurry up and go to the house and tell mama. But I was too scared to move as I looked down at the ground and saw all the blood. Sis kept yelling for me to go to the house.

I was walking like a duck and lead the trail of blood to the back door of our apartment. Sis ran in the house to get mama and Simon ran to go get Ernestine while I stood outside crying with my little brother and little Ernestine trying to comfort me. Mama came outside and by the look on her face you would have thought that I had two heads; my lips were probably big enough for two heads. Mama first tried to stop the blood so she could see how much damage I had done to myself. What happened was all she kept asking. Sis had to explain as I tried to mumble what happened and mama couldn't understand me. Mama was still trying to get the bleeding to stop when Ernestine had arrived.

Ernestine took one look at my lip and said, "Oh she'll be fine. She doesn't need to go to the hospital. You can take care of that yourself." Just get a spider web and put it on her lip." My eyes got big as fifty cent pieces. Did I hear this woman correctly? A spider web on my mouth; who does that? We go to the doctor around here. Aint nobody doing no back woods cure over here. I was waiting for mama to tell us to get in the car so we could go to the hospital so the doctor could sew up my lip. But instead she just keeps trying to clean up the blood off my mouth. After she stopped the bleeding mama took a closer look at my mouth. "Well, you chipped your tooth." She told me. Okay so can we go to the hospital now because I can live with a chipped tooth but I don't want to be walking around with my lip dangling from my face? Needless to say we didn't go to the hospital and mama doctored up on me for the next couple of weeks minus the spider web. I was left with a big lump on my lip that never fully receded back into place. The lump got smaller as my lips got fuller as I grew older.

Things got back quiet for a while and life went on as usual. Peter popped up in town that following summer and what would happen in the next couple of days would change our lives forever. Mama had come to us one day and asked if we wanted to move to Florida. My first thought was yes so that we could finally really get away from Big Willie because if they let him out on early release; he gonna kill all of us, including Peter. I figured if we moved it would be a way of hiding from Big Willie while he was in jail and he would never be able to find us again. This way we could move in the middle of the night and no one would be the wiser.

What on the other hand, did we know about this man Peter? All I knew was his name and that he liked to clown around a lot and talk in this funny voice character called Mr. Bill. Who Mr. Bill was I don't know but Peter sounded funny doing it. I knew Peter was sneaky and that meant he could be very manipulative. But on the other hand he really hadn't done anything to me. I guess everyone had their own personal reasons for wanting to go or stay. It didn't snow in Florida so that meant no more making snow angels in the fresh soft snow. After a couple of days after mama asking us the question; we had packed up all our stuff in a small U-haul moving truck and headed down to Florida.

On the ride down to Florida, Peter talked me and my little brother into riding down with him in the U-haul truck. I sat in the middle while by little brother sat by the door. I thought it would have been more comfortable for my brother to sit in the middle since he was smaller; giving Peter more room to shift gears. But Peter insisted that I sit in the middle by him while he drove. Sis rode with mama in the baby blue Impala. I didn't think that old car was going to make the trip. She did and that was her last.

The ride in the U-haul was interesting. Somehow Peter kept missing the gear shift and his hand would end up in my lap. At other times his hand would just rest on my knee. I didn't say a word but would play it off by moving my legs closer to my brother. After two hours of trying to pretend that Peter wasn't trying to feel on my thighs I had had enough.

When we stopped for gas I got out the U-haul and got in the car with mama and Sis. I told mama that I wanted to ride with the girls and to let the boys ride together. She thought it was a cool idea and thought nothing of it. There was no use of me telling mama what had been happening in the U-haul for the past two hours. If she would turn her back on God for Peter, I knew she would do the same to me. We got back on the road and continued to head down south.

The whole time that we were riding behind the U-haul, I was looking up into the sky praying for my little brother. I was hoping that Peter wasn't doing anything strange to him like he had been doing to me. I was also watching the sun and I noticed when we turned it turned. When the trees would try and block the sun its sun rays would still peek through the trees branches to let me know it was still there. And when we would go through a tunnel and it got completely dark; when we came out the sun was still there.

I asked mama was the sun following us. She told me yes. I only hoped that God was doing the same.

# Chapter 14

**AFTER A COUPLE** of days driving, we were in Haines City, Florida. Peter didn't have his own place so we ended up staying with his mama. I guess that's what men do down south. My question is how you going to move a woman and her three kids and don't have a place to put them. I guess Peter and mama didn't discuss that part the night that they were getting all touchy feely with each other. Besides Peter living with his mama so was his niece and two nephews. The story with Felicia and her younger brother was that their mama left them there and never came back for them. I don't know what Bernard's story was. They all seemed to be pretty good kids. So why would their mama leave them. Maybe she was running behind some man. That seems to be a trait with women. They lose their mind over these men. I hope I wouldn't make the same mistake when I grew up and have kids of my own.

It was summer time and there were always a lot of kids at Peter's mama house, so there always someone to adventure out into the neighborhood with. Me and Sis became close with Peter's niece Debra. She was around our age and lived a couple of blocks over. Debra had an older brother but we hardly ever saw him because he was off at some basketball camp. Tony was his name. Other cousins and friends lived nearby so grandma's house was the place for everyone to hang out. But there was nothing to really do but go outside and kick the ball around in the street. That got very boring after the third day. And the Florida sun was not nice at all. I think that this is as close to hell as I'm going to get if I can help it.

There were three bedrooms and one bathroom in Peter's mama's house so I wondered where all these kids were going to sleep. With Peter's mama having her own bedroom that only left two bedrooms and three beds for two adults and seven kids to sleep in. well needless to say; mama and Peter slept in Peter's bedroom of course and that left us kids. The bedroom only had two beds; one twin and one full. Boys slept in the twin bed while we girls slept in the full size bed. I was just hoping that my little brother was okay with the situation because it was said that one of the boys was still wetting the bed. At his age I took it as him having a nervous side effect. I must say; it was crowded but I guess it was better than being on the floor.

Florida was hot and to make matters even hotter; there was no air conditioner anywhere. One day it was so hot, we all piled in the car after Peter suggested we go swimming. Hooray, alright good clean chlorine cold blue water was what I was looking forward to after enduring all this Florida heat. So you could image my surprise when we pulled up roadside to a lake. Not a beach, but a lake. People were actually swimming in the lake as if they were at the beach. I wanted us to pack our things and go right back to Detroit right that very second. I couldn't believe what my eyes were seeing. Um where is the swimming pool. Are you serious right now? I looked over at my sister who had the same stunned look on her face as I did mine. What in the world had mama gotten us into? It was bad enough we all had to sleep in a bed with strangers. Now we are expected to swim in a lake.

After being in shock for a good twenty minutes and listening to Peter convince mama that it would be fun for us and that's what everyone one does around these parts; we all decided just to make the best of a weird situation. Bernard, Felicia, her brother and another of their cousins; Debra had come along for the adventure. They ran out into the water like it was nothing. I guess they were used to swimming with the fish and crab in all that brown seed weed grass but I wasn't.

I looked at Sis and she looked at me as if to say; are we really doing this? I walked to the edge where the water started and I stopped. I looked out at this mass space that was covered with water. You couldn't see through to the bottom like you could a pool. There were things floating on top of the water; leaves, sticks, grass and creatures that I could not identify. I started walking into the water and I came to grass that came up to my calves and yes when I looked down and looked very closely; there were little fishes swimming around my ankles. The water looked dirty but as I looked around at everyone splashing around in the water no one seemed to care.

I was too scared to move. Do fish bite? Seeing me just standing there; Debra waved for me and Sis to come into the water further where she was. The closer I got to Debra, the less grass I was standing in and the less fish I saw. I still couldn't see my feet because they were cover by the dirt at the bottom of the land. I guess they called that sand around these parts. The water was nice and cold; I must admit that. It took my mind off the Florida heat. Even though we were out in the water you could still see the shock and hesitation on Sis and my face. We would just look at each other and laugh because we really couldn't believe that we were doing this.

Sis dared me to dunk my head under the water and open my eyes. She knew that I couldn't pass up a dare. So after getting my nerves together I pinched my noise together and got a mouth full of air; I dunked my head under the water and opened my eyes. That was a bad idea. It looked like I was looking through a glass of tea and the tea bag had busted in the glass. I quickly snatched my head from the water. I told Sis she could go under but whatever she does don't open her eyes there was no point; you can't see. And not to open her mouth or she would get a mouth of stuff.

After a while with all the splashing and playing I forgot about being in the lake and just enjoyed the cool water. Peter thought that it would be fun to toss us kids in the water since there was no diving board to jump off of. We all lined up to get a turn. Watching everyone else get tossed into the water by Peter did look fun until it was my turn. Of course I was hesitant I didn't want Peter to drop me and he promised that he wouldn't. Not knowing that that would be the least of my worries; I took my turn and let Peter toss me in the water.

One hand he put on my arm and the other hand he put between my legs. I thought that was an odd way to hold a girl. Peter lifted me up and tossed me in the water but not before he rubbed his thumb against my privates. Why did he do that? Maybe I was heavier than he thought and so his hand had slipped; so I thought. By the time I hit the water; it was too late for me to react. When I jumped up from underneath the water and stood on my feet, I looked around at everyone who was busy laughing and playing. Everyone was still lining up to be tossed in the water.

I looked over at Sis; she looked normal. Maybe Peter didn't rub his thumb up against her privates. She was lighter than me even though she was taller than I was, so maybe his hand didn't slip with her. I looked over at Debra; she looked normal too. No sign of foul play on her face.

It was my turn again for Peter to toss me in the water and yet again he rubbed up against my privates and this time even harder. When I came from underneath the water and stood to my feet; I looked at Peter who had this devilish grin on his face. I had seen the grin many times before on Big Willie's face. I knew then that Peter was doing this on purpose; there was no slip of his hand. I knew then that we had made a mistake moving here to Florida with Peter.

I thought to tell mama what Peter had done. But as I looked over at her drying my brother off with a towel and laughing with him, I didn't want to spoil her moment of happiness. To see my mother smile lite up my world and it had been a minute since she had a reason to smile. If I tell her would she believe me? I really didn't want to take the chance and find out. I didn't want to be the one spoiling anyone's day at the lake. Needless to say, I didn't give Peter a third chance to toss me. The ride home from the lake was a little awkward for me. As I sat in the back seat wondering if I had did any of us any favor by not telling mama what Peter had done; I watched him as he kept his composure and acted as if nothing had happened. I didn't know if by not telling mama it told Peter that I was capable of keeping secrets from her for him. I didn't know if it showed Peter how much I didn't trust my mother enough to trust that she would do what was best for her children in any given situation no matter her personal sacrifice. Peter knew what he had done and even worst, he knew that he had gotten away with it.

Down south in Florida; what I considered as country life, the people were totally different than what we were used to. The way they ate and what they ate; a whole slice of fried ham, grits, eggs and greasy sausage. What the heck is a grit? Where is the cream of wheat at? The way they talked; total strangers said hello to you while you walked along the street as if they've known you all their lives. I came to figure that country folks are very noisy. They try to make it come off as being friendly. They say hello and as soon as you say hello back to them they start with a hundred questions. Who you some kin to? Where you live at? Do you know the Patterson up on Fifth Street? Who your mama people? My question to them would be, why are you asking me all these question;

I don't know you. The rule; never talk to strangers does not apply down south.

They didn't say pop here, they called it soda. Pickled eggs and pickled pig feet were their favorite snack. Do they pickle everything down here? Who would want to eat a pig's feet knowing where it had been. No thanks, I'll stick with cookies, cakes and jello. Their daily activities were nothing short of having none. They would wake up in the morning eat breakfast than be outside playing all day until it was time for dinner and then go to bed. No one read a book or played a board game; you know do something that causes you to have to use some brain cells. And the way they discipline the children someone should have definitely been calling CPS. You would have thought that by me getting beat with a weight belt and an extension cord that I wouldn't be surprised by anything that an adult would use to whoop a child, but I was. When they got a whooping, they didn't go outside and get the switch off the tree in the backyard or go and get the belt. What they got a whooping with was with a piece of a two feet long, one inch thick water hose that had been cut from the eight foot water hose that was bought from the store to water the grass. Do you know how thick a water hose was? To me it was worse than getting a whooping with an extension cord. It sounded worse too.

To hear the wind after the water hose was whipped through the air to land on somebody's behind or body part that wasn't being covered up sounded so painful. The sound that it made when it made contact with skin was unbelievable. You think a jumping bean can jump around; just witness someone getting whooped with a water hose. Jumping Jack Flash ain;t got nothing on them. One thing about country folks; they didn't mind whooping their kids in front of people. Up north we did it behind closed doors but down south the kids get it right where they cut up at.

This county living was just too much to take in all at one time. Mama knew that we weren't use to this. She knew that we were totally out of our comfort zone. But she never came to us to comfort us. She never ensured us that this living arrangement was only temporary. Mama never said a mumbling word.

Peter's mama's house to me looked like someone took half of one house and half of another house and glued it together to make one house. It was no longer or wider than a school bus on each side. In the front of the house on one side was the living room and literally next to it was a bedroom. You had to walk through the living room, through the bedroom to get to the kitchen which was a straight shot towards the back of the house. The house had two front doors as if at one point in time another family was living on the other side and when they moved out Peter's mama turned that side into two more bedrooms and there was the bathroom. The way the house was set up I think both families shared the kitchen and bathroom. I couldn't imagine how a family of six could live in such a small space. I'm so glad that I didn't grow up in the south. It looked like they lived a real rough life.

Well the way the house was arranged, the side that the two bedrooms were on; if you came in that front door you walked right into Peter's bedroom. You had to walk through the second bedroom to get to the bathroom which as I mentioned was in the back of the house. There were no doors to any of the bedrooms, so when it was time for me or Sis to change our clothes we went in the bathroom. There were only four doors to this whole house; two front doors, a back door, and a bathroom door. There was no privacy in this house and Peter took full advantage of that fact.

It had been a long day. Everyone was settled down and even off to sleep when I suddenly felt a tug on my foot that woke me up. I thought that it was one of the others girls kicking me or something in their sleep. It was the four of us sleeping in the bed together so it didn't give us much elbow room to stretch out. Without opening my eyes I just moved my foot over out of the way and fell back off to sleep. Moments later there was another tug on my foot but this time it was harder and I knew it wasn't one of the other girl's foot kicking me but someone's hand. I sat up in the bed and looked around but no one was there. I looked over at Sis, Felicia, and Debra but they were all still asleep. I even looked over to the boys' bed; they were dead asleep too.

Our bed sat against the wall and was the first bed when you came out of Peter's bedroom. So I looked over at his doorway to see if someone was standing there; it was empty. I could only see the shadows of the darkness. I know I wasn't crazy, I know I felt someone tug on my foot. After seeing no one, I laid back down but I didn't go back to sleep. I gently moved my foot under Sis's so that way if it happened again her foot would have to be moved and she would wake up too. That way I would have a witness that she felt something too and that I wasn't crazy.

I laid still and after some time I heard popping and crackling noise and then I heard footsteps. Someone has bad knees, I thought to myself. I figured it was Peter walking around since everyone else was sleep. I lay still as the noise got closer and closer; suddenly it stopped. I figured Peter had been just playing around on his way to the bathroom and now he was on his way back to go get back in the bed with my mother.

It was still quiet when I felt Sis's foot being lifted ever so gently away from mine. I was screaming in my head for her to wake up. Wake up; please wake up, but she didn't. I felt two hands grab me by both my ankles and slowly pull them to the edge of the bed so I could be away from the others. Without opening my eyes I knew for a fact it was Peter. Oh my God, I thought to myself; is this man crazy? What is he doing? Does my mother not know that this man is missing from their bed? I was scared. I lay ever so still pretending to be asleep. Peter spread my legs open; I could feel him crawling onto the bed and positioning himself in the open space that he had made. Peter is much stronger than me, I can't fight him. I was frozen with fear. Is this man going to rap me in front of everyone? It was too many witnesses for that; he can't be that brave or crazy. Isn't he worried that someone is going to wake up and see him. Or has he done this before and gotten away with it so he was confident in himself.

Why me? Why did he choose me? Was it because I didn't tell mama about what he had done at the lake, so he figured that I would keep my mouth shut about whatever he did. I hope that he didn't take my silence as a weakness. My not telling my mother wasn't to benefit him, it was so I won't feel rejection from my mother again because of a man. I couldn't believe that this was happening. Is this what we left Pennsylvania for? I've gone from getting beaten to getting molested. Mama needs to pick her men a little bit more carefully. I had literally left the room and my body with my thoughts. If I scream now everyone will wake up and the little that I know of Peter; he will deny everything and mama will do nothing. Then again mama may tell us to pack our stuff, that were leaving and not know where the hell we going because we are new in town and have no money or family down here. Maybe we end up going back to Pennsylvania and wait for Big Willie to get out of jail and commence to beating on me again. But I knew that my mother was not going to help me; I had to help myself.

I was back in my body again and just in time. I felt Peter pull my panties to the side and then I heard a click. Still to frighten to move, I could feel a light being shined on me. The clicking noise was from Peter turning on a flash light. This man had a flash light; are you serious. I felt as Peter touched the lips of my private and spread them open with his fingers. Every muscle in my body froze in fear. Peter began to examine me as if he had never seen female private parts before. I was in so much disbelieve that a grown man was doing this to a little girl. He was in his mama's house with a room full of people and he had no concerns of being caught. I couldn't let him continue what he was doing. I couldn't let him go any further. I didn't want to find out; if given more time, what Peter would do. Yes I was scared, but my innocence was mine to keep and not for him to take.

I started moving my arms and elbowing Felicia and Sis in the hopes that they would wake up. I was still surprised that no one had. Or had they? Had they seen what was going on and was glad that it wasn't them this time? Did they lay there only pretending to be asleep all this time? And why didn't mama notice that Peter was missing from her side all this time? I continued to move around and I heard the flash light click again; this time it was off. I started moving my legs to close them which made Peter move from in between them. I slowly pulled myself back to the top of the bed. I sat up and looked around the room with so much anger. I was angry because no one woke up. I was sad because I had the feeling that Peter had done this many times before to someone else and had gotten away with it. As quick as he had come into the room; Peter had left it. As I sat there; I knew Peter could feel the fury of my anger coming from me through the wall that separated the two rooms. I became a different person that night. I was no longer my mother's child.

# Chapter 15

**THE WEEKS HAVE** gone by and I've seen less and less of Peter. I don't know whether it was because I was avoiding him or that he was avoiding me. I just know that he wasn't around and neither was my mother at this point. To make the best of the situation that mama has now put us in, I sat the incident of the other night on the shelf in my mind to deal with it at a later time. Out of sight out of mind is what Peter was to me.

Something bad must have kicked off early one afternoon between mama, Peter and his mother because as we were walking down the street coming back from hanging out at Debra's, you could see all the kids outside playing in the road and them three standing outside arguing. All I could make out was that Peter's mama was very mad and mama was trying to plead their case but Peter's mama didn't want to hear nothing that my mother had to say. I heard Peter's mama tell my mother to get her kids, her stuff and get out of her house. The next thing I know we were in the car; stuff and all riding around town trying to find a place to stay.

Mama and Peter weren't saying much to each other. After riding around for a while we made a stop at Peter's brother's house which was really a double wide trailer. I heard of people traveling with them to go on vacation, but I never known for people to really live in them. Peter's brother was in the army and his family was leaving for Germany soon. Peter's brother let us stay with him for that week; that was the best he could do for us. I felt so misplaced. The trailer was pretty much empty. Only the kitchen table, a sofa and loveseat were in the living part of the trailer because they had packed up everything and shipped it to

Germany. Peter's sister-in-law acted like she didn't want us there. She acted very high class and sophisticated. She didn't want us to touch anything; especially the walls. She never let her daughter play with me or Sis as if we weren't good enough. She would look at us as if we were trash that needed to be sat out by the curb. But what she didn't know was as much as she didn't want us there; we didn't want to be there. We slept on the cold floor covered by the one or two blankets that she supplied. The house wasn't the only thing that was cold around there. When she served us breakfast in the morning we only had a certain time to eat because after a certain time the kitchen was closed whether you ate or not. I was so glad when that week was over. I would have slept in the car than spent another night at her house; I mean trailer.

We were back in the car again riding around trying to find another place to stay. I don't know what happened to the U-haul of stuff that we had but thank God we didn't have it because we didn't have anywhere to put it. Hell, we didn't have anywhere to put ourselves for that matter. Peter had another brother who had a two bedroom apartment. We all watched from the car as Peter got out and talked to his brother in the front yard. We couldn't hear exactly what was being said but we knew when Peter fell over with joy and his brother reached out his hand to help his brother off the ground; that we had a place to sleep for the night.

Peter's brother was very nice to us. He told us we could stay there as long as we wanted and if there was anything that we needed to let him know. We got settled in. We slept in the bedroom while mama and Peter took the living room floor; I think it should have been the other way around. One night I was in a lot of pain because somehow or another I had developed something on my foot called a ring-worm. Not taking me to the hospital yet again, mama listened to some country back wood remedy way to get rid of it. Something to the effects of cut my skin to open it and pour some liquor in the wound to run the worm out. I just think the worm got drunk from the liquor because all it did was move around in a circle. And when it was moving that's when it was hurting and for some reason it only wanted to move at night; late night. It was itching so badly that night I couldn't take it anymore. I had suffered in pain for at least an hour before I went looking for mama so she could give me something for the pain. I didn't have far to look because when I opened the bedroom door there her and Peter was all naked for God and everybody to see doing only God knows what looking like a black Adam and Eve before they ate the fruit from the tree.

I just stood there and shook my head at them as they tried to cover as much of their body as they could with their two hands. Thank God Peter's brother didn't walk out his room. I was losing more and more respect for my mother if I hadn't completely lost it already. I was sick to my stomach now. I didn't care about the pain in my foot I just wanted to go back to bed. The worm could have eaten my foot off that night, I didn't care. After seeing what I saw, I didn't want my mother to give me nothing.

After some time mama even enrolled us into school; I was twelve years old and in middle school by this time. After school I was so bored because Sis and my little brother's school schedules were different than mine, so that left me with no one to play with or talk to for an hour or two. Mama suggests I go outside and play. With whom I asked her. Trying to make my situation better, mama walked me to the door and pointed to the monkey bars and swings that I could play on. Who wanted to entertain themselves in this hot behind heat? I really didn't. As we were talking a young girl passed by and she must have heard part of our conversation. "I'll play with you." She said. Shonda was here name. She was the first friend that I made in Florida. Shonda was a nice girl and she even went to the same school as I did. We became friends instantly.

Another summer has come and the Florida heat is not kind at all. Getting bored with our surrounding, Peter suggests another playground for us to play at. He gives us directions and so we're off onto our new adventure. We're so excited for something new to do. We took the instructions that Peter gave us which the more and more we walk, I discover that he was sending us in the direction by my school. We have to walk down a steep hill to get to the playground. But it wasn't a playground, it was just a baseball field without a tree in sight and one set of benches three tier high. That was a long walk just for us to be so disappointed when we had our hopes up so high. I could have cussed Peter out. It was too damn hot to do all that walking for nothing. Not even a cast of a shade to hide from the Florida sun. After standing there for ten minutes with nothing to play with but the dirt and grass: we had enough and decided to head back home. We were so hot, mad and tired when we got back home. Mama asked, "How was it"? We didn't say a word and I think I rolled my eyes at her as I passed by her on the way to our room. We all just fell asleep from the heat.

Towards the end of the summer, we had moved into our own place in a city called Bartow. We were now living in our own two bedroom apartment. It seemed like we had nothing but the clothes that were on our backs. It's kind of rough having to start all over. We didn't have beds so we made do with what we had. Instead of sleeping on the floor, we slept in our camping sleeping bags that we used one summer for church camp. So we wouldn't be completely on the hard floor even though there was carpet, mama bought blow up air mattresses to lay the sleeping bag on top of.

We didn't have any furniture to sit on so we sat on iron milk crates to watch television. Mama bought little cushions to put on the crates to make them more comfortable. Sometimes we would argue over who would get to sit on the crates because some were more comfortable than others: if that was possible. But most of the time I just soon sat on the floor. We couldn't afford a vacuum cleaner so every weekend mama had us on our hands and knees picking the rug of any trash. It felt more like picking cotton to me. There we were all three of us in a row from one end of the living room/dining room to the other until we were done. Along with washing down the base boards and going outside to pick the weeds. We had our weekend choirs to keep us busy. I hated going outside to pick weeds. We lived in a nice apartment complex that cut they own grass, why did we have to go out and pick weeds? We never picked weeds before coming to Florida. See that's that down south country mentality rubbing off on mama. I hated picking weeds because it was hot. It seemed like the sun just found a spot on your back and stayed on it. To me the Florida sun was only good for one thing and that was to make some good sun ice tea. Mama had a large gallon glass container that she used to make the tea. She would put eight large tea bags in the water and sit the glass container out on the wooden fence post for an hour or two in the sun. Anticipating its every drop sometimes we would just sit and watch as the sun brewed the tea turning what was once just plain water into gold. Boy that was some good sun ice tea after mama added in her sugar.

That summer we also joined the local YMCA summer programs where I got a small part in a play that they put on every year at the end of the program. I played a Queen's maid, which was a far cry from being the Mother Mary when I was up north. Mama was so proud of me that she made me this beautiful spaghetti strap dress with a short sleeve half jacket to go with it. Mama came to see the play and she was very disappointed. I only had one line and mama said that I didn't even say that clear enough. Well, at least I got a part in the play. What did Sis get? I don't know but my attitude was just horrible that summer. The girls at the YMCA were so mean for no reason and it seemed like mama just kept making us go even though we didn't want to. My attitude was so bad that one day I got in trouble and mama tried to beat the black off of me. I probably had said something smart knowing me and didn't care. Mama sent me to my room and she didn't stop beating me with that extension cord until she got tired. I was throwing up and everything; she just kept swinging that extension cord and told me that it was just the hell coming up out of me. The more I tried to block the licks, the more and harder she went to swinging. After a while it didn't seem like she was beating me but fighting me. I can honestly say that I did deserve that whooping, I just didn't want her to kill me in the process. Because the look in her eyes was that she really wanted to.

Since our baby blue Impala had given it all she had, we had to put her to rest. Not having a car meant that we had to walk everywhere we went which wasn't new to us but everything was across the bridge. I was just glad that everything was close by. Mama even got a job at the Payless shoe store which was in the same plaza as the grocery store that we went to also across the bridge.

Things started to change for the better for us. Mama bought some furniture for the living room which got us off the crates but we still had to sit on the floor because mama wanted the furniture to last. Mama even saved up enough money to put a down payment on a car. It was a gray exterior, burgundy interior small but big enough for us station wagon. It wasn't new but it was better than what we had which was nothing. Mama had surprised us with it one day.

We started this weekend like every weekend; having to go grocery shopping and that meant walking over the bridge. Mama told us to get ready that we were going to the store. So of course we prepared ourselves to walk over that long bridge. But when we got outside the apartment instead of walking our normal trail of the sidewalk and through the wooded path that had been formed by residents of the complex as a short cut to the bridge; mama proceeded to walk into the parking lot. Where was mama going, we asked each other? We were all puzzled looking at each other for the answer. Mama just smiled and continued to walk until she stood by her pride and joy. We were so excited that we didn't have to walk anymore. I think mama took it to another level though. She kept that car so clean and smelling good that you could live in it if you wanted to. Sometimes I think it did become her second home.

Later mama even bought some beds which got us off the floor and out the sleeping bags. Me and Sis were getting older and turning into young ladies. Mama figured that we might need a little bit more privacy but with our little brother sharing a room with us, that was almost impossible. And only having one bathroom and tying it up just to change our clothes when we could just change in our rooms was a better solution. When we did kick our brother out the room so we could change he would get mad as if we were kicking him out of his room for good. So, mama had an idea to turn the back storage room into my little brother's bedroom. It was big enough to fit a twin bed and space for him to hang around in. Just the thought of having the hot water heater in your room was kind of weird to me, but mama fixed it up nice. She was good at doing that. Since there was no door mama hung a curtain up in its entry way so my brother could still have some privacy.

Now that me and Sis had our own bedroom, we decided to personalize it with some drawings. We started to develop our drawing skills. We would draw any and everything. I think we got the gift to draw from our daddy who loved to draw and paint mama told us. Bunnies, cats, dogs with fluffy long ears; anything we could think of, we drew. I once drew a lady sitting at a café having tea with her fancy lace umbrella shielding her face from the sun. She wore a long pretty dress with lace gloves. We would hang our pictures over our beds on the wall and then argue who's was the best. I always thought mine were better.

By mama working, that left Peter home alone with us at times. One weekend while mama was at work Peter made sure we still did our chores of picking the rug and weeds. I felt something crawl on me and bit me on my back. My little brother looked on my back but he said that he didn't see what had bit me. But something had to be there because it was stinging. It must have fallen off when I stood up and reached around to scratch my back. Whatever it was had me itching so bad that I couldn't wait for mama to come home to see what it was. I went to Peter to tell him that I think that something may have bit me on my back.

Peter hadn't done anything to me since we left his mother's house and matter of fact he had been kind of nice to us. Playing kick ball outside in the yard with us and stuff like that, so nothing came to my mind that he would do anything stupid. I felt that he had changed. I was hesitant about asking Peter to check to see if he could see what might have bit me but I was in a lot of pain. It could have been an eight eyed African spider that bit me for all I know. I took my little brother as back up when I went in the house to ask Peter for help. We found Peter and stood in the hallway as I told Peter what had happened outside. Peter told me to turn around and he lifted my shirt only a little so he could check the lower part of my back. Me and my brother kept eye contact the whole time. Yeah, something had bit me alright. Peter said he could see where my skin had turned red from being irritated.

Peter went and got some alcohol from the bathroom. When he came back he told my little brother to go and take out the garbage. At the same time Peter told me to go lay on my bed so he could put the alcohol on my back. We both did as Peter had instructed for us to do. Peter did put the alcohol on my back where whatever had bit me and it did stop itching. I appreciated him for that but at the same time I was hoping for my little brother to hurry up and come back. My brother was taking a long time to come back and I think Peter was counting on just that. After putting the alcohol on my back Peter told me to turn over and lay on my back. I did but at the same time I was thinking; why did he want me to lay on my back when the problem was on my back and he couldn't put more alcohol on my back if I was laying on it. Peter said that he wanted to put alcohol on my chest and he proceeded to crawl on top of me. I told Peter that I didn't need any alcohol on my chest; that nothing had bit me on my chest. Peter seemed to be up to his old ways again. I guess a snake never bites his tongue. I pushed Peter off of me and ran out of my room.

At that time I heard the front door close and I thought it was my little brother finally coming back from taking out the garbage but I ran right into my mother instead. Out of breath; I began rambling on to mama about what had just happened. She acted like she didn't understand a word I said. I know she heard me but I'm thinking she really didn't want to believe that Peter would do something like that. If she only knew what Peter was really capable of? But I think the frustration of having a long day at work and then having to come home to some foolishness was not on her agenda for today. In all of my rambling she asked me to repeat myself. By this time Peter had come out of the room and was standing in the hallway entry way. What was the use? I thought to myself. It wasn't like she would believe me anyway. I told her never mind and went to my room. My little brother followed me and asked if I was okay. I wasn't, I felt trapped in my own skin. As we sat in my room; you could hear mama and Peter in their bedroom arguing about what I had just told her. I thought for sure mama was going to put him out. Peter denied it of course and mama believed him of course. I didn't expect anything less or more for that matter.

Weeks had passed and though mama was giving Peter the silent treatment and the evil eye; he managed to get back on her good side after a while. Peter walked around the house with this stupid smirk on his face knowing that he had mama in the palm of his hands and that there was nothing anyone could say or do to pry her out of them.

Money was tight and so Peter tried to help out where he could since he wasn't working. One time Peter took all of us to the Salvation Army to shop for clothes. Even though it was his idea I thought mama had bumped her head for going along with it. Was he crazy, because the idea of us buying anything out of the Salvation Army sure enough was? I knew we weren't rich but we weren't dirt poor either. Peter acted like we were at Macys or somewhere like that; telling me and Sis to look around that we might see something that we like. In here, I don't think so. We walked around the store only to entertain him but touching nothing. He walked rack to rack pulling clothes out that he thought that we might like. I don't know what gave me the idea that we would like anything in here. Every time he would hold something up to show us; me and Sis would just shake our head while making an ugly face at the clothes he was picking out and kept on walking like he didn't say anything. I guess mama thought that we were being a little too harsh to Peter and asked us to look around anyway.

So that we wouldn't hurt anyone's feeling and break their pride, we stroked Peter's ego. Sis and I agreed that she would get a pair of pants and I would find something to go along with it. She did, she found a pair of brown slacks so I found a beige vest. It really didn't match and I didn't care because we weren't planning on wearing it anyway. But Peter told us that we could put it together and have one outfit. The shit didn't match, who was going to wear it. So we bought the pants and vest. Peter stood there with a big grin on his face. Can we get the hell out of the Salvation Army now that Peter's ego has been stroked? Me and Sis just shook our heads about what had just happened. The things a woman would do for her man.

With Peter finally getting a job working at Burger King which he rode his bike to everyday; things had gotten a lot better but we weren't exactly out of the woods just yet. When the new school year started mama didn't buy me and Sis our own wardrobe, we shared. Mama bought about five shirts that me and Sis had to take turns wearing. I bet that was one of Peter's bright ideas because mama never made us share clothes before. Even when we were broke we at least had our own. God forbid that we might have wanted to wear the same color shirt on the same day. But we got lucky with the pants because Sis was a slim 7-8 and I was a thick 9-10 with hips and butt. And when it came to the shoes we shared also. You would think by mama working at the shoe store and getting a discount we should have a closet full of shoes and wouldn't have to share; but that wasn't the case. We had to squeeze into a narrow size nine because that's the size mama wore. Me and Sis had our daddy's feet; we needed a size more.

I hated going to school in Bartow. The kids on the bus were so mean. And even though me and Sis had to share clothes, the kids thought that we were rich because we wore nice clothes and shoes and that we lived in an nice apartment. I guess it don't take much to make a good impression on country folks.

# Chapter 16

**ALONG WITH OUR** weekend chores that we had to endure, nothing was worse than sitting in our family meetings. We would sit around and discuss any issues that we may have had. Nothing was ever resolved just orders were given out and expectation of us. Some meetings were short and others were hours long. One weekend we had our usual family meeting and this one no one saw this subject coming. Peter wasn't included in this family meeting for whatever reason. Mama started the meeting off by asking us how we felt about her and Peter getting married. Is she serious right now? She really wanted to marry this man. What is she thinking? My head just went to spinning. Mama even said that we could call Peter daddy. I think I threw up a little bit in my mouth. I would never call Peter my daddy for the simple reason he was not my idea of what a daddy was and anyway; I already have a daddy. And what if we did said no, that we didn't want her to marry Peter; would she marry him anyway. To me she already had her mind made up. Why would the thought of marriage come up anyway? I thought people married for love. And it was obvious that Peter didn't love mama because if he did he wouldn't have done the things that he had done to me. To me mama and Peter never looked like two people in love; just two people together for convenience.

No one answered mama's question right away. We all just looked at each other waiting for someone to be the first of us three to speak up. After sometime of dead silence; Sis spoke up and said that she didn't care if they got married. My little brother was happy to have a man in the house so he also agreed that they could get married. Everyone looked at me awaiting my response. I on the other hand didn't want them to get married. But on the other hand I didn't want to rob mama of the happiness that she thinks that she may have found. If Sis and little Willie said go right and I knew it was better to go left; I would still to go right so not to break up the pack. I didn't want to be the deal breaker; all for one and one for all. So I said that I didn't care if they to get married.

A week later mama and Peter were married at a courthouse. None of Peter's family was there. Sis, little Willie, and myself and two clerks of the court was mama's wedding party. I wore the unmatched outfit that we got from the Salvation Army. I thought it was the proper thing to wear for the occasion; an unmatched outfit for an unmatched marriage. Later that summer we even took a family portrait to make it legit. We really looked unmatched and no one even smiled in the picture. But we did go to Disney as a family, that was fun I must admit.

After mama married Peter we didn't get to see much of her anymore. They just stay locked up in the bedroom all the time. Things were quiet now; Sis, little Willie and I seem to only have each other. We count, depend and take care of each other. One good thing is we laugh a lot. But there was one day that I would have given anything to hear my sister cry.

Like any other night me and Sis were laying in our beds after our adventure filled day was over and we were up laughing and talking up a storm like we do every night before drifting off to sleep. My sister had a little habit that I didn't know about; she kept sewing needles tucked in her mattress. I can't remember exactly what she said but it was so funny and she had me laughing so hard that I reached over and hit the edge of her mattress with my hand and said to her something like, " girl you so crazy." So when she realized that I had hit her bed where she had stuck a needle and the needle was no longer there, she asked me if I was okay. Is told her sure, not knowing just yet why she was asking me that.

After she fumbled in the dark to check her bed and told me that the needle was gone, she jumped up and turned the light on to double check her bed; the needle was definitely gone. She panicked and told me to check my hand. I did front and back and there was no sign of any needle sticking out of my hand and my hand wasn't bleeding. I made a fist with my hand and opened it back up. Nothing was stopping me or poking me as I made a fist; so the needle couldn't have went in my hand. I told her that I was fine that maybe the needle went down in the mattress further. I asked Sis was she sure that the needle wasn't still stuck in her mattress. She checked again and it wasn't. There was no needle sticking out of my hand or the mattress so we came to the conclusion that I must have hit it and the needle went down into the mattress. I told her that that was a dangerous habit to have and that what if one night she forgot where she stuck the needle and rolled over on it. but she assured me that she would never do that. That she always kept them up somewhere by her pillow so she could reach for it quickly. I asked Sis why she kept needles in her bed anyway. She never answered that question. Needless to say we went back to laughing and talking into the night until we fell asleep.

As the days went on I noticed that I could barely close my right hand into a fist or write my name. After a while I couldn't use my right hand at all. I had to go and tell mama what had happened several nights ago and tell her that I might have a needle stuck in my hand. I didn't want to get Sis in any trouble so that's why I waited as long as I could. But when I couldn't use my hand anymore I knew the situation had gotten serious. Maybe mama would understand that it was just an accident. I told mama and she didn't seem too happy but the next day she took me to the doctor where an x-ray was taken of my hand. And there as big as the moon was a sewing needle stuck in my hand. The doctor said he would of course have to perform a small surgery on my hand to remove it. At the time mama seemed calm; at least I thought that she was calm. She made an appointment for the surgery. But when we got back home mama's calmness went right out the window.

Mama took out her frustration on Sis. She didn't whoop Sis with a belt or an extension cord; she whooped Sis was a water hose which was even worse. You see the thing about Sis was she never cried or yelled out when she would get a whooping and I never understood why. Unlike me I be yelling, hooping and hollering, running, fighting back, pleading for my life. Not Sis, she would just stand there and take it. And you know as a parent when they are whooping you they want to know that it hurts so they know that they're doing their job.

Sis would never cry out so her whooping's would last longer until the person giving the whooping got tired. Someone must have trained her how to stay silent no matter how much pain she was in or the situation would be even worse for her or harder the next time. So Sis held in her pain. But that day I wished I could have heard my sister cry so mama would stop whipping her with that stupid water hose. I watched as mama stood in the middle of the living room and beat Sis. I watched my sister as she moved her body to endure the pain. Tears began to roll down my cheeks for my sister as I watched my mother beat her until she got tired of swinging that piece of a water hose. She didn't deserve to get a whooping for something that was clearly an accident. I again later on asked my sister why did she have the needles stuck in her mattress. She said it was for her protection because someone kept sneaking in our bedroom at night messing with her. Another trick she would do was put a glass of water behind our bedroom door at night. If she woke up the next morning and the glass was knocked over, she knew that someone had tried to come in our bedroom while we were asleep.

1984 school was back in and I was glad. Mama use to get up in the mornings with us; make us breakfast, pack our lunches and get my brother dressed and do me and Sis's hair and see us off to school. All that stopped after her and Peter got married. Now we get ourselves ready and off to school. Mama can make a peanut butter and jelly sandwich taste like it came right out of heaven's kitchen my sandwich on the other hand taste like it was made three days ago and was left sitting out on the counter. But mama did make sure we had a lot of good stuff to put in our lunch boxes.

I loved going to school, the kids on the other hand were something to reckon with but I learned early on how to ignore simple people. I had one class that I looked forward to everyday and that was music lyrics class. I became so interested in music and I loved how it made me feel. Our lyrics teacher picked a different song every week to teach us about and get the real meaning of a song and understand what the artist's message was in the song. Donna Summers' *She Works Hard for the Money* was a big hit at the time. The country group Alabama had a big hit too. I learned about all types of music. And Lionel Richie had a song out *You are the Sun You are the Rain* which was the first song that I ever learned every single word to. I loved that song so much; I wrote the lyrics out on my yellow music class folder. Peter didn't like that I wrote all over my folder but yet again, I didn't care; it was my folder. I've came to love classical, gospel, and r&b music. Music would ease my spirit in troubled times and it still does.

Receiving the gift of music was not the only gift that I received that year; Mother Nature presented me with a gift of her own. Yep, this was the year that I became a young lady while at school mind you. I was scared. I grabbed some paper towels and lined my panties with them so that I wouldn't make a mess for the rest of the day. I was excited that Mother Nature had finally come to visit me; I no longer carrier the title little girl. I couldn't wait to get home and tell mama but when I told her, she wasn't happy at all. I didn't understand why not. But I know now. Other body parts would soon start to develop. I don't know but Mother Nature's gift had me feeling like I could breathe now and enjoy life. But the strangest things started to happen; even though mama had made the back storage room a bedroom for my brother she would move him back into me and Sis bedroom every couple of months or so. I guess she was sensing something about Peter. It was about time.

Peter quit his job at Burger King but not before he saved up enough money to buy himself a car. Peter later joined the police academy to my surprise. Are you serious, that's all we need; a fool with a gun and a badge to hide behind? With all his training he wasn't home and I was able to let my guard down. So did Sis; she didn't put any more glasses of water behind our bedroom door. This gave us time to think and focus on other areas of our young lives.

I always thought that I was fast and much of a tomboy, so I joined the school track team. Sports were one of Peter's favorite things. So when Peter came home on the weekends, he would help me run drills to improve my speed. Mama would stand off to the side with the stop watch as me and Peter would make a b-line as fast as would could down the street. Peter ran track and played football while he was in high school, so you know speed was in his blood. Keeping up with him was not an easy task at all. I must say, the academy was doing Peter some good. You could really see a change in him. When it came time for my first track meet Peter went out and bought me a fancy looking running shoes; gold, white and red they were. I took this gesture as him apologizing for the bad things he had done to me. But I never got to wear the shoes because the day before our first track met at practice I quit the track team. I didn't think that I was fast enough and the other team's mates didn't think so either and they didn't mind voicing their opinion. I could hear their comments as I passed the finish line after running my drills. Girls in middle school can be so mean. Mama and Peter were disappointed that I had quit; I could tell. But they did encourage me to find something else that I might like and try out for that.

Not finding anything that spark my interest; there was no more staying after school for me. So one day when I came home from school Sis wasn't home and neither was Peter to my surprise, I thought since he had a two week break from the police academy that he would be home trying to catch up on some of the rest he lost having to get up at 4am in the morning for his daily exercise at the academy before he started class. And with mama working late hours at the Payless now that she had a car, I knew she wouldn't be home. I wondered where Sis had disappeared to. I figured Peter was off doing something that pertained to his police training. About an hour later Sis and Peter walked in the door.

I asked Sis where she had been. Sis said that Peter had taken her to the movies for her birthday. Wow that was nice of him. I must admit I was mad that Peter didn't take all of us. I went to Peter and asked why he didn't take all of us. Peter said he would make it up to me and my brother and take us that weekend. I was satisfied with that. I went back and asked Sis what movie did she go and see. She said it was the new movie, *Ghostbusters*. I was jealous. I asked her what happened in the movie. I had seen little clips of the movie being advertised on television but I wanted to know the other good parts because it did look like it was a good movie by what the y were showing on television. Sis could tell me nothing about the movie. She fumbled over her words and she only told me the parts that we had already seen on the television. How could you sit through a movie that was more than an hour long and not be able to tell me anything about the movie. My heart dropped into my stomach. I got the feeling that my sister didn't have such a Happy Birthday after all.

Peter kept his promise and took me and my little brother to the movies that weekend. We went back and forth on which movie to see. After finally deciding just to go and see *Ghostbusters*. I wanted to see all of what Sis missed. Maybe the movie was boring and she couldn't remember it. What other reason could it be that she couldn't tell me about the movie? We got settled in with our drinks and popcorn in the theatre. The lights went out; I was sitting on one side of Peter while my brother sat on the other side of him. Fifteen minutes into the movie, Peter pulls out a blanket from a back pack that he was carrying. He proceeds to cover all three of us up with the blanket. I must admit it was cold in there but who brings a whole big old blanket to a movie theatre. A jacket yes, not a blanket; you take blankets to picnics. After being covered with the blanket for about five minutes, I felt Peter's hand rub between my legs. I immediately threw the part of the blanket that covered my lap back off of me. I jumped up out of my chair, looked at Peter and yelled, "No."

I grabbed my popcorn and drink and sat next to my brother who was still covered by the blanket and startled by my outburst. I see why Sis couldn't tell me anything about the movie; she probably didn't get to see it. I could only imagine the things he did to her under that blanket. After about five minutes, Peter put the blanket away and we watched the rest of the movie in silence. That jackleg aint changed one bit. That would be the last time that Peter tried to put his hands on me. I didn't care if Peter was going to see the Wizard about getting a pot of gold; I never wanted to go anywhere with him again. The ride home was very awkward. I didn't say a word and neither did Peter. But my baby brother was going a mile a minute about the movie *Ghostbusters*. When I got back home I could only look at Sis. She looked at me and we didn't say a word. She knew that I now knew the truth. But it seemed that Peter had more tricks up his sleeve. Before the school year was over, Peter started teaching Sis how to drive. When Sis was telling me how Peter was teaching her how to drive by having her sit on his lap I just shook my head. Trying to imagine that scene was giving me a major headache. I made up in my mind that it would be a snowy day in hell before I would give Peter the chance to teach me how to drive. Riding the bus for the rest of my life didn't sound so bad. I've rode the bus before. It's not half bad if you get a window seat.

# Chapter 17

**AFTER WEEKS OF** training, Peter finally graduated from the police academy. We went to the ceremony where he was issued his certificate and badge; yeah we were there looking like the perfect family. We were truly proud of Peter and his hard work and what he had accomplishment despite how we felt personally about him. Even a wet dog deserves to shake himself dry. Peter was later assigned to his police department and that meant that we had to move. Back to Haines City is where we ended up. That's funny because that's where it all began.

Moving to Haines City would be a major part of my life. Here is where I would make friends for life and maybe a couple of enemies too that I wasn't aware of. I would be introduced to the crazy and sometimes wicked world. I would become a young lady having to deal with grown woman issues. I've always said, the best lessons learned are the ones that you teach yourself.

We ended up moving to a townhouse; Yet again a place with only two bedrooms. Did Florida not have any three bedroom apartments or a house that we could move into that you couldn't see underneath straight across to the neighbor's yard. There were no houses in Florida, just a whole punch of wooden shacks. Never the less, we made do with what we had. The bedrooms were separated by the bathroom which you could enter from either side. Scared that Peter would say that he accidently walked in on me while I was undressing to take a bath; I would triple check the bathroom door that lead to their bedroom to make sure that it was locked. But all and all we settled down for a minute and things were good.

With Peter being assigned to his department us moving around became very regular, but I was able to complete a school grade while living in the townhouse. The school was literally in my backyard. Only a fence separated the two. It would only take me two minutes to get to school. In the morning that was great, I didn't have to worry about getting up early and trying to have to walk to the bus stop. But in the afternoon after school I didn't like it so much because I got home too fast and no one would be home yet. But one afternoon when I came home from school someone had come to leave a couple of packages on our door step.

I'm walking around making sure bathroom doors are locked; mama should have been checking Peter's closet for any skeletons that may have wanted to fall out. Knowing Peter as long as we have; maybe two years now we discovered that he had been keeping a little secret from us. Or should I say two little secrets. Besides the fact that he was a pervert; Peter had a set of twins a boy and a girl they couldn't have been no more than two years old. Surprise, surprise, surprise; I say in my Gomer Powell voice. My first question to myself was why he wasn't with the baby's mama. And how did he marry mama when obviously he already had a family of his own. I guess the baby's mama got a scent that Peter was back in town and since he was playing daddy to someone else's kids, she thought it only be right that he play daddy for his own. At first they were dropped off only on the weekend then the weekend became the summer.

Mama did like a good stepmother would; she made sure they had everything that they needed and more. She bought them new clothes, shoes and toys and not from the Salvation Army either. Oh no, Peter's little rug rats was too good for that. I thought how strange it was that he violated her kids but yet she loved his. I guess he never heard of; treat others in the way that you would like to be treated.

The summer was over and we were on the move again. One good thing about this move was that we were still in Haines City, the bad thing was we moved into yet another two bedroom apartment with only one bathroom. The apartment was way too small for five people. Where we moved to was a huge apartment complex so it was kind of hard for me to believe that there wasn't a bigger apartment available. I later learned from the kids in school it was for the fruit pickers and their family if they worked in the orange groves. Kids would ask me where I lived and when I told them Park View Village they would laugh and say that we picked fruit. I guess picking fruit was as degrading as picking cotton. I always found myself defending my honor and reputation. So I would always have to go into this long story how no one in our house picked fruit and that we were only living out there was because my stepfather was on the police force and was part-time security for the apartment complex. Another officer on the police force and his wife managed the property. So I also learned early on its not so much what you know that will get you places, it's who you know that will get you very far in life. But trying to explain that for three weeks straight after arriving to a new school became very tiring. But the message got out very quickly that me and my sister were the new girls on Powerline. One thing about PVV; I made a lot of friends. That was kind of surprising to me because we were only allowed to come outside on the weekends and we couldn't go any further than the front porch. Anyone who wanted to see us had to come to our porch. I hated the fact that we couldn't leave off the porch. What was the purpose of going outside if all you can do is sitting on the porch. And what made matters worse was our apartment was the very first apartment in the complex, so we never really got to get to know the neighborhood until much later when moved into our four bedroom apartment. Yeah you heard me four bedrooms. Needless to say; there was a new sheriff in town and we were about to put Park View Village on Powerline Road on the map for all the right reasons.

1985 I was attending my last year at middle school and Sis was in her third year at the high school. Mama had got a new job working for Mickey Mouse in one of the many bakeries at Disney and Peter was getting his feet wet at the Police department. My little brother was somewhere in the mix going to elementary school. Everyone had their own busy schedule as life continued on.

Mama and Peter had been arguing about something one evening when she had gotten off of work. The argument went well into the evening. Realizing that we hadn't ate, mama decided to take us out for a quick bite but I think Peter wanted to continue the discussion. Mama told us to get ready so that we could go. We could still hear mama and Peter in their bedroom having words. As we walked through the kitchen mama had stopped arguing but Peter wanted to have the last word. Mama proceeded to the back door as she reached for the door knob Peter knocked her hand away from the door and they had a couple of words. Me, Sis, and little Willie just stood there in the kitchen and watched as all this was unfolding. Mama proceeded again to reach for the door and this time she managed to open it but Peter stood in front of the door and wouldn't let us leave. When mama tried to walk out the door as if Peter wasn't standing there, Peter pushed her back. I had never seen any man put their hands on my mama not even Big Willie. Peter and mama were now in a shoving match and none of us was doing anything to help her. Despite my feelings towards my mother, I still had the sudden urge to protect her. I had become overwhelmed by many emotions and I let out a warriors cry.

I ran to one of the kitchen drawers that had the big knives it in. I slung it open so hard that the whole drawer came out and fell to the floor. I picked up the largest knife that was there. I ran towards Peter with the knife. Somebody had to do something; enough was enough. Mama saw me coming with the knife in my hand and she started yelling for me to stop. I was confused; I'm trying to protect her and yet she's protecting him. Peter managed to grab the knife out of my hand and push me back. With everyone realizing that this situation had reached a very dangerous level; almost deadly, everyone froze in their tracks. Suddenly there was a knock at the front door.

It was the police. I guess one of the neighbors heard all the yelling and commotion so they called the police. Peter answered the door as two police officers stood there on the porch. I remember the tall white police officer doing most of the talking while the other officer who was black just looked around. After being invited in and seeing that no one was physically hurt, they took mama and Peter in the bedroom while we sat in the living room. You could hear Peter yelling that he didn't want any paperwork done on the situation and that he didn't want the other officers at the police department to know that police had to come to his house. He got his wish. I learned that night that the police do take care of their own. And once Peter discovered the type of power his badge held, he seemed to be untouchable.

After that night mama seemed to throw herself into her work at Disney. She would work longer hours and many days. I thought I didn't see her before; I really didn't see her now. There were many days when I didn't see my mother at all. By the time we got up in the morning she was already gone to work and by the time we went to bed at night, she hadn't made it home. Peter's shift changed every week, so he and mama were like two ships passing in the night. No one was ever home and it almost cost my sister her life.

Sis had gotten very sick and for the most part she suffered in silence until one day the pain was too much for her to bare. Sis went to mama telling her that she was hurting. Sis stood there in the middle of the living room crying, short of breath and balled over in pain. Seeing the extreme pain that Sis was in mama immediately took my sister to the emergency room. They were gone for hours and when mama returned home from the emergency room, she was by herself. The doctor had kept my sister in the hospital because she had gotten a very bad infection. The doctor said if they would have waited a day or two longer that the matter would have been worst or even deadly. My sister would have to have an operation in order to save her life and preserve her chance of having babies. It frightens me the thought of losing my sister. It saddens me that she chooses to suffer in silence. Who was she trying to protect? How did she get that way? Sis didn't have a boyfriend, not that I knew of. We were not allowed to leave the porch so she wasn't seeing a boy. So my question was how did she get this infection? After I found out the details of my sister's condition, my suspicions went right to Peter as the main suspect. After mama told us what was going on with my sister and that she would have the operation soon; Peter looked like he had swallowed a roll of quarters. I watched Peter for the next couple of days walk around in silence and have this worried look on his face. I don't think the worry was for my sister but for his self. Mama never knew of my thoughts or suspicions of Peter. I could only figure that Peter had been sweating bullets and hoping he wouldn't get sick.

After her operation my sister came home, but she wasn't the same to me. She was weak and had no energy and she took a lot of medication. She slept a lot and stayed in bed. For weeks because of her surgery my sister walked around the house bent over like an eighty year old lady with a walker because she couldn't stand up straight. It pained me to see her in so much pain. On her good days when she had enough strength we would sit on the porch. As much as I use to hate when we use to have to sit on the porch before; I seemed to not mind it as much at all that I was now sitting here with my sister. Sometimes it felt like I was babysitting because if she needed anything I would have to go and get it for her. But I didn't mind, I knew she would have done the same for me. Sitting on the porch with my sister I would catch myself starring at her. I tried not to ask too many questions. I was just glad she was here and alive. My sister got better and so did mama. In the back of her mind I know the thoughts that crossed my mind about my sister's condition crossed hers; whether she wanted to admit it or not. Out of sought out of mind is the approach I think mama took. If me and Sis weren't around Peter so much he couldn't bother us. So mama gave us some freedom; we were allowed off the porch and free to roam the neighborhood. We had to be home when the streets lights came on. We became the joke of the complex for that. At first I didn't like getting teased about it but I rather be known as the street light girls than some other names that the other girls were being called who stayed out way after the street lights came on.

Even though Mother Nature had paid me a visit and mama freed us from the front porch; I was still trying to hold on to my tomboy ways. Two large braids to the back and a bang across the front of my forehead was the hair style that I rocked. That's the only hairdo that Sis could do with no problem. Sis had to do my hair a lot since mama wasn't home to do it.

Basketball became a major sport for me. And it helped that the complex had a basketball court. All the kids hung out there whether they played or not. On the weekends the guys would get together and put together two teams and really play basketball. You would have thought the Bulls and Lakers were playing. I quickly made a lot of friends in the neighborhood. One day while I was hanging out on the basketball court just shooting hoops by myself, I saw the most beautiful thing that I had ever seen in my life and his name was Jeffery.

Oh my God. He was tall, handsome, milk chocolate with a pretty white smile and he had good hair; I think I'm in love. He was older than me; eight teen I think he was. I was only fourteen, matter of fact I had just turned fourteen. I was just shooting hoops at the basketball court one day when he passed by. I guess love feels like butterflies in your stomach because that's what was going on with me as I watched him make his way to his front door which was the apartment next to the basketball court. You mean to tell me that the love of my life had been that close to me all this time. Weeks went by and there wasn't a day that I didn't miss an opportunity to see Jeffery playing a game of basketball. I didn't want to play basketball anymore; I wanted to be the basketball in Jeffery's hands. I knew I was in love when I started putting more detail into what I was wearing to the basketball court. I traded my tomboy wear for pink shorts and red nail polish.

I hate to admit it but he had a younger sister about fifteen but seemed more mature for her age. If you didn't know better you would think that she thought that she was above you. She was always talking about her big dream of becoming a model. And so she always talked down about the other girls in the neighborhood as if they were beneath her and since she was the only one who felt that she had dreams and plans for her life that she didn't want to waste her time hanging out with the crickets in the neighborhood. Her attitude caused a lot of people not to like her and someone always wanted to fight her. Fake it till you makes it; I always say. I just became friends with her just so I could have a reason to come over to the house and see Jeffery. One day I got brave and knocked on Jeffery's door; his mom asked the door. Instead of asking for his sister who I would normally ask for, I took a chance and asked was Jeffery home instead. He was and he came to the door. I asked if he wanted to shoot some hoops; he smiled and told me sure. I admit love will make you do some crazy things. Jeffery knew that I had a crush on him and he didn't act like a jerk when he broke the news to me while we were shooting hoops that he had a girlfriend.

So my first encounter with love didn't go as I would have like, but I would live to love again.

# Chapter 18

**IT WAS THE** end of the school year at the middle school when I learned that the ninth grade would be at the high school instead of the middle school. Mama didn't seem too excited about the idea. She thought thirteen was too young to be around older experienced teenagers. On the other hand, I was very excited about going to the high school a year early; that really meant I wasn't a little girl anymore and plus I would get to go to school with my sister which hadn't happen since we were in Catholic school. I missed being able to see Sis passing in the halls and giving her that sisterly smile.

We never see much of Peter anymore since he's on a new shift at the police department. Don't worry, he's not missed and we only see mama on Thursdays when we ride to Disney with her to go and pick up her check. We never really go into the park just to the back of the property to where all the business buildings are. Having to take that long drive and never getting to go into to the park was not the making of a nice drive.

Arriving at Haines City High School for the first day of school made me feel like I was a star arriving in Hollywood for the first time. By Sis being a senior, I got to know a lot of them and hung out with them more than I did my freshman classmates. Soon as we would speak to say hello, people knew that we weren't from the south. Our proper English and pronunciation of words usually resulted in a giggle or two from others. I may be in the south but in will always be a Yankee to my heart. The school did do their part to keep lower classmen separate from the seniors in the hopes of not exposing us to any of the upper classmen's bad habits. But occasionally there were a couple of classes that the freshmen took that were upstairs and I was one of the lucky ones to have a class up stairs.

The seniors walked the halls with much pride with their head held high and a stride in their walk. They didn't run up and down the halls like crazy kids with no home training. Not like us under classmen who were not sure of ourselves. I just loved the seniors' attitude and level of sophistication. The seniors wore the latest trends in clothes, shoes, and hair. Every day was a fashion show. Kids were divided into social groups. Of course you had your popular, the geeks, the nerds, the out-siders, the lost, the wannabes and oh yeah, let's not forget the jocks and the cheerleaders; who I always thought were in a league of their own. The first time that I saw our school cheerleaders in their green and white uniform with their crisp white tennis shoes and embroidered jackets with their name on them; I was taken back to when we lived in New Castle, Pennsylvania. The cheerleader walked through the halls with books in one hand and their big fluffy green and white pompoms in another that is if they didn't have one of their football boyfriends carry-ing their books for them. They looked like the perfect married couple; with matching jackets instead of rings. With every fiber in my body, I so wanted to become one of them; a cheerleader that is.

After seeing the football players, I quickly learned what I liked about the opposite sex. And it seemed my tomboyish ways have gotten away from me completely now. No more basketball for me unless I'm watch-ing from the bench. Strong muscular arms, washboard stomachs, and a chest that was ripped right off the body of a Greek God; Hercules, Hercules; I could only imagine what poor Venus had to go through.

I can't remember whether mama talked to me and Sis about the birds and the bees or if I found out about them myself. That Fall, my at-tention quickly turned to another nice looking boy who I later learned played on the high school football team. And with him my flower blos-somed. Unknowns to him that he was my first and I must admit he was a gentleman throughout the whole experience. Me on the other hand I was so nervous and I didn't know what to expect or what to do. It was kind of hard for me to enjoy this magic moment. I thought I would see fireworks and unicorns drifting across the sky as they jumped over rainbows. If there were, I was too nervous to notice them. I guess that comes later when you know what you're actually doing. I thought that he would be mad when he found out that he was my first. And yes he was a bit taken back after finding out. But when it was all over he walked me home and made me promise to call him the next day in the hopes that I would see him again.

I went straight to my room and didn't tell a soul. I felt funny; I didn't understand what was going on. All I know is that I was so hungry and that I had to pee real badly. I paced back and forth in my room; was I pregnant I thought to myself. I had heard that it only takes one time to do the do and you can get pregnant. I ran to the bathroom to pee than to the kitchen to sneak a piece of bologna out of the refrigerator. I couldn't be pregnant; mama would kill me. I snuck back to my bedroom with the bologna hid under my shirt. If I wasn't pregnant than, why was I so hungry. Was the baby hungry, I thought? Did I need to feed the baby that was growing in my stomach? I don't know but I knew that I had to pee again. After emptying my bladder for the third time I sat on the bathroom floor eating another piece of bologna that I had stolen from the fridge. I was deep in thought but I could still hear Peter in their bedroom talking to someone on the phone. I had my own issue right now and I had better figure out how to tell mama that I was pregnant. After much thought I realized, there was no baby; it was just my uterus expanding after all the exercise it had just had. Relieved that I had solved my own problem I sat on the bathroom floor with my ear pressed against the wall listening to another problem.

Peter was on the phone talking to someone and the conversation had gotten really heated. Apparently Peter was seeing some girl who went to my school and he had sent her some roses. The girl's father found out and gave Peter a phone call. He told Peter to stay away from his daughter and if he didn't that he would have Peter arrested. I knew the girl that Peter and the man on the phone were speaking of. My thought was though if Peter was going to do all this cheating on my mother than why marry her. Before Peter got off the phone he had to promise not to call, see, talk, or send anything else to that man's daughter and Peter did promise to do so. After hearing all of that I quietly went back to my bedroom and forgot about my own issues but was saddened about my mother's issues.

That Monday when I went to school, I saw her walking down the hall. She was tall and skinny with long black hair. She was only a child and was the same age as my sister was. I couldn't be mad at her; she was the innocent one. But for a split second I thought to say something to her to defend my mother, but then I thought it was my mother who had to speak up for her. But how was my mother to even know. I never told her. Not right away anyway. I think the subject came up years later in a casual conversation one day that we were having.

The school year went on and so did my blossoming friendship with my special friend. My close friends and sister really didn't like the idea and at first I didn't understand why, but I would soon find out. By him being on the football team, it made him a girl magnet. He had way too many girls liking him and he liked them back. I started to feel like the last chip in the bag; you only want me because I'm the last one here. I dealt with it for a while then I decided that I didn't want to be last anymore but first. So I jumped out the bag. I made up in my mind right then that I would be second to no one and that no other girls flower smelt sweeter than mine. But as far as mama knew, my flower was still just a seed.

My grades were very important to me so I always liked doing my school work. As and Bs were what I mainly brought home on my report card. My freshman year at the high school was a blast. Yeah I learned a lot and everything that I learned didn't come from a book.

I hadn't fell in love yet so I knew that I still had a lot to learn and Sis was the oldest so she would lead by explain. Sis fell in love and went slap crazy. My sister was quiet in school and she didn't hang out with the popular kids like I did. But she did have a couple of admirers and one of them she admired back.

I don't know, the only way that I can describe this incident is that my sister went koo-koo for coco puffs. I don't know if one day mama told my sister that she couldn't see this boy anymore or whether my sister went to see him and didn't want to leave him. Anyway one night mama came home from work very late one night. We were all already in bed sleep; so I thought. I was awakened by mama asking me where my sister was. I was totally confused by the question because my sister's bed was only two feet away from mine, so I don't know how mama could have missed her. We had to go to school in the morning so I know she was sleep. Where else would she be two o'clock in the morning.

I looked over at my sister's bed and she wasn't there. Lord, what done happened now. Maybe she went to the bathroom. I told mama that I didn't know where she was. By the look on my mother's face; that was not the answer that she wanted to hear. Mama went around and turned on every light in the apartment. I might as well wipe the sleep out my eyes and sit up. Mama went room to room looking for my sister. In a two bedroom, one bathroom apartment; that wasn't a long look. When mama came back to our bedroom I had managed to make it to the side of my bed to put my slippers on. Mama asked me again where was my sister and again I told her that I didn't know; I really didn't.

Mama came up with the bright idea that since I knew where she hung out at that I should go look for her. Are you serious; right now I thought to myself? I got to get up in four hours and get ready for school. Did she forget that it was two o'clock in the morning and that it was pitch dark outside? The whole time that I was getting dress, I was hoping and praying that my sister would walk through the door. For one; to know that she was alive and safe, at least until mama got a hold of her and for two: so I could get back in the bed and take my butt to sleep. But she didn't.

Mama had allowed Sis to have a boyfriend and she did give her at decent curfew; no more being home when the street light came on. After all, the girl was seventeen. It wasn't like her boyfriend was a secret. He would come over to the house and at times Sis would spend her days over at his. So, I really didn't understand why mama just didn't go over to his house and see if she was over there. Why was she sending me out to the wolves? Yes, I understand that she is a little pass curfew and that it is a school night; but can we not panic. Let's just have some cake and wait.

No cake: mama and Peter are in the bedroom arguing and I'm out here walking the neighborhood streets looking for my sister. I started close to home first to save myself some time because her boyfriend lived in the back of the apartment complex; I mean way in the back. I went to the basketball court; she wasn't there. I went to the playground; she wasn't there. I went to the park; she wasn't there. I went to the laundry mat; she wasn't there. I went to the wreck room the door was locked and the lights were off; she wasn't there. I even went by the big green electric box that everybody likes to sit on and hang around at; but she wasn't there either. Now I was getting mad because I really didn't want to walk to the back of the complex but I knew if I returned home without my sister mama would somehow blame me for her absence. I didn't know where the hell this girl was at and I didn't feel like explaining her absence tomorrow in school.

I thought that I would take a break after all that walking so I went back home. Mama and Peter were where I left them; arguing. Where is she? mama asked me once she came up for air and realized that I was standing in the living room alone. I told mama that I didn't know that I had looked for her everywhere. That wasn't good enough. Mama then asked me where Sis's boyfriend lived. The next thing I knew we were standing at his front door. At least I didn't have to walk.

His mom answered the door of course; this time of night I'm surprised that she didn't come with a shot gun. I explained to his mom what was going on and that we were looking for my sister and asked if her son was home and could we speak to him. After a ten minute wait which seemed like a life time; she finally got him to come to the door. I asked him had he seen my sister, he told me yeah that he had seen her earlier that day. I asked had he seen her any that night and had she mentioned about going anywhere. He told me no that he hadn't seen her. Mama had had enough of this dead end trail and told ole boy if he does know where she might be to let us know and if he did see her to tell her to come home. We left, but I thought it was kind of funny that he was fully dressed two o'clock in the morning; jacket and all. Look at me being detective.

Mama began to be sad as we sat in the car. She took a minute before starting the car and going back home. When we got back home, Peter wanted to know what happened and by this time my little brother had gotten up. We all sat in the living room as mama told Peter what she knew, which was nothing. Mama couldn't keep still; she just kept pacing back and forth. It was three o'clock in the morning and I was really ready to go back to bed but I knew that wasn't going to happen until we found Sis. Maybe she came back while we were gone my mother said; convincing only herself. My thought was if she had come back while we were gone Peter would have said something when we got back or Sis would have had her butt sitting on the couch.

Mama sent me back to our bedroom to check once again. I went to the room looked at my sister's bed. She wasn't sleeping in it or sitting on it. She aint here, hell; I thought to myself. I went back to the living room and told mama that she wasn't in the room. I guess I must have come back too fast; mama told me that I hadn't looked good enough. Huh, how long does it take to look in a room that's the size of a restaurant's freezer? You tell me. Mama flew past me mumbling something as she headed to our bedroom to look for herself; as if I was lying. I'm ready to go to bed hell; why would I lie about Sis not being in the room. It wasn't my fault the girl wasn't here.

I followed mama back to the bedroom; I guess she knew something I didn't know. Mama went over to my sister's bed and threw back the covers as if a body would appear like they do on the magic tricks. She wasn't there. It was obvious that the girl wasn't lying in the bed. Sis was skinny, but she wasn't that skinny. Then mama looked under the bed; no Sis. At this point I thought that my mama was losing her mind. Mama looked around the room at the walls as if Sis would be hanging on one like a picture. Mama seemed desperate. Mama looked over at the closet as if it were a locked safe. She went over to its doors and snatched them open. At first glance the closet was dark. Mama moved the clothes that hung on the rail as if it were the red sea. Low and behold there sat Sis in the back of the closet in a row of shoes fully dressed in the sitting fetal position. Where the hell did she come from? You mean to tell me she been sitting in the closet all this damn time since we got back home and hadn't said a mumbling word. I know she heard mama fussing; hell the whole neighborhood heard mama fussing.

I was glad to see that she was safe but I wanted to cuss her out; I'm going to bed. Mama and Sis had a very long talk that night. After I was sure that mama wasn't going to kill my sister; I fell off to sleep.

In a way, what my sister did that night by running away made my mother realize a few things. One, she was working too much. Two, her daughters were growing up and needed her. Three, as well as having a job she had a family. We were all stressed out about everything that was going on and even things that weren't going on but should have been. We all handled the stress different. My sister spent more time at her boyfriend's house, I got more involved in school and having a social life and my little brother, well my little brother turned to food to help him deal with the stress at home.

I must say, he was getting a little thick around the middle. Peter thought it would be a good idea to sign him up for football so to get the extra weight off. My brother didn't seem like the sports type. He was more of a jokester and likes to disassemble things then put them back together. So, I was wondering how this was going to play out. A couple of weeks later, there he was in his little league football uniform. I don't think my little brother was thrilled about the situation. He played okay if running up and down a field of grass and landing on people is playing; go little bro. mama never missed a game. My little brother never really took a liking to the game but Peter was determined to make a football player out of my little brother even if it killed him; my little brother that is. My thing was if my brother doesn't want to play, don't make him. Go and get your son and run drills with him until his picking his butt up off the ground.

One game after my brother had made a hit and took a bad fall, he hurt his ankle. My brother was in a lot of pain. His ankle was swollen really badly and he couldn't walk on it. Mama had to help him to the car; Peter was too busy walking behind them fussing. I guess he seen my brother's football career flash before his eyes. Oh well, we all know that he didn't want to play in the first place, but you didn't want to listen. To me ever since we knew Peter, he always thought of my brother as weak and now that my brother had gained weight I think Peter thought of him as lazy too. Seeing that my brother was about to cry; Peter told my brother to suck it up and put some ice on it when we go home that he would be okay. I just looked at my little brother in so much pain. His face looked like it was just more than a sprang ankle.

On the ride home mama kept asking my little brother if he was okay and his answer was no every time. Peter felt like my mother was babying my little brother. Every time mama would check on my brother Peter would answer and say that he was fine that the boy just sprung his ankle. When we finally got home, my brother couldn't even walk. I watched as he hobbled to the front door. I just looked at mama. Are you going to help him; I thought to myself. Or are you going to let him suffer just because Dr. Peter diagnose that my little brother only has a swollen ankle.

My brother finally made it to the bedroom after much agony. He propped himself on his bed with tears just running down his face. I felt so bad watching as my brother suffered. I went to get him a bag of ice. Mama had finally decided to go check on my brother after her and Peter had finished having words. What was there to discuss I wondered. Your son is hurting, why are you even wasting your energy arguing with Peter about your son's well-being. Mama gently took my brother's shoe off. I don't think that was such a good idea. My brother's ankle was the size of a grapefruit. Sprung ankle my ass, I thought to myself. Tears ran down my brother's face even more. I think it's broke my brother said. Mama touched my brother's leg as gently as she could, checking to see if she could feel any indication of a broken ankle. But with every touch she caused my brother pain. Hell, he'll be fine once the swelling goes down Peter said as he stood in the hallway. I really wish he would shut up; I thought to myself.

And I really wished mama wouldn't have listened to him but she did and for a week my little brother hobbled around the house in pain until mama finally realized the swelling wasn't going down. She finally took him to the doctor. My brother came back with a cast on his leg because despite what Dr. Peter said, my brother did break his ankle. I hope my brother leg don't heal wrong just for the simple fact that my mother waited too late to take him to the doctor.

I was so disguised with my mother for letting my brother suffer for the past week the way he did for no reason. This boy had been making the best way he could around this place and suffering in silence every night because she wanted to listen to Peter who said my brother's leg was just swollen instead of listening to my brother who said that he thought *his* leg was broken. I just wondered when she was going to stop listening to these men when it came to her taking care of her children. When was she going to stop putting her men's needs before ours: her children? When was she going to start listening to us and putting us first. Eventually my little brother's leg did heal and the cast was removed. But, he never played football again or any other sport for that matter. I told you, he was more of a book worm. At this point I have lost total respect for my mother for not listening to my little brother. I made a vow to myself; that when it was my turn and I was blessed to be a mother; that I would always protect my children from whom ever and whatever.

# Chapter 19

THE CITY IS humming because everyone is getting ready for the annual holiday parade. Local businesses participate by driving nice cars with their business logo on the side of them and others companies made floats which had some of the employees riding on them handing out candy. The high school marking bands, cheerleaders, flag team and dancers from all over the county joined in. the ROTC would march as they carried their riffles. Local neighborhoods had their organization groups like the Boys and Girls club, YMCA and the neighborhoods had their own dance group made up from the neighborhood kids. It was a big deal and the whole city looked forward to it.

The holiday spirit must have gotten into mama too; she put up a Christmas tree. She surprised us all one day when we came home from school and saw it. Mama hadn't put up a Christmas tree since the incident of the missing candy canes when Big Willie was going to damn near kill everybody. The tree was white and stood three feet all. Mama had it sitting on a table making it look five feet tall. A white Christmas skirt covered the bottom of the tree. She decorated it with red flowers and red lights. It was pretty; it was something.

After Sis's little runaway adventure that night; mama had made a two hundred and twenty-five degree turn around. She started taking an interest in us. She surprised us again by letting me and Sis join the dance group that Powerline had. The group was made of about twelve girls ages five to seventeen. PVV is what they called themselves. Our first year was fun because a lot of our friends were already on the team, but it was a bit unorganized for mama's taste. We had white t-shirts and wore whatever colored shorts you could find with white socks and shoes. About six girls who were around five years old didn't know the routine so they would mess up a lot and would only walk half the way of the parade. So at times we didn't look like a good unit. We didn't have any music to dance to; we would just start dancing whenever the parade route would pause so the bands could perform. It was a hot mess, but it was something to do and we were just glad to be part of one of the biggest events in the county.

The following year mama took over the dance group. She had uniforms made for us; our colors were burgundy and gray. We were the *shit*. We had our gray cheerleader skirts, burgundy pull over sweaters with the letter PVV in white ironed on the back. We wore burgundy leggings, white gloves, socks and shoes. And oh yeah our shoes had gray and burgundy pompoms on them. We had music and our dance routine was on point. We felt like new money; crisp and clean. When we would stop in the parade and dance you could hear the crowd cheering us on. We did the latest dance moves and put our little twist on them. Mama had made the dance team practice every day for two hours. No one missed a step; mama made sure of that. I can still hear the music playing. We became the talk of the town that year. I wasn't ashamed anymore to say that I was from Powerline. When we would returned back from holiday break; people didn't call us by our names but we were now known as the PVV and we were proud. That just jumped my popularity status up two levels; now everyone knew who we were and Powerline was seen in a different light. We would be part of the dance group for the next two years with mama directing it of course. But where there are a lot of girls, there's a lot of drama I quickly learned. Yeah, some girls could dance better than others and they let the others in the group know it. New friendships were made some old friendships were broken. At times it was sister against sister; and that didn't exclude me and mine. Some girls would end up dropping out while others would end up taking over.

Mama took her new found interest and her family one step further. She started holding dances on Saturday nights at the apartment complex's wreck room. Word spread about the Saturday night dances and Powerline was now on the map as the place to be. Mama paid the latest music and sold sodas, chips, candy, pickle sausage and eggs. It was a good place to hang out and dance; that is if you weren't too shy to. We had a lot of fun at the dances and even looked forward to Saturday night. Mama even put on a talent show once. Me and Sis performed to a song called Sukiyaki by the group A Taste Of Honey. We had our Chinese fans as part of our act. The dances went on, the crowds grew and so did my respect for mama. Mama's attention to detail towards her kids was great, but I think it was a little too late for her marriage. Mama and Peter started to seem more like roommates who split the bills in half and less like a married couple who were in love.

We finally moved out of that two bedroom apartment and into a four bedroom. I thought the move would be a good thing for us, but it wasn't. Six months later me and Sis were still sharing a bedroom; don't ask me why. My only thought was that mama felt that we would be safer that way. And we were for the most part; but I would have loved having my own room, my own space. In the new apartment we saw less and less of mama. There was no more dance practice since we didn't march in the parade anymore and mama didn't put on any more weekend dances. It was fun while it lasted. One weekend mama didn't even come home. We asked Peter where was she, but he said that he didn't know. She didn't even bother to call her own children that whole weekend to let us know that she was safe or where she was. I didn't have the feeling like she was dead or anything bad had happened to her, but she could have let us in on the joke. I felt so abandoned. Mama finally did come home and acted like everything was normal; like she didn't just leave her kids with this man who was not our father or something. Never the less, with all the yelling and screaming that she and Peter were doing; I was able to make out that mama had gone on her own little adventure and spent the weekend with a male co-worker. Oh great mama; way to fix the problem. Yeah, go do what he did; and how is that supposed to help the situation. Two wrongs definitely don't make a right. I guess mama was thinking more along the lines of; what's good for the goose is good for the gander.

Things were changing and so were me and Sis. Our minds were different and so were our bodies. We were getting older and our bodies were starting to develop. Body parts started getting bigger and more noticeable. Around this time for some unknown reason, Peter started walking around the house in nothing but a small white towel. I swear he got the smallest towel out of the closet that he could find. Didn't nobody want to see him. But I think he got a thrill off of the reaction he would get from me and Sis when he would unexpectedly walk in the living room with nothing but a towel on after he got out the shower. Nobody is looking at him like that. Sometimes I think he wish the towel would accidently untie and fall off. I'm so glad that it never did. At first it was just when he got out the shower; then it just started being all the time. I don't even want to think about what he was doing in his bedroom laying around in his towel all day. I thought that it was very rude and disrespectful of him to be walking around exposing himself like that to us. I felt that he had gone too far.

Me and Sis started staying in our bedroom with our door closed so we wouldn't have to see him. I guess he went back and said something to mama about us closing our bedroom doors because after a while mama came to us and told me and Sis that we couldn't have our bedroom doors locked or closed unless we were getting dress. I can only assume Peter left out the part that we were tired of looking at him walk around the house in nothing but a towel; yeah I know he did. He gets on my nerves. Our silence towards him and the things that he had been doing was only making him stronger. He knew that we weren't going to say anything to mama because we knew that they were already having marital problems and we didn't want to add fuel to the fire by telling her what he had been doing. But, I'm tired of this crap now. When he married mama that's who he married and that's all that he is entitled to. Me and Sis are not substitutes for when mama can't or chooses not to carry out her wifely duties. I didn't want to know mama's business; and Peter was mama's business.

So I told mama what Peter was doing because obviously she didn't know or she would have said something to him about it I would have hoped. And apparently she did say something to Peter about walking around the house in nothing but a towel because he stopped. Now he just walks around the house in his tight white thigh length boxer underwear that clearly shows his male bulge. I think mama should have been more specific and just told him to put on some clothes. Wow really, what's next? There was no use of saying anything to mama about this because I really didn't want to know what Peter would come up with next.

Mama's frustration with Peter was starting to spill out over on us. Mama started whooping us for every little thing. Her weapon of choice was a cut off piece of a water hose that was about eighteen inches long.

On the weekends we had to be up and out of bed by nine o'clock.

Peter didn't believe in lying in the bed all morning; at least not us kids. One Saturday morning mama came in me and Sis bedroom. We were already woke. You know that first wake up you have in the morning; you hear the sounds of the new day but your eyes aren't quit open yet, you're still peeking to see if your ears are deceiving you. Well anyway, mama had come in the room and told us to get up and she left again. We stretched and yarned for a little while before our heads left the pillows. I finally sat up and made it to the side of my bed still holding my pillow so I could remove it from the bed so to make it. I looked back at my ruffled sheets and was deciding on the quickest way to make my bed. Sis was standing by her bed when mama came back in the room. Mama had the water hose in her hand, for what I don't know. The next thing I know, she went to yelling. "I thought I told yall to get up". Yeah you did five minutes ago; is what I was thinking to myself and we are up, so what's the problem? Mama looked at Sis then at me. I guess we weren't moving fast enough for her. I guess she wanted us to have made our beds, washed up, eat breakfast and cleaned the kitchen since the five minutes she last saw us. I guess I should say that I hadn't move fast enough for mama. Mama raised that water hose above her head and made it land right on my bare chest. It felt like a thousand bees had just stung me all at the same time. My first instinct was to come up off that bed and punch my mama in the face, but instead I gripped my pillow and held it tightly to my chest to try and ease the pain. But nothing could ease my hurt. Mama looked at me dead in my eyes and I looked right back into hers and for a minute the world stopped. Without saying a word mama knew that she had gone too far and what she had done was wrong. I know when she looked in my eyes she saw black because when I looked at her I saw nothing. She again no longer looked like my mother but only a stranger to me. I wanted to hit her so bad in that split second. I had left my body to remove myself from the pain that I was feeling; both physically and emotionally. Mama looked at me but her daughter was no longer there. I watched from above as all of us occupied the room. I had to remind myself that she was my mother. Mama left the room without saying a word.

Sis turned and looked at me; she could tell that I wasn't myself. I don't know if I was angry because I didn't do what I wanted to do which was punch mama in the face or if I was just shocked that it came so easy for her to cause me so much pain. I sat there on the edge of my bed trying to decide what to do with all this frustration that had just gathered up inside of me. I didn't speak to mama for the rest of the day.

The next week mama tried to make it up to me by giving me my own room. She asked us all what colors we wanted for our rooms. Of course my brother chose baby blue. Sis chooses pink and I choose white. I choose white because the angels wore white and angels were pure. I decided long ago no matter what this world did to me; I wanted my heart to stay pure. Mama did our rooms real nice. Mama found that there was more than one way to skin a cat. Since Peter was still walking around in his tight white underwear; mama hung curtains up to our bedroom door that was the same color as our room so even though we couldn't close our door we didn't have to see Peter walking around in his underwear and he couldn't complain about our door being closed. But nothing could block out the sound of his crackling knees when he walked the halls late at night. My only hope was that he would never stop at my bedroom door.

Me having my own room was great but I had labeled myself the black sheep of the family before I even knew what that phrase really meant. I just knew it felt like mama like picking on me. Maybe she knew that I didn't respect her so her way of getting back at me was to pick on me.

For example; I remember when the *Jerry Curl* first came out. It was the answer to every black person's hair problem. Little curls all over your head that were permanent for a good six months; you just had to keep it from drying out and all you needed for that was some liquid activator. You know what I'm talking about class of 89. Anyway, mama got Sis's done first of course; why would I expect anything less. It looked good and it was the latest thing. But mama told me that she wasn't going to get mine done, at least not my whole head. She was only going to get the bang done. Now how stupid does that look? I'm walking around with half my head done. Now how fair was that? I was fourteen and I had out grown these two braids and a bang; I'm in high school now. I didn't want to wear this hair style for the rest of my life. I went in the bathroom and cried. I starred at myself in the mirror and imagine how my hair would look with just my bang in a *Jerry Curl*; stupid. I was so mad and it wasn't fair that Sis got to get her hair done and I didn't. I was tired of looking like a little girl. I starred at myself in the mirror some more. If mama wasn't going to get my whole head done she wasn't going to get the bang done either. I decided that I was going to cut my bang off. I washed my face and came out of the bathroom and went to the kitchen and got the scissors out the drawer and headed back to the bathroom. Mama and Sis were sitting at the kitchen table. Mama asked me where was I going with the scissors and I told her that I was going to cut my bang off because it was going to look stupid with just my bang in a *Jerry Curl*. Fact of the matter is; it was going to look stupid with me not having any hair in the front of my head but at the time I didn't care.

I went back in the bathroom and starred at myself again in the mirror. I put the scissors to my hair several times but I knew if I cut my hair I would really look stupid. Then I thought well if I let mama do the bang with only the *Jerry Curl* than she would see how dumb it looks and then she would have to get the rest of my head done. I walked out of the bathroom thinking that I had just out foxed the fox. When I went to put the scissors back in the drawer mama said that she was only playing with me, that she had planned on getting my head done when she got paid next week. Wow, really. What a way to play with someone's emotions.

While I was in the bathroom contemplating whether or not to go bang-less; mama and Sis had got out some makeup and mama decided to make up Sis's face. Thirty minutes or so she worked on Sis's face; she did a good job. Mama put the make up on my face too, but when she got done it had a green tone and not a brown tone like Sis's did. It took mama all of ten minutes to put the makeup on my face. I wondered if that may have had something to do with it. Mama favoritism is really starting to show. She made me feel like she just threw anything on my face and not take the time to match anything. If she had taken the time and care that she took with Sis I wouldn't be here looking like Ms. Incredible Hulk. After having the makeup disaster; mama went on to describe our face structure. Mama said Sis's face was shaped like a triangle. She went on to say that my face was round but not like a circle but more like a monkey's face. Sis and mama started laughing at me. I didn't see anything funny at all. My feelings were hurt. I left the kitchen and went to my room before they could see me crying. Wow mama really; a monkey.

The following week; mama kept her word and got my hair done like she had promised. Sis's boyfriend's aunt was a hair dresser and she lived out there on Powerline way in the back. When she got finished that walk home didn't seem to bother me at all because my hair was done and I was feeling fabulous. I had a smile plastered on my face that spread from ear to ear. At least until I got home to show mama my hair.

Mama was in the kitchen when I got home. The house was quiet and nothing seemed out of place but yet something seemed wrong. Mama was standing fidgeting with something in her hands. I had told mama that I was back from getting my hair done but she never really looked up to see. Mama started to say how she wished that she would have had just her first child and went on with her life. That was a very hard pill for me to swallow; hearing my mother say that to me. To know that she didn't want me or my brother was a bit much. She even admitted to me that shortly after my brother was born that she got pregnant again but decided not to keep the baby. She said she couldn't see herself with four kids. Mama just walked out the kitchen almost in a daze as if she was in mourning. I stood there in silence just wondering if my ears had just heard the confessions of a woman.

I never repeated what mama had told me to my little brother or Sis. That night I went to bed only to awake three o'clock in the morning. The things that mama had said to me just kept playing over and over in my head. I found myself in a very dark place and I didn't want to be here anymore. I felt tired now and so alone. I didn't care to see tomorrow because I knew it would be a repeat of today. How could I look at my mother knowing that she didn't want me? Maybe that's why she never hugs me or kisses me on my forehead. I remind her of her mistakes.

My thoughts became; how could I ease her pain. My only thought was if I wasn't here anymore than she would be happy. What my little brother would do about his part in this problem I didn't know; I can only fix the pain that I have caused.

I had left from my bedroom and made it back without making a sound. I sat on the floor at the head of my bed. I felt a tear roll down my face. If mama didn't want me here then I didn't want to be here either. This world had never been nice to me so I didn't owe it anything. Would she even miss me when I'm gone? I pulled the biggest and sharpest butcher knife that we had in the kitchen from under my night shirt. I had learned that the fastest and quickest way to bleed was to slit my wrist.

I could feel more tears as they filled my eyes and ran down my face, but this was something that I knew that I had to do. Kill two birds with one stone; isn't that what they say. I could stop the hurt that I was feeling and I could stop the hurt that I was causing mama. I laid the sharp edge of the blade of the butcher knife on my skin at my wrist. I had to make sure I laid it just right so I could cut the vain real deep with my very first stroke. I sliced my wrist like a butcher does when he's trimming the fat off a prime piece of meat. I didn't bleed; my skin did not part. So I did it again, making sure to put much pressure on the butcher knife. Yet again; I did not bleed nor did my skin part. I know that I was doing this right. I had seen it done so many times on television and I knew this was the biggest and sharpest knife we had because when we would be in the kitchen helping to cook; mama would always warn us to be careful and not cut ourselves. This was mama's best knife. She had this knife for many years. I took the knife away from my skin and looked at the blade. Yeah this was the knife mama would always warn us of when we pulled it out the drawer. I pulled back my curtains from my bedroom window to use the light that shinned so bright from the moon to make sure I could see what I was doing. I proceeded to try and cut my wrist three more times. But neither time did I bleed nor did my skin part. You stupid knife, I said to the black handle tool of steel. Why wouldn't it cut my skin? Disappointed; I made my way back to the kitchen and threw the useless thing back in its drawer.

Oh, I was not finished yet. I was determined to end this pain. I wasn't letting myself off the hook that easy. I was going to make mama happy even if it killed me. I went to our bathroom; being careful to lock the door behind me. I searched and searched under the sink for some type of bathroom cleaner or Drano. All I could find was a brown bottle of peroxide. I figured poison would be quicker and there wouldn't be any clean up; if peroxide can kill germs it should be able to kill me. I drunk more than half the bottle than filled it back up with water so no one could tell any was missing. I quietly made it back to my bedroom even holding my breath to be sure no one heard me. I laid down in my bed like people lay in a casket. I folded my arms over my chest; I said my prayers and closed my eyes. I made peace with myself knowing that I wouldn't see the morning and I only wondered who would find my lifeless body.

As I laid there in my bed my stomach started to hurt. I knew it was the poison doing its work. Tears started to roll down from my eyes even more, for I knew this was the end. I began to become sad because I hadn't said goodbye to my baby brother. I hoped that with me being gone that mama wouldn't start taking out her frustration on him. The pain was getting worse. I held my stomach tight so that I would endure the pain until it passed. I felt myself drifting off. I asked the Lord to forgive me of my sins and would he look after my little brother.

Thirty minutes later I woke up. Instead of being dead I found myself running to the bathroom throwing up. Thinking that I still had enough poison in me to carry out my plan, I went to lie down until I would hear the angels come and get me. At five-thirty a.m. it wasn't the voice of angels that woke me; it was my stupid alarm clock. I was so mad that I was still alive. I heard a voice say; no you still have work to do. As I lay in the bed starring up at the ceiling I could only wonder what was it that God wanted me to do. I was only a child and I had no means of anything. I got up and got ready for school as usual. I didn't want anyone to know that I had tried to kill myself not once but twice and failed. My stomach didn't hurt and there were no marks on my wrist; almost as if I had only rubbed a feather across it several times instead of a sharp butcher knife. Why was I still here? Why wasn't I dead?

I didn't do much talking that day in school all I kept thinking about was how I could kill myself and why my last two attempts didn't work. Running in front of a bus didn't seem to be such a bad idea; there were definitely plenty around for me to do so. Then I thought how I would look like road kill after being hit by the bus. As I walked to class something in the hallway bulletin board grabbed my attention. In big black bold letters it read: **CHEERLEADING TRYOUTS** Friday after school in the gym. I figured since I was still here on earth; I might as well try to have fun and make the best of it. A smile came from inside of me and planted itself on my face.

Forgetting about the night before, I was so excited and ready for school to be over so that I could get home to ask mama if I could try out for cheerleading. It was late when mama got home that night. I became hesitate about asking mama if I could try out for cheerleading because we rarely got to do much of anything unless she was involved. Mama had got herself settled at the kitchen table with some paperwork. She was probably making the schedule for all the cookies and stuff that they had to bake tomorrow for the park. I waited for a moment while I somehow mustard up some courage to ask her .Without hesitation or looking up from her papers; mama said yes. My soul jumped out my skin and back in again as I did a little dance all the way to my room. I was glad that death had not answered its door the other night when I came knocking; Grace and Mercy had already answered it for me.

# Chapter 20

**I GOT THE** feeling that life; no matter how crazy at times it may seem that it all served a greater purpose and that I had a part to play in it. I know God had spared my life for a reason but for what reason I did not know. And I wouldn't know for a very long time.

I looked forward to going to school every day because I had cheerleading practice and plus it was an escape from what was going on at home. Mama and Peter were no longer trying to hide the fact that they were having serious martial problems. At times it seemed like they wanted us to choose sides. But my thing was; that was their marriage and it was up to them to fix it.

I was getting older and my interest in boys was getting greater. I wasn't allowed to have a boy's company. You know the kind that would be allowed to come over and sit on the porch and visit but not be out of your parent's sight the whole time that they were there. Well, that wasn't allowed for me yet. I wasn't even allowed to talk to a boy on the phone. But I got smart. When my sister would go over to her boyfriend's house, I would tag along. I would hang out with his younger brother and listen to music; LL Cool J song *I Need Love* was a hit. Nothing ever got serious between me and Anthony we were just friends. But some boy company was better than none at all because for a minute there I was about to question my sexuality because all I was hanging around with were girls.

Because no one ever saw me with a boy; word seemed to get around school that Peter was keeping me for himself. I was so hurt one day at school when some boy came up to me and tried to talk to me and I denied him and he made that remark. I denied him because he wasn't my type not because of any untrue arrangement. Even though that was the first time that anyone had actually said it to my face; I always felt like that was the way others did think too. Every time a boy would approach me the first thing they would say; oh you Peter's stepdaughter. You're off limits. Isn't he a cop? I think Peter being a cop kept them away too. I will admit that being the daughter of a cop had its perks at times; but this was not one of those times. Regardless of which fact was true; I hated the rumor. I ran home and told mama of the rumor that was going on around school. She didn't say much but I know she was concerned.

The graduating school year of 86 was whining down and the seniors were whining up. A lot of crazy things were happening at school. Seniors were passing around their yearbooks so that they could be signed. And there was another book that was being passed around. In that book; you hoped your name wasn't in it. Boys were getting caught in the girl's bathroom together. Fights were breaking out; if you had beef with anyone all year, this was the time to set it straight. Senior skip day was a big event. How is it senior skip day if everyone knows you're skipping. Everyone was getting ready for prom and all the end of the year balls. Peter's nephew was a big star on the high school basketball team and so they threw him a huge block party because he was going off to college right after graduation. You would have thought that he was already signed to the NBA. They had closed down the whole street for this party. I wondered whatever happened to Tony.

Because it was the end of the school year, some classes started to be combined with others. So my nine grade P.E. class was invaded by the seniors P.E. class. In P.E. in order to get a grade you had to run four laps around the track. At the completion of each lap; coach would hand you a stick. You were to get four sticks a day. Well, I wasn't trying to run and get all sweaty because I had another class to go to after P.E., so I always walked and only collected two sticks. I still passed that class for the year. Anyway, one day when I was minding my own business to start walking my first lap with my friends. Suddenly I heard a voice from behind me and asked me why I wasn't running. I didn't know him, so I figured that I didn't have to answer him. I turned around to this cute guy who was running in place behind me; he introduced himself as David. He asked me again and I just giggled and looked over at my friend. I finally told him that I didn't want to. To my surprise he made me a deal.

He said that he was going to run his lap and when he came back around that I was going to run the next one with him. He stood there so sure of himself. I only told him okay so that he would leave me alone because I wasn't running; I was going to walk my two laps like I did every day before today. Who he thinks he is; my boyfriend? David took off running and left me standing there with my friends. One of my friends knew who he was. She told me that he was a senior, in ROTC, was on the football team and went with one of the popular girls in school but heard that they had just broken up. All I know was that he was cute and he took the time to notice me.

After running his lap; he did just what he said that he was going to do. He caught back up with me and after some deal of persuading; he got me to running. We ran together and when the lap was over, a relationship had begun. David was the first real boyfriend that I had. Mama allowed him to come over the house and see me. And not just sit on the porch either; he got to come in the house. On the weekends when he was able to get his mom's car, he would come and get me and we would go for rides through to the city. Even though David was my boyfriend he was older than me and that didn't allow for me to do a lot of things with him. My curfew was nine and his was midnight. But one night mama made an exception for me.

It was New Year's Eve and David had stopped by. We were busy cleaning the house before the New Year came in because it was said to be bad luck to start the New Year with a dirty house. So David asked Mama if I could go with him to ring in the New Year. He never really said where we were going and mama well; she never said no. So David sat on the couch in the living room and waited for me as mama finished handing out our task and we completed them. Peter was very irritated that David was there for me. Peter kept following mama around the house asking her was she going to let me go with David. Mama would never answer Peter and you could see the steam rising off the top of his head because he was so mad. Mama didn't allow Peter to intimidate David either. She made it very clear to Peter that David was my boyfriend. Mama told David that I would be with him in a minute. That he couldn't take me anywhere but that we could spend some time together in the parking lot and not on the porch. David was very happy with that idea so he waited patiently. I was just laughing inside as I watched Peter's face expressions as mama just refused to answer him.

At one point I think she told him that it was none of his business. Peter wouldn't even go in the living room and speak to David. If the rumors that they were spreading around in school, weren't true; to see the way that Peter was acting, a person might just think that they were. Peter just kept following mama around the house like a little puppy. When I got done cleaning up; I went and freshen up and changed my clothes. I greeted David in the living room and as we walked out the front door, I turned around and smiled at Peter with biggest grin that I could manage up. I was letting him know that by the time I came back into this house that I would be damaged goods to him. I was going to make sure of it that night.

To this day, I don't know what it was about David that made me want to run that day. It must have been the way he showed that he had confidence in me even if I didn't have it for myself. And for that very reason, I didn't want to disappoint him. Or was it the fact that he ran with me letting me know that he would support me, that I didn't have to attempt this task alone. Or maybe it was the fact that he didn't let me sell myself short. Or maybe he was just being a boy and flirting, but since I thought he was cute; I gave in.

It was Prom time and Grad Night after that so mama was busy getting Sis all ready. I was the least of mama's concerns. She made a big old fuse over Sis. It was more like she was getting married then just graduating from high school. Mama made Sis this beautiful white silk dress for her prom. But something went wrong when Sis went to go and get her hair done. You see the one thing about a *Jerry Curl* is that you can't put a perm in your head until the *Jerry Curl* has completely grown out. Too much processed hair is a formula for disaster; and that's exactly what they had. Sis found out the hard way and ended up going to prom with a mini afro. She looked nice in her dress though. Sis went on to graduate mini fro and all. I don't remember going to her graduation ceremony and watching her walk across the stage to receive her diploma. I don't know why we didn't go.

At the end of the school year everyone went their separate ways to start their adult life. Me and David never really broke up. After graduation he went off to college and we tried to keep in touch as much as we could. I would call the college dorm where he was staying and whoever would answer the hall phone would take a message that I had called and give it to him. It was hard to catch up with him because he had such a busy schedule but every once in a while I would hear his voice on the other end when I would call. David did come home to visit that fall when college let out for semester and he came by to see me. He told me that he wasn't going back to college but enrolling into the army instead. I knew then that I would never see him again after that. Before the summer was over, I had a new hair dresser and a new boyfriend. Mama found me a new hairdresser since our old one had moved away. Mama and the new hairdresser hit it off well. By the end of my hair appointment mama had gave the hairdresser our number and promised that I would call her son and if I didn't definitely have him call me. Yeah, he came and brought me a soda while his mom was doing my hair; but I didn't think that a soda deserved a date.

Well Bob did call and we dated that summer. He was okay. Took me to Disney, we went out to eat, and went to the movies a lot. He always made sure that he had me home by curfew. Mama really took a liking to Bob. As if she knew that I would always be safe with him. I spent a lot of time at Bob's house that summer that's why one day when I came over to see him packing I was surprised. School was about to start in about another week and Bob said that he was leaving for Philadelphia. He never said when he would be back, so I just assumed he wouldn't be. The whole time that Bob was gone he never called me so I figured that we broke up so I moved on.

I tried out for the cheerleading team and yup; I made the team. Ironically I had the number one, so that meant that I had to go out first and do all the cheers, jumps, and spirit fingers that I had learned over the past four weeks. The gym was packed and mama and my little brother sat in the crowd. My number was the last one they called to say that I had made the team. It didn't matter to me that they called me last; as long as they called my number. I just figured that they saved the best for last. At that very moment when they called my name and number; I felt like everything that had been taken from me a small piece of it had been given back. I looked into the crowd of people and there I saw my mama for the first time cheering for me, supporting me. I ran to her with tears flowing down my face. Mama embraced me as I cried in her arms. I could feel that five year old little girl inside of me doing cart wheels.

I went off to cheerleading camp that summer which was held on a college campus. So I got to experience some of what David had gone off to college. The family music group the *Jetts* had a song out called *I*

*Got A Crush On You* that we did one of our cheerleading routines to. If you ask me; they were the Spanish version of the family signing group *DeBarge* .

When I had come back from cheerleading camp my sister decided that she was moving out. She said that she was going to move into a one bedroom studio with some white girl that she knew from school. In my mind I was trying to see how was that going to work out with only one bed; but my mind wouldn't let me go too far. I couldn't believe that she was going to leave me alone here with mama and Peter and their foolishness. I really didn't blame her for wanting to leave; I just didn't want her to leave me. Mama gave Sis some money. She told her that it was her last two social security checks that she would receive since she was graduating. Unknown to me until that very second; every month mama received two checks a month, one for my sister and one for me due to our father's death.

I know I heard what mama had told Sis but that couldn't have been true. How was she getting checks for us every month and we're walking around here sharing clothes and shoes that are a size too small? We found ourselves sleeping on the floor in sleeping bags because we didn't have a bed. If we got a check every month why was she taking us to the Salvation Army to shop for clothes? In my opinion; she had us around here living like poor pigeons. Mama would only buy us five outfits to last us the whole school year. Packing lunches and sitting on milk crates instead of furniture. I know mama wasn't getting a check for us; but indeed she was. You would have thought mama had just given Sis a million dollars.

Either the world couldn't handle Sis, or Sis couldn't handle the world because she was back home in eight months. When Sis came back home she was a hundred pounds heavier and looked like she had been through the ringer; more than once. She didn't even look like my sister. I didn't even recognize her. I would catch myself starring at her when she would walk by to make sure that it was her. Sis had gained so much weight that she couldn't fit into any of her clothes and mama had to let her borrow some of hers. Her butt was so big; it looked like someone had tied two sand bags to her back side. If leaving home does that to you then I don't want to go. That girl was out there balling. Any meal that she thought she never had; she made up for it. When Sis left the house she was a stick now she was the size of an elephant tree.

Well cheerleading camp was over and in a week I would start my second year at the high school. Sis got back settled in at home and got a job at McDonalds and later got herself a 79 red Hugo, so I hardly ever saw her any more. Me and my little brother never saw each other because our schedules were so different and he always stayed in his bedroom. Cheerleading became such a big part of my life once school got started; practice was every day and a big game every Friday. Cheerleading kept my mind off the fact that I was living in a broken home. But we did keep up appearances for Peter's sake since he was a pillar of the community being on the police force and all.

And since the cat was now out the bag and I knew about the money that mama had been getting every month for me and my sister; this year to my surprise (not) mama took me on a shopping spree. I didn't have to repeat an outfit for school for a whole month. I had so many clothes I almost didn't have enough room in my closet to put them.

The old gang of seniors were gone, so it was a bit quiet this year around school, but it was still fun. Being on the cheerleading team had its many perks and benefits. I had a few male admirers this year that didn't mind letting me know. I was smart in the books and my grades were awesome. I felt like a million bucks my whole tenth grade year. I felt like a star walking the red carpet. And when I put on my green and white cheerleading uniform, I was taken back to the times when I would watch the cheerleaders walk down the hall in catholic school wishing that I was one of them. And now I was. I even had the jacket with my name on it and the big pompoms to prove it. I had a lot of friends. I was even invited to sit on the popular side of the cafeteria at the senior table at lunch time. That was a major deal. I'm not saying that everyone liked me; but if they didn't, I didn't know about it. This was the year that I felt like I came into my own. This was even the year that I was able to give out my phone number to boys.

I had my high school crush on a popular football player. One day he was supposed to come over to my house and meet my parents. He had ridden my bus home and everything. When we got off the bus, instead of walking with me to my apartment he suddenly got a case of cold feet and instead walked over to one of his homeboy's house with him. I was so mad at his bow-legged ass for doing that to me. Mama had come home early from the laundry mat so she could meet him and he gonna act like that.

The only thing that I didn't like about my tenth grade year was the walk home after cheerleading practice. That was a very long walk to Powerline from the high school. Mama and Peter were always at work when practice was over and no one lived out that way. I walked it every day. It was rough at first. I got use to it but what choice did I really have. It definitely kept me in shape.

Sometimes I didn't go home right after practice. What was the rush of me going home; no one was there to ask me how my day was or if I needed any help with my homework. And when mama was home, she would let her frustration out on me. I guess something around the house wasn't done that she asked someone to do. I know she didn't ask me because I was hardly home. Anyway, it was the weekend as usual and mama was in her wicked witch mood. She was going through the house ranting and raving about whatever as she swung that water hose around. And of course I was standing next to her when she came to a halt and the water hose landed on the side of my leg leaving a dark mark that was the width of a ruler and half the length of one.

I was furious and mama knew it. I looked down at my leg and then looked up at mama. I just went to my room and cried; I was getting tired of this. How was I going to hide this mark when I wear my cheerleading uniform; my skirt don't go down that low and my socks don't come up that high. I just starred at the mark on my leg and cried. I hated my mother for what she had done. The next day while we were out at the store mama had picked up a coca butter stick and told me to rub it on my leg for the next couple of days; that the mark would go away. I took it as a gesture of her apologizing. I figured if she didn't care she wouldn't have even bothered. Yeah, I remember my cocoa butter days from when I was a little girl. I knew exactly what it was used for. And the mark on my leg did disappear like she said just in time for my Friday game.

I could never find a way home from practice, but it was funny to me that after every football game when I had to cheer Peter would be parked out front of the school waiting to pick me up. I think it was just for show. I'm quite sure everyone got the message. Sometimes people would come to find me to let me know that my step-father was out front waiting for me in his police car. Where the hell was he when I got out of practice and had to walk nearly twenty miles to get home? Mama never came to any of my games too watch me cheer. And after a while

I got use to her not being there. I guess that was too much to ask for. Sometimes though having her not there took the thrill out of putting on that green and white uniform. To me it became just another missed opportunity for us to form a mother and daughter bond.

# Chapter 21

**NOW THAT CHEERLEADING** season was over for football and basket-ball, I was home a lot and I noticed that mama wasn't. This left me with a lot of responsibility and my brother had a little but when he didn't do what he was supposed to mama felt it right to hold me responsible and not him. One day my brother didn't mop the kitchen floor like he was supposed to so she started yelling at me. I felt it would have made more sense for my mother to just ask my brother to come in the kitchen and mop but instead she felt the need to whoop me. I wouldn't have had a problem mopping the floor if she would have said so but she act like that wasn't even an option.

I guess she must have had a bad day at work or something. Mama told me to go and get a belt. She stopped using the water hose after it had left a mark on my leg the last time she hit me with it. My brother took off to his bedroom and closed the door and I didn't move from my spot in the kitchen. I just couldn't believe that she was really going to whoop me over what my brother didn't do. Why wasn't she whooping him if she wanted to whoop somebody so bad. Oh no, she wanted to whoop me and I really didn't feel like getting a whooping today and nor did I feel that I deserved one. She turned to me again and told me to go and get a belt and again I did not move; for I heard her the first time when she said it. Mama started to leave out of the kitchen to go and get the belt herself.

I still didn't know why I should get a whooping for something some-one else was supposed to do and didn't. I'm tired of getting in trouble because of him; were my thoughts but somehow the words came out of my mouth and mama heard me. She stopped dead in her tracks. I didn't mean for her to hear me but maybe it was good that she did. What did you say, she asked me as she was half way down the hallway. Well since she asked, I figure I might as well tell her. I shouldn't get in trouble for something that my brother was supposed to do and didn't. I guess she didn't agree because when she came back in the kitchen a few minutes later, she had a belt in her hand. Mama don't hit me, I asked her. Mama looked at me as if I was speaking another language.

She raised the belt up over her head and as she began to bring it down; I caught the belt in midair. "Mama don't hit me", I repeated. Mama told me to let go of the belt and I did. But again she raised the belt over her head and again I caught the belt in midair as she tried to bring it down. I'm not going to let you hit me for no reason; I told her. Mama looked at me and didn't say a word. I let go of the belt that mama was still holding over her head. Mama let the belt fall to her side. She just stood there with a blank look on her face. I left her standing there and walked over to the sink to fill the bucket up with water so that I could mop the kitchen floor. I could hear mama leaving out of the kitchen. I never looked back at her to see if she would try and hit me while my back was turned to her. Seconds later; I heard her bedroom door close. I proceeded to mop the kitchen floor. When I got done mopping the floor the mop water was just as clear as it was when it came out of the faucet. The kitchen floor never had a spec of dirt on it in the first place.

That was the day that I found my voice. Not because I talked back to my mother, but because I talked up for myself and right was right and even she couldn't deny me that. The tension in the house was ten times as worst for a while. Mama had put me on punishment since she couldn't whoop me. That's the only reason that I could think why I was confined to my room and told that I wasn't allowed to leave the house. Mama wasn't talking to me and I wasn't talking to her. We became two strangers in my own home. Weeks had passed and nothing had gotten better between us. One of the biggest events of the year was approaching; my best friend Wanda was throwing her birthday party. Wanda's birthday parties were always a big deal and this year would be even bigger because it was the big sixteen. I went every year and I didn't see why this year should be any different.

I went to mama and asked her if I could go to Wanda's birthday party. Mama knew that Wanda was my best friend and I figured mama wouldn't deny me not going to her party. I asked mama could I go but she held her silence. I went to my bedroom and got dress for the party any way. I figured if mama saw me dressed she would say something and let me go. I could hear outside my bedroom the music playing from the party. I knew this one was big because usually Wanda held her birthday parties at her house but this year she held it at the rec room at the complex. I walked around dress and ready to go. Peter even seemed concerned. He had heard me ask mama if I could go and he had heard that she didn't answer. Peter asked mama if she was going to let me go to the party; again she did not answer. I found myself sitting on the side of the bed that night listening from my bedroom window; as Wanda's party go on without me and despising my mother for it.

It took mama a long time to realize that I wasn't a little girl anymore. And though I would never disrespect her, I had the right to become the person that I was to be. My body was going through changes also. She realized that too. So much to the point that one day when we were passing each other in the kitchen, she made a comment; "you're going to put somebody's eye out with one of those things." She was referring to my breast which had gotten to the size of grapefruit and my butt was getting bigger. Peter noticed too. I would always catch him staring at me like a dog at a bone. He made me sick with that. I was already feeling awkward; I didn't need him staring at me. I think mama caught him staring at me a couple of times too.

Mama started giving me my space and one night she even let me go out to the rec but only if Sis came along. I didn't mind at all hanging out with my sister, I was just glad that mama let me go so I could get out of the house and away from Peter's drooling stares.

On Friday nights everyone usually hung out in the parking lot on 11th street. It was just a vacant parking lot where everyone would park and sit on the hood of their cars and just hang out with friend. If you weren't hanging in the parking lot; you were doing a slow drive by to see who was and so they could see you. We weren't allowed to hang out in the parking lot but it was fun to drive by just to see who was. The older kids played music from their cars. Everyone just hung out and had a good time. If you were too young to go to the club; the parking lot was the next best thing.

But then there was the civic center or the "Rec" as they called it. During the day it was like a YMCA but on weekends it turned into a dance club for the teenagers. That was always packed too. One night me and Sis went dressed like twins. We had our powdered pink dresses on with a white blazer jacket and white flats to match. Sometime during the night I guess Sis got hot under her skirt because she disappeared on me. When the dance was over and the rec was closing; I went and stood by the car to wait for her. Unknown to me, she was gone. She could at least tell me that she was leaving. Did she forget that she was my ride home? I had waited there by the car for a while. As I was leaning up against the car I noticed that it wasn't parked where we had parked it earlier when we first arrived. I thought that was very strange. It was getting later and later and everyone was almost gone and there was still no sign of Sis.

I started to get worried and by that time mama and Peter had drove up. I guess they were just in the neighborhood, yeah right. You know how parents are when you go on your first date at the movies; you're on your date while your parents are five rows back to make it seem like you're really on your own. I was glad to see them though, because I didn't know where the hell Sis was at and that's exactly what I told my mama when she asked me where she was.

When I got home mama drilled me about where my sister was. I told her that I didn't know because I didn't. She thought that I was lying and she noticed that my dress was dirty. I told her that it came from me leaning up against the car but she didn't believe me. I guess she thought that I had been with some boy and got my dress dirty. Mama started calling me a hoe and ripped my clothes off my body like she was peeling a potato. I couldn't believe her rage. Mama left the room and I just stood there looking in the mirror at my torn clothes that hung off my body like rags. I couldn't believe what had just happened.

Mama couldn't take her rage out on Sis even though that's who she was really mad at. Sis really in a since was grown. She was nineteen, had a job, had a car and paid her own phone bill and pretty much paid her own way. It was time for mama to except that. Sis didn't come home at all that weekend so she was never able to defend my honor. It wouldn't be until I got to school on Monday that I was able to solve the mystery of the disappearing sister.

That morning in my drama class a friend came up to me and told me that she had seen me and my sister Friday night at the Rec and said that she liked our outfits. Then she asked me why I didn't go with my sister.

"Go where?" I asked her. I told her that I didn't know that my sister had gone anywhere until the Rec had closed. She hesitated and then said that she couldn't tell. It was only after I promised her that I wouldn't tell that she told me and after I told her what my mama had done to me when I had got home that night; did she agree to tell me. She told me that she knew that my sister had got in the car with some of her friends and that they all went up to Kissimmee. The name of the city that she had said sounded funny and I had never heard of it before. I asked her to repeat what she had just said. I couldn't believe what this girl was telling me. I was scared that I wasn't going to be able to remember the name when I got home so I made myself break it down; kiss-a- me I told myself. I couldn't get home quick enough when I got off the bus that day from school. I felt like a firecracker ready to burst into the sky. Now I had proof that I wasn't lying.

I walked into the house and mama was in the kitchen standing at the sink rinsing out a cup. I wasn't expecting to see her as soon as I walked in the house because lately she had been confining herself to her bedroom with her little brown box; never the less I was glad she was even home. I don't remember if I said hello or not I just started unloading the information that I had received from school that day as I sat my books on the kitchen table. I paused to look at mama to make sure she was paying attention to me because at this point she hadn't moved from the sink or turned around to neither face me nor ask me what night I was referring to. She just continued to rinse out her cup. I starred at the running water that was coming from the faucet I hoped that it wasn't drowning me out.

I continued on with my story. I was proud of myself that I had re- membered how to break down the name of the city that my friend had told me. I told mama that Sis had went to Kiss-a-me that night. Mama must have heard me talking then because she turned around from the sink with a smirk on her face and said, you mean Kissimmee. At first I wasn't sure if I was happy because she had heard of the town that I was talking about or that she knew that I couldn't have just made up that story up and that I wasn't lying about Sis leaving that night. Oh she said as she starred out of the kitchen window. She responded as if she already had heard the story. Mama just left me alone standing in the kitchen as she went to her bedroom and closed the door.

I stood there in the kitchen yet again amazed by mama actions. She didn't say sorry about what she had said and did to me the other night. She didn't fuss due to the fact that my sister left me alone that night. No acknowledgement of what I had just told her. I had a witness that saw my sister get in another car and leave. This is not just coming from my mouth; I'm the messenger. I had proof that I wasn't lying and didn't deserve to get treated the way that I did that night by her. And all I get is a correct word pronunciation and an; oh from her. Okay maybe she didn't want to admit that she was wrong when she thought I was lying. Okay maybe she didn't want to admit that maybe she went overboard when she ripped my clothes off and left me standing in the middle of the room half naked as I tried to cover my body and recover my dignity. But say something besides oh.

Honestly in my whole life up to this point I never recall my mother ever saying that she was sorry. I guess those words were not in her vocabulary. I guess her actions had to speak for her. For the next couple of weeks mama let me go to the Rec by myself; I guess that was her way of apologizing.

The Home Coming dance at school was right around the corner and I just knew mama was going to make a big fuss over it for me the same way she had done for Sis the year before. So I asked mama if I could go and she told me yes. I was so excited. I pictured in my head the dress that I wanted her to make for me. It was a week before the dance, and mama hadn't said a word yet about making me a dress or even buying me a dress. Thinking that maybe she had forgotten, I went to her and asked her about a dress for Home Coming. To my surprise mama told me that she wasn't going to make me a dress or buy me one. So my thought was how on earth you are going to tell me that I can go to a dance and not supply me with a dress. She told me to pick something out of my closet to wear. But there was nothing for me to pick from. My heart dropped. I didn't have anything dressy like that to wear to a dance.

I just looked in my closet and starred at it; I had nothing to wear. Why wasn't she going to make me a pretty dress like she had made Sis last year? Since mama wasn't going to make me a dress I asked her if I could wear Sis's dress. That was the only other option that I had. It was either that or don't go to the dance at all; no that wasn't an option either. Mama seems to not be changing her mind about not making me a dress for the dance. She told me that I would have to ask Sis if I could borrow her dress for the dance. And so I did. I swallowed my pride and asked. After some deliberation and making me almost beg; she said yes that I could borrow her dress.

The night of the dance came and I can say that I understood how Cinderella felt the night of the ball. I knew I had borrowed my sister's dress but the night was mine. I danced all night long. The dance was finally over but I didn't want the night to end. The crowd inside made its way outside as we all waited for our rides to arrive. You could look around and tell that everyone was still in the party mood. One by one I watched as everyone got in their cars as their parents arrived to pick them up. I just knew mama would be here early to pick me up. I was surprised that she wasn't already waiting for me when the dance was over. But there was no sign of her.

I was standing alone by a parking post when Nathaniel came up and stood next to me. He told me how pretty I looked in my dress. I wasn't about to tell him that it wasn't mine and that I had borrowed it from my sister. I don't think it would have really mattered, but I got the feeling that guys didn't care too much about stuff like that. I just smiled and told Nathaniel thank you. Nathaniel was always easy on the eyes and tonight by the stars and moonlight made it ten times better; if that was even possible. Nathaniel was fine as hell; if I do say so myself, and I do. Nathaniel asked me if I he could keep me company while I waited for my ride and of course I said yes. When me and Nathaniel started talking that night; I didn't care if mama never came to pick me up. A little of the party crowd was still waiting on their rides too as the night went on. We had been talking for a good while when a car pulled up next to us. I figured it was mama but it wasn't; it was Nathaniel's ride. Nathaniel told his ride to go on without him that he was going to stay behind and wait with me for my ride to come. I literally melted in the inside.

Nathaniel and I talked so much that when I looked around, I realized that everyone was gone but us and mama still hadn't arrived to pick me up. Seeing that I was cold, Nathaniel took his football jacket and put it on my shoulders. To me, that was better than Cinderella's glass slipper any day.

Mama finally came to pick me up. I dared not ask her what took her so long to come and get me because I was glad she took so long. I stuck my head in the car and told mama that we had to take Nathaniel home. He was being such the gentlemen to stay with me and wait until she came to pick me up, it was the right thing to do. And mama agreed that it was. I guess he was making up for the time he chicken out on me when mama was supposed to meet him the first time. Whatever his reason, I was just glad he stayed.

Me and Nathaniel sat in the back seat. I swear it felt like I was riding in a chauffeur limousine or in Cinderella's case; a pumpkin carriage pulled by white horses. We laughed and talked about the dance. When we finally reached Nathaniel's house he told me good night and my mom thank you and got out the car. As he was walking away, I asked mama if I could get out and tell Nathaniel good night. She told me to go ahead. I jumped out of the car hoping to catch Nathaniel before he reached his front door.

I called him back to the car. I just wanted to thank him for waiting with me until my ride came. I gave Nathaniel a hug. You're welcome, he whispered in my ear. I had my prince that night. Time stopped and the stars in the night sky seemed brighter. Nathaniel said good night and headed toward the house. I got in the car with stars in my eyes. I didn't say a word all the way home. I just kept reliving that night over and over again. Every now and then I would look over at mama. She never said a word; she only had the biggest smile on her face. I think she knew that tonight was a magical night for me.

# Chapter 22

**EVERYTHING WAS CHANGING** now and the school year has come to an end. New people were moving into the neighborhood while old ones were moving out. I had no direction or idea about anything at this point in my life. I could only wonder what my junior year in high school would be like.

When someone has a crush on you but you don't like them, is it wrong to go with their brother? Well that's exactly what I did. My friend Sac had a crush on me but he wasn't my type. I let him down easy and he turns around and introduces me to his older brother RJ. I never knew that Sac had an older brother. You see, Sac and RJ lived in the same apartment complex out on Powerline but they didn't live in the same apartment. RJ lived with his mother and little sister while Sac lived around the corner with his dad and stepmom. Me and RJ hit it off and became an item right away.

Three months later Sac had got shot and killed. When I heard the news I ran to RJ's house thinking that maybe it was just a rumor because Sac was always getting into some type of trouble but never anything so serious. Sac was a jokester who kept everyone laughing. When I got to RJ's house he wasn't home. I found his little sister sitting on the couch crying; I knew then that the rumor was true. When I finally caught up with RJ to tell him that I had heard the news, it had spread around the whole complex. It was a very sad day.

After that, I started spending a lot of time with RJ to comfort him in his time of lost. RJ started to become my whole world. I was spending more time at RJ's house than my own. It became very apparent to me that Peter didn't like that idea so much. Why because he wasn't able to stare at me anymore and have his fantasy thoughts and no one was there anymore for him to parade around in front of in his tight white boxer underwear.

One day on my way out Peter was sitting in the living room cleaning his police gun. As I passed by on my way to the door he looked at me and I looked back at him; neither one of us said a word. Soon as my hand touched the door knob to open it Peter told me to come here; that he wanted to talk to me. I looked back at him in the wonder of what was it that he could possibly want to talk to me about. I went and sat down on the couch as Peter continued to clean his gun. He talked never looking up from it at first. To me he looked like one of them cowboys in one of them old western movies spit shinning his riffle. Peter would hold the gun up in the air occasionally to show off the shininess of the heavy steel and the power of its barrel along with the strength of its black handle grip. He laid the gun down gently as if to intimidate someone but only to pick it back up again and balance it in his hand. I didn't care if he had a bazooka; he didn't intimidate me at all. I wasn't studden Peter or his gun. "Where are you going", he asked me? I told him that I was going to see my boyfriend RJ. "Who is this boy that you are seeing?" Peter wanted to know. I never once have mistaken his questions for concern because I knew that they weren't. I told him who RJ was and anyway what business is it of his; mama had already met RJ.

"Why are you seeing him", was what Peter asked me next. "Because I like him", I told Peter. "Do you think that you should be seeing a boy?" I don't see why not but I'm quite sure you could come up with a few reasons why I shouldn't; is what I was thinking to myself. "I don't think you need to be seeing a boy, you should be concentrating on your school work"; Peter went on to say. At first I just sat there in silence. Has he even seen my report card? I'm getting all A's and B's. I think I'm doing just fine in school. I was not about to let Peter dictate my life. I told Peter that I was going to continue seeing RJ and that it really didn't matter what he said or whether he like RJ or not. I told Peter that it wasn't his choice that it was mine. Peter continued to clean his gun in silence. "What you see in this boy", Peter asked. "He's nice to me", I told Peter. And at that time in my life; that was something that I needed. Peter said that he wanted to meet RJ as he laid his gun down again and looked over at me. I told Peter okay. Not that I needed his approval anyway.

Me and RJ had been going together already by this time for at least four months. I was still going to see RJ whether Peter took a liking to him or not. Peter picked up his gun and started cleaning it again; "you can go now", he said. He didn't have to tell me twice; I didn't want to talk to him in the first place.

The following weekend, RJ came by the house to meet Peter. That was the first and last time RJ came to the house. Peter was not welcoming at all; to tell you the truth he was very intimidating to RJ. I don't know if the thought of Peter being a cop made RJ so uncomfortable. RJ was so nervous that he had a seat on the floor and not on the couch next to me. I just looked at RJ in stock as he sat on the floor like a little boy Indian-style. Are you serious right now; I thought to myself. Don't buck up on me now. I needed RJ to show that he was an upstanding good guy. Peter spoke to RJ in a weird tone that I had never heard him in before. I guess it was his police voice. It sounded like a lion in the jungle that was marking his territory.

Peter told RJ to get up off the floor and sit in the chair. Peter didn't bother to say hello or anything. When RJ extended his hand out to shake Peter's hand, it was just left there alone. And that was that, Peter left out of the living room without saying a mumbling word. RJ stayed for a while and watched television but I could tell that he was uncomfortable. I don't know if I was more embarrassed by Peter acting like a lion marking his territory or RJ acting like a little boy sitting on the floor. I thought it best that we better go before Peter brought his gun out and start swinging that around.

I spent every waking moment at RJ's house. When I would get home from school I would do my homework and chores then dart out the house to RJ's. I wouldn't return home until it was time for me to go to bed at night. That would explain the fact why I didn't notice my sister was getting bigger and about a have a baby.

As usual I was over RJ's house and we were sitting on the bed playing cards. Suddenly there was a knock at the front door so RJ went to go and answer it. It was my mother at the door asking RJ had he seen me. He told her that I was there. The bedroom window was up so I could hear her yelling for me to come on as she headed back to the car. See, that's why I was never home now. Mama was always yelling about something instead of talking to you about something. I looked out the bedroom window to see what all the yelling was about. I opened up the curtain and told her I was coming. She looked back at the window and told me to hurry up and put my clothes on and come on. What in the world was she talking about; I was already dressed. Really mama, could you embarrass me any further in front of the whole neighborhood. That just shows you just how much attention this woman pays to me. She didn't even notice that I was fully dressed. Its three o'clock okay in the afternoon, why would my clothes be off anyway. And all because I'm over my boyfriend's house doesn't mean I'm having sex all the time; get a life. "Your sister is about to have her baby", she yelled.

I did have my shoes off because no one wants dirty shoes in their bed. I just sucked my teeth, rolled my eyes and snatched up my shoes while running pass RJ who was still standing at the front door. I told RJ that I would call him when I got back home. I got in the car with my shoes in my hand and slammed the door. I asked mama why she said what she had said. As usual she didn't answer. She obviously should have recognized that I was already dress if I came out of the house in two minutes. But no there was no apology from her for embarrassing me. I'm used to it now. Or do you ever. My little brother was in the back seat looking worried, while my pregnant sister was doing some funny breathing exercise. Sis didn't seem to be much in a panic so the ride was quiet but very long. I was feeling hot like fish grease still mad at mama; I just got in the car and sat back until we got to the darn hospital because mama had bigger fish to fry right now.

We finally arrived and drove up to what looked like no hospital that I had seen before. It was a building with a construction trailer attached to the front of it. Mama got Sis out of the car very carefully. Me and my little brother were a little anxious and scared at the same time. We couldn't wait to see the new baby but hoped that nothing would happen to our big sister. We all made our way to the trailer which served as a waiting room and where you checked in at. Mama got all the paper work done with the lady who sat behind the desk and then they wheeled my sister away down some hallway. We thought the ride was long; that was nothing compared to how long it took Sis to have the baby. When we got there it was day light. It was dark now and still, no baby. Me and my little brother kept ourselves entertained with each other; laughing and talking about any and everything. Every couple of hour's mama would come out to the waiting room and check on us; but still no baby. Later on that night; if it wasn't already midnight, my sister finally gave birth to a baby boy. Making me an aunt at the age of sixteen and my brother an uncle at the tender age of eleven was pretty exciting. I hope she knew who the baby daddy was because I figured he should have been here. As a matter of fact I didn't recall Sis even having a boyfriend. I never saw anyone come around for her. But then again I was never home myself anyway.

A couple of days later Sis came home with her new born baby. Mama turned my bedroom back into her sewing room so me and Sis were roommates yet again. So it was a little crowded in the room with all the baby stuff. Sis told me that I could look at the baby but that I couldn't touch him. That's because she was still mad at me about an argument that me and her had a couple of weeks ago. She had overheard me and RJ arguing one day on our back porch. RJ was mad because I had bought me a new pair of Pumas and didn't buy him a pair. Sis had gotten me a job at McDonalds working on the weekend, so with my very first check I bought me this new pair of Pumas. My check was only but so much; I could only afford one pair. Sis told me that he shouldn't have been talking to me like that and that she was going to let him know. Yes I can say now that she was right and she was just being a big sis being protective but at the time I didn't see or understand that. All I saw was her saying something to RJ and him getting mad and break up with me and I didn't want that. RJ was my only freedom from this mad house and she was trying to take it away. So in anger I told her that if she said anything to RJ that I would kill her. And when I said it I could feel the rage show itself in my face. The look on her face told me that she knew that I was serious. But that next second after the words came out of my mouth; I wanted to take them back; but it was too late the damage was already done. But after sometime eventually Sis did let me hold my baby nephew after mama had a talk with her.

That fall Peter got himself in some trouble on the police force. He supposedly destroyed some evidence in a case trying to keep his bad behind nephew from going to jail. They asked Peter to resign with incident from the force and if he so no charges would be brought against him and so he did. Peter was never the same after that. I think he was a little depressed. I was sad for him because I knew how hard he had worked to get on the force and I knew how much he loved being a police officer. Now all this hard work went down the drain for what? His nephew still got into more trouble after that and ended up in jail anyway. Family; you got to love them.

Sis and the new baby were taking up a lot of mama's time and attention. I had posted an event flyer on my bedroom wall for all that was going on this school year. I would stare at the flyer knowing the dates of the events were near. Grad Night was coming up and I really wanted to go. Grad Night was always held at the theme park Disney World. You got to ride all the rides all night, eat and see several mega stars as they had a concert. Last year dreamy *Ready for the World* r&b singing group was there and some other big names. I know Sis had a blast with that. I asked so many questions the next day when Sis got home from Grad Night; you would have thought that I was a reporter for the local newspaper. This year I wanted to see some stars for myself.

Mama and Sis were in mama's bedroom with the baby just laughing and talking so I thought that I better go and ask if I could go to an event now and not wait until the last minute. That way she would have time to have the money together. I stood at the bedroom door for a moment watching them just playing and laughing with the baby. I knew mama saw me standing in the door way but she didn't acknowledge me. I stood there I know for at least ten minutes. That was another reason why I spent so much time at RJs house; I got tired of mama acting like I didn't even exist.

After having enough of obviously being ignored by mama; I asked a question. I asked my mother if I could go to the Grad Night. She never even answered me; she just kept laughing and playing with the baby. Wow, that was rude. She could have at least looked up at me. But to totally ignore me as if I wasn't even there was so wrong. So I asked again just in case she didn't hear me over all the laughing and talking that she and Sis were doing. Still, there was no answer from my mother.

I went back to my bedroom. The more I looked at the flyer hanging on my wall and listened to Sis and mama laughing in the next room; the madder I became. If she would have just said no that I couldn't go to Grad Night because she didn't have the money for my ticket and pocket money that would have been just fine with me. Maybe she didn't want me to get a bad reputation for being a party girl because she was allowing me to go to the rec a lot. Maybe she thought I needed a break from the party scene. That was fine with me, I would have understood that but say something. Don't just act like I didn't exist. I stood in my bedroom and the more they laughed the more I felt like they were laughing at me. At that moment I just felt like she was only concerned with the baby and Sis anyway and that she could careless about whether I was there or not. I felt not. Mama never even came out of her room and into mine to check on me to even see why I was standing at the doorway even if by chance she didn't hear me earlier; I knew she saw me.

If mama didn't want me here, then I wasn't going to be here anymore. So I made up in my mind to do my mother a favor; I'll leave. That way her and Sis can laugh and play with the baby all they want without any interruption from me.

I went back to mama's bedroom and stood at the doorway again and I just came out and told her that I was running away. It didn't sound funny to me when I said it but I guess it did to mama because all she did was laugh at me and told me to go ahead. This time she looked up at me. Did she hear what I just said; I thought to myself. Is it just that easy just to let your child go and you don't ask any questions? At least act like you're concerned and don't want me to go. But my mother didn't and that made me even madder than before.

I went back to my bedroom in complete shock with many tears in my eyes. I just grabbed the biggest gym bag that I could find and just started snatching my clothes off their hangers in the closet and stuffing them in it. When that one was full; I filled up another. Wasn't she going to come and stop me? I just told her that I was running away from home. I guess she wasn't going to stop me because before I knew it, all my stuff was packed. I took a second look around my room to make sure that I wasn't leaving anything behind. I took my bags and put them by the front door thinking that all the noise that I was making going in and out of my room would get my mother's attention. She never came out of her bedroom. I went back to my bedroom pretending that I had left something behind so to buy my mother some time so she could realize that I was really leaving. I was trying to give her a chance to stop me showing me that she didn't want me to go; that she did love me. I just stood there in the middle of my bedroom listening for a sign; but all I heard was more laughter.

Was my mother really going to let me walk out of here was all that ran through my head. Where will I go? I guess I'll go back to Detroit. How was I going to get there; I didn't know. And by the way mama was treating me I didn't care just as long as I got there. I'll hitch hike if I had to. Not being able to stand the laughter any longer; I went back to mama's bedroom door. I stood there for a second before saying a word. She never lifted her head from looking at the baby. Yet again, she acted as if I wasn't there. I'm leaving, I told her. She looked at me laughed and said bye. She went back to playing with the baby. My eyes filled with tears; I turned away before one would drop. I didn't even say good bye to my baby brother who was shut up in his bedroom as usual. I went to the front door, threw the heavy bags over my shoulder and walked out of my mama's house.

As I left the porch and then the front yard and now standing in the middle of the road; I was hoping to hear my mother's voice telling me to come back. But there was nothing but silence. I looked back at the front door and it had remained shut. No one was standing there like I hoped that they would. It was late and I was scared, but my pride would not let me go back into that house where I knew that I wasn't wanted.

No one was outside. I walked to the basketball court and it was empty. I needed to give my arms a rest from carrying those heavy bags so I sat them down on the bench and I sat beside them. The night was dark and only a street light kept me from blending into its shadow. The thought of going back home passed through my mind as I sat there shivering from the night air. But then that famous scene from the movie *Carrie* began to play in my head. You know he part when Carrie's mother tells her, *"they're going to laugh at you, they're going to laugh at you..."* Not wanting to hear mama laugh at me, I sat at the empty basketball court even longer.

It was getting late. As I sat at the basketball court I never heard anyone calling out my name as if they were looking for me. No one was walking around the complex in search of me. I was expecting the same search team out looking for me like we had looking for Sis when she ran away. Where is the love I wondered? But then again I never had it to begin with. Sitting at the basketball court I began to get sleepy. The night was quiet and I was very scared but I refused to go back home. I picked up my bags and I just started to walk. Maybe I would sleep on the playground. I looked over in that direction but there were no lights on there. As I walked down a couple of streets, I caught a view of my apartment; there was no light on over there either. Peter was home now; he had parked next to mama. It seemed as if everyone just went to bed. I dropped my head and began to cry; as if I ever stopped. If she doesn't want me there, I won't there; I kept reminding myself. I just couldn't get over the fact that she let me walk out the door. She didn't even try to stop me or come looking for me. I walked around the apartment complex for at least another hour until I came to rest at RJ's front door.

RJ opened the door; I was still crying. He looked at me seeing that I had bags sitting at my feet. He asked me where was I going and what was going on. I told him that I had left home and would be headed to Detroit. RJ grabbed my bags up and told me to come in. At that very moment I felt the same way RJ did when he came to meet Peter for the first time; unsure. This time I took a seat on the floor when I entered into the house. RJ sat down on the floor next to me. I put my head on his shoulder and just cried. He didn't say a word. He just sat there and let me cry as long as I needed to.

It was three o'clock in the morning. For the next two hours I sat with RJ had told him everything that had happened and how I just felt like the black sheep of my family. RJ could see that I was tired so he told me to go and lay down in his bed so I could get some sleep. I told RJ that I couldn't stay there that I had to start making my way to Detroit. But the thought of me on the side of the road in a ditch after someone hit me with their car on the back road made me not want to move from my spot on the floor. I told RJ that I couldn't stay there that his mom wasn't going to allow that. Without asking his mom's permission RJ assured me that she wouldn't mind me staying. But I wouldn't move until I was sure it was okay. I made RJ go and ask his mom anyway. Leaving me in the living room with only the television on to give me some light; I could hear RJ talking to his mom. Minutes later RJ came back in the living room. RJ stretched his hand out to me to help me up off the floor. He told me to come on so I could lie down and get some sleep. RJ told me his mom said it was okay for me to stay. I reached for his hand.

RJ's mama was totally different from my mama. As long as they didn't burn down the house, she really didn't care what they did. We quietly made our way to his bedroom. I told RJ to leave the bedroom door open. We just lay across the bed. I began to cry again. RJ just held me as I cried myself to sleep.

The next morning it was Saturday and I wasn't feeling any better about my situation and was in no condition to make any decisions, so I decided to make breakfast instead. I figured it would be a way for me to show my gratitude for him and his mother for taking me in for the night. Pancakes seemed to be simple enough. I made my way to the kitchen. I grabbed the heavy black skillet and turned the stove dial on seven. I had never seen a pan like that before; it was black all over even the handle. The skillet had to have weighted at least twenty pounds. I was use to the silver pans with black handles that weighted about two.

I was mixing up my pancake batter while the skillet was getting hot. After a minute I threw some butter in the skillet. The butter dissolved in less than half a second and formed a big cloud of smoke. I quickly turned on the stove fan so it would clear all the smoke away but more smoke kept coming from the skillet. I thought the smoke would clear once something was in the skillet to cook. So I poured some batter in the skillet, more smoke came from the pan. By this time the whole kitchen was full of smoke and RJ's twelve year old sister walked in.

Getting something out of the refrigerator; she kept one eye on me and one eye on the skillet on the stove. I was fanning the smoke with my hand trying to clear some of it away and trying not to choke on it. What are you doing she asked me. I'm making pancakes was my response. She looked at me then at the skillet, than looked back at me. You might want to turn the dial down she said as she walked out of the kitchen shaking her head. Oh that's why it's smoking so much, I thought to myself. Well at least I knew to flip the pancake over when all the bubbles in the batter had popped. I learned that in school in home-economics class. But what good that did because when I flipped the pancake over it was just as black as the skillet. I was so embarrassed.

RJ came in the kitchen. What are you doing he asked as he turned off the dial on the stove, removed the smoking skillet from it and grabbed a towel to fan away the smoke. Yes, here RJ was again rescuing me in between laughs and fanning smoke. I was trying to make you some pancakes for breakfast but the skillet was cooking too fast; I explained to RJ. That's because you had it turned up too high and you're using the wrong skillet. RJ went to the cabinet and pulled out a pan that I was used to seeing. Here you go, use this pan. It was the gray black handle pan that I was used to seeing sit on the stove. I never cooked that much when I was at home just cleaned, Sis did all the cooking. I may have boiled an egg or two but that was about it.

RJ's mom came in the kitchen and asked what was going on and where was all the smoke coming from. The woman let me spend the night now I'm about to burn down the place. RJ's little sister came back in the kitchen to put her cup in the sink and told her mom that I was cooking pancakes. Your stove is different than ours; were the words that I heard coming out of my mouth. I know I sounded dumb saying that but at the time that was the only excuse that I could come up with for all the smoke. It wasn't the stove RJ's sister commented as she left the kitchen rolling her eyes at me. RJ's mom finished up her coffee and was headed out the door for work. She told me that I could stay as long as I wanted to but for me not to cook anything. We all looked at each other and laughed. RJ finished cleaning up my mess and his little sister cooked all of us breakfast. As I looked down at my plate of the unburnt food; I realized that I didn't know how to cook so I had better stick to cleaning.

# Chapter 23

**DAYS TURNED INTO** nights and before I knew it, I had been at RJ's house for at least a week. I had even forgotten about my own home for a minute. I had missed school so I was wondering who miss me. No one had come looking for me still. I never left RJ's house for any reason and I only left the room if I had to use the bathroom or shower. RJ never left my side. Thou I was safe at RJ's house I was still sad. I kept the curtains closed to the bedroom so no one walking around outside could look in and see me. I had gotten so paranoid since I had left home. Even when I was in a deep sleep, the slightest noise would wake me and bring me to my feet. Sometimes I would scare the mess out of RJ the way I would jump out of bed too quickly. I had needed to stay hidden until I was ready to go home and deal with things.

Me and RJ were always in the room playing cards; and this day was no different. There was a knock on at the front door. I had gotten into the habit of peeking out through the curtains whenever I heard a knock at the door before RJ would go and answer it. Peeking, I could see my best friend Macey standing at the door. I was glad to see Macey; it just let me know that someone cared but then I panic because I couldn't believe that she was standing there. I quickly closed the curtain and told RJ who I had seen. There was another knock at the door but this one was even harder. Don't let her know that I'm here; I instructed RJ. By the third knock at the front door, RJ was leaving the room to answer it, but only after assuring me that he wouldn't let Macey know that I was here.

I listened closely as RJ opened the front door to greet Macey; I listened closely to them talking. I could hear the concern in my friend's voice. She asked RJ what happened and had he seen me. She mentioned that she had also spoken with my mama. Macey was concerned that I had missed school and wanted to know where I was. She wasn't giving up so easy even though RJ told her that he hadn't seen me. Every now and then I would peek out the curtain but I would quickly snatch it close when Macey would look in the direction of the bedroom window. I swear it seemed like she could see right through them. RJ continued to ensure Macey that he hadn't seen me but if he did that he would let me know that she was looking for me. Macey ended her conversation with RJ but as she walked away from the front door she passed by the bedroom window and yelled; "I know you're in there". She stormed off and I got the feeling that I would have more visitors real soon. And I was right the next day there was a knock at the door.

Doing my usual routine of peeking out through the curtains before RJ answered the door; I knew Macey had went with her gut feeling about RJ lying that he hadn't seen me and she spilled the beans. To my surprise there stood mama and Peter. Peter hadn't walked up to the front door; he stood back in the parking lot keeping his eyes open for anything suspicious; once a cop, always a cop. Being careful to only use half an eyeball so Peter wouldn't see the curtain move; I watched as he paced the sidewalk as if he was concerned about my well-being. Then mama came into my view. I looked at her face and you could tell that she had been crying. It wasn't a just this morning cry that was on her face. It seemed like she had cried for everyday that I was not home. Her face seemed bathed in worry. Seeing her still made me not want to go back home. She went out of my view and I heard another knock at the door. I carefully closed the curtain. I again told RJ who was at the door. His eyes got big as dollars coins.

I sent RJ to go and answer the door but not before I gave him the same instruction that I had when Macey was at the door. I listened as RJ went to the door. I could hear mama and Peter talking to him; asking him if he had seen me. Really; you mean to tell me after two weeks then you finally come looking for me. I didn't want them to know that I was there. I was even holding my breath as I listen scared that they might hear me breathing. Mama was crying so Peter would take over the conversation when mama's crying became so bad that you couldn't understand a word she was saying. After about forty minutes of interrogation from Peter and begging by mama RJ closed the door after continuing denying that he knew my whereabouts. I was still watching from the window. Mama took a couple of steps away from the door, and then broke down in Peter's arms. At that moment I couldn't tell you what she was feeling; the regret of letting me walk out the door or the panic of not knowing where I was and if she would ever see me again alive. I really didn't understand my mother's tears. She let me walk out the door, told me to go ahead, never tried to stop me and didn't bother to come after me. Why isn't she laughing now like she was the night I left? And in that same moment I couldn't decide whether I felt sorry for her or if I wanted her to suffer. I guess I wanted her to feel all the pain that I had felt for so many years for so long. I watched as they walked away out of my view. I began to breathe again. RJ returned to the bedroom with a look of concern on his face. I just laid down on the bed in deep thought wondering if I had made the right decision to stay hidden.

As days passed by going home became the least of my concerns. My focus was on how I knew that I was missing a lot of school and falling behind in my grades. Being book smart was one of the things that I prided myself in and I knew that I had nothing but my education that was going to help me in this world; education and God that is. But at the time I wasn't in the mood to return to school yet. I think the shame of running away was bearing on me. I had heard bad things about girls who ran away from home and I didn't want those things to happen to me. I didn't want the kids at school to think that those bad things had already happened to me since I had been gone so long either.

My Saturday started out quiet but by midafternoon all that came to a halt. There was a loud knock at the door and before I could get to the window and peek out all I heard was, "Antoinette, I know you're in there and I'm not leaving until you come out". It was my best friend Macey again yelling at the top of her lungs. Oh my God, could she be any more obvious. More banging and yelling continued at the front door. I told RJ to go and answer the door before she draws the whole neighborhood to the street. I never answered Macey; I stayed hidden in the room. When RJ opened the door, all I heard was Macey saying; "where is she at? I know she is here". RJ didn't say a word. I just figured he didn't have the energy to lie for me anymore. All I can say is a real friend knows her own friend. Macey was my best friend and she knew me very well that's why she knew where to find me and she wasn't taking no for answer. "You might as well come out because I'm not leaving until I talk to you"; I heard Macey saying. In her voice I knew she meant it. I didn't move; I didn't even blink. "Antoinette, I know you hear me". The whole neighborhood can hear you; I thought to myself. I heard Macey say that mama had come by her house looking for me. RJ didn't say a word. I thought to myself that I at least need to let someone else know that I was okay and let RJ off the hook. He had kept my secret long enough.

I got up the courage to face Macey and came out of my hiding place. Macey was standing in the middle of the living room with her hands on her hips. For a second Macey took on the role as mama.

"What happen? What's going on? Your mother came to my house looking for you and asking me if I had seen you. She asked me if I knew where you were or could have been. You've missed so much school and everyone is asking about you. They didn't know if you were sick, dropped out or pregnant. Why aren't you at home? What are you doing here? When are you coming back to school? How long are you going to be here? When are you going back home?" I don't think Macey took a single breathe the whole time.

I explained to Macey that I got tired of being left out feeling like I wasn't wanted. And that I had been feeling that way for a very long time. I got tired of only being allowed to do stuff when mama felt guilty about how she mistreated me. "You need to go back home", was her answer to everything. But why would I go back to a place where I'm not wanted was my question to her. I told Macey that I wasn't going back home and I meant it. But somehow as I watched Macey walk out that door; I knew that I would surely see my mother at RJ's door again.

The knock at RJ's front door that I wasn't looking forward to came to pass a couple of days later. I wasn't surprised when I saw that it was mama and Peter standing at the front door. I knew that if mama continued her search for me that she would go back and see Macey again. I knew my best friend and I knew that she would do the right thing and tell my mother where I was.

This time when I had looked out I saw a mother who was in need of her child. Peter looked so helpless knowing that he couldn't comfort her. Knowing that the only thing that would stop my mother's pain was finding me and he couldn't give her that. When I saw mama, I knew she had suffered enough and I didn't want to be the reason for her sadness anymore. I gave RJ permission to answer the door and tell her that I was there. RJ went and answered the door while I got dressed.

Preparing myself for what was going to be an awkward situation was not easy. I got myself together and my mind clear. Maybe this could be a new beginning for me and mama. I came in the living room, RJ stood by at the opened front door while mama and Peter stood outside. I didn't know exactly what their conversation was about if any; I had heard nothing. As I approached the doorway I looked at RJ and he looked at me. "Are you sure you are ready for this?" he asked. I wasn't but I nodded my head yes anyway. He assured me that he would be right there if I needed him. I knew that I couldn't turn back now; I was already in my mother's view. To know that I was only twenty feet away from home all this time and the fact that she couldn't find me made my heart ache. I no longer felt as if I was her child. I felt like she had traded me in for something new. Mama stepped towards me for a hug but I quickly stepped back. I was confused by her gesture to comfort me now after all this time. "Can we talk", she asked. I guess that was the least I could do since she had come all this way four weeks later.

As I stepped outside, I looked at Peter then at my mother who no longer looked like my mother but just a woman. I sat down on the cement park stoop being careful not to stray too far from RJ's front door. My focus was on the ground below me and not on the two people who stood in front of me. Even though Peter was standing by my mother's side; I wondered if she knew that he was pure poison. Did she realize how much damage he had done to our family and yet here he stands with her with his poker face of concern. I hated Peter. I hated that my mother was still with Peter. It irritated me to know that Peter had gotten away with doing so much and that he still had that stupid smirk on his face.

Mama began to talk saying how much she missed me and wished that I would come home. Well we all know that I didn't believe that. Did she really miss me or was she just feeling guilty. Yeah, for a second I felt bad because I saw my mother in pain but that was the quickest second of my life. "Come home", she begged me. I told my mother " no, that I wasn't ready to come home". Come home for what, I thought to myself. Nothing was going to change or get better if I did. Peter is still going to be disrespectful and walk around in his boxer drawers showing off his package that you can't help but see because it right there in front of you big as day. You're never home and when you are home you're either yelling about everything or locked up in your bedroom with your little brown box. Or you and Peter are arguing or fighting about stupid stuff and he's always trying to handcuff you to the bed. No one wants to hear all that. And the only time I do see you when is the weekend when you're off and you're hanging out with Sis and the baby. I never see my little brother because he just stays in his bedroom all the time away from all this craziness. And my sister has a baby and a job so she doesn't have time for anything else but that. Who wants to come home to that? That's not my idea of a home. No I don't want to come home to that. I'm sixteen years old and I have to ask can I get a glass of water, if I can go outside, or go over to my friend's house. I have to ask if I can make a sandwich if I'm hurry, I have to ask permission to watch television. What kind of life is that? No thanks; I think I'll stay out and enjoy the fresh air.

Mama continued to plead her case but it just fell on deaf ears. So when she realized that I was serious about not coming back home right now, she asked if I would stop by and just say hello now and again to let her know that I was still alive. I looked up at her and for a moment i saw my mama. I told her yes that I would stop by and say hello. She just smiled at me and told me that I could come back home at any time; when I wanted to. I stood up and told my mother good bye. I did that so I couldn't give her a chance to change my mind. My mother walked away like a mother who had just given birth to her new born baby but had to leave the hospital without her. But as mama walked away I just wondered why she never asked me why I left that night.

I walked pass RJ who was still standing at the front door. A tear ran down my cheek but I quickly wiped it away. I knew as I walked away from my mother that I was walking into a different stage of my life. I was sixteen years old and I felt like I had to take control of my life and what happens in it.

I was no longer in hiding and over the next couple of months RJ's large family quickly became my own family. They welcomed in with open arms and I really felt like I belonged. Things had settled down and began to feel like normal. I had even got a job working on the weekends at the local Popeye's. I worked the night shift so if any chicken was left over, you were allowed to take some home. I ate so much chicken while working there; I think I grew a couple of feathers. It wasn't anything for me to grab a two piece and a biscuit for a late night snack. Sometimes the chicken that I brought home was all that there was to even eat. RJ didn't have a job so my income was all the money that we had.

I went by to visit mama to let her know about my job and to let her know that I was doing okay. I got my mind right and returned back to school. Everyone was happy to see me and I was just as happy to see them. They had a lot of questions for me some I answered and others I didn't. I had a lot of school work to catch up on so that's where I put my focus. All my teachers were very helpful in getting me caught up but it would be my Algebra teacher Ms. Beswick who I would never forget and have so much respect for because she wasn't there teaching just for a paycheck, she was there teaching to empower lives and I will always treasure her for that. She wanted her students to make it in life and it showed. Towards the end of the week upon my return to school, Ms. Beswick called me to her desk and told me to pull up a chair. With about fifteen minutes of class still remaining; the rest of the class kept themselves entertained. Ms. Beswick expressed to me how happy she was to see me back at school. She told me that I was one of her favorite students. She went on to say that she hoped that everything was okay at home and that if I needed someone to talk to that I could come to her. It was touching to know that someone did care about my well-being. Ms. Beswick pulled out her grade book and showed me my grades from the first part of the year and the half of the second part of the school year; it was all A's. She also showed me several spaces in her grade book that were empty next to my name. She told me that she wasn't going to but any zeroes there where the empty spaces were, but she was going to give me time to do the work. Ms. Beswick told me what lessons had to be done and gave a quick review of each one and told me when the lessons were due. She knew that I was smart and would understand easily.

For the next three weeks my nose stayed in my books and I stayed up late a lot of nights getting my work done. That meant very little or no time at all for RJ. Four weeks were left before school would be out and I had turned in all my work for Algebra and even did my final exam. The next time Ms. Beswick showed me her grade book; six A's stood in a row. She told me that she never doubted for a minute that I could do it.

While I was busy catching up on a lot of other work I didn't go outside as much. In the afternoon when I would get home from school I would dive right into my books. A lot of times time would pass by so fast that the next time I would look up from my books; it would be dark.

One evening while I was doing my schoolwork; a funny feeling came over me. I noticed that RJ wasn't home so I decided to take a break and get some fresh air; so I went for a walk.

It was still early dawn so the sun was still making its last pitch to light up the sky. I went by my house to see my mama. She was in the kitchen cooking when I got there. We talked for a while and then I left. As I left my mother's house that strange feeling that something was wrong was stronger and wasn't sitting well with me. I continued to walk around the apartment complex thinking that the walk would do me good and clear my mind. Maybe I was working too much, I thought at first was the reason why I was feeling weird but deep down I knew it was much more to it than that. I was hoping to run into RJ hanging out with some of his friends but that wasn't the case. After I was about to make my second round of the complex I ran into some of RJ's friends but he wasn't with them. I asked them had they seen RJ but they told me no. I just figured that I would hit a couple of the spots were I knew he hung out maybe he would be there and we could walk home together.

He wasn't at the big green electric box. RJ wasn't at the basketball court. He wasn't at the rec center. He wasn't at the playground or the laundry mat. In my walking I came across one of RJ's buddies. I asked him had he seen RJ he told me no but that he had heard that he was around at Ann's house laying that pipe; those were his exact words. He told me to promise not to tell RJ that I had heard that from him. The whole world had just stopped on its axis. RJ's buddy just left me standing there in shock. He walked off like nothing was wrong as if he had told me that he had seen RJ at the ice cream truck. But I was still trying to really process what I was just told. I looked around and now it was really dark so I knew that I had been looking for RJ for a while and was puzzled why I still hadn't found him. The headlights of passing cars seem too blind me as I stood in the middle of the road in their path. Did he just say Ann, I asked myself. The only Ann that I knew that stayed out here with us was my best friend Macey's mom. I just knew he wasn't over there doing what his buddy said that he was doing. RJ wouldn't do that to me, hell Ann wouldn't do that to me; I was her daughter's best friend. Me and Macey were almost like sisters. What I just heard could not be true.

Why would RJ buddy even say something like that and where was RJ anyway? I was starting to get tired of looking for him. I've been looking for RJ now for over an hour. I became dizzy and scared all of a sudden. I found myself back at my mother's front door. We sat at the kitchen table as I told her what I had heard. She told me not to believe what anyone said and for me to ask RJ for myself. I told her that I couldn't find him, that I had been looking for him for over an hour. She stressed to me to go back and look for him and not to stop until I found him. I did just that.

On my way back to look for RJ I ran into Macey and I asked her had she been home and she told me no. I asked her had she seen RJ and she told me no. Just at that moment something caught my attention. It was RJ coming from the direction of Macey's apartment as he walked through the open grass. Macey turned around noticing that she no longer had my attention and that something else did. She saw RJ walking towards us and seeing the look on my face she knew that something was going on. Macey politely walked off and caught up with another friend leaving me and RJ to talk. RJ had a look on his face as if he was surprised to see me just as much as I was surprised to see him. My world with RJ that I thought was so safe just came to an end.

Not wanting to know the truth or hear the truth or to think that what RJ buddy had told me was true; I just stood in silence. But deep down; I already knew. I approached RJ very slowly and in a concerned voice I asked RJ where he had been. RJ just replied that he had been hanging out with some of his friends. What friends, I asked RJ because all the friends of his that I asked said that they hadn't seen him. RJ eyes dropped in the direction of the ground. I could no longer look into his eyes and see his soul and it tell me the truth. I told RJ that I had been looking for him for over an hour; where had he been. But he just continued to look down at the ground and not say a word. I started to weep because his silence spoke louder than any words he could now say to me.

Why are you crying he asked me? I told RJ what was told to me by his buddy. RJ denied it, but that wasn't good enough for me. I needed him to keep my trust and the only way that was going to happen was for me to ask him the same question in front of Ann and him deny it in her face and see her reaction; then I would be able to tell if he was telling me the truth or not. That he didn't do what his buddy said that he had done. I told RJ if it wasn't true to come with me. I just couldn't wrap that picture around my head that a grown woman would have sex with my eighteen year old boyfriend. I guess she wanted to see for herself if the rumor was true. Everyone always said that RJ had a big kick stand.

Not much of a conversation was going on between me and RJ as we walked over to my best friend's house. I just kept hoping that the rumor was a lie. Somewhere along the walk Macey joined us. "Where you going", she asked. "To your house", I told her. She looked puzzled and asked, "For what"? "I need to ask your mom something", I told her. Not wanting to lose focus or say anything out of angry to my friend; I didn't look in her direction. It took everything that I had to hold my peace and wait to see if the rumor was true. But what I wanted to do was turn around and tell my friend what I really thought of her mother. But I had to wait before I put my foot in my mouth and destroy a friendship over nothing but a rumor. How did I know that RJ's buddy wasn't just saying something stupid so I could get mad at RJ? Then when we broke up and RJ's buddy would try and talk to me. Maybe that was the plan behind what he told me. But the closer we got to Macey's house I could feel myself getting nervous and sick. RJ followed without hesitation so my second thought was that the rumor couldn't be true because who would willingly volunteer to walk into the fire pit. But maybe he just went along because he didn't think that I would do it.

We reached Macey front door. My heart stopped beating and I stopped breathing; at least that's how it felt. Macey opened the door and went in but I wasn't ready to go in just yet. I needed to make sure that I was doing the right thing. Do I just believe RJ and live with the fact that I would never know if he lied to me or not. I wouldn't be able to look at him without wondering. No, I wouldn't be able to look at myself in the mirror knowing that I would never know the truth. It was now or never. I couldn't turn back now; I had to know the truth. We all walked into the living room which was lit up by the kitchen light and a table lamp that sat in the corner. Macey's little brother was sitting in a chair playing with some toy. I looked around expecting to see Ann but she was not in sight. I asked Macey where her mother was but with Macey not knowing; she had to ask her little brother who replied that she was in her room. I asked Macey to go and get her mother because I had to ask her something. I took a seat on the couch and waited. RJ didn't try to talk me out of talking to Ann nor did he try to leave. I could only start to believe that maybe the rumor wasn't true. That maybe RJ came along because he had nothing to hide. Or maybe he knew that Ann would lie for him and keep his secret. Maybe he was trying to teach me a lesson with all this. Maybe he was trying to show me that if I wasn't going to pay him any attention that he could easily find someone who would. I was confused and only time would tell his real reason for coming along.

Ann walked into the living room. She was a very slender woman with a short haircut. She weighed maybe a buck and five soak and wet. She had the attitude of a tinny bobber in their blossoming young years. I really think in her mind that she was the age of her teenage girls. I had heard some things about Ann but I never really took them to heart. She was always nice to me and I respected her because she was my best friends' mother. I figured she couldn't be that bad if she had raised a good girl like Macey and her sisters.

Ann took a seat in one of the empty chairs as if she was the queen of Sheba who was sitting on her throne and looked upon us as if we were her royal court or town peasants. She lit a cigarette and crossed her legs.

I looked around the room; Macey and her little brother were still there. RJ sat down on the couch next to me without saying a word. His silence was really getting to me. It was time for me to get this over with. I told Ann that I needed to ask her something in private. I looked over at Macey who got the hint and left the living room with her little brother following close behind. When I was sure that only the three of us could hear what I was about to say; I proceeded on. I told Ann of the rumor that I had heard earlier that evening and I asked her was it true. Ann looked over at me and then looked over at RJ. She looked me dead in my eyes and said "yes I sure did and what are you going to do about it". Those were the words that came out of her mouth and she puffed on her cigarette. She tossed her head back with her nose high and blew smoke in the air as if to dignify herself in the situation. I looked over at RJ; he just dropped his head down and starred at the floor. This was one cold bitch; I thought to myself. Did she say what I think she just said? How could she? She knew me and RJ were going together. Everybody knew that RJ was my boyfriend. RJ was only a teenager while she was an older woman. In her way she was letting me know that she was grown and that I was only a child and that she could do who she wanted when she wanted regardless of what. RJ sat there the whole time and didn't mumble an uttering word.

As if admitting to having sex with RJ wasn't enough; Ann went on to give me a reason why; as if there was one that would make me understand this craziness. Ann went on to say that she wanted to see for herself if the rumors about RJ were true. Are you serious right now; was all I could think as my jaw hung. Yes granted, RJ was well endowed but he was always a gentleman about it. The rumors made it hard for him to have a girlfriend before I came along. But I wasn't worried about what was in his pants I was worried about what was in his heart. But that was no reason for Ann to do what she did. People in hell want ice water. Maybe Ann should go check out that rumor and take them some. Well wow Ann, that's really was a good reason to sleep with an eighteen year old boy who was the same age as your oldest daughter and you're walking around here at the age of thirty-four for crying out loud. And let's not forget he has a girlfriend. Yeah, good answer Ann.

I was so hurt and lost for words. I just looked at her. I learned that night just how dirty the real world was and the people who walk around in it are. Dirt is dirt no matter how you mold it and dress it up. I just got up off the couch with the dignity that I had left and walked out the door. I never stepped foot in my best friend's house again. And I would never trust RJ again or anyone else for that matter.

Even though I was out living on my own I realized too that I was still only a child. RJ followed behind me but it didn't matter because just like a shadow at night; he did not exist. I blindly walked back to RJ's house with tears in my eyes. What I really wanted to do was run to the arms of my mama, but I wasn't sure if she would open the door and comfort me. I felt like a zombie. I felt nothing, I heard nothing, I could think of nothing.

When me and RJ got home I walked straight to the room and sat on the bed. A rage was boiling up inside of me as if I was possessed with a demon. I was beside myself. How could RJ betray me like this? I didn't know if I was mad because it was my best friend's mother. Would it have mattered if it was some other woman that I didn't know? Or was it the fact that RJ said nothing to deny or defend himself. Or was it the fact that I had said nothing in my defense or honor. My defense; what the hell was I defending? I didn't do anything wrong. I was at home doing my homework trying to stay in school and get an education despite my circumstances. And this fool who I trusted is out here slinging dick around like he doesn't got a PYT lying next to him at night. Oh hell no.

It was just me and RJ in that room. I looked at him as he leaned against the closed door. Tears started to run down my face. All I kept hearing myself say to him was how could you do this to me, I trusted you. And all he would say was that he was sorry. But his sorry did not soothe my pain. So I would ask him over and over again but his answer would be the same and it still had no effect on me. But then he began to apologize and try to explain. Nothing RJ said made matters better. The more he tried to apologize and the more I refused it; the madder he and I became. There was no fixing this. There was nothing RJ could say that would satisfy me and he knew it; so he stopped trying. After an hour of me yelling, screaming and crying, I guess RJ had had enough. At one point RJ grabbed me by the arm shaking me like a rag doll and shouted I said I was sorry. RJ grabbed me by the other arm and put us nose to nose. I said that I was sorry he yelled again and pushed me down on the bed. He pushed me down so hard that I bounced up off the bed, flipped over and landed on the other side of the bed on the floor.

There I lay crying and scared. Not knowing what RJ might do next while I was down on the floor I heard the words; don't hurt my baby come out of my mouth. I had missed my period that month so I thought that I might be pregnant. And if RJ thought I was I sure hoped that he wouldn't hit me. I found myself repeating those words holding my stomach and crying as RJ stood over me. I think what I was saying may have shocked him because he ran out of the room. I just laid there on the floor in disbelief that RJ had put his hands on me. He didn't hit me and I hoped that he never would. I cried myself to sleep that night alone. RJ's guilt had changed him.

For the next couple of weeks RJ didn't leave my side and if he did he wasn't gone for more than fifteen minutes. I guess it was a small comfort to know and a bigger one to know that I wasn't pregnant. But all good things must come to an end as they say. I guess RJ had gotten cabin fever and he wanted to go out one night. It wasn't the fact that he wanted to go out I wanted him to go; it was the fact that I didn't trust him to go out and not do something stupid again. RJ proceeded to leave out of the bedroom and make his way to the back door in the kitchen. And I was there with him step for step. RJ said that he would be right back but couldn't tell me where he was going. He reached for the door and opened it only for me to run and slam it shut. I told RJ that he wasn't going anywhere if he couldn't tell me where exactly he was going. He wouldn't tell me and so I only thought of the worst.

Me and RJ played tug of war with the door. RJ was losing until he picked up a bb rifle gun that was sitting by the back door. He had been shooting out in the woods earlier that day. Seeing RJ pick up the rifle and place it by his waist side made me slowly back off and go to the other side of the kitchen. Not being scared of him but the rifle that he raised and pointed at me. I still had words for him and so I took a couple of steps toward him. RJ eyeballed me through the rifle as he focused it on me. RJ had already caused me pain by cheating on me, there was no way he would dare cause me more pain by shooting me with this bb rifle. Then I thought the worst thing that a person could do to someone that they were in a relationship with was to cheat on me. RJ had already done the worst to me so what made me think that he wouldn't do greater. Ignoring his warning and calling his bluff; I took two more steps toward RJ. The rifle went off.

I felt an awful pain in my face. My hands went immediately to my right eye. I let out a howl like a wounded animal. RJ's mom ran into the kitchen after hearing the awful sound. She saw me holding my face and RJ holding the rifle. She asked me if RJ had shot me in the face. Through my pain and shock I was able to answer her with a yes. She turned and looked at RJ in disbelief and asked him was he crazy but RJ didn't answer her. She yelled at RJ to get out of her house and that she was going to call the police on him. In a panic of what he had done and what his mother had just told him; RJ dropped the rifle and ran out the back door.

For a moment I felt dazed and scared to remove my hand from my face in fear that my eyeball might be in it. He shot me, he shot me; I cried. RJ's mom had to pry my hand from my face to make sure she didn't have to call the paramedics as well. It was just my luck; RJ had missed my right eye by three millimeters. Do you realize how small a millimeter is? Do I realize how lucky I am? I was that close from having only one eye. RJ's mom took a good look at my face; you're okay she told me. You're okay she ensured me. I ran to the bathroom to see for myself. Yeah, I still had two working eyeballs but you could see where the bb had hit me in the inner corner folds of my eyelid. The police finally came and talked to me. I told them what had happened. They assured me that they would surveillance the apartment complex until they arrested RJ. That didn't make me feel any better. Even though RJ had done something bad to me; I didn't want anything bad to happen to him.

Something very horrific had just happened to me; but I never once thought to go and pack my things and go home. I didn't realize that I was slowly becoming a victim of domestic violence. That was mistake one, two and three for me. Instead I just went back to the room and threw myself across the bed and cried. I didn't realize that I had cried myself to sleep until I heard a tapping on the bedroom window at three o'clock in the morning which woke me up. Pulling back the curtains I saw RJ's face. I was glad to see him because that means that the police hadn't shot and killed him in the dark. But that didn't last long because I remembered why he was on the other side of the glass and I was mad again. I asked RJ where he had been because the police came by and they were looking for him. RJ said he had been hiding in the woods and that much I figured because it was the best place for a black man to hide from the police.

"What are you doing here", I asked him and then I answered my own question. Um, he lives here; oh yeah I forgot. "You better leave", I told him that the police where still looking for him. But RJ didn't want to hear about all that, he just wanted to plead his case and apologize to me for shooting me in the face with the bb rifle. He sounded so sincere and for a moment I wondered if I had pushed him too far. That was mistake four, five and six for me. He begged me to let him in and so I unlocked the window and let him crawl in so he could get some sleep. Picturing RJ hiding in the woods all night cold, wet, and hungry made me feel sorry for him. He wasn't a criminal and I wasn't going to treat him like one. Mistake seven, eight and nine; I forgave him.

Even though I forgave RJ our relationship had changed and not for the best. RJ knew that I would never look at him the same. I would trust no one. I would depend on no one. RJ was no longer my life line. He only became tolerable. My independence started to show and RJ didn't like it. One day we got into a heated argument and RJ open handedly slapped me across the face. I scrambled to get to the phone to call my mother as I watched RJ do what he normally did when we got into an argument; he ran to hide.

Mama listened in silence as I told her of all the things that had been going on in the past few months. "Come home baby", she told me before she laid down the phone. And yes I went home and things were good; for a while any way.

___

# Chapter 24

**THE PAST YEAR** had been a world wind for me. I had left home, moved in with my boyfriend, his mother and little sister. Dropped out of school but went back and even got a job. My boyfriend cheated on me and now the guilt has caused him to become I guess you can say abusive. He shot me in the face with a bb gun and now he's starting to hit on me. So now; I'm back home.

I would see RJ around in the neighborhood after our last incident. I didn't go to the court appearance so they dropped the charges against him. I had had a long talk with my mother before I made the decision not to go to court. Mama seemed to have had some experience in the matter. I told my mother that I didn't want RJ to get in trouble and go to jail. His mother had lost one son to the streets and I didn't want to be the one responsible for her losing another to jail. I told mama that I didn't want to ruin his life by putting him in jail. I felt like yes he hit me but I'm okay so no damage done, right? Mistake number ten; eleven, and twelve, I'm starting to lose count. Mama went on to explain to me that if I didn't want RJ to get in trouble just don't show up at court. She told me that they couldn't make me press charges against him if I didn't want to. And I didn't so I didn't go.

Weeks passed and I guess RJ finally got the courage to come and talk to me. We talked and he apologized to me several times for cheating on me and told me how much he missed me. And yes, I believed him but I wasn't ready to go back with him; I was enjoying my new found stage of independence. RJ said that he was angry at himself for cheating on me and that he was sorry for taking it out on me by hitting on me. RJ promised me that he would change if I went back with him. He promised that he would never put his hands on me again. That he would get a job and even go back to school. You see, it wasn't until a couple of months into our relationship that I had learned that RJ had dropped out of school. He later told me that he dropped out because he didn't like it but I always felt that there was more to it than that. So I told RJ that I would go back with him but not move back in with him. That being at home was okay and things were quiet now. What number am I on?

And RJ did just that; he got a job through the city summer job program. The only bad thing about that was when the summer was over so was the job. RJ was being very nice to me. There was no fighting or arguing. I had even started sneaking RJ into my bedroom at night after everyone had gone to bed. I had this little white fan that would make a lot of noise when it rotated. So I always made sure it was on so it would drown out any unusual noise coming from my bedroom. RJ would wait until around two in the morning and tap on my window to let him in. we would sleep on my bedroom floor under the moonlight. Sometimes at night from underneath the door (I was allowed to close and lock my bedroom door) we could see Peter's shadow pass by as he walked the hallway. We were careful to be very quiet. Sometimes he would even stop by my door but he never came in; thank God. Around five in the morning he would leave before anyone saw him. But as we all know there is nothing that's done that someone doesn't see. But we never got caught by my mama or Peter so that's all that mattered to me. But I think mama may have known something was going on. She never said anything to me she just changed my bedroom back into her sewing room and moved me back in the room with Sis and the baby.

When it came time to go back to school; RJ ran from the idea. RJ had let a lot of people down by not going back to school. His mom had gone and spent a lot of money on school clothes for him. Everyone was willing to help him with his studies or whatever he needed for school. I was so disappointed by his decision not to go back. I knew how important it was to have an education and he was not going to not get one just because of; what again? I think the pressure of letting everyone down had gotten to him because RJ's old ways were starting to come back. I could tell that his self-esteem was low and that he had insecurities about himself; he had no job and no education. RJ started to take his frustration out on me.

My independence from RJ had gotten stronger and he didn't like it at all. Every day we seemed to be getting into arguments about every little thing and I mean every single day. The arguments became fights. At first it was a little pushing and shoving. Then that turned into hits and then that turned into punches. It had got so bad that RJ started fighting me like he would another man. And I learned very quickly how to give as well as I got. I could always tell when I got a good lick in on RJ because his next punch that he would deliver to me would always be critical. Sometimes it was as if I was in the boxing ring. RJ would be Joe Frazier and I was Ali. This was crazy, but not one time did I think to break up with him. But I did need a break from all this arguing and RJ's fists; so I started not to visit RJ as much and stay home and lay low for a while.

I had tried to get RJ to understand that I was on his side; that I was willing to help him do whatever he needed me to do; that I wasn't his enemy. I think that jealousy only blinded that fact. I truly think by me working and having my own money and going to school that he thought that I was leaving him behind. I think he felt like he wasn't good enough for me or that I didn't need him anymore. When I first meet RJ I had nothing and he provided me with everything. He gave me a place to sleep, something to eat, a friend to talk to, he protected me and even nurtured me, and he supported my decisions and never questioned my actions. But now that I was doing those things for myself he was lost. But I still needed him; I needed my friend.

With me slowing things down with RJ that meant I was home a lot more. I decided to quit my job at Popeye's and put all my time and energy into my school work. Having the family all together again, I think mama thought that it was time for a fresh start. Mama and Peter went and bought a new house built on the out skirts of Kissimmee in a new subdivision. We all went and toured the house when the construction was finished. The house was huge and nice and for a moment I think everyone was on the same page with mama; a new house, a new town, a new start for the family. Mama had pointed out who would have which bedrooms. Of course mama and Peter would have the master bedroom with the bathroom in it. That was my very first time hearing of a bathroom actually being with the bedroom; I thought that was fancy.

Sis would get the largest of the three bedrooms remaining since she had the baby; which made sense. My bedroom would be next to Sis's but across the hall from the master. And my little brother's bedroom would be next to the master on that side of the hall closest to the living room.

Everyone was in agreement with the bedroom layout. But since there was only one bathroom for the three of us kids to use, Peter thought it best for *him* to come up with a bathroom schedule for *us*. Not a good idea. We were old enough to figure out how to utilize the bathroom for ourselves. Peter made the statement that me and Sis could be in the bathroom at the same time. I couldn't imagine it but I know that he could. Once a pervert always a pervert; I say. Me and Sis looked at each other; we knew that wasn't going to work. But Peter was serious about the idea. He even went into detail about what we could be doing in the bathroom together. He went on to say, "Oh one of you could be brushing your teeth while the other is taking a shower". Okay I thought to myself; Peter, hold that thought. I needed my privacy; hell, I wanted it. We were young ladies and not little girls. All flowers don't smell like roses.

Me and Sis looked over at mama for some female support on this issue to let Peter know us utilizing the bathroom at the same time was not a good idea. But mama just looked on as if nothing was said. I guess she didn't want to break the good mood that everyone was in before Peter opened his mouth. And because mama didn't say anything; there Peter stood with that stupid smirk on his face as if he was getting off on the idea just standing there. New house new town; same old problems. Now I understood the statement; you should never put new wine in old bottles. It will leave a bitter taste in your mouth. After touring the rest of the house and the neighborhood, we headed back to the apartment.

Over the next couple of days we did some light packing nothing major just little odds and ends that we knew that we wouldn't be using. During my packing I noticed that some pictures that I had hidden under my mattress were no longer there. I knew that there could only be one person who had them and that was Peter. I waited up all night for mama to come home that night and as soon as she hit that door I was up. She was still coming down the hallway headed to her bedroom with purse in hand when I stopped her. I told mama that I had had some nude pictures that I had taken when I was staying with RJ hidden under my mattress and that they were gone. I didn't mix any words and I told her that I knew that Peter had taken my pictures.

Mama called from the hallway for Peter who was in the bedroom. Mama didn't mix any words either. She got straight to the point and asked Peter if he knew what pictures I was talking about and if he did to give them back to me. Peter just looked mama in the eyes and he knew she was not in the mood for any foolishness. He didn't even deny that he had taken the pictures. He just went back in the room and where ever he had them hidden he went and got them. When Peter came back into the hallway mama just snatched the pictures out of his hands. She took a quick look at them before she handed them back to me. About five pictures in all. Some I had on a blue silk lace night gown and others, well let's just say I was in my birthday suit and my flower was on display for the whole world to see and obviously for Peter to get his rocks off on. Mama looked at Peter with total hatred and then handed the pictures to me but not before she asked me a question. She asked me where I got the idea to take pictures like that. I told her that I had gotten the idea from her. One day when I was getting my mother Bible to read some pictures had fallen out. Some were of her and some were of Peter and they were both in their birthday suit. I always thought mama was a beautiful woman and those pictures of her didn't change my mind I just thought she should have found a better place to hide them besides in her Bible. I think mama was shocked by my answer. She mumbled something but I couldn't understand what she said. Mama handed me back my pictures. Her and Peter went back to their bedroom where they stayed at all night; arguing. That was one argument that Peter didn't win. I hated hearing them argue but Peter deserved that one.

Weeks later the storm was over and the smoke had cleared and it was time to move into our new house. I hadn't seen RJ much but I had told him about the new house and that we would be moving I just didn't know exactly when. So the day we decided to take some stuff to the new house I went by RJ's to tell him not goodbye but that we were moving. I don't know what RJ heard or thought I said but that conversation ended with me being slapped around because I wouldn't do him a *little favor* before I left. I didn't not have the energy or will to fight with RJ. After about the third hit from him I told him that I was calling the police and of course he ran out the door. When the police arrived RJ was long gone. I gave the police my statement and went back home. I was so ready to move into the new house and get as far away from RJ as possible. I didn't care if I never saw him again. I know I didn't do anything to deserve RJ hitting on me.

We didn't have a moving truck so the little boxes and bags we did have we just loaded Peter's and Sis car up with and headed to Kissimmee. Mama was at work so Peter had to show us how to get to the house and let us in. Sis wasn't as eager to move as I was. She hesitated at times to make the trip back and forth. At one point she just got frustrated with the whole idea of moving but with no other option her only choice was to move. In her hasty decision making she decided to throw her mattress on top of the roof of her car and tie it down with a rope. I asked her was she sure it was a good idea. With her short answer she told me yes so we got in the car. Her driving was not its best because she was so upset. Sometimes the speed of the car was fast and others were normal. Half way to the new house Sis's impatience got the best of her and she started speeding and that's when the mattress broke loose and took flight. Thank God no one was immediately behind us or she would have caused an accident. We quickly jumped out the car and secured the mattress back onto the roof of the car. Sis drove slowly to the house. It was late so Peter suggested that we all spend the night at the new house. Mama would join us when she got off. I thought it was a good idea, but Sis didn't. Sis made every excuse why she needed to go back to Haines City. I tried to talk her into staying but my words fell on deaf ears. I begged her to stay the night at the new house. Sis still frustrated; grabbed up my baby nephew and jumped in her car to go back the apartment. Twenty minutes later Peter got a phone call from the Sheriff department saying that Sis had gotten into a car accident and flipped her car.

Peter ran out of the house leaving me and my little brother behind to tell mama what happened when she got home from work. But there was no need because about an hour later Peter returned to the house with Sis and my baby nephew who were unharmed. Sis just took my nephew and went straight to her room. I gave her a minute to herself and then I went and checked on her. I knocked on her door and stuck my head in; she was putting my nephew to sleep. I walked in and sat at the bottom of her bed. I asked her if she was okay and she said no. She wasn't physically hurt it's just she didn't want to be here. But I couldn't resist telling her that I told her not to leave. My sister looked up at me with a twitch in her eye. I quickly exited her room without saying another word.

---

I think it was a week or so later and we were completely all moved into the new house. Everybody likes new things but keeping them looking new and clean was a different story. Some were better at it than others. I turned my bedroom into my own little sanctuary. Everything in my room was still white. I had bought a television, television stand and a stereo for my room. But the best part of my bedroom was my bed. I had a least ten to fifteen stuffed animals and cartoon characters that I would neatly place on my bed every morning. That looked like they were sitting on a cloud. I always kept my room spic and span. Others on the other hand; well that was a different story. Flies started to be in their bedroom and I was mad because I didn't want any to come into mine. I can only assume it came from having dirty diapers lying around. When you change diapers you have to put it in one of those Winn Dixie plastic bags; you know the ones I'm talking about and then throw it away in the garbage can outside. You can't sit a dirty diaper on your dresser or throw it away in a waste paper basket in your room and then leave it for two days. Oh no; that's not going to work. When you open the bedroom door the flies are going to come out and so is the smell.

Flies and dirty diaper weren't my only concern. Because the subdivision was new construction and fields were still being cleared by bulldozers. So whatever was calling the field home got evicted and had to find shelter where ever they could. So just so happen that while I was in the bathroom using it minding my own business; a rat ran across my feet. I was too terrified to go in the bathroom and sit on the toilet for a while. I had gotten so paranoid that I would stuff towels under my bedroom door so just in case the mouse came out the bathroom; it wouldn't have a chance to run into my room. A mayonnaise jar became my best friend. I didn't mind going in the bathroom to brush my teeth, take a shower, or do my hair; but sitting on that toilet was out of the question. That was until I heard the sound of a mouse trap go *snap*. That was music to my ears.

In the new house mama was home a little bit more and Peter wasn't around as much. I guess the tables have turned. By mama moving closer to her job that meant less time in the car trying to get home instead of being home. I like mama being at home. She kept the house so clean that sometimes you thought that you were in a museum. You were too scared to touch anything in the fear that you would put it out of its place. But to this day; that is exactly how I keep my house. I liked seeing mama walk around doing laundry and stuff around the house; it made me want to be like that when I grew up. We never got any new furniture though so the big house did seem empty. But when mama wanted to have the house have a new look; she would put slip covers over the furniture. When mama was home she cooked. I use to love going into the kitchen and seeing her very expensive lightly tinted glass cookware sitting on the stove top. I use to love watching the food cook through the glass.

Because mama was a baker at her job she had all these fancy cooking and baking tools around the kitchen. We loved mama's peach cobbler and when she had time she would make us one. We all helped mama make one that night. When it was all done and in the pan and ready to go in the oven; my little brother grabbed one side of the pan and I grabbed the other so we could put it in the oven. As we were putting it in the oven just before sitting it down on the rack; my brother moved the pan over so to not burn his hand on the side of the stove. But in doing that he moved the pan over making my hand hit the side of the hot oven. When my hand felt that heat it quickly let go of my side of the pan. And needless to say; the peach cobbler ended up on the floor instead of on the oven rack. To our surprise mama wasn't mad; she just started laughing at the spilled cobbler on the floor and began cleaning it up. That night she made us a cake instead. Mama might not have been upset but we sure had our mouth fixed for some cobbler. And maybe mama was upset but she saw no need to show it. It would be many nights when it was just us three in the kitchen talking and laughing with mama.

For the most part; we all did try to make the best of a new situation but all our friends were in Haines City and there was nothing to do here. Me and Sis tried to hang out with each other but she was a mother now and that meant she didn't have time to hang out. But she did transfer to a new McDonald's in Kissimmee and later got me a job there working weekends. Me and my little brother who is about twelve now hung out at the pool a lot. There weren't any kids in the neighborhood our age so it was just me and him for a while. And I hated when Peter would find us at the pool. He would call me out of the pool, have we walk all the way over to him and ask me a dumb question. Oh, you all out here swimming or why you all hanging out with these people. What did he think they built the pool for? So for the residents who didn't choose the house plan that came with a pool could swim. And who did he want us to hang out with, him? I think not. I know Peter only wanted one thing when he would call me over to him and that was to see me in my bathing suit. He would look me up and down as I walked toward him and I could feel him starring me down as I walked away and got back in the water. He would never use his key and just come inside the gate and talk to me while I was in the pool. He always made me get out and come to him. He would never call my brother and those dumb questions he was asking me could have waited until I got back home.

I guess Sis couldn't take being way out here with nothing to do any longer so she moved out. Mama turned her room into an exercise studio for herself. I hung in there a little bit longer but then I started missing RJ and the freedom that living with him brought me. We had gotten a new home but we still weren't a new family. I was seventeen years old but I felt like I was being treated like I was ten. I couldn't use the phone to call anyone and I wasn't allowed to give out the phone number so someone could call me. Mama didn't feel comfortable with the house number just floating out there for everyone to know. Who was she afraid was going to call? Still having to ask for every little thing was driving me crazy. So some days after work; I would catch a ride to Haines City and visit RJ. I would make sure that I made it back home before mama or Peter got home from work. It wasn't long before I went back to Haines City and moved back in with RJ.

With me only working weekends and school was about to start in a couple more weeks; I knew I wouldn't have enough money to buy myself some school clothes. So I gave my mama a call. By the tone of her voice, I could tell that she was upset because I had left home after she tried to make a fresh start of things. But she did give me some money; only two hundred dollars and told me to do with it the best I could and hung up the phone. And I did just that. I bought myself about five shirts and three pair of pants. One thing about life; it will teach you what no book can.

I went back to school but it just wasn't the same. Everyone had gone and there were so many new faces; I felt like I was left out. I felt like I didn't belong there anymore. Yes, my classmates were there but it was like I didn't know them anymore and they didn't know me. It felt more like two siblings separated at the age of five and given up for adoption. You know each other exist but you just don't grow up together. Then fifteen years later you're reunited. You recognize each other but you just don't *know* each other. I know that there were so many rumors put out about me because no one had seen me around but I didn't come back to school to do rumor control. They would just have to believe whatever they wanted to believe. They could shift through the truth on their own time. But this year school was hard and I had lost all interest in it. I had started missing a lot of days and then weeks at a time. So after only a few short months; I dropped out and started working full time.

RJ always made sure that I made it to work. I didn't know how to drive so I was at his mercy. He wasn't working and so yet again I was our only source of income. This kind of put a strain on our relationship. Not really knowing how to mentally handle not having a job; RJ resorted in other measures to let out his frustration. I can only guess that RJ felt less than a man because he didn't have his own money. RJ would make an argument over anything; if the ice machine was making ice that became an argument. If the bus stopped at the bus stop, that was an argument. If the street light came on; that was an argument. If I needed to go and do laundry, that was an argument. I just refuse to argue with RJ about anything because I knew it wasn't because of me that he was feeling this way. I would just look at him and listen. I felt my second time around here would be better but I knew that some changes had to be made.

While I was gone RJ's oldest brother had moved in but he had since moved out again. So in RJ's bedroom were two twin beds that we ended up pushing together to make one. His little sister would hog up the television in the living room so I decided to by a television for our bedroom. So that Friday when I got paid RJ's older brother took us to the store.

Everything was fine. RJ and I were laughing and talking the whole while that we were shopping. When we finished shopping and got to the car, we found out that the television wouldn't fit in the backseat of the car so we decided to put it in the trunk; but that was a problem too. The television box was just too big. Even though we left the trunk open and secured the television down with a rope; we still didn't feel comfortable driving home. We all sat in the parking lot coming up with ideas on how to get the television home but none really paved out. So RJ suggested that he would sit on the edge of the trunk with the television just to be able to tell his brother if he was driving too fast and making the television come lose. I told RJ I didn't want him to ride in the open trunk; for his safety. I didn't want him to feel inadequate; as if he was being thrown in the trunk like a bag of used clothes that was about to be dropped off at the Goodwill. But he insisted that would be the only way to get the television back home. So RJ did just that; sat in the trunk with the television. That was the longest ride ever.

RJ and I walked in the house going to the bedroom to rearrange it so we could find a good spot for the television. RJ and his brother carried the television in the bedroom and set it up. Satisfied that everything was in its place big brother had to leave to run his own errands. I saw it only right to thank him for his generosity and time so I handed him a couple of dollars on his way out the door. As soon as I closed the door and turned around, I was greeted by a punch in the chest by RJ.

I was stunned and confused. "What was that for?", I asked RJ after I had time to catch my breath. RJ had no answer for me. I was so mad. We were just laughing and talking just a few minutes ago and now he was hitting on me. For what is what I want to know? I can only assume it was because he was sitting in the trunk with the television; but that was his idea and I told him that he didn't have to do it. Or was he mad because he didn't have any money to help pay for the television; so he felt less than a man. Did he feel bad because he couldn't give his brother a couple of dollars and that I was? What was the problem? You know what; it didn't even matter because there was no reason or excuse for RJ hitting on me. I charged at RJ and pushed him. It was on and popping from there. At this point I was tired and fed up with RJ picking fights and arguing with me because of his insecurities. I had had enough of this foolishness. We fought from the front door to the back door, down the hall to the room and back up the hall. I wasn't about to back down. A good fifteen minutes into the fight, RJ somehow got me pinned down in a chair that sat in the hallway. The next thing I know his little sister was sitting on top of me holding a knife in her hand. I guess she heard all the commotion from her room and she wanted in on a piece of the action. Or maybe she thought her brother seemed to be getting his butt whooped and she was coming to help. She put the knife up next to my face. I hesitated for a second because I didn't want to hit her because this was not her fight. But when she cut my face I started choking her. Two on one, oh no; I was not about to let this happen. I started choking her even harder so she would drop the knife. RJ realizing that his little sister had no reason in the middle of our mess, told her to get up. When she did I pushed RJ off of me and ran to the bathroom. I had a mark on the side of my face the size of a cat scratch. Oh hell no; this little bitch cut me. I called the police and RJ took off running before they could get there. His sister went back in her room and locked the door.

Twenty minutes later the police arrived. I told them all what had went on that day about us going to buy a television earlier and about the fight which his sister had jumped in on to help her brother. It wasn't until I was standing there answering all the questions that the police officer was asking me that I realized that I had become weak and a victim of domestic violence; I had somehow become my mother. Why hadn't I stood up for myself against RJ before? I guess because I never thought it would get this bad. Maybe because I believed him when he told me that he would never put his hands on me again. Maybe because I wanted the old RJ back and I was willing to wait for him no matter how long it took for him to get back to his good ways. I stood there with a cold washcloth pressed up against my cut while the police officer handed me a booklet of domestic violence with a case number written on the back of it. One of the police officers asked me if I wanted to press charges against RJ's sister. I told them no because she was only a child.

I couldn't continue to allow this to happen to me. All the arguing and fighting day in and day out had to stop. But when the police officer asked me if I wanted to press charges against RJ; again I said no. I guess I wanted to handle the situation in my own way. I would break the cycle of being a battered woman myself. The officer asked if I was going to be safe staying there and if I had anywhere else to go. I told him that I would be safe. I knew RJ wasn't coming back anytime soon. I knew that he was somewhere hiding and whenever he did decide to return I knew he would be oh so apologetic. And as far as his sister was concerned if she came out that room starting anything I wouldn't hesitate this time to knock her out. Her brother wouldn't be around this time to pin me down. The police officers left wishing me good luck.

For the next couple week's things were quite between me and RJ that's because bigger things were brewing; his little sister was pregnant. RJ had seemed to have hung up his boxing gloves for a while and so I starting concentrating on getting back into school. But it wasn't shortly after the birth of his nephew that RJ decided that his boxing gloves needed to come out of retirement. I guess with everyone's attention on his sister and the new baby and me juggling work and school; RJ felt that he was being ignored.

It was Sunday; me and RJ were home alone. It was like any other Sunday morning; got up late, got some breakfast and then off to the showers. I got out the shower and went in the bedroom to get dress. RJ had begun getting dress already so I walked to the other side of the room. Soon as I got to my side of the bed RJ started arguing at me about something. I really didn't know what he was arguing about because I wasn't listening to him on purpose. I knew he had just wanted to pick a fight because we had barely said two words to each other all morning. I just ignored RJ and continued to dry myself off. I think that I was ignoring him too good because he came over to my side of the room and pushed me while I was bent over drying off my legs. He almost made me fall over. I stood up and wrapped the towel around my body and asked RJ what his problem was. I pushed RJ back of course and he slapped me; of course. I was stunned; not by the slap because I knew RJ had no guilt about hitting on me but the fact that we were fighting and I still didn't know why. But I knew also; RJ didn't need a reason.

Emotionally I was drained by all this fighting and arguing with RJ. But it seemed to me that RJ loved it and looked forward to it. I really just had enough of it all. I just wanted to get dress at this point and leave. I had just enough time to put some panties on while I was crying and saying a few choice words to RJ before he punched me in the arm. Three seconds later, me and RJ were in the middle of the bedroom duking it out. I don't know but lately when me and RJ fight; I feel like I'm fighting for my life. I know people will never understand the mind of a battered woman. Don't worry we don't understand it ourselves. I just knew that my heart would not allow me to hate RJ no matter how much harm he had done to me. But I just felt like I needed to fight back and not just take it. If I didn't fight back I could only blame myself for what happened to me. I would be weak in my own eyes.

We tore that bedroom up. But once again RJ got me pinned down on the bed. RJ was sitting on my chest and with each one of his knees holding my arms down so that I could not move. I felt like a trapped deer. At that point RJ was looking down at me with much rage in his eyes. I was so scared. I thought that he was going to kill me. I thought that RJ was going to choke me to death. I thought about my mama and I knew that I didn't want her to get the news that I was dead. I recalled a book that I had read a couple of years ago called *The Burning Bed* and I knew that I had to fight for my life. I couldn't move my arms and RJ was too heavy for me to buck him off of me. The only weapon that I had was my mouth; so I used it. I turned my head to the left and bit RJ in the meat of his thigh. I bit it like I was taking a bite out of a Big Mac. RJ let out a yell like a wounded dog. The next thing I know, RJ came down on my face with full force with his fist. I heard a loud pop. He hit me so hard; I fell half way through the two twin beds that had been pushed together. I let out a scream. My scream frightened RJ so that he jumped up off my chest. He knew he had hurt me real bad this time. I immediately went to grab for my eye but something was in the way. I couldn't see my hand because my eye had swollen shut in a matter of one point three seconds. The room was spinning, I was dizzy and my head was hurting. I was in so much pain. As I slowly tried to pry myself from in between the two beds, I could see RJ grabbing the rest of his clothes and shoes and running out of the room. I waited until I heard the front door close and then I stumbled to the bathroom. I was horrified by what I saw looking back at me in the mirror. I couldn't believe that RJ had done this to me. My eye was the color and size of a plum.

I had to get out of this house. I had to leave before RJ came back but knowing his track record he wouldn't be back anytime soon. I wasn't safe here anymore. What made me think that I was in the first place? I stumbled back to the bedroom crying and in so much pain. I managed to finish getting dress as best I could. I collected some extra clothes and grabbed my school books. I made my way to the nearest pay phone hoping that no one would see me in the process. The sun was so bright that it was hurting my eyes. I was so nervous and so scared. I was just fumbling through all my things looking for a dime so that I could call the police.

# Chapter 25

FINALLY FINDING A dime, I made the call. I told the police that me and my boyfriend were arguing and that it turned physical and that I needed help. I hung up the phone and slide down the wall to the ground in total disbelieve that the same person that once protected me is now the one causing me harm. It seemed like only seconds before the police had arrived.

Two police officers got out the car. The looks on their face as they approached me said it all; I was in bad shape. They asked me if I wanted to go to the hospital. I told them no that I wanted to go home. One officer went around and started picking up my things that I had neatly sat in a pile while the other officer helped me to the police car. They wanted to know who had done that to me and was he still around. I told them RJ's name and told them that he was long gone. I sat back and rested my head. I felt safe now. I just wanted to get as far away from RJ as possible. I never wanted to see him again.

The police didn't take me home instead they took me to the police station. They asked me again if I wanted to go to the hospital. But again I told them no that I just wanted to go home. The police were very nice to me I must say. They gave me something to eat and drink and an ice pack to put on my eye. I felt so ashamed and ugly the longer I sat there having both of them looking at me as they asked me so many questions. But when they took a picture of my battered face I felt like a victim because now there was proof of RJ's rage against me. I sat there for so long at times I even got sleepy. They finally asked me who was my next of kin so they could contact them so that they could come and get me. All I could do was tell them that my mama worked at Disney World. I didn't know her work number, I didn't know our house phone number and I didn't know the address of the house in Kissimmee. I had been sitting at the police station for hours. When we got there it was early afternoon; its night time now.

I was back in the back seat of the police car and on my way home, so I thought. I wasn't fully paying attention while I was in the back seat because I was so sleepy. We drove up to this huge house; but it wasn't mine. It was dark so I didn't know where I was exactly but I knew it took us a long time to get there. The police officers got my belongings out of the car and headed to the front door. They hadn't said much if anything during the ride and they weren't speaking now even after I asked them where were we. One officer knocked on the door and we were greeted by a young lady who after talking with the officers for a brief moment; lead me to a bedroom with three beds in it. Two of the beds I could see that someone was asleep in them. She showed me to the empty bed and told me to get some sleep and that we would talk in the morning.

I slowly crawled into bed. I looked around the room but it was so dark I couldn't really make anything out and only having one functional eye didn't help much. I was just wondering why wasn't I at home. Why hadn't the police taken me to my house? Even though I didn't know the address I could have still shown them the way. Did they call Disney and get in contact with my mama. Why didn't she come and pick me up from the police station. Maybe she didn't want me back home because I had left the last time. I starred up at the ceiling not knowing what tomorrow would bring. Then I did something that I hadn't done in a long time; I began to pray.

Early morning came quickly. I was sleep but suddenly awoken by the quiet sturring around of the girls that I shared a room with as they got up made their beds, got dressed and left. I still didn't know exactly where I was but I knew that I didn't want to get up this early hell; it was still dark outside. What was I getting up early for anyway? I had no plans to go anywhere. I could see other girls walking up and down the hallway getting their day started. I looked around but never letting my head leave my pillow. I finally realized that the girls were getting ready for school. I figured when everyone left I could get some peace and quiet and some sleep.

"We don't sleep all day around here", I heard a voice say twenty minutes after I had fallen back off to sleep. Well that scratched my plans for the day. I went to open my eyes but only one would open; I forget one was swollen shut. I was able to make out that the voice came from the lady from last night who was now standing in the doorway of the bedroom. "Get up and get some breakfast", she told me. "Make your bed and get dress, then meet me downstairs". She was gone as quickly as she came.

Feeling a little light headed and drowsy, I found my overnight bag amongst my things and found my way to the bathroom so I could freshen up. It was when I looked in the mirror to wash my face that I didn't recognize myself. I just starred at the reflection in front of me and wondered how I ever let myself get here. I splashed my face with water hoping that the damage to my face would go down the drain with the water that fell to the sink. But when I looked back at my reflection the damage was still there. I was digging in my bag looking for my toothbrush and I am across some black shades. I found an answer to hide my eye but not my shame. Forgetting about my eye for the moment; I gave myself a once over and began to push my teeth. The black shades hide my eye but not the tears that oh so silently ran down my face. I felt so alone.

I made my way back to the room where I had rested my head the night before. I sat on the end of the bed. I was suddenly frozen with fear. I didn't know what was going to happen to me from this moment on. Had this place become my new home? I couldn't stop the tears at this point nor was I trying. Eventually after some time I got up, made my bed, got dress and made my way downstairs in search for the kitchen. As I looked around I could tell I was the only one left in this huge house. I followed the only light that was left on downstairs and that led me to the kitchen. There sitting on the counter was a load of bread. I wasn't really hungry and not knowing where everything was; I just made myself some jam toast and had a glass of juice. After about twenty minutes of just sitting at the table, I cleared my place. I wondered around the house for a little bit until I came upon this room that looked like a study or home library. It had a huge window that let in a lot of light in the room. I found a comfortable spot on its window seat. I was alone with my thoughts just staring out the window as life was passing by me so fast. Looking around; I wondered if this was a runaway house and if this was where I had ended up for the rest of my life. I knew I should have hitched my way back to Detroit a long time ago. At least I would have been with family instead of here alone.

Hello, my name is Tina; I heard a voice say. I looked away from the outside world and in the direction of the doorway and there again stood the lady. She must be the only adult who lives here. Tina smiled at me but because of my uncertainty; I could not return one back to her. "Do you know where you are", she asked. I just shook my head no. "You're in a woman's shelter for abused women", Tina explained to me. My uncertainty became even stronger. I was only seventeen and not a woman by any means and yet here I was with a black eye in a woman's abuse shelter. I thought it was some type of halfway house for runaway girls, I could have accepted that better. But to be put in a woman's situation when you're only a child is a bit scary. I can't believe this is where I have ended up.

Tina began to say that the police weren't able to get in contact with any of my family last night; so they brought me here. I was dying inside and losing all hope of being able to go back to a normal life. Tina went on to say that after the police dropped me off there that she did her part and was able to get in contact with my mother. But by it being so late and she assured my mother that I was now safe, she arranged for her to come pick me up this morning. But because the location of a woman's shelter is a secret, the police would have to come and get me then meet my mother at a different location so she can pick me up. I became overwhelmed with relief and was able to return a smile. Tina left the room saying that she had to go and finish some paper work but that she would come back and check on me later. Looking back out the window I could see that life had slowed down a little and was waiting for me. An hour later, just as Tina had promised a police car was there to take me to my mother.

After about a thirty minute drive the police pulled into a McDonald's parking lot then minutes later I saw mama and Peter pull up. Before I was let out the car; mama, Peter and the police officer talked for a while. Watching them talk made me feel like I was a hostage that was able to be released because the ransom had been paid. Finally I switched cars trading one back seat for another. Mama asked me if I was hungry I told her no, just that I was tired and ready to go home. Mama said that was fine and that we could go home. I didn't have much to say if anything as I hide behind my black shades. But Peter on the other hand had plenty.

Peter was not at all being sensitive to the whole situation and let peace and quiet have its moment. He just kept going on and on about the night that they received the phone calls. Peter just would not shut up. He acted as if he was trying to get a reaction out of mama to stur things up. But mama sat quietly in the passenger seat as did I in the back. Peter talked about how mama had been crying all night long. How at first when she got the call that she thought they were calling to say that I was dead. Peter mentioned that the police officer had told mama that I had been shot in the eye with a bb gun and mama thought RJ had shot my eye out. Peter was saying some more stuff as if he wanted a reaction out of me. I just tuned Peter out as I looked out the car window and started counting all the red cars that I could see. Before I knew it, we were pulling up to the house. I went straight to my bedroom and closed the door. I imprisoned myself there for the next several weeks until my eye went down. I would walk around the house in my shades if I had to leave my room for any reason. Mama knew that I had needed my space so she would just check on me periodically but never question me. I really appreciated her for that. This overwhelming feeling of shame would not leave me alone. A couple of weeks had gone by and my eye had completely healed. Mama had given me some fade cream so that I wouldn't be left with a black circle around my eye. But even though my eye had healed I still wasn't ready to face the world.

Another month or two had gone by and it was time for me to make my way back into the swing of things. Life does go on after a tragedy and it stops for no one; not even little old me. Mama decided that it was time to get me enrolled back into school. The vibe at the new school was totally different; I was almost scared to stay. There weren't a lot of black kids that went to the school so I pretty much stayed to myself. The kids here in the County were much different from my friends in the City. Here instead of forming friendships they formed gangs. And I don't know what it was about exam time but these kids took it as an opportunity to schedule fights instead of study group. But about three weeks into school; I realized why mama was such in a rush to get me back. She had received some papers from CPS. I assumed the incident that landed me in the woman's abuse shelter kicked up some dirt. Unknown to me I had some type of protection order on me. The State was filing and charging RJ with domestic violence and assault because of it. I now had to sign a paper letting CPS know that I was going to school and living with my mother or my checks would stop. At least that's how mama explained it to me.

Since I wasn't hiding in my bedroom any more, I was able to wonder the neighborhood and it had changed while I was gone. More houses had been built so more families had moved in. Since my brother had already established himself in the neighborhood, I just piggy backed off of him when it came to making friends. I hung out with the older sisters of his friends. Another thing had changed while I had been gone, I noticed that there had been pad locks put on mama and Peter's bedroom door but even stranger than that, on the refrigerator. I've always known for mama to lock the deep freezer in the garage; but to put locks on the refrigerator seemed a bit much to me. Who does that? I asked my little brother why were there locks on the refrigerator. My little told me that Peter had told my mother that he was eating up all the food at night while they were in the bed sleep.

I can only assume that my mother did not stand up for my little brother and tell Peter that as long as she was buying groceries that he could eat whatever he wanted. Even if she had believed Peter and thought that my brother was eating at night while they were sleep; she could have had a talk with my brother and told him to ease off on the late night eating. But to just throw locks on the refrigerator seemed like you didn't even try to resolve the situation. So my next question was where the keys were; around Peter's neck? Other than that, I didn't understand why the refrigerator was locked during the day. I know mama didn't expect for me to go along with this foolishness.

If I didn't eat lunch at school I would starve until the time I got out of school which was at one thirty until the time mama got home from work which would be at six or seven depending on traffic. Sometimes when mama would leave the lock off the refrigerator I would scramble me a couple of eggs to hold me over. Other times when I didn't eat lunch at school; I found myself going over to one of my friend's house to eat. Mama would only leave the refrigerator unlock when there was nothing left in there but a pitcher of water, a carton of eggs, and a half gallon of orange juice which no one was allowed to drink but Peter. That was always the number one rule in the house since mama and Peter got together. I never understood why he was the only one allowed to drink orange juice when mama had been buying groceries with me and Sis's check. I mean I can understand if she had bought his own personal orange juice and then bought the kids theirs. But to sit up there and buy this man not one but sometimes two cartons of orange juice and put it in the refrigerator and then tell us we can't have any; knowing he aint bought none and that we paid for it. I feel that was a slap in the face and a bit much. But that's mama doing for her man.

After seeing that the lock situation had no intention of changing I knew then that I had to keep a job in order for me to eat. So yet again big sister got me a job at her McDonald's. I only worked weekends since I was back in school and that all worked out just fine because some money was better than no money around here. Overcoming little obstacles and getting use to the County life; I had forgotten all about RJ. My life actually seemed normal except for the part of having to buy my own food and stash it in my bedroom closet. I continued decorating my room since it was truly my sanctuary. I bought two straw high back round chairs and spray painted them white to match my room.

The New Year had come in and things were still going okay. Mama and Peter were like two ships in the night. Peter worked the night shift and mama worked the day shift. That helped kept the peace. I really don't know how much damage was done to their marriage but it didn't seem like either one was willing to fix it. But that was their problem; I had my own problems to figure out.

I was eighteen years old about to graduate from high school, what was I going to do with my life. Mama hadn't asked me that question so I didn't know if she had no advice for me or that she wasn't concerned. She never talked to me about going off to college or what my interest were. I knew that I had always wanted to be a business woman. You know the kind that would pull up to her office in her red sports car and get out in her six inch stilettos, three hundred dollar tailored pants suit carrying her briefcase; yeah that was me. I wanted to be an accountant. I had always heard if you do a job that you love, you'll never work a day in your life. I loved math; math was my thing. But the sad thing was mama was never around to ask us about our dreams or goals so I didn't know how it to get there. She never encouraged us or pushed us to do anything. It seemed she only pushed us away. I needed her. I needed my mother to give me direction. We all know that without direction you can end up anyway.

With no help from my mother, I turned to my guidance consular at school for help. That night I was lying across my bed going over some pamphlets that she had given me when I heard a tap on my bedroom window. At first I ignored it thinking that it was a bug hitting my window being blinded by the moonlight. When I heard the tap again I figured maybe one of my friends was out late playing around throwing pebbles at my window as a joke to scar me so I again ignored it. But when the tapping continued I had to go to my window and see what was going on.

I turned my light off in my room and went over to my window slowly opening my blinds. Looking into the dark I saw nothing with the help of the moonlight. Then I caught a figure out the corner of my eye. I focused in and saw that it was RJ. What the hell was he doing all the way up here? More so, how the hell did he know that this was my house? Matter of fact; how the hell did he know that this was my bedroom? Had he been watching me all these many months and I didn't know it. I never thought that I would see RJ again in my life. I had completely gotten him out of my head. What was he doing here? Shocked that he had even come all this way because the City was thirty minutes from here and the fact that he didn't have a car confused me. "Go away", I told RJ. But he didn't, instead he pleaded his case and told me how sorry he was and that he missed me. I just wanted RJ to go away. Then again I thought he was crazy to come all this way. But I still wanted him to go away and I made that very clear. When RJ knew I was serious he made his last plea. He could have saved his breath. I motioned for RJ to go away now and I slammed my blinds closed and got back in my bed.

During the week I assumed my normal routine, but it was the damn Saturday night that was ridiculous. Every Saturday night for the next three weeks, I got a tap on my bedroom window from RJ. And every Saturday night I told RJ to go home after he would plead his case to me. But no matter how many times I would tell RJ to go away, he would come back the following week. November came around and the nights were cold but that didn't stop RJ. Like clockwork there he was Saturday night at my window. I began to feel sorry for RJ; he had come such a long way in the cold. My heart hadn't turned as cold as the night so I pulled back my blinds and let RJ crawl through my bedroom window so that he could warm up. And for the next four weeks I quietly snuck RJ out of the house when the morning came.

The back of the house was very dark at night so I know no one could see RJ crawling in my window at night and think that it was a burglar or they would have called the police by now. But to see RJ crawl out of my bedroom window at seven in the morning would have been a totally different story. So we had to tip-toe pass mama and Peter's bedroom door, pass my little brother door, down the hall; being oh so careful not to walk on the plastic runner that lead to the front door. Thank God we didn't have an alarm system that I would have to turn on and off. Peter would have heard me pushing buttons in his sleep. It seemed like it took us forever to get to the front door. I was so scared of getting caught. I didn't want to make a peep. I would hold my breath to not make a sound. Making it to the front door I would direct RJ in which direction to go so he wouldn't pass by mama and Peter's bedroom window.

Had I forgiven RJ for giving me a black eye, maybe? Had he seemed like he changed his ways and was a totally different person, maybe. Was I being a fool for getting sucked back into his grasp, maybe? Will I live to regret this later, maybe? Why I went back continuing to see RJ, I really couldn't tell you. Maybe because with RJ, I had freedom and there were no locks on the refrigerator. But being with RJ my freedom came with a price. One Sunday morning when it was time for me to get RJ out of the house he decides that he was too tired and worried that he wouldn't be able to find a ride back to the City. He told me that lately it had been hard for him to find a way up here to the County so a lot of times he would walk. I felt so bad but what was I to do. I couldn't leave him here in my room; I had to go to work. I asked RJ where he was going to stay. He told me that he would just hang around the neighborhood until I got off of work. That wasn't a good idea. This was not the neighborhood to just be hanging around in. We were the only black family in the neighborhood and everyone knew that there were only two black kids in the neighborhood. You walking around all day looking suspicious will get the police called on you in the quickness. I told RJ that there was no way he could stay here. He convinced me that he could get a ride from someone who worked at my job that lived in the City. Feeling sorry for RJ and going against everything that I knew to be right, I let him stay. But on one condition; that he stay in my closet out of sight until I got off of work and the coast was clear. RJ agreed and said that he would just sleep until I got off of work. I told him if he got hungry or thirsty that I had some cookies and juice on my shelf; for him to help himself. I must have been crazy because I left for work leaving RJ in my closet.

Drive-thru at work was my spot and I loved it. My day was going normal and busy like any other work day. I had forgotten all about RJ hiding in my closet that is until I got a phone call half way through my shift. It was the police on the other end. The police officer explained to me that my little brother had called them saying that someone had broken into the house and was hiding in my bedroom closet. "But when I question the young man in the closet he said you gave him permission to be there. So I'm calling to clear this up before I make an arrest", the police officer went on to say. I removed the phone from my ear and placed it on my stomach because that's where my heart was at. My life flashed before my eyes because I knew that I was dead if mama and Peter found out that I was seeing RJ again let alone sneaking him in the house and then leaving him in my room to hide in the closet. I already saw myself lying in my casket.

The officer's voice yelling hello brought me back to the present. I wasn't dead yet but I will be if I didn't clean this mess up and escape with my life. I explained to the officer that I did give RJ permission to sleep in my closet while I was at work, that he wasn't a burglar. I asked the officer to let me speak with my brother. The officer put my brother on the phone and before he said a word I already knew what he was going to tell me about how he ended up in my room in the first place. My brother knew that I kept snacks in my closet; he didn't know that I kept boys in there too. He went on to say that he and his friend went in my room to get some and that's when he stumbled upon RJ asleep in the closet. "Why didn't you call me before you called the police", I asked him? He said he was scared and didn't know my work number. I had bigger problems to worry about because I knew that my little brother was going to tell my mother and that was one fire I didn't want to get burned by. I knew that there would be no recovery from this with my mother. I told my brother that RJ didn't break in that I had let him in and told him to stay in my closet. My little brother just said oh as if he just realized how much he over reacted by calling the police and not me instead. I didn't think that I could trust my brother not to tell my mother what I had done so I went into panic mode. The only thing I knew to do was to pack my stuff and leave. I told my brother to hand the phone back to the officer. I told the officer that it was okay for him to leave and that I was on my way home.

I hung up the phone. Oh my God, I am a dead woman. I turned

to my manager and told her that I had an emergency at home and that I needed to leave right away. That was such an understatement; I had more of a crisis on my hands. She told me okay that I could go home. Then I told my ride to work that I needed a huge favor from her. I needed to get out of the County fast and in a hurry. We clocked out and we headed to my house.

When we arrived at the house it looked like a crime scene. The front door was wide open and people were standing in front of the house all in the road. People where asking questions amongst one another. I saw my brother and his friend Steven come out the house. I jumped out the car and I could see RJ coming up the road. "Tell mama that I'm sorry", I told my little brother as I passed him on the sidewalk headed towards the house. I knew that I had very little time before mama or Peter was due home from work. I went straight to my bedroom and just started grabbing stuff hoping that it would fit in my friend's car trunk. I didn't have a choice if I wanted to live; I had a better go with RJ. I had a better chance of surviving. RJ might beat on me if I leave with him but it would be mama who would kill me if I stayed. I grabbed my clothes out of my closet along with the stupid cookies and juice that my brother was after. I made a couple of trips back and forth to the car loading it up just throwing everything in and not caring how it landed. "What are you doing my brother asked?" I handed him the two packs of cookies and eight juices that I had. I told me that I had to leave I knew mama would never forgive me for this. I wish that I would have stayed around long enough to ask her. RJ helped me finish packing up the car and apologized to my brother for scaring him. With much regret I got in the car and back to the City I went.

# Chapter 26

**MOVING BACK IN** to the City was total chaos. I was seventeen; three months from being eighteen and now on my own. Mama wasn't around the corner anymore, she was far away. And for the first time things seemed real. I must say though the best lessons learned are the ones you teach yourself. But those lessons can be the hardest. School was the farthest thing from my mind. I had to go to work and make some money because now that I was eighteen I was expected to take care of myself. Again I was living with RJ at his moms. And maybe I was a fool yet again but I did believe RJ when he told me that he would never hit me again. With things going good between us I had to find another job. His aunt got me a job where she worked cleaning rooms at a hotel resort in Kissimmee. Here I was almost eighteen making beds for a living. Every morning meeting when they would hand out the clipboards with assigned section of rooms to clean I would just look around as I stood there in my brown housekeeper maid uniform dress. I was standing amongst woman who were twice my age. They would get mad if someone else got their routine section because they knew if they had cleaned the room all week when the guest would leave they would leave the housekeeper a good tip. I learned; don't mess with a housekeeper and her section.

These were grown woman. They had kids, husbands, and a household to run. Listening to them talk about their everyday life; made me want to run and go hide under a rock. I was only seventeen I didn't want those kinds of responsibilities. I should be somewhere in college with my nose in a book. But I think I may have missed that train. The job was kind of hard for a young girl like me. But some of the ladies were nice to me and trained me showing me short cuts on how to clean rooms so I wouldn't be killing myself. Every day when I got off of work my feet and back would be hurting so bad; but what else was I qualified to do without a high school diploma. The only thing I like about my job was the free lunch. We got to eat at the resort buffet that they prepared for the guest.

I had been working at the resort for a good six months when I came across my sister who had been living back in the City since she left the house. She said she was doing okay but had been looking for a job. So I got her a job where I worked after talking to my boss. One thing about my work place was that immediate relatives were not allowed to be employed there. So it was hard to convenience my boss and everyone who asked that me and Sis were cousins and not sisters. Hell we looked just alike. But we pulled it off and she got the job.

I was working and even RJ was working but then the arguing started. I can't quit remember but I think it went along the lines of RJ's mom had put him out but said that I could stay. She said she couldn't deal with all the noise and handle having to deal with the new grandbaby. She said her nerves were already bad. I felt bad that RJ got kicked out, so we decided that maybe it was time to stop living with his mom and get our own place. But the only place that we could afford was this well-known rooming house on six street. It was definitely not he Ritz and Donald Trump was not a resident there. I called my mother and told her I was moving. We made small talk and she agreed to come help me move. It was a "rooming" house; there wasn't much if anything to move. It was just big enough for a bed and two dressers and they were already in the room. There was one bathroom at the end of the hall that everyone used. But mama did just that, she came and helped me move my clothes along with my television. Mama took one look at the place and I knew that it wasn't a place that a mother would want to leave her child. But what choice did she have. I didn't want to go back home with her and live in a museum with locks on the refrigerator.

RJ and I were the youngest couple there. Mostly it was men who had just gotten out of jail that lived there or just people down on their luck. RJ knew one of the guys that stayed in the room next to us. He could tell that I wasn't use to this side of town. He and RJ assured me that I would be okay and that he would look after us. Oh yeah right, that put all my fears at ease. I was worried that someone would try and break into our room and steal our television and stereo since we were the only one to have one. You would see the occasional crack head or lady of the night hanging around outside the building handling her business, but for the most part no one bothered anybody. I was scared; I'm not going to lie. I had never been exposed to the night live before. I felt like I was living in the gutter. But I was getting an eye full of real life up close and personal. One day RJ had to go work so I was alone. I was sitting on the bed folding laundry and watching television when all of a sudden something ran across the floor. Pets weren't allowed so I knew it wasn't a cat but it was the size of one. I jumped on the bed and started screaming at the top of my lungs.

RJ's friend from the room next to us came running in asking what was wrong. I told him that I saw something run across the floor. He casually stated that it was probably a rat. He said that they have been known to run around. He said it as if it was okay. But it wasn't okay with me that a rat that was as big as a cat was running around my room. I started to cry and told him that I had needed to get out of there. I told him I would go across the street to RJ's aunt house and sit with her until RJ got off of work. I didn't want to stay there with the rat. He told me he would stay with me while I got some things. I got what I could as I reached into the dresser draws, grabbed some stuff off the bed and ran out of the room. RJ's friend asked if I was going to lock the door. I told him nope without looking back. I didn't care about the television, stereo or anything else that was in that room; the rat could have it for all I cared. I just wanted to get away. I ran across the street to RJ's aunt house. Thank God she was home.

She was surprised to see me because I hardly ever visited her without RJ. I told her what had happened. She just laughed and told me to stay until RJ got off of work. Oh believe me, that was my plan. I went in her bathroom to take a shower and as I was getting dressed I realized that I didn't grab any panties but RJ's underwear instead. I was one fruit of a loom wearing chic that day because I wasn't going back to that rooming house where that rat was at for nothing; and I meant nothing. As I sat at his aunt's house watching television, I was hoping that she would invite us to come and stay with her but I knew she didn't have any room. But she did tell me that I could come over anytime and sit over there until RJ got off of work. That night when RJ off of work; he came to his aunt house to get me. He said his friend told him what happened and where to find me. We went back to the rooming house to our room and to my surprise everything was exactly how I had left it. We stayed at the rooming house for another week or two but RJ knew that I couldn't take it anymore so we moved back in with his mom.

That was okay for a little while, but we still wanted our own place. So we ended up moving in with my sister. She had told me that she wanted her own place too. I think at the time she was living with her mother-in-law. She had already gotten the apartment but hadn't moved in yet. She only had one rule for me. Knowing me and RJ's history she said that there could be no fighting and if there was that she was going to put RJ out. I could understand that she didn't want all that around her baby. I really didn't think that we would have a problem because I had explained to RJ our situation and that we couldn't keep staying with his mom so he better not mess this up for us; he agreed. But just like the clock strikes twelve twice a day; so did RJ.

We weren't living there a good month before me and RJ got into an argument. He had gone off somewhere and came home two o'clock in the morning and I refused to open the front door for him. He came to our bedroom window and started hitting on it. I told him where ever he had just come from to go back and I meant it. We argued through the window some more. I was tired and had to go to work in the morning so after thirty minutes of listening to him begging me to let him in; I did. The next day after me and Sis got home from work she told me that she heard me and RJ arguing and that he had to leave. I knew that was coming. But then she turned around and said that I had to get out too because she said as long as I stayed there that RJ would come around and she didn't want to deal with that. That was so cold blooded. At this point I was really getting tired of being put out on the street. I didn't know whether I was mad at RJ for getting me put out or my sister for putting me out. With nowhere to go; RJ and I ended up moving back into his moms.

A couple of weeks later while I was at work, my sister was telling me that my mother had been looking for an apartment by where she lived. I guess her and my mother had been keeping in contact for a while because my mother hadn't reached out to me and mentioned anything. I wondered why she was looking for an apartment; was she finally leaving that scum bag for good. It was shocking to me but it was true. The following month mama got a two bedroom apartment. I left RJ and moved in with her. It was actually a lot of fun living with mama. We shared a bedroom so we seemed like roommates in college. My brother was enjoying being away from Peter. I never really asked her what happened between her and Peter but she just said that she needed her space.

I had come in from work one day and mama wasn't home, it was just my brother. I asked him if he knew where mama was. He said that she had left a note saying that she was going to see Peter. I had gotten a bad feeling after I read the note. I didn't think that she should be with Peter alone. I knew how manipulative he could be. I didn't feel that she would be safe with him alone. I was right. The next time I saw my mother she was limping. Peter had hurt her somehow and I think in a very bad way. I was so mad. I felt so helpless. I knew Peter would have hurt her if she was alone with him. I asked my mother what had happened to her. She only said nothing and that she was okay. But I knew she wasn't. Her spirit had been broken, I could tell because she never looked me in the eye. I wanted to find Peter and kill him for hurting my mother. But my action would have been for nothing because a month later mama said she was moving back into the house with Peter. Why was she going back to him after what he had done to her? Did he threaten her; is that the reason why she was going back. I didn't want her to go. I wanted her to stay here with me; we were having fun, right? I couldn't afford to keep the apartment on my own and I wasn't about to go back and live with mama at the house not after what Peter had done to her. So I was back to square one living with RJ's at his moms.

Moving back in with RJ at his mom's took me down memory lane and I knew that I didn't want to be there. I realized that I didn't love RJ and that I never did. RJ was just an escape for me. He was a way out and away from all the drama and madness that I had going on in my own household. But with RJ; I had developed my own drama and for a while I was trapped, but not anymore. I realized that this was not the life for me. This was not the life that God had planned for me. I was eighteen years old and I still had a chance to know what his plan was. So I quit my back breaking job at the resort and when school was back in around August so was I. When I started going back to school so did the fights with RJ again. I didn't want another cycle of this so my approach to the situation was totally different. It was only after seeing what happened to my mama that I finally saw myself.

I went and got my old job back at McDonalds working only on the weekend which was just fine. I went to work that weekend and confided in my friend Stacey. Stacey told me that I had needed to meet other people and get away from RJ. She told me that she would come by one night and take me out so I could get some "fresh air" is how she described it. Hesitant at first, but it did sound like a good idea so I agreed. Stacey gave me a word of advice that I will never forget; once a man starts hitting you, he never stops. And she was right; no matter how many times RJ promised me that he would stop hitting me, he didn't. And I so wanted to believe that he would. It had gotten to the point of me and RJ having so many fights that I just didn't have the energy to fight back any more. I was at my wits end; RJ had beaten the fight out of me. I now started to feel resentment towards RJ because I realized that I didn't deserve what he had done to me. I know that I had made the decision several times to go back to RJ but it was not for him to use my disposition to get his gratification. He figured if he could beat me down than he wouldn't be at the bottom. But I decided that I wasn't made for the bottom either. But I wasn't going to beat anyone down; I was just going to pull myself up.

It was Friday night and Stacey came by to pick me up and we went to a local spot in the City. I had always heard of this spot but I had never been in before. It was just a small neighborhood club that everyone went to. I had never been out to a club before so the atmosphere was a bit over whelming for me. I felt like I had been kept away in a cave for the past two years and now I had escaped. The club was dark and the music was loud. Red and blue lights lit of the dance floor. As me and Stacey sat at a very small table I observed the people around me. Everyone looked like they were having such a good time. It wasn't long before I was sitting at the table by myself. Stacey asked me to watch her drink as she was whisked away to the dance floor. I was drinking a coke but I think Stacey had a little bit more than that. I had a good time just watching everyone else. Then the lights came on and the party was over. It was two o'clock in the morning and it was time for the spot to close. You didn't have to go home but you had to get the hell out of there. Everyone was headed towards the door to make their exit. Stacey asked me if I was okay and if I had had a good time. I told her that I did; it felt good to get some "fresh air".

But just as soon as I walked out of the spot there was RJ waiting for me. I didn't even know that he knew where I was because when I had left the house and he asked me where I was going I just told him that I was going to hang out with Stacey. Which I was because she never even said where we were going. Had he followed us here? Had he been in the dark in a corner somewhere spying on me? Had he been driving all over town looking for me? He looked like a stalker tracing my every move. As I passed by the crowd he grabbed my arm. I quickly yanked away from him. "What are you doing here"? I asked him. He said he was coming to pick me up. I told him no, he wasn't and that I had come here with Stacey and that I was leaving with Stacey. I knew if I had gotten in the car with him with the look that was on his face; it wouldn't have been a quiet ride home. I walked off ignoring him for the most part even though I did make eye contact with him on my way to Stacey's car. Stacey drove me home and didn't leave until I assured her that I would be okay.

RJ had gotten home before me so as soon as I hit the front door the fighting started and lasted all night but at this point I didn't care anymore. I had had enough. I told RJ whatever it was that he was going to do to me to do it. I was willing to die that night if that's what it was going to take to end the abuse. Nothing was going to stop me from speaking up for myself and putting an end to all of the abuse that I had endured from him. I told RJ that he couldn't keep beating me down in order to make himself feel better about the choices that he had made. They say misery loves company; well I don't love misery so scratch me off the guest list. I told RJ that he wasn't mad at me but only mad at himself for his short comings and failures. I told RJ to stop taking it out on me, that he may beat me down but that I will always get back up. I refused to be his bunching bag any longer. There was that voice that I had heard oh so long ago.

The following week I went to school and that weekend Stacey came by again to pick me up and we went to the spot. And again I would just sit and watch as everyone enjoyed their night. This went on for a couple of weeks. Finally RJ got the message and he was no longer standing in the crowd spying on me at the end of the night. Instead he would stay up all night until I got home. I didn't care if he acted like a watch dog that was his problem. I hadn't danced with anyone, given anyone my number, kissed or went home with anyone, drank any alcohol or smoked something while I was at the spot. So if he wanted to play watch dog that was on him. RJ would just stare at me without saying a word following my every move as I prepared for bed. I could tell that he wanted to say something but he knew I wasn't afraid to stand up for myself anymore so he said nothing. RJ could see that I wasn't that scared little sixteen year old girl that he once knew. With every day that passed I felt myself getting stronger and wanting something better for myself than this. But I still couldn't see my way out of the situation that I was in. Every morning when I saw the light of day I prayed to God to help me find a way out.

One night at the spot while Stacey was sitting at the table with me resting her feet; I got a tap on my shoulder. I looked up to see it was my old hair dresser's son and summer boyfriend Bob. I guess he did come back to town after all. The spot was about to close so the DJ announced that it was the last call for alcohol and last song; Bob asked me to dance. I was hesitant at first but Stacey encouraged me a little to go ahead and so I did. I really didn't mind too much, it wasn't like he was a complete stranger who would be groping all over me while we were dancing in the dark. Bob was a complete gentleman. We danced and had small talk while the music played then the lights came on; the club was closing. Bob asked if I was going to be at the spot next weekend. I told him that I didn't know that it was up to Stacey because she was my ride. Bob turned to Stacey and told her to make sure that she brought me back next weekend. Stacey told Bob don't worry that I would be there. I felt like I was present at my own arranged marriage. I looked at Stacey with that girlfriend look of surprise. Me and Bob said our good night. Stacey and I giggled like little school girls on my way home about what had just happened. Even when I walked in the house nothing could wipe the smile off my face not even RJ and his arguing.

I was looking forward to the weekend; I was glad that the week went by fast. I think that RJ had noticed a change in me. I was spending less time at home. School, work and very little conversation with him is how my week would go. I could feel myself pulling away from RJ little by little and not too soon, if I say so myself. Just as Stacey had promised we were at the spot and so was Bob that weekend. Soon as we got in and got a table Stacey disappeared off onto the dance floor leaving me to watch the drinks. For a moment as I looked around I wondered to myself what was I really doing here? And I heard *the voice* say; trying to get your life back. And I chuckled at the thought; how was I going to get my life back by sitting in a club. My life had been in a tail spin for the past two years and I saw no hope for my future. I had been left feeling empty and numb. But I knew if I had a chance to get out of this situation with RJ I promised myself that I would never let it happened again.

The sound of the music brought me back to the spot. Not being a drinker at all, I took a sip of Stacey's drink; who still hadn't returned to the table since she left. The drink was sweet; not bad though. I had saw Bob earlier when we first arrived but he somehow had disappeared into the crowd. Stacey finally returned to the table looking like she had took a couple of rounds on the dance floor and won. Catching her breath and a couple of winks from an admirer; she was gone again back on the dance floor. Stacey was a little fire ball, I had fun just watching her have fun. Then suddenly there was a tap on my shoulder; it was Bob. "Is this seat taken" he asked, pointing at the chair where Stacey had been sitting only seconds ago. Doubting that Stacey would be back anytime soon; I told Bob that he could have a seat. Seeing that I didn't have a drink Bob asked me if he could buy me one. I told him that I didn't drink but thanks anyway. "Well do you eat?" he asked. A little giggle came out before my answer did. "Yes", I told him. "Well, let me take you out to breakfast". I told Bob okay that nine a.m. tomorrow would be fine. Bob laughed and said that he was meaning that he wanted to take me to breakfast now after the spot closed.

Breakfast with a gentleman at two thirty in the morning sounded nice. And at this point I was ready for something nice. The spot was about to close in about thirty minutes so I thought why not. I told Bob that I hadn't been living the night life but that I had heard rumors about it; or were they. I was still young and that I wasn't trying to become a hoe by any means and that breakfast was all that I was interested in tonight and that if he was interested in anything else that I didn't want to waste his time; for him to choose someone else. Bob agreed; breakfast it was. Bob got up from his chair and whispered in my ear that he had to handle some business but that he would come and find me when the lights came on. I watched as Bob worked his way through the club like a star with status and then he disappeared into the crowd. I was smiling so hard on the inside I just knew that it had to be showing on the outside. I took a sip of Stacey's drink hoping that I didn't just say yes to the wrong person.

Bob did just what he said, he found me when the lights came on. He told me where he was parked at and to wait for him by the car while he told a couple of folks goodbye. Before I headed out to his car; I found Stacey and told her that I was leaving with Bob and that he would drop me home. She asked me if I was sure and I told her yes. Stacey gave me a hug and her girlfriend stamp of approval and then disappeared into the night. I walked to the parking lot following Bob's direction of where his car was parked at. Standing by the car, the early morning air of November was a bit cold. So many thoughts were running through my mind as I stood there waiting for Bob. The love of my father; I would never know. The love of my mother would seldom show. That which I thought at first was love from my boyfriend would only turn out to be bitter and end in blows. But I refused to give up on finding what I knew was rightfully mine and that was to be loved by someone. I could only wonder if he would be the one.

There was no arguing, screaming, or fighting just laughter as Bob and I played catch up with each other about the past two years over omelets and cheese grits at Denny's. Bob was truly a breath of "fresh air". I never told him about RJ's abusive ways just that I had left home and had been in and out of school, lived in Kissimmee for a little while and that I was now back in the City. I did tell Bob that I had a boyfriend but that our relationship was over even though I was still living with him; I had one foot out the door. Bob told me that he had just ended a relationship himself so he understood how difficult it could be to end. Time got away from us as we enjoyed each other in conversation. It was four thirty in the a.m. when Bob happened to look down at his watch and decided that he had better get me home but not before he stopped at his house and switch cars.

Bob had a baby blue late model Pontiac Impala whose trunk went on for days. You could lay straight down in there and still have room to put a top hat on your head. But his car didn't have a heater in it and his brother's car did. We sat in his brother's car talking some more as we waited for the car to heat up. I guess Bob preferred some body heat at this time because suddenly he leaned over to kiss me while we were talking. I quickly pushed him away. No matter how bad our situation got; I never cheated on RJ and I wasn't about to start now. I told Bob that and he said he would respect my decision and not pressure me to do anything that I didn't feel comfortable doing. That was the Bob that I had remembered.

My long ride to Powerline line seemed short as me and Bob listened to music on the car radio while still laughing and talking. But when we made it to Powerline my reality hit. I didn't want to be disrespectful to RJ so I asked Bob if he would not drop me off in front of RJ's apartment. It was bad enough that I was coming home five o'clock in the morning and that I had been out to breakfast with an old boyfriend of mine. So I thought it would be a bit much for a man to drop me off to another's house. I thought it best for Bob to drop me off two streets over. Bob asked if I was sure as he was concerned for my safety having to leave me at night or early morning dark. His concern flattered me but I told him that this was best and that I would be okay. Bob handed me his phone number and insisted that I call him if I needed him; I agreed.

I think that I might have said a little prayer as I made my way to the apartment. As I approached I noticed that all the lights were out. Looking down at my watch I was concerned that I only had two hours before it would be time for me to get up and go to work. I had prepared myself for RJ's arguing but wanted to limit it to thirty minutes. But there was none. RJ was asleep when I enter the room but he wouldn't be for long. He awoke as I was getting undressed. He asked me where I had been. I told him that I had gone out to breakfast with an old friend after the spot had closed. RJ asked me who this old friend was. I told him it was Bob. RJ asked me who dropped me off; I told him that Bob did. Silence filled the room. I told RJ that we both knew that our relationship was over that it had been over since this last time that I came back to live with him and that it was time for me to move on. At first RJ just sat there with this bizarre look on his face. But his normal quick to draw was slow; was it because there was another male that was now involved in the situation and so now he didn't seem so mighty now. But as long as it was weak young me he felt like mighty Joe Frazier. RJ had a couple of heated sentences to say but I told RJ that I wasn't in the mood to argue so could we please just save it for tomorrow. The last thing I wanted to do was lay down next to RJ feeling the way that I did but I didn't want to sleep on the for floor either. I had just purchased a brand new queen bedroom suite so I might as well use it.

The next morning I went to work and as soon as I got in the car Stacey wanted to know every single detail so I spilled my guts. On my first break I gave Bob a call just to let him know that I was okay. It was good to hear his voice again. Bob asked if when I got off of work would

I stop by and see him. I told him that I would have to ask my ride because it would be a little out of my ride's way. Bob told me to tell Stacey not to worry that he would give her some money for gas for bringing me to him. I asked Stacey if she would take me after work. Seeing how excited I was to know that Bob had wanted to see me again; she said she would. Bob said that he would be waiting for me.

Work couldn't go by fast enough for me nor could the ride to the City. Before I knew it we were parked in front of Bob's house. I was so nervous that I didn't want to get out of the car. It was broad daylight and I was at another man's house. In my mind I questioned myself if I was making the right decision or not by being here. But I couldn't make a clear decision so I turned to Stacey who already saw the uncertainty on my face and before I could get a word out she started pushing me out the car before I chickened out and tell her to start up the car and go. I was so nervous but I did remember the promise that I had made to Bob and Stacey had already used her gas to get here so there was no use of wasting it. I got out the car still in my work uniform smelling like French fries. I took a couple of steps as I headed to the front door. Every other step I would look back at Stacey who was cheering me on and waving both her hands giving me the signal for me to go on. I began to laugh because the look on Stacey's face was that girlfriend look of; your crazy if you don't, but if you don't I will. But it only took a couple more steps and I was at the front door and knocking on it.

I stood there waiting but it didn't take long before I heard Bob's voice from afar saying come in as if he knew that it was me at the door. I opened the door for myself and stepped into the house. Bob was sitting amongst his friends. He greeted me with a smile as he motioned for me to come and sit next to him. With the aroma of French fries still on me and I didn't think that it was a sexy allure; I politely declined and stayed by the door. But he asked again and I didn't want to be rude and just knowing that he really wanted me there made me slowly shuffle towards his direction and sit next to him. Bob's smile got even bigger now that I was by his side. He told me that he was glad that I had stopped by to see him. I was glad that I had stop by too, I told him. But I just couldn't stop thinking that I wished I had stopped by the apartment first; took a shower and changed. Bob could tell that I was a little uncomfortable. He introduced me to his older brother who I never got to meet when we first went together in high school because he was already out of the house and on his own. Then he introduced me to his brother's girlfriend who seemed very nice. I said my hellos then me and Bob made our way out to the front porch.

"Sorry that I smell like French fries", was the first thing out of my mouth to Bob. "You're okay" he told me, "I like French fries", he said. We both just laughed. "Stay here with me; I'll take you home later tonight". Mama and Peter's relationship, marriage, arrangement; or whatever you want to call it was far from perfect but I learned one thing from it, how a lady should always compliment the relationship. Always making it look good from all angles. When you go out you are to compliment his outfit with yours. You are to compliment his appearance by your own. Hair, face and attitude are always to be on point. And my mama did it well, very well. And at that moment I knew I was not in my lady swag. I had to fix this and with the quickness. I told Bob that I had needed to stop by the apartment to take a shower and change. Bob said okay but I had to promise him that I would really come back. I had to say it three times before he would let me out of his sight.

I got in the car and told Stacey that Bob had wanted me to stay but that I insisted that I go to the apartment and take a shower then return to him. "What are you going to tell RJ if he ask where you going", Stacey asked. Silence filled the car; I haven't even thought that far. I didn't want to lie to RJ. I hadn't done that before. I told Stacey that I didn't know. Seeing that I couldn't come up with a lie quick enough, Stacey suggested that I just tell RJ that I was going shopping with her. I was so deep in thought that I hadn't notice that Bob had come to my side of the car. Stacey on the other hand was excited enough for the both of us that she told Bob that she would bring me right back. I had butterflies all the way to the apartment.

It was hard for me to determine whether I was excited or scared. Maybe I was a little bit of both; I was excited to be seeing Bob but scared that RJ wouldn't let me leave without a fight. But to my surprise, RJ wasn't home. Good, that kept me from having to lie to him. I jumped out the car telling Stacey to give me twenty minutes. She nodded and turned the radio on. I didn't see RJ'S mom's car when we drove up and there was no sign of him when I went in the bedroom. I couldn't tell if he had not too long ago left or if he had been gone for most of the day. I jumped in the shower and was out in ten hoping the whole time that RJ wouldn't show up before I was able to leave. Twenty minutes later shower done, I'm dressed, hair done. I was out and there was no sign of RJ. I jumped in the car with Stacey. It felt like a Thelma and Louise moment. We made our way back to Seventh Street without a hitch.

Bob was exactly where I had left him; sitting on the porch. He came to the car to greet me and to assure Stacey that he would take good care of me and get me back safely. He thanked her for the past couple of weeks and gave her some money for the gas. Stacey gave Bob the evil eye and told him that he had better take care of me; putting her girlfriend infuses on "better". Yeah, I felt like the little baby chic leaving the nest for the first time. Stacey drove off leaving me in good hands.

The rest of day was spent laughing and talking with Bob as a lot of his friends were stopping by the house for this and that. His phone would constantly ring and whoever he was on the phone with he would tell them to swing by the house because he had company, so it was no longer a secret that I was there. It began to get real late and Bob said that he was hungry and asked me to accompany him to dinner and I done just that. There was no rush, time seemed to slow down and at times stop. I didn't have to work the next day and there was no school for two weeks. Dinner was lovely and though I was having fun, I didn't want to be rude. I knew that I had to go back to the apartment where I called home whether I preferred it or not. There were still some lose ends that I had to be tied up for good. Me and RJ hadn't officially called it quits so I still needed to show him some ounce of respect. I knew RJ had to have been wondering where I was since he hadn't seen or heard from me since seven o'clock that morning and that was on my way off to work. Hating to end the night I told Bob that I had needed to head back to the apartment. Reluctant to let me go but knowing my position and knowing that I wanted to do the right thing under the circumstances, Bob agreed. He said first that we had needed to stop back by his house so he could switch cars with his brother. I had gotten use to Bob doing that so I didn't object. Keith Sweat played on the car radio in the background while me and Bob talked and laughed.

When we got to the stop sign at the corner of Bob's street we stopped but as we turned the corner onto his street, I noticed the car behind us that was still sitting at the stop sign; it was RJ in his mom's car. I got the eerie feeling that RJ had been following us for some time or least since we left the restaurant. Not wanting to kill the mood but I had to warn Bob. "He's following us", I told Bob. "Who", he asked. "RJ", I said to him. "He's sitting there at the stop sign". Bob turned around to look back in the direction of the car at the stop sign. "Oh, that's who that is; he's been following us for a while". Bob pulled in front of his house but parked across the street. RJ pulled up behind us.

Bob turned the car off and we both just sat there for a minute. "Are you okay?" Bob asked me. I turned around and noticed that RJ hadn't gotten out of his car yet and the look on his face was not a happy one. I pleaded with Bob not to get out of the car. I told him if we were to get out of the car that RJ was going to fight me. Bob looked at me in shook; "he's going to do what?" Even though Bob and I had talked, I never told him how abusive RJ was to me and that's why I was leaving him. But in the following thirty seconds I told Bob everything. I found myself repeating to Bob that if I got out the car I knew RJ was going to fight me. I again begged Bob not to get out the car. I figured if we didn't get out the car that eventually RJ would just drive off and go home and I would just have to deal with the situation when I got back to the apartment. I didn't think that it was fair to Bob that he be put in the middle of our mess. Bob reached for his door and I reached for Bob's arm. I told Bob that I didn't want RJ to hurt him. Bob let out a little chuckle; "he's not going to hurt me and he's not going to hurt you anymore either". Bob grabbed my hand and told me that he wouldn't let RJ touch me ever again. That after tonight I would never have to fight RJ again; that he would protect me from him. That I didn't have to go back home with RJ if I didn't want to and that if I said so that he was my boyfriend now and that I would stay with him at his house. In that moment I was free and I told Bob that I didn't want to go back to RJ. Bob said okay that the matter was settled. He made a little joke amongst all the chaos because he said he loved to see my beautiful smile and for us to go in the house; that we couldn't stay in the car all night. But I still was unsure of things.

Minutes later there was RJ standing on my side of the car beating on the window with his fist yelling for me to get out of the car. I looked down at the door to make sure that it was locked so he couldn't just yank my door open. I wouldn't open my door so RJ went to try and open it but he couldn't. Bob yelled for RJ to get away from me and that if he wanted to talk, that RJ would have to talk to him because I had nothing else to say to him. RJ didn't move. I looked at RJ and yelled through the window for him to go away and to leave me alone. RJ said that he just wanted to talk to me but the look on his face said that he wanted to do more than just talk. RJ began to bite his lip and I became scared for my life. Bob yelled for RJ to get away from his car but this time Bob opened his door to make sure that RJ knew that he meant business and for him to moved away. I reached for Bob's shirt but it was too late. RJ had ran around to Bob's side of the car and soon as Bob stepped out the car RJ slid in behind him slid across the front seat, reached over and punched me in the face. Bob quickly reached in and grabbed RJ by the back of his neck, dragged him out the car and threw him down on the ground.

RJ got to his feet and told Bob that he only wanted to talk to me; well he already proved that wasn't all he wanted to do. Bob told RJ that I didn't want to talk to him. Bob closed the car door so that RJ couldn't get to me again and I reached over and locked it. Bob and RJ exchanged words again then RJ made the mistake of reaching for the car door trying to open it and Bob punched RJ in the face. The next thing I know; RJ and Bob were in the middle of the street fighting. I guess Bob's brother had heard all the commotion; he turned on the porch light and opened the front door. Bob had two guard dogs so when his brother opens the door to come outside; so did the dogs. Bob was holding his own and getting the best of RJ. The dogs ran out to the street and stood their position next to Bob as they barked and growled even circling the two waiting for Bob to tell them to attack.

RJ couldn't handle Bob anymore, so he backed off. RJ again said that he just wanted to talk to me as he tried to catch his breath. Bob looked over at me as I was still sitting in the car. He asked if I wanted to talk to RJ. No, I cried out to him. Bob told RJ to leave but he wouldn't and I knew he wouldn't until I said something to him. Despite everything, RJ did deserve the proper break up from me; it was only right. With all the commotion going in the middle of the street things got a little wilder because more of Bob's family had pulled up in a van. I became nervous, I didn't want RJ to get beat down and become part of the asphalt. My thought was I better help him before they kill him; I didn't want him to get jumped because of me. I slid over to the driver's side of the car and rolled down the window a little bit. I still wasn't sure that RJ wouldn't try to hit me but he would be crazy if he did. I yelled for RJ to go away and leave me alone and that it was over between us. RJ was still insisting on talking to me; I couldn't believe him. Bob walked over to the car and I looked up at him and explained that I knew RJ wouldn't go away until I talked to him. Hesitant, I reached to unlock the door and got out the car.

Bob stood by my side as well as the dogs. Bob told RJ that he could talk to me but that he had better not lay a hand on me. Everyone was standing guard just in case RJ didn't follow Bob's strict instructions. I made two steps forward towards RJ. I was soft spoken but meant every word. I looked into his eyes and told RJ that it was over that I didn't want to be with him anymore. RJ told me that he was sorry and asked me if I was sure that we were over. Like so many times before he promised that he would do better. He promised to get a job and even go back to school. He promised to never hit me again; oh, how many times had I heard that one before. RJ went on to say that we could work it out, but we couldn't and we wouldn't. I had already freed myself from RJ and I wasn't going back. I didn't want to spend the rest of my life hiding black eyes behind dark shades and ending up in protective shelters. Maybe the next time I wouldn't be so lucky to be in a shelter but end up in my grave; I wasn't willing to take that chance with my life anymore. My life was mines to keep. I told RJ that it was too late to try and that it was truly over.

I turned and walked back to Bob where I now knew that I was safe. RJ called out my name but Bob interrupted him and told him to leave now. The look of defeat showed on RJ's face. When he realized that this was really final and for real he became vindictive. He yelled for me to come and get my stuff out of the apartment or he would put it out on the street. Bob told RJ not to worry that I will be coming to pick up my things in the morning and that nothing had better be wrong with my stuff and that it had better all be there. Bob reminded RJ that I didn't want him anymore so for him to leave. The tone in Bob's voice made it clear that he wasn't going to ask RJ to leave again. Knowing that he had lost this fight; RJ got in his car and finally left.

I looked up to the sky and I told God thank you for keeping me alive and safe until I was able to see my way out of the situation that I had put myself in. I heard a voice say; that he would never leave me nor forsake me. The stars seemed to shine a little bit brighter that night. There wasn't much sleeping going on that night. Me and Bob talked about our plans for the future. Bob went in his pocket and pulled out a wad of money and dumped it in my lap. There had to be at least two thousand dollars there. Bob told me that he wanted to take care of me, that he was willing to give me all his money in order to do that. I scooped up all the money that was in my lap and put it back in Bob's hands. I told

Bob that I didn't want his money that I wasn't a gold digger and that even though I had heard that his pockets were deep because he was successful with his hustle of living off the land, that wasn't the reason why I wanted to be with him. I explained to Bob I just wanted him to love me, do right by me and promise that he would never lay a hand on me. He promised.

Dreading the task ahead, the next morning I was back at the apartment to get my things. But instead of arriving with Bob, he sent me with one of his friends to help me. Upon his mother's request not to go with me because she didn't want Bob fighting with RJ because of me and end up in jail. His mom made the statement that she wasn't sure if I was really leaving RJ or we were just having a lover's quarrel and maybe me and RJ would make up later and be back together. There was no chance of that but new mother-in-laws; you got to love them. I was busy carrying my things to the car while RJ was following behind him begging me to give him another chance. I really couldn't believe he was still carrying on the way that he was. Did he see that I came with a truck to get my stuff? Did he see the big guy that Bob sent with me to get my stuff and to make sure that he didn't bother with me? RJ finally got the message when he was told by Bob's friend to help him load my bedroom set onto the truck.

I left with my things loaded up in a truck, but more important I left with my heart not harden by the past two years. The truth be told, protecting myself is a one man's job; mine and from here on out I plan on doing my job.

# My Own
# Beginning......

# PART III

# Chapter 27

**THE FIRST TWO** years of me and Bob's relationship was wonderful. We were truly in love and inseparable. Young love is a beautiful thing. Bob even asked me to marry him but I told him no but that didn't stop him from continuously asking every couple of months. We had so much fun together. We went clubbing and partying all while living life without a care in the world. We hung out a lot in Davenport where Bob grew up and his mother still lived in the family house on Fuller Street. From the early morning until late at night we were there. I got an eye full of the street life and learned quickly life was no joke. I hadn't talked to my mother in a while so I gave her a call to let her know that I wasn't with RJ anymore and that I was now safe and going with Bob. She sounded very relieved but told me that I had needed to get myself together. So I took her advice and got myself back in school but that didn't last long because I couldn't stand being away from Bob.

It doesn't take long for reality to rear its ugly head and throw you a couple of curve balls. The house that Bob and his brother were living in was being reclaimed by the owner so we had to move. I didn't know where we were going to live. His brother was going to move in with his girlfriend and we couldn't stay with them. Bob seemed to not be concerned at all about the situation; I guess that was just his character; not to panic. I was the total opposite. Frantic and unsure I needed to go for a ride. I wasn't but halfway down the road before I started crying and asking the Lord what do I do now. Aimlessly driving and crying; the Lord guided me to a new apartment complex. I went in and applied for an apartment and to my surprise; I got the apartment. I rushed back to the house to tell Bob that I had found us a place to stay.

Life brought about changes; some I was ready for and others I wasn't so ready for. I quit my job at McDonald's in the County because I needed more money to pay the bills. So me and Bob got a job together at a new restaurant in the City. We were one of the young couples living in our own apartment. We had no furniture; only the new bedroom set that I had. Eventually Bob had found a dinette set to put in the kitchen so we could sit down and eat. We always eat at the restaurant so there was nothing but juice in our refrigerator. It would be a couple of months later before I would be able to afford to get some living room furniture. The world around me was moving fast and our lives were starting to intermingle with others' lives. I learned; when other people get in your personal business; it's no longer your business. Other people caused friction in our relationship but we did work our way through it.

After about a year, Bob lost his job at the restaurant and things started to fall apart. He tried to go back to his old hustle but not having a car to get to Davenport made it almost impossible. Money issues started to cause static between me and Bob. I didn't want to be poor; I made that very clear to Bob on more than one occasion. I had lived that life and I didn't want to relive it any time soon. But I found myself carrying the load of two much longer than I had cared to. Bills were coming in and I was the only one paying them and that left very little in my pockets. Bob did end up finding another job for a local furniture leasing company. But it was too late; eviction notices had been placed on the door. I moved out of the apartment, quit my job at the restaurant and moved in with Bob at his place. We lived in an old boy's school from the sixties that was converted into small apartments with no heat. We were cold but at least we were together; we would keep each other warm.

Young and in love is what we still were but it wasn't easy. We were still trying to figure out who we were as individuals. But Bob was always trying to keep a smile on my face. One day he surprised me with the cutest long ear puppy I had ever seen. I was sitting on the toilet; I couldn't finish peeing for trying to get to my new puppy. At times living on our own became a struggle and I had to call my mother for financial help. Bob and I shared a bank account put he really didn't understand the whole concept. You can't take more out then what you put in and you can't take money out the bank without writing it down so the next person can know what's left so they won't over spend. When I was getting returned checks in the mail, I didn't understand why until I sat down one day with my mother and went over my bank statement and all my bad checks. I just started to cry after I realized what had happened. I immediately took Bob's name off the bank account and that was the last time I mixed my money with a man.

Every now and then mama would slide me fifty dollars so that I could buy groceries. Things started getting harder for us when Bob car broke down and we couldn't get it fixed. We managed to scrap up three hundred dollars to get a car from a buy here pay here lot. Bob's license was suspended so that left me to get the car in my name. I didn't know you couldn't buy a car with only restricts but the salesman gave me the car anyway and just told me to go and get my driver's license within the next thirty days. That's when I discovered that a pretty smile and big boobs can get you far. I tell you; Life is the best teacher that you can have.

Having a car gave me so much freedom. With Bob hanging in Davenport so much which quickly became overrated to me and I had had my fill of seeing the street life and I knew I wanted no part of it; I would grab some of my girlfriends and head up to my mother's house and hang out at the pool. But my freedom was cut short when I flipped and totaled my car one day when I was taking my friend job hunting. I think I drifted off for a second and the car started to drift off the road. When I tried to drive the car back onto the road I turned the wheel too hard causing my little Horizon to slowly flip. It was turning so slow I thought it was going to change its mind and land on all fours. But instead it sat with all fours in the air. I thought I had killed my friend who lay still on the side of the road after I had pulled her out of the car. After a day in the hospital and a free ride from the ambulance and she was fine.

A couple of weeks later I went and found a job and Bob found us a new place for us to stay. There was a three bedroom one bathroom house that was for rent that was across the street from where he worked. I remember mama telling me that I needed to do better and so I figured that I was but I didn't have any money for a deposit for the house and first month's rent. But I knew I wanted to live in the house, I was tired of living in that cold apartment; so I gave her a call. The following week she met me at the house with the owner. Mama gave me the money that I needed to get the house; I guess it was about three hundred dollars that she gave me. As mama was driving off, she told me not to ask her for anything else. She acted like the money she gave me came out her pocket but I figured it didn't because I know she was still getting checks for me. And if the money did come out her pocket than all she was going to do was put it back in her pocket later when she got my check the next month. But I did as she asked.

Me and Bob moved into our new place. With no car, thank God that everything was just across the street; Bob's job, the grocery store, Eckerd's and the laundry mat. After catching a ride to work for about eight months; I finally got up two hundred dollars for a down payment for another car. Things were going good, so good in fact; that Bob talked about wanting to start a family. We tried for several months with no success. I didn't think it fair to deprive Bob of having a child to carry on his last name, so I gave him permission to get another woman pregnant. But he only told me that if I couldn't have kids then he wouldn't either.

In the summer of '91 I became very ill with what I thought was the summer flu. I was throwing up everywhere, not able to keep anything down. Not even the special tea that Bob had cooked up for me to drink; five minutes later it came back up. But I was so weak at times that I couldn't even walk. Bob would have to help me across the street to use the phone to call into work sick. Unknowns to me it wasn't the flu that had me so sick; I was pregnant. They called it morning sickness but they should have named it; all day sickness. Some days I felt as if I was going to die. It had gotten to the point that I didn't want to be left alone. So Bob would leave me at his sister's place so she could keep an eye on me while he went and ran the streets. This went on for weeks. I was so happy that I was pregnant and so was Bob, but I don't think that he was as ready for parenthood.

My idea of a happy family quickly started to be tarnished by Bob's obsession with me paying him back every time I got money from him to buy something for the baby; what father does that? I thought both parents were financially responsible for the child; I quickly found out that Bob didn't. Then a couple of months into my pregnancy he stopped being home after work. As soon as he got off of work he would come home; take a shower, change clothes and be right back out the door. He always had somewhere that he needed to be besides home. It got to the point I wouldn't see Bob until two or three the next morning. He started partying with his friends a lot. And we all know what goes hand in hand with partying. It got so bad Bob started making excuses to get out the house. Once he said that he wanted to take up boxing so in order to get in shape he wanted to start jogging at night. Bob use to leave eleven o'clock at night to go jogging. I have yet to see Bob in the boxing ring. It was obvious that Bob was hanging out with just more than the boy's. There was a note left behind by one of his female admirer's on the car. According to the note she left behind, she was mad that Bob didn't show up for one of their nightcaps. Yes I was hurt by the letter and I told Bob that he needed to handle the situation. He did but it wasn't long before he was back at it again. At one point Bob wouldn't use an excuse at all he would just have someone come and pick him up and he would literally run out the house. I mean literally run and jump in the car that was waiting for him. By me being six months pregnant; running wasn't one of my functions so by the time I would get to the front door all I would see is tail lights and sounds of screeching tires.

I was seven months pregnant when there was an eviction notice placed on our door which was a surprise to me because Bob never mentioned that he hadn't been paying the rent. When we first moved into the house me and Bob agreed that he would pay the rent and I would take care of utilities and food. I guess with all the partying that he was doing; he forgot our arrangement. I was able to talk the landlord into an agreement that I would divide up the past due rent and include it in future paying of the rent that I would now pay. He agreed and we didn't get kicked out. But I don't think that putting a pregnant woman out on the street was something that he wanted on his conscience. So since I took over paying rent; Bob took on the responsibility of paying utilities and buying food. Eight months pregnant and I was sitting in the dark; Bob didn't pay the light bill. I was devastated and disappointed with Bob. I felt like we no longer had a home. I began to understand that I could no longer depend on Bob to do right by me. I started to form my own since of security for myself.

With no money to get the lights turned back on, Bob asked his aunt who also had his dad living with her because Bob's parents had gotten a divorce; if I could spend the night. Seeing my condition of course she said yes. Bob didn't stay; he went back home. What he did or where he stayed that night; I really couldn't tell you. Bob made me feel like a load of clothes he had just dropped off at the cleaners and would be back tomorrow to claim. Bob left without looking back. That evening I sat on the porch enjoying the cool breeze and listening as Bob's aunt and dad gave me a few pointers about how life worked. I finally understood that Life didn't play by any rules but its own and because it did; it could change them at any time. That Life only had to answer to itself and that it didn't have to answer for anything if it didn't want to. Life was not fair because it was not asked to be. Life was not concerned with my well-being or my happiness. Life's only job was to be and nothing else.

I took a shower, ate a little something and got ready for bed. I stood in a dark room feeling just as empty as the night air. I was in a stranger's house because of her kindness but I was feeling alone and abandon. Bob said that he would protect me, take care of me. But here I stood with our baby forming inside of me without him. I felt like he passed me on to someone else to be responsible for me. Feeling weary and broken; I pulled back the sheets to crawl into bed but, I fell to my knees instead. I noticed a bible which sat on the night stand. I called out to God for his name was all I could utter. I cried as I rubbed my stomach remembering the promise that I had made to myself when I was a little girl; that I would be a better mother than my own to my child than my mother was to me; that I would let no one harm him or allow harm to come to him. I bowed my head over the bible and watched as my tears landed on its cover. I flipped the bible open to nowhere particular and in His word he reminded me that he had never left me and I could call on him anytime and he would be right there to comfort me. I prayed to God hoping that he would understand that I didn't know what I was doing and that I didn't know what tomorrow held for me but if he would just guide me through that I would follow him. I crawled into bed rocking my baby and myself to sleep.

In the next couple of weeks a lot had changed. Bob's dad had bought and moved into his own house and Bob sister moved in with him. Me and Bob were back at home now and Bob had an idea to rent out a room to one of his friends to help us out with paying the rent. Having strangers in my house didn't sit well with me being that I was mostly home alone all the time. But for the most part Bob's friend was quiet and always paid the rent to Bob on time. When you're pregnant your hormones changes your normal senses into mush. I don't know what brand of shaving cream Bob's friend would use but it would make me sick to my stomach every time he would use it. And let's not talk about the cigarettes he smoked that would make a dead man gag. He tried to stay isolated in his room when he did smoke but it didn't help. Late one night about two in the morning I was in the kitchen getting a glass of water. The front door came open and there was Bob's friend pushing a mountain bike into the house. I stood quietly in the dark drinking my water watching him. I knew that he didn't own a bike so it seemed kind of strange to me. But then whose bike was it? It belonged to the blonde crack head prostitute he was sneaking into my house two o'clock in the morning; suddenly I wasn't thirsty anymore. My jaw dropped when I saw her. It was dark but I could tell that he was still dirty. I watched on as he told her to try and be quiet as they tipped toed to his room; bike and all. I ran back to my bedroom where Bob was in a deep sleep. I woke him up and told him what I had just saw and told him that he had three seconds to go and tell his friend to get that crack head and her bike out of my house. Bob did it in two.

A couple of weeks later Bob's roommate was gone and we had a huge Doberman pinscher mix guard dog that we named Precious. Bob had gotten her from one of his friends. She was a beautiful and gentle dog and kept me company many of nights when Bob wasn't home. The funny thing about Precious was that she didn't like white people. I thought that was funny because that's who Bob got her from. The only time we had trouble out of Precious is when Bob's friend from work Donny would come over. She would never let him step foot in our yard. We always knew when Donny was outside because that's the only time Precious would bark. She was loyal, I have to give her that much. Precious would get up every hour and make her rounds about the house and then come and lay by my side of the bed. I had isolated myself to my bedroom because the house seemed too big for me to be there alone, plus it was closer to the bathroom. My poor bladder wasn't dependable for more than two feet. I was scared of Precious, I will admit because she was so big but she protected me never the less.

Bob's dad use to come by in the early evenings at least twice a week looking for Bob but he was never home. Bob's dad would try to make the best of his trip across town and we could talk about whatever events were going on. I felt bad for his dad after coming all that way for nothing. There were times when I would go and hang out at Bob's job for the last couple of hours of his shift just to see him. Bob and his boss became very good friends so he didn't mind me being there.

St. Patrick's Day came and went no baby like the doctor had told me only labor pains that came every ten minutes which I had Bob scribble down each time. My sister-in-law asked me if I wanted to go to the hospital I thought I better. But not being two cm dilated; the doctor sent me back home. Day two of labor my sister-in-law had me walking up and down street hills but with no progress just more labor pains. Day three of labor my labor pains left me speechless, but my mother-in-law insisted I not go to the hospital until I passed a plug; whatever the hell that meant. I didn't lay in a hospital bed that night instead I laid in hers trying to sleep through the pain. With every pain I felt it woke me and my vision was fixed or a needle point rug with the face of Jesus that hung on the wall. My only words were, "yes Lord" when I was awaken with pain and He was the only one I saw and in the room with me at my most tender moment. On March 20th first day of spring when everything is new; God blessed me with a baby boy. As my son entered the world; tears of joy streamed down my face as my baby boy took his first breath. He was three days late but as I lay on the delivery table hearing my son's first cries. All I could remember saying was, "do you hear my baby? Can you hear my baby?" His cries were the sweetest sound to my ears. The doctor placed my baby in my arms. A beautiful gift was entrusted to me. Bob was there in the delivery room as the proud daddy he was and of course we named the baby after him. I was grateful to Bob for not letting me go through that alone. I couldn't wait to take my baby home and start our family.

That day would come after a three day stay at the hospital. We arrived at the house and learned that the electricity had been cut off that morning. I felt defeated and wondered how Bob was ever going to make a place for his family to stay and grow. I knew he wouldn't be able to. So, I made up in my mind that I would have to be the one to do it because now I wasn't just responsible for myself; I had someone else depending on me; my son. But until then we stayed at his mothers who made us sleep in separate rooms. Which I didn't understand at all; we had a baby together what more harm could we do. I gave my mother a call to let her know that I had had my baby. She came to visit me and stayed all of five minutes. She came baring no gifts for her second grandson and her third grandchild. She didn't even bother to hold him. My mother just commented on how my baby had fat feet. That night all I could do was remember that my baby was my first priority. As I lay their starring at the ceiling; I noticed a spider the size of my hand crawling across the wall above us; my mother instincts quickly kicked in. I was afraid but I had to protect my baby. I grabbed my shoe cursed the spider as I mashed it against the wall killing it. I looked down at my baby as to say; "you're safe, mama's here".

My hormones were so out of control all I did for the first couple of weeks after my baby's birth was cry; I was so miserable. Bob wasn't there much during the day; he was too busy hanging out in the streets. He would come through every couple of hours and stay for five minutes and then back outside with the boys he would go. One night Bob on his run through visits, he handed me the phone saying that someone wanted to talk to me. Puzzled that someone would be calling me, I slowly received the phone. It was two giggling chicken heads calling the house saying that they had a baby from Bob too and wanted child support. My blood started to boil because I knew that I was the only one who had a child by Bob but people like to play jokes and I knew better. I asked the chic on the other end of the phone; what was she calling me for than?, to call Bob. Better yet go to his job. But that I better not see her there or I was going to beat her down. I told her I didn't know whose child she had but it wasn't Bob's. I threw the phone back at Bob because I was mad at him for even handing me the phone knowing what was going on.

I already felt so unequipped for motherhood. My own mother left me with no words of wisdom and Bob's mother didn't make matters any better. She was always talking down to me when it came to matters with the baby like I didn't have common sense. I know this was my first baby, but I knew where the bottle was supposed to go. And after only two weeks she wanted to add cereal to my baby's formula. I think if I would have stayed any longer she would have had him sitting at the table eating grits. I was willing to take my chances and learn by trial and error; I was ready to go home. First thing first; I had to introduce my new born son to a friend of mine. Easter morning I stood in my Lord's house with my head bowed; tears running down my face and my new born son in my arms. I stood there thanking God for keeping me, asking him for forgiveness, and promising him my life.

Eventually me and Bob made our way back to our house with our new baby. The lights were back on and now I had to make this house a home for my family. But it wasn't as easy as I thought it was going to be. Bob still wasn't staying at home and I got tired of being home alone, so I found myself hanging out with my sister-in- law at her father's house.

This was a very bad idea. I started to look for and found company with someone other than Bob. Where do broken hearts go? I know it was wrong and I was weak, but it served him right for leaving me alone all the time. Well, one night the shit hit the fan. When the dust settled a boot was left lying in the middle of the street with no one around to claim it. In a way I was a glad that Bob found out. It made him straighten up and pay attention to his family more.

Settling into motherhood wasn't hard at all with time I got the hang of it. My son was three months old and things were good, that was until one day I got a knock on my front door. You nor I would have guessed in a million years who was standing on my front doorstep when I opened the door with my son in my arms; it was Peter. I didn't even know he even knew where I lived. What the hell was he doing at my front door? I stood there staring at him as he made small talk with me. I felt scared. I didn't know if he would try to come in my house and do something to me. I could only remember feeling like this when I was a child waiting for Big Willie to come and whoop me with that thick weight belt. But then I heard a voice say, "you're not that little girl anymore; you're a mother now." My mother instincts kicked in; I had to protect my child but also show Peter that I wasn't that scared little girl. I smiled at Peter and introduced him to my son to let him know that I had something important in my life. Peter showed no interest and kept going on about nothing. It was almost as if he came to apologize but he couldn't find the words to. I told Peter that I had to go and that I would appreciate if he never come to my house again. He said he could respect that. I closed the door and locked it. I squeezed my son so close to my chest; I didn't know if I was assuring him that he was okay or assuring me that I was.

Dj was six month's old now and Bob had been hanging around the house more since he lost his job at the furniture place. A couple of weeks have passed and he hasn't found a job. That's because he hadn't been looking. I've been doing the best I could with paying the bills and buying food for the house. I couldn't afford the furniture anymore without Bob's store discount so I had to let it go back. After sitting on the floor for a week or two; Bob had brought home a small ugly green square couch and love seat that he had found on a garbage pile. I was so horrified by the thought that we had gotten that poor that he was picking through trash piles to survive. I didn't say anything to him; I just made the best of it because he seemed so proud of the fact that he had solved our problem of not having any furniture. The one couch he brought home had a big dip in it so I had to pile pillows underneath the cushions so we wouldn't fall in when we sat on it. This was not what I had pictured for my life so I thought that I had better have a talk with him. We talked, then that turned into an argument, which turned into me breaking up with him, which turned into me kicking him out, which turned into him making promises to find a job, which turned into us making up and out. Dj was eight months old and I was pregnant again and homeless.

Bob decided that we needed a fresh start while he looked for a new job. We put our stuff in storage but I told Bob to throw that ugly green sofa and loveseat back on the trash pile where he found it and we moved in with his father. It was a tense situation. His father hadn't had the house for long before his daughter had moved in and not long after that his own sister moved in. It was like he never got a chance to enjoy his new house before everyone decided they wanted to move in; now here we came with a baby and a big dog. Some relieve came when his sister had moved out and got her own place and his aunt who I had spent the night with that one time; she had moved in because the house that she was living in she was going to buy but the owners changed their mind. We decided on the amount that I would pay Bob's father every two weeks. I could tell that his father really didn't mind us there but preferred for us not to be but the money that he was receiving from us was too good to pass up. Bob eventually got a job where I was working but I still continued to pay his father because Bob felt he shouldn't have too. The first couple of months were okay but then things changed. Every time I would pay the rent for the week Bob's father would find a reason to get upset and want to tell us we had to get out. That was confusing to me because we hadn't done anything wrong. He didn't want us sitting in the living room. The television had to go off when he went to bed. Every day when he would come in from work, he would check the refrigerator to see what food we ate or any juice we drunk. One day he even fussed at me for washing my hair in the kitchen sink. I've never known any place else to wash hair. My mama always washed my hair in the kitchen sink. Dirty dishes and dirty dish water, uncooked chicken and fish could be put in the sink, but he had a problem with me washing my hair in the sink. To me with all the shampoo lather; that helped cleaned the sink out. But I wasn't just getting grief from his father; Bob started acting up when he bought himself a car.

He had bought this canary yellow 83 Cadillac; you would have thought this boy had a Porsche the way he was carrying on. Then to make matters worse, he put rims on the car and had a red light for the interior.

Bob loved his car so much that he wouldn't park it in the driveway; he parked it by the bedroom window in front of the house. Every night around two in the morning you would see headlights on the bedroom wall because Bob was just now coming home and parking his car. He never let me drive it and I was rarely in it. Only when we went to Kissimmee to take DJ to visit my mother; did I get a chase to ride in Bob's prize possession. Because mama never came to visit me, I could tell that we didn't have a strong relationship and we hadn't for a long time. Her and my sister on the other hand had a great relationship. It seemed like once my mother left Polk County she had no intentions of coming back.

One night while Bob was at the club someone stole his car. He was sick for two days, I mean literally sick. He would not eat and he was glued to the phone waiting for a call from the police to tell him that they found his car. It was a sad sight watching him mope around. He didn't hold his son, he didn't feed his son, and he didn't even talk to his son or even me for that matter. His only concern was for his car. It was pitiful to see a grown man mourn over a material thing then he would pay attention to his family. I thought it served Bob right that his car was stolen; something needed to get his attention away from that car. He was a father now but he hadn't been acting like one; going out every night and coming home in the mist of the morning dew. I didn't feel sorry for his lost because he treasured that stupid car more than me and his son. Two days later, he finally got the call that he was waiting for and miraculously he came back alive. He recovered his car, cleaned it up and picked up his activities right where he left off. He didn't learn a damn thing. He didn't see what was more important than that stupid car. But his reunion with his car would be short lived; it was stolen two more times and after the third time, Bob had finally had enough. When the police found the car and told him of its locations, Bob went there and just took any personal belongs of his that the thieves may have left behind which wasn't much of anything. I had just bought DJ a very nice car seat and they took that. I could only assume the thieves had a baby too. Bob walked away from his car leaving it in its woody grave. Bob wrote it off and said that the car was bad luck.

I was at my wits end with the way Bob's father was treating me and the way Bob was treating me and our son. I had to take charge of my situation. I learned that when people think that you need them they think that gives them the right to treat you any kind of way but, God bless the child that got his own. I didn't want Bob to disrespect his father but at least speak up for his family; but he did neither. He just sat there while his father treated us like we weren't family. I wasn't going to continue to let him throw our not having a place to stay or go in our face. I went to my sister-in-law so she could school me.

Since I was a single parent; there were a lot of programs to help with housing, food, and school and I wanted to know it all. She pointed me in the right direction. I reminded myself that I was only going to be in the system until I could do better. I quickly learned and understood the system and even worked it. Everyone knew that the girlfriend and her babies got the apartment; meantime the boyfriend stayed under the radar while "visiting". The system was made to help people get on their feet. But unfortunately a lot of people have chosen to make the system their lifestyle and sit on their butts. I put down a deposit with my last paycheck from work along with my first welfare check and got the lights turned on for my one bedroom apartment for me and my baby. I asked for a two bedroom but there wasn't any available so I got put on a waiting list and moved into the one bedroom. Rent was only twenty-five dollars a month and Bob refused to even cover that. He was still doing his Davenport hustle, so it wasn't like he didn't have the money. If there was one thing that Bob was good at; it was hustling. But I never understood why he wouldn't go and get a job. I guess he figured since my welfare check covered all the bills that he didn't have to work. But I made it very clear to Bob that I didn't like him hustling. There was a time and a place for everything. I could understand when he was single and not responsible for anyone but himself; that was his choice to put his life out there. But now that he has a baby, another one on the way and a girlfriend; his life was no longer just his. At one point I thought all boyfriends hustled. All the girls I knew their boyfriends hustled too. I figured only married men with a house and kids had jobs.

When I moved into my one bedroom; there was no lock on the

door; not even a door knob, but I didn't care. Bob said that he wasn't going to stay there and I told him that I didn't care but that I was. There was a broken stove that sat in the middle of the living room. When Bob left; I closed the front door, pushed the broken stove in front of it, made a pallet on the living room floor with some blankets that I had brought, said my prayers and me and my baby slept under the stars by the sliding glass door because I had no curtains to hang. I was so proud to be in my own place and I knew God would keep us safe. I didn't care that there was no door knob or lock on the door. I would have lived in a cardboard box then to stay one more night with Bob's father; and he called himself a Christian.

Two days later the maintenance crew came to put locks on the door. They were shocked when they learned that I had stayed there. They were going on and on how brave they thought I was for doing that. If they only knew at that point it was either the apartment or a cardboard box under the bridge. Bob helped me move the little stuff that we had in storage into my apartment. The only thing I really had was my bedroom suite that I had when I had left RJ, dishes and some towels. Again I found myself making a place a home. Sheets hung to my windows in the place of curtains for a while. Donated furniture came from his sister and at first I politely declined the idea but Bob insisted. The furniture came with its own family of roaches. It took me two months to evict them.

I was twenty-two years old with a twelve month old and I was three months pregnant with another one sitting at home. The first two weeks of the month everyone would be happy and outside moving around. BBQ grills would be going. Much shrimp, steak, and ribs were being eaten in the projects. Then about the third week things got quiet. Food stamps started running low and money even lower. About that fourth week, you could hear a pin drop. There were times when I didn't even have formula to feed my baby. I found myself doing things in order to survive. It became hard for me to even look at Bob in the face and acknowledge him as the man in my life. When I was six months pregnant Bob went back to his old ways and started coming home two o'clock in the morning. Since I was paying all the bills and the rent; I saw no reason to give Bob a key to the apartment. One morning when he knocked on the door so I could let him in and then knocked on the bedroom window so I could let him in after I didn't answer the door; I told him to go away and never come back. That me and my babies would do just fine without him. So Bob found himself back at home with his dad and aunt. That night I sat in a chair starring into the dark night sky with only the moonlight shinning on me. I prayed until the sun came up.

With me going on maternity leave from work, I quickly fell into a daily routine for me and my baby and for the most part I was content with the situation. I cooked eggs, bacon and toast every morning for breakfast. We watched our morning cartoons along with the kid's shows like Nick Jr and Sesame Street. Then it was time for morning game and talk shows and then DJ would lay down for his afternoon nap. The news would come on then around one o'clock it was time for lunch. Something like a cheese toast or a ham and cheese sandwich. And then my stories- Young and the Restless, Bold and the Beautiful, As the World Turns and the grand finale the Guilding Light. They would have my full attention for the next four hours. When the stories went off more talk shows came on and it was time for me to prepare dinner. By the time the evening news came on, it was time for dinner. After cleaning up the kitchen it was time to have a relaxing evening watching sitcoms. This went on for the next two months without a snag and I enjoyed every minute of it. Saturdays were a little different only because it was laundry day. I had no car so finding a ride is where Bob would help out at occasionally when he was in a good mood.

But then there I was like everybody else at the first of the month waiting on the mailman. Walking to the food stamp office and waiting in line to pick up my stamps became so dreadful. Eight months pregnant and DJ barely beginning to walk made the trip ten times worse. There I was walking along the street with one baby on my hip and the other on my bladder. I saw myself becoming exactly what I said that I didn't want to be; some chic living in the projects with kids and no daddy. I guess one weekend I had over done it, I started having labor pains. I went to the phone to call Bob at his dad's but of course he wasn't home and his aunt answered the phone. She insisted that she come and get me and that I stay with them until the baby was born. It did make sense because I was scared. Me being there with Bob didn't slow down his partying. He still stayed out all night, drinking and doing whatever he was doing. Bob never asked me if I had needed anything for the baby while I was there. So I suggested that he buy the baby basinet and get back in good grace with his aunt because she was not pleased at all with the way her nephew had been carrying on for the past few months. Two weeks had passed and Bob still had not bought the basinet. My second child was due September 4; I ended up buying my baby's basinet September 1st when I got my monthly check; Bob was not wearing fatherhood well at all. Bob not buying one thing for the baby did hurt me but it was what he didn't care to do; that would make me build a wall between me and Bob forever.

I was awakening from my sleep late one night; not for any other reason but that I had to pee. I noticed that Bob wasn't lying in the bed next to me but I wasn't surprised, he was doing what he did best. I couldn't go back to sleep so I went in the living room and watched television. I looked at the clock it was September the fourth, five after one o'clock in the morning. When the clock hit two, Bob walked in the door and I started having contractions at that very second. It was as if the baby was waiting for his daddy to come home. Bob went straight to the bedroom as if he didn't see me sitting in the chair next to the door and threw himself across the bed and passed out. I sat there in the chair to make sure what was happening was really happening. And it was; my baby was coming.

I went and took a shower and got dressed. I went and sat back in the living room in the chair by the door. I said a prayer and then I went to wake Bob up to tell him that it was time to take me to the hospital because the baby was coming. Bob just mumbled something and rolled over. I went back to the chair in the living room and quietly sat there as tears ran down my face. It was three thirty now and the contractions had not stopped. I looked in on Bob as I passed by the bedroom on my way to his aunt's room; he was still passed out. I knocked on his aunt's door and told her what was going on. She asked where Bob was, I told her he was in the bedroom. She got out of bed calling for Bob. When he didn't answer her she went to his room and there he lay like I had left him. She called his name again but louder. He rolled over to look at her or at least in her direction. She told him that he had needed to get up and take me to the hospital, that the baby was coming. But she only got a mumble as I did earlier and he rolled back over. His aunt was very upset by Bob but right now he would have to wait. I just stood there looking at Bob as he lay drunk strolled across the bed. I was in a lot of pain so I went back in the living room and sat in the chair by the front door. I rocked through the pain and prayed through my displacement, anger, and confusion. Aunt Lola went and got dressed but afterwards she took one last chance to wake Bob. She saw that he was in no condition to drive so she suggested that she drive and he at least ride to the hospital with us and that his father would watch DJ until she got back. Bob never moved. When she realized he wasn't even listening she told me to come on so she could take me to the hospital before I had the baby on the living room floor waiting on Bob and his drunken ass. She just shook her head and grabbed her car keys. We got in the car and Aunt Lola drove straight to Bartow without stopping. I swear to you every traffic light was green straight through. I knew then that God was with us and was making a safe path for me to make it to the hospital with my child.

We arrived at the hospital and I was checked in. Aunt Lola looked so worried and upset. I could see the disappointment in her eyes at the whole situation. I grabbed her hand and held it. I reassure her that I was okay and I thanked her for bringing me to the hospital. I told her to go home now and for her to get some rest. She squeezed my hand and smiled. The nurse wheeled me to my room and tried to get me comfortable. It was four o'clock and I was in so much pain that the medicine that they gave me just made me pass out. When I awoke I had an oxygen mask on my face and the nurse was telling me that it was time for me to push. My second son; Dominique LaMar Penick was born two o'clock that afternoon. When the doctor showed me my new born son, he was the splitting image of his brother. He wasn't crying but when I looked into his eyes I said "yes, this is my child". It was just me and him in that very moment.

Later as I lay back in my room recovering from the birth of my son, I was saddened because I was alone. I was mad because Bob couldn't get his self together enough to be there for the birth of his second son which he named. Tears fell as I wondered where my life would go from here. I remember looking up at the clock; it was four o'clock in the afternoon and the phone in my room rang. I answered and it was Bob on the other end. He asked me how I was doing but I had no words for him. Just the sound of his voice made me cry. I was so devastated and my heart was filled with so much pain. I remember the promise that he made to me and I realized then that promises were made to be broken. Bob asked me about the baby but I only sat there in silence because my pain became too much for me to handle. I finally let myself speak to assure him that his son was just fine and I hung up the phone.

They didn't bring me my son right away for his first feeding because the doctors informed me that he was having trouble keeping his body temperature. Around eight that evening the nurse bought me a baby but it wasn't mine; it was a white baby with beautiful blue eyes. I was in a panic and I alerted the nurse and demanded her to go back to look for my son. Where is my baby? Is someone else holding him? Is he crying? I had planned on breastfeeding him so I hope no one was feeding him. Minutes later she did come back with my son and assured me that he was safe because he was still in the nursery. I looked the baby over before I reached for him from the nurse and yes it was my son. I looked down at my son; he seemed to be a gentle soul. He was a little thing and he was quiet. We bonded in our moment and I promised him that I would always be there for him and his brother; that I would scale the end of the earth to get to them and dared anyone to stop me. That I would protect them in life; even if it meant giving up my own. That they shall be free to laugh and play. Allowed to develop their mind, build their body and protect their soul. I know my strength shall come from the sound of their laughter. My arms shall extend to them for comfort, my mind open for understanding and my heart shall endure. I would make a place for them that was free from fear; this was a mother's love.

A couple of days later Bob arrived at the hospital to take us home. Bob thought it be best that we stay at his dad's house for a couple of weeks instead of my apartment. When Aunt Lola saw my baby for the first time, she gave him the nickname Survivor; recalling the chaotic night of his birth. But still not being over the pain of Bob not being there at the hospital of Dominique's birth, there were very few words spoken between him and myself. My pain was still so deep and fresh that even when Bob did try to talk to me the sound of his voice made my claws come out and I just wanted to attack. I could feel the dark and angry being that I had buried away in me so long ago start to take form in me again. And I started to welcome it. I was weak and vulnerable; I needed something to protect me now. I felt like up to this point I had been silent and nice and that my kindness had been mistaken as a weakness.

I guess Bob's dad had got the impression that we were trying to move back in with him but he was so far from the truth. He started acting like he was irritated by our presence in his home. I overheard him and Bob having a conversation in the kitchen. He told Bob that he couldn't afford to feed me and my kids. But the funny thing was, I never recalled anyone asking him to. I told Bob that I didn't want to be a burden to anyone and for him to take me home to my own apartment. I thanked Aunt Lola for all her help and kindness packed up my things and my two babies and went home; Bob came too.

It was the four of us in a one bedroom apartment. When my baby boy turned six weeks old, I quickly returned back to work. My mother never checked on me or came to see me while I was in the hospital, so my baby would be two months old before she would see him, and that's only because I took him so she could see her grandson. She spent plenty of time with her other grandchildren so I didn't understand why she never made an effort to spend time with mine. But I guess that's a matter for another chapter.

Going back to work was bitter sweet; I had to put my babies in daycare while I worked. Dropping them off to strangers was the worst feeling but knowing that I would be back to pick them up when I got off of work didn't make the situation any easier. I would wonder all day if they were being treated right; was someone changing their diaper, singing and talking to them or feeding them at the right times. Or were they just lying around starring at the ceiling waiting for me to come back and get them. Needless to say; Bob and I were making it work with our little family but I could feel that I had lost faith in him. I no longer believed that he could be the man in my life for me or the father to his children that he needed to be. Bob is not willing to help financially and I'm not willing to beg him to. It had gotten to the point that I paid for everything. Bob kept his money in his pocket for his recreational purposes which literally kept his head in a cloud of smoke. My disappointment with Bob has turned into anger and resentment. But I refuse to let my kids suffered for his shortcomings and do without. I even would wonder if I would be better off with another man. My mind would picture me in a relationship with another man but I could never take my sons away from their father. So I stayed with Bob. There is tension between us but, my house was filled with the laughter of my children and their diapers and I loved being a mama. It wouldn't be until early one cold November morning that I would find out just how much.

We were all dressed and ready to head out of the door so that me and Bob could go to work right after dropping the babies off at daycare. The morning was very chilly so Bob thought to kill two birds with one stone; let the car warm up and pack up the car. Bob had experiences in the past with people stealing his car so he would park his car at our patio door in the back of our apartment building instead of in the parking lot. So Bob went outside to start the car so it could warm up and he took DJ with him who at the time was only two years old. I stayed behind in the apartment getting the diaper bag and the baby ready for daycare. After about ten minutes Bob came back in to see if I was ready to go. I asked him where was DJ and he told me that he had already put him the car. I looked out at the car and you could tell that it was still cold by all the smoke that was coming out from the exhaust pipe. I gathered up a couple of things and threw the diaper bag over my shoulder and went to pick up my baby boy from off the couch as he laid there asleep all wrapped up. Bob went to check the front door to make sure it was locked and I started to head to the car. I must have only taken two steps onto the patio when the next thing I knew the car that was once parked I watched take off.

I screamed for Bob as I watched in horror as the vehicle took off ahead of me. With my baby boy in my arms and still screaming for Bob; I ran after the car. Seconds later; Bob joined me in the chase. I saw that I couldn't catch the car so I stopped running and let Bob take suit. In a panic I ran back in the house to lay my baby boy back down on the couch. When I came back outside I could see that Bob was still chasing after the car with my little boy DJ in it. The car had run through a chain linked fence. Bob never stopped running after the car. I watched as if I was looking at a movie but then somehow I became the narrator. The car was headed straight for a tree and I knew if the car was to hit the tree at the speed that it was going that my little boy who was now standing in the driver seat looking back as his daddy chase the car; would fly through the front window and I didn't want that to happen. I did the only thing that I knew to do and that was talk to God; my Father which was in heaven. No I wasn't praying; I was talking to him. Lord; you are my way maker.

I said, "Lord, dont let my baby boy hit the tree." And before my eyes the tree split in half and the car went straight through it and never touching its sides. My heart stop for then I knew God was with me. All I could say was thank you Lord. The car was still racing forward and Bob was still chasing behind it. At one point he managed to get beside the car. Trying to catch the door handle; Bob would reach out, but the car was too idled up to slow down that he would miss. Something caught my eye as I looked ahead at the path in front of the car. There sat the large green electric box and I knew if the car were to hit it that there would have been an explosion and I didn't want that. I said, " Lord, don't let my baby boy hit the electric box." And at that very second it was as if the Lord took a hold of the steering wheel of that car and steered it to the left. The car went right pass the electric box. My spirit rejoiced for I knew that God was with me. But the car was still racing and Bob was still chasing the car and there Ahead laid the busy highway of 544. I knew if the Bob didn't catch up to the car soon that there would be a terrible accident and I didn't want that. So I said, "Lord, don't let my baby boy go out into the road." The car was full speed by this time and it looked like Bob was out of breath but he never stopped running. The car went down and came back up out off of the side road ditch as if someone had shot it out of a canon. But at that very instance when the front wheel touched the white line of the border of the road, it was as if God had pressed the pause button because that car did not move. Even though the engine was still running that car was frozen in its place. My soul cried out because I knew that God was with me. No one has to tell me about God because I know him for myself. I Am... My Father's Child.

Bob finally caught up to the car and dove in the driver's side window that was down. He quickly put the car in park and got my son out of the car who was laughing never thinking that anything was wrong but that daddy was playing a game with him. A couple of days later I went and stood by the tree that once was parted into two before my very eyes like the waters were for the children of Israel. I gently rubbed my hand across its trunk where there was no evidence of any parting or splitting. I let my eyes slowly glance at it as it stood before me whole and standing tall with its roots planted deeply beneath my feet. Oh, what a mighty God we serve.

Christmas was coming and it would be the first time that we would celebrate in our very own place. I wanted our Christmas to be just as wonderful as the Christmas when my mother had put up the white Christmas tree and decorated with red flower lights; so I called her and asked if I could borrow her tree. I was excited for the kids but disappointed with Bob when he came home from Christmas shopping for the boys. Bob had gone to the Dollar Tree and bought DJ a bag of wooden blocks and a bag of dinosaurs; total cost two dollars. Are you serious; this is your first born son and his first real Christmas and all you find fit to spend on him is two dollars and ten cent. I was so hot I could've fried fish in my mouth. The white Christmas tree was up and presents were under the tree but the tree didn't look as pretty and it just wasn't the same feeling; I knew then that I had to make my own memories and experiences for my own children. That nothing borrowed can be made to be my own. I wanted happiness in my life and for my children. I had no focus or goal before, but when I looked at my babies while they slept; I now found two.

The New Year was in and new things were happening and some of the old things were too. I started going to church and occasionally Bob would come along. I got promoted at work and my sense of independence started to form. I even went and got myself another car. Bob tried to redeem himself with me and ease some of my disappointment in him, so he went and bought me new furniture. I thought it was a step in the right direction. He knew how much I hated the furniture that his sister gave us and he knew what my standards were. My thought was all because you lived in the projects, you didn't have to look or live like you were poor. Some gave that way of living the term; ghetto fabulous. But I just called it living a good life in a not so good situation. If you do the best with what you have, then better will come. Then somewhere in the middle of the year things turned upside down.

Bob had lost his job a couple of months ago and I tumbled down some stairs while at work and broke my ankle. I could no longer perform my duties at work so for six weeks I sat home while my leg healed; the worst pain ever next to having contractions. The first four weeks of healing was the longest weeks of my life. Dominique had just started to learn how to walk when I first broke my ankle; so that was good because there was no way I could carry him around and walk on crutches. Even though I wasn't working, I did keep the kids in daycare so I wouldn't lose their spot while I was out of work. There was no real reason to take them out anyway. My thought was while I was healing, they could be learning. That way when I did go back to work; I wouldn't have to look for new day care. They had already bonded with the workers and I trusted them with my children, so as they say; if it ain't broke don't fix it.

In the time while my leg was healing I decided to try and heal something else that was broken; my relationship with my mother. My mother had moved several times through the years after her and Peter's divorce and she even had a new boyfriend which he remained no interest of mine. Over the few years I had heard of his name mentioned by my sister. She and I stayed in touch very loosely also. My sister had moved to Kissimmee shortly after I left the job that she and I had worked at together. My sister had a new baby girl and a husband so she made a home for her family there. Shortly after my mother divorced Peter she lived with my sister for a while until she got on her feet. My brother meanwhile was in and out of trouble a lot. Once or twice I did find myself at his court hearings so my mother wouldn't have to go alone. At one court hearing I ended up breaking down after the judge read my brother his sentence. All I could see was my brother following in his father's footsteps and I so didn't want that for him but it would be up to him to make that decision for his life. My mother said once when my little brother got in trouble they forgot to pick II after his name and they pulled up his father's rap sheet; they were ready to give my little brother twenty years until my mother cleared up the clerical error.

The men my mother had in her life weren't good role models for my brother or anyone else for that matter. I was no longer a child or living in my mother's house, so I was able to make my own decision whether or not to get to know her new boyfriend; I choose not. On one of my many visits to see her while I was in the fifth week of healing my broken ankle he was there. He said something to me but I only ignored him. While I was there at my mother's apartment, she noticed that I was admiring a picture of Jesus that she had hanging on her wall. He had caramel skin and his hair looked like wool. I could not take my eyes off of him. When I got ready to leave, mama surprised me by taking the picture off her wall and giving it to me. In this life time that would be the best gift that my mother could ever give me. Not the picture, but introducing me to God and I made sure I passed that same gift on to my children.

As much as I gave an effort to go and see my mother to try and mend our relationship; the favor was not returned. I would learn by the slip of my sister's tongue that my mother had come to town over the weekend and spent the night at her house. My feelings were deeply hurt because in order to get to my sister's house; you would have to pass by mine. And my mother would do just that and never stop. Just knowing that she had been in town and no one even called me to tell me to come over hurt even more. It made me feel like I wasn't wanted around. Again I felt like that hurt little teenage girl. There would be several times that my mother would come to my sister's house and I wouldn't find out until my mother was already back home. One time when Bob was coming to pick me up from work and we were riding down the road, I happen to notice my mother's car headed in the opposite direction headed out of town taking the route that would get her back home. I told Bob to turn around so to flag her car down. Yes, it was my mother headed home after spending another weekend with my sister. Not even a phone call did I get and here I was on the side of the rode talking to my mother as if I was a stranger to this town who was lost asking for directions. I hide my disappointment to my mother's face but when I turned to go and get in my car after our ten minute conversation; tears ran down my cheek. Bob could see that I was upset. He consoled me and told me not to worry about it and I did just that. I focused on my own family once more.

The kids were at the day care, the house was clean, and it was a quiet day. I was feeling a little sad, depressed, and a little discouraged as I stared out the sliding glass door into the sunny afternoon. There was just an open field of grass with sidewalks that lead to other buildings in the complex. The sky was blue and only a few white fluffy clouds accompanied it. I stood there wondering if this was all that this world had for me. I decided to lie down and take a nap. In the middle of my nap, I heard someone call my name just as clear as a glass of water. I sat straight up in the bed. I knew that no one was in the house. It wasn't Bob's voice or any other man's voice that I had ever heard before. I know that I heard someone call my name. Was it the voice of my daddy letting me know that it was time for me to get up; I believed that it was. I called out to him but when he did not call my name again or answer I started to cry. I wanted so badly to hear my father's voice again. I looked over at the picture of Jesus that my mother had given me, for I too had hung it upon my bedroom wall. Was that you God; I asked. There was no answer, but I knew that he was there in the room with me. I thanked him for letting me hear my father's voice. It's time for you to get up; I heard a voice say. "Yes Lord" I said, "yes Lord". You have things to do; you can't sleep your life away. I began to cry again.

A week later I walked into a class room on crutches so I could take the test to get my GED. When I received my High School Diploma (that's what it read on the certificate) I was so proud of myself and I knew that it was the beginning of something. I knew that there was more to do but how to get there I didn't know. But for some reason I became comfortable with just living in the projects. I found myself being content with just getting my AFDC check every month; it covered all my bills. Food stamps and WIC feed us. But then there would be hours on end when I would just watch in silence as my boys would play in the yard where the grass didn't grow and only a dirt mound remained. With their faces covered in smut looking like a child from a third world country; I had no right to get comfortable. I had to give them a good head start in life. To let them know that there were other places to play and live outside of the projects.

A week later my cast came off and there were no more crutches. Crutches were replaced by a walking boot. Weeks went by as I stayed home and wondered what to do next. Staying in the house was driving me crazy so one day I decided to take my babies to the playground. I will never forget how the sun shined so brightly and the wind blew ever so lightly as I watched DJ run from slide to swing laughing and playing and his baby brother trying his best to keep up as much as his little legs would let him. For a moment I was content with the two decisions that I had made in my life thus far. But as I watched my babies play innocently, I knew that they didn't know what this world had to offer them and that no fault of their own, that they already had two strikes against them. They were black and they were males; and society had already profiled them as failures and troublemakers. They didn't deserve to be a statistic and I wasn't going to have them bare a strike three by living in the projects and becoming a product of their environment; I knew what I needed to do now.

I decided in enroll into college. I didn't know how I was going to pay for it but I would believe and ask God for what I would need. One day while I was picking up my baby boy from daycare there was a green flyer written in black ink on the bulletin board that caught my attention. It was saying something about a program through one of the daycare programs called Heartland. Heartland would pay for my education, give me gas, and pay for daycare; what else could I ask for or need. God had taken care of everything for me. I've learned that When God calls your name; it's best that you answer.

My focus was on college and raising my two boys. So you could just imagine how horrified I was one day when I noticed my son's DJ head one day when I got him home after picking him up from day care.

His head was looking deformed. It was as if someone had hit him in the head with a hammer and left about four big knots in his head. I took DJ in the bathroom and upon further examination of his head I noticed that these were sores; pusing sores at that. I called for Bob since he was such a county boy and asked him what it was. He said that it could be ringworm but that he wasn't sure. I didn't think that it could be ringworm because I made sure that they took a bath every night. DJ and his brother would spend a whole hour in that tub. So I knew it couldn't be that. So I doctored on him the best that I knew how with the little supplies that I had. I didn't have any bandages so I just covered his sores with squares of toilet paper that were taped to his head. Don't judge me.

The next morning when I checked my son's head it seems as if the pusing had gotten worst. So I put some more ointment on his head and covered his head with one of Bob baseball caps and spent him off to school. I got a call a couple hours later from the daycare telling me to come and pick up my son and that he could return to daycare until his head had healed. Well I thought that was rude because I figured that's where he got it from in the first place and now they going to put him out. Oh well the following week I took my baby to the doctors. After the doctor examined my son head he told me that where the knots were my son's hair would never grow back. I had to fight back the tears of the vision of that. My son was going to have to walk around with patches of hair missing from his head for the rest of his life. The devil is a liar.

I got home from the doctors that day and called my mama crying about what the doctor had told me. I felt that I was a bad mom for not noticing the condition of DJ's head sooner. Mama told me that the only thing that she could advise me to do was pour peroxide on his head; peroxide will kill anything. When I got off the phone with my mama I took DJ in the bathroom and stood him over the toilet while I poured peroxide over his head crying and praying for my baby hair to grow back. I did that for a whole week. I had prayed, cried and poured so much peroxide on DJ head that his hair turned red. But a month later the sores were gone; his hair was black and two months after that he had a head full of hair. I wouldn't be surprised if one day his hair got so long that he would wear it in twist that would drape down to his shoulders and rest between his shoulder blades across the middle of his back; it did. You can't tell me what God can't do. Lord, you are my healer.

Bob couldn't get his head out of the cloud of smoke long enough to realize that life was passing him by and so was I. Bob never did go and find a real job. He just kept hustling until one night I put my foot down because it had gone too far. At first there was a tap on our bedroom window two o'clock in the morning asking for Bob followed by three different knocks on the door within an hour and a half. I was alarmed when there was a knock at the window and Bob answered, sending them away with what they asked for and coming back to bed. I asked him who it was because I knew that I had told no one that he lived with me. He only brushed it off and said it was no one. So I became no longer concerned. But the constant knocking at the door got my full attention. After figuring out what was going on and that Bob thought it more convenient to have his "aquatints" come to him where he could be warm instead of waiting for them to come to him in the cold night air; I made it crystal clear that night to Bob that I didn't care what he did in the street but not to bring that crap to my front door where my babies lay their heads. Bob knew I serious and it never happened again. After that night Bob stopped hustling and stayed home to help me with the kids. At the beginning of my second year of college and after being on the waiting list for a two bedroom; we finally moved to the back of the complex into a new apartment. But along with a new apartment came new neighbors and new problems. Me and Bob had our arguments; some big and some small. On the big ones the police were called and Bob went to jail.

Somewhere along the way I found myself working and going to school. Bob watched the boys at night while I went to work. That was the least he could do since he still refuse to help financially. When I would get off of work it would be time for me to go to school. That situation became too much for me so after three months of that I decided just to concentrate on college. I started giving God a lot of my time as well. I was so deep into the church that every time the doors open, I was there. At first Bob would come along but that was soon short lived. Bob would just stay home and watch the football games and except for me to cook when I got home from church. One Sunday morning Bob had got me so heated before church; I dumped all the contents that where in the refrigerator on his lap. He was just sitting there all smug like he was pimp of the year demanding me to cook him some breakfast before I left for church. If I didn't leave when I did; let's just say thank God for his Holy Spirit because if I would have stayed it wouldn't have been nothing holy going on in there.

At one point I looked at my life and saw that everything was in order but the fact that I was not married. I didn't feel comfortable anymore running to church and then coming back home to Bob and living in sin. I thought if we got married that Bob would stop smoking that stuff and be more of a father for his kids and a husband to me. A girl can dream; can't she?

Keeping my head up and focused; every day on my way to college I notice that there was some new construction going on. It seemed that it was something major and I wanted to be part of it. There were no signs to say what the construction was; all I could see from the road was a large white building that sat away from the main road on top a hill. I would pray to God every day when I passed by the construction site on my way to class; telling him that I wanted to work there one day. March of '96 I graduated from two year college with my Accounting degree.

I hadn't found a job yet but my welfare checks were still coming in and Bob was still working doing odd jobs making very little money, so when the local paper put out an employment aid for the new construction site what was now known to be a major company warehouse; the city was jumping. Me and Bob went down to the local unemployment office where they were accepting applications for the new jobs. When we got there, the line was wrapped around the building. There had to have been at least two hundred people there. Needless to say after much processing June of the same year I was working in that white building on the top of the hill and Bob was very disappointed that he wasn't. He took not getting a job at the new warehouse very hard. He kind of went into a depression almost. He started smoking a lot. I felt sorry for him because I could see how much he was hoping that he would get a job. But a couple of weeks later he hooked up with some guy named Smitty and started working with him.

Smitty drove around in a flashy mobile detailing van; it was the first of its kind I had ever seen or heard of for that matter. If you were at your office and you needed your car cleaned he would come to you. If car dealerships needed all the cars washed on the lot, Smitty was the man to call. When they weren't washing cars they used the equipment on the van for pressure cleaning and painting buildings. Smitty took his business to the next level. His punch line was he could teach you how to own your own mobile detailing business by buying one of his video tapes. So since no one was buying his videos that he had packaged he stuck to car detailing and pressure cleaning in order to make some money. And Smitty never let Bob forget that that was his van. After washing cars all day Smitty would pay Bob fifty dollars, but that would be all gone up in smoke the time he got home. One or two days out the week Bob might make it home with some money. And when it was cold and no one was calling for pressure cleaning or details for their car; Smitty passed himself off as a model agency. His only model was he girlfriend who no one ever saw him with. With Smitty's new found adventure; this would leave Bob looking for work with an opportunity that could make him some money.

There would be times when Bob didn't work because no one could find Smitty. Some of the other guys that worked with Smitty would come around looking for Bob asking where Smitty was because he hadn't paid them for their last job. You wouldn't see Smitty for a couple of months after he had done disappeared in the middle of the night. But when he did surface he would have all these jobs lined up and he would convince Bob that he needed him to work with him because he was his right hand man and he was the only one that he could trust. Smitty made it sound like that he had so much work lined up that he couldn't keep up with the paper work. So he asked me would I keep his books for him. It wasn't like he was some major corporation even though he would have liked to have been. What books he had, a five year old could have kept. I knew Smitty was slicker than spit but I needed proof so I could tell Bob. So I told him the only way I would work for him was that he had to pay me in cash. I didn't care about the money, I had a job.

Smitty had an office in some business district that he rented out. It was nothing fancy; it smelled of mildew and was really no bigger than a broom closet. Smitty talked big and he could sell you your own shoes right back to you if you let him. He once told me that he wanted me to contact Jessie Jackson and Al Sharpton so he could do a commercial with them. Smitty believed his own hype not just half the time but all the time.

His work ethic was weird because he had no money in the bank. When he would bid on jobs and get them, he would have to get half the money up front so he would be able to buy supplies for the job. And when the job was finished he would get the rest of the money. Now granted Smitty had his own exspenses; his fancy sports car was about to be repossessed, he was behind on child support; and not from his current girlfriend. He was still paying for the van; which he lied and said that it was paid for. And he had rent to pay on a condo that he passed off as his own but come to find out was owned by some snow birds. And he only ate at the finer restaurants. So when he got paid he didn't pay the guys. Smitty never had enough for payroll so he would get another job and pay them some of their money from their last job and buy cheap supplies to get the new job done. I watched him do this for months. I knew Smitty was just a wooden nickel hustler because where he comes from two plus two always equal seven.

I tried to tell Bob but for some reason Bob couldn't see past his crap because Smitty kept him buttered up by making him think he was partners with him. Smitty would send Bob out on jobs as if he was sending him to look over the place to see if it would be a job they might be interested in. Smitty would tell Bob that he would meet him at the job site and Bob would go with his clipboard in hand and a pencil tucked behind his ear. Smitty would never show because he was at the real job site making a bid for a job without Bob. After that job Smitty paid Bob fifty dollars and disappeared into the night. And Bob would sit around the house moping.

A couple of months later Smitty did surface but this time he had a new hustle; he was in the cleaning business. When people would move out of their apartments the leasing office would call him and have him clean the apartments. He lured Bob into that too by telling him that he could head up his own cleaning crew. But Smitty didn't have a clean-up crew to begin with. So Bob asked me to help him clean apartments. So standing by my man and supporting him even though I told him that I didn't think it was a good idea, I went. While I was cleaning the apartment, Bob was painting it. Smitty only paid Bob seventy five dollars instead of the one hundred and fifty that he had promised. I never cleaned another apartment again. I would just look at Bob and shake my head and wonder when he was going to see this guy for what he really was. I couldn't waste too much more time or energy on the situation because I still had to hold things down at home.

Two weeks after working on my new job my way of thinking quickly began to change. I noticed that there were a lot of men who were working and they weren't married. But that they gladly came to work every day and took their paychecks home. I wanted the same for myself. I was mad that I was the only one working on a real job. So when I would go home after work and asked Bob why he wouldn't go find a real job, it would just end up with us arguing with one another. I started to feel like there was someone else out there other than Bob for me who I could be happy with. I wanted to find someone who had their shit together. Where was I going to find someone like that; I didn't know? So when my neighbor asked me to go out with her one night to a famous club; I agreed and decided that would be a place to start. I went a couple Fridays in a row and all I saw were wanna be players in the club. They were just looking for something to scoop up for the night. I remember one night an eerie feeling came over me while I was just standing there watching everyone dancing and drinking around me. All I could think of was if God was to come right now; we all going to hell. I never went back to the club again.

Bob clearly stated that he didn't want to clock in and out on no one's job. He wanted to be his own boss. I thought that was funny because that was the same slogan that his partner Smitty had on the side of his van and label of his video tapes. But I personally believed that Bob didn't want to get a job because if he did, he would have to give up his favorite past time of smoking that "green stuff." He knew if he didn't stop smoking and was sent for a drug test; the test would definitely come back dirty and he wouldn't get the job anyway.

But if it was Bob's dream to have his own business; I wasn't the one to keep him from that. It's just in the seven years that we had been together I had never even heard him mention anything about wanting to have his own business. So it was kind of hard for me not to believe that Smitty hadn't gotten in his head and planted that seed so he could make some money off Bob.

While Bob was off trying to learn how to be his own boss, I was working and buying things for the apartment trying to make the projects look like we were living in the pent house at the Ritz Carlton. Things were beginning to change for the better. We never had a dining room table before; so I bought one. When we lived at the old apartment it was too small for one. Our apartment seemed to not accommodate me anymore. I bought new dishes, glassware, and silverware along with pots and pans. I rented a standup washer/dryer unit since it wasn't convenient or time saving to go to the laundry mat. The washer was detachable so you could hook it up to the kitchen sink with a water hose and do your laundry. Then there was the issue of drying clothes. When you ran the dryer it made the apartment into a sauna. I would complain to Bob about it all the time. With all the improvements done to the apartment, you could tell things were going well. Christmas that year was off the chain. I bought my very own Christmas tree and there were so many presents; that the pile was taller than the tree. You would have thought Santa Clause stopped by our house two or three times.

While out and about doing whatever it was he was doing and still not financially contributing to the family; Bob came across an apartment that was for rent. He gave me the address and told me to go and take a look at it. February of 97 we moved out of the projects.

# Chapter 28

IT WAS A new year, a new beginning and we were in our new apartment on the other side of town. Things were good between us and we were happy and so in June of that same year; me and Bob decided to get married. Funny thing I remember how Bob got nervous when he was filling out the paper work for the marriage certificate. He seemed to get irritated when the clerk asked him if this was his first marriage. We didn't have a church ceremony; just a good old fashion court house wedding. I was disappointed that I wasn't going to have a church wedding with flowers, bridesmaids, and a beautiful wedding dress; every little girls dream, but Bob said it would cost too much. When I told him how much a wedding cake would cost, he had a fit. Though I did have a wedding cake; the square one, without the top only because I paid for it. Come to think of it I paid for our wedding rings too.

We quickly got to know our neighbors and their friends and became good friends with them. You will come across some strange characters in your life time; but that's what makes life exciting. Bob had a real job now and was bringing home his money. I thought it was time that I loosen my load a bit and let him handle a few small bills. I took care of the rent while he was responsible for paying the utility and the furniture bill. Bob was my husband now and that's how I looked at him. In my mind, he was the man of the house; he was the head of the household; regardless of what. I never questioned him about whether or not he paid the bills; it wasn't my place. I just trusted that he did because he was now my husband. I took great satisfaction in making my home beautiful for my family. I was a wife and a mother now. When I was a child

I wasn't allowed to do childish things and I may never recover from that. My own priorities were the well-being of my kids and husband. I only went to work, the store, the boys elementary school, occasionally church and home. Everything seemed to finally come full circle.

Sometime later on that year, my sister fell on hard times so she came and stayed with us for a little while. It would have been longer but her and Bob got into a big argument which ended in her packing up her things and storming out the house in her pajamas and robe. The stupid thing was that they were arguing over a decision that I had made. You see, I looked at the whole situation of my sister coming to stay with me as me helping her. So I told my sister not to give me any money on any of the utilities just for her to save her money. My understanding is how you can call yourself helping someone if you're taking money out of their pockets that they could be saving. But Bob felt that she should pay. And we all know why because that would have been less money coming out his pocket and more for his beer and cigarettes. But the way I looked at it was those bills were there before she came to stay with us and they would be there when she leaves.

And it wasn't like she was taking up any extra space because she and my niece and nephew where sharing a room with my boys. It wasn't like she was eating up all our food either because she bought her own. I was sick that morning when they were at each other's throat. All I could do was stand in between the two of them so it wouldn't get physical. My sister had had enough of Bob's mouth. I begged her not to go but she thought it be better that she did. Bob had a way of saying things and rubbing people the wrong way. She said she couldn't stay there any longer because she didn't want to do anything that she might regret later. I told Bob that he was wrong for even stepping to my sister about something that was between me and her. It was a sister-sister situation. I could understand if she was doing something in the house that was putting our life in danger, then yes I would expect for him to speak up. But that wasn't the case.

That summer I realized how much I had let myself go. My weight had gone up while my style had gone down. But one day while doing laundry I passed by the mirror and I really saw me for the first time. I had let myself go and not in a good way. I don't mind sharing with you because in order to understand me; you would have to know all of me. My good, my bad, my flaws, my digressions, and my insecurities; is what makes me the person that I am.

Bob never complained about my weight but I felt that it would make me an even better wife if I was to lose the weight. I was getting ready for work early one morning and a diet pill infomercial was on. I had seen bits and pieces of the infomercial several times before but I thought if I was going to try and lose weight that I should do it the natural way. I even ordered Billy Banks workout tapes once and worked out to that. But it started to be like every time I would put the tape in the vcr; everyone would suddenly gather in the living room and watch me do my exercise as if I was putting on a Muppet show. When you're exercising you already know that you look crazy and you feel awkward because you're not kicking and punching as high or as hard as the people on the video. You don't need an audience telling you that. I did away with the Billy Banks video tapes. But there was something about the diet pill infomercial this morning that made me actually sat down and watched the whole thing. It couldn't hurt to try it; I convinced myself. I ordered a couple of bottles and waited for them to get delivered.

There were three different pills that I had to take three times a day. The nastiest taste that you could imagine was left in my mouth. No matter how many times I brushed my teeth, chewed gum, gargled, or ate mints; the taste stayed in my mouth. I can say though, the pills were doing their job; I didn't want to eat. They gave me plenty of energy. If I doing anything simple like washing the dishes or any type of housework, I would sweat like a pig. When I would go to work the sweat was ten times as worst because the warehouse was already hot and on top of me sweeping the dock after shift, it just intensive. I had started carrying a washcloth from home to work with me. One day I sweated so bad and had to wipe my face so much, I had formed a whelp across my forehead.

To get some type of manual exercise in I went and bought an ab cruncher and a gadget called the wheel. I would do at least a hundred sit-ups a night. That was the only exercise I really did and drunk lots of water. Within six months I had lost thirty pounds.

I was still wearing my regular clothes to work until one morning I got up as usual and was getting ready for work. Trying not to make too much noise as to wake the boys because they had to go to school; I tipped toed through the house. Three o'clock was a bit too early for me and I'm grown, so I know it would have been for them. I managed to get half-dressed without making a sound; still having to put my pants on. I went in the bathroom just to double check my hair. I guess I must have caught a side view of myself out of the corner of my eye as I was passing by the mirror. I stopped in my tracks and faced the mirror; I looked at myself from head to thigh. I was skinny; well not skinny -skinny like a toothpick skinny but I could tell by looking that I had lost some weight. Oh my God, I did it. I said to my reflection. My boobs were still huge and I figured it would take a miracle directly from God to get rid of them things. But at the same time they kind of became my trade mark. You know how when someone is trying to describe to someone else someone that they don't know; the girl with the big chest would be the next sentence out of someone's mouth after saying my name. I got use to that. But my waist was smaller. I was in total shock at what I was seeing. I stood in the mirror amazed and crying, I did it.

After a few more moments, I finally pulled myself together and went to my closet and got my favorite pair of black jeans. It had been awhile since I was able to wear them because they had become too tight in the thigh area. I put the jeans on and to my surprise; I needed a belt. I didn't even own a belt because before now my expanded waist line kept my pants up. I hadn't worn a belt since before my kids were born. I borrowed my son's belt. Still being in shock that I even needed a belt; with every loop I put the belt through I was more amazed.

I fastened the belt going to the last hole, but the pants were still too big in the waste. I cried some more. "Oh my God," I said as I turn around and catch a view of myself from every angle. I just couldn't believe it. I hadn't been that small in years. I had to get my butt to work before I was late. After our morning meeting we all were picking up our paperwork, everyone just stopped and it got real quiet. No one said a word I just noticed that everyone was just looking at me. I knew they had noticed what I had seen that morning in the mirror.

Soon as I got off of work I went to the store and tried on a different or should I say a smaller pair of jeans. The fitting room attendant probably thought I was crazy because I just kept talking to my reflection in the mirror about being able to fit into a smaller pair of jeans then what I had put on that morning.

I was enjoying my new body. At night I would lie on my side and just feel the difference in my thighs. It now felt like a small hill and not a huge mountain. Or how my stomach had gotten flatter; it didn't stick out as far like before. I had thirty pounds gone and fifteen more to go. But they never went. Not matter what I did; I couldn't lose those other fifteen pounds. What's wrong? What happened? I was still taking the diet pills even though they didn't let me sleep some nights because they would give me the jitters. When my jitters would get real bad, I would have to have one or both of the boys rub my whole arm up and down until I fell asleep. That was the end of the diet pills for me. Six months later the weight came back. I never had low self-esteem so I made up in my mind that I was meant to be a beautiful black full-figured woman. But always in the back of my mind; I never wanted to be a fat mom.

98' and Bob hasn't worked in the past two months. He had been sitting around the house having a pity party for himself. On his good days he goes out and goes back to what he knows; hustling. Bob got in late the night before and the next morning I was greeted by a large zip lock bag of "collard greens" sitting out on the kitchen counter for the world and my children to see. With the steam that was coming out of my ears I could have cooked those "collard greens". I woke Bob up at three o'clock in the morning and told him through my teeth while smiling; that I didn't cook those types of "collard greens" and that I had not ever see them on my kitchen counter again. All I could think of was what if one of my boys would have gotten into the bag and ate some of the "collard greens". For all they know; everything in the kitchen is eatable. Bob tried to apologize and explain but I didn't want to listen to his excuses because someone had to go to work to keep the lights on.

Bob's pity party lasted for a couple of weeks more. Since he was home a lot, he started hanging out with a neighbor across the way named Eric. Eric was a Puerto Rican from the New York Bronx. He, his wife and two boys moved to Florida about five years ago. For the most part Eric was okay to me; he was the typical Puerto Rican father. Eric just smoked like a chimney and seemed to always be in a lot of pain. He introduced Bob to his friend Bobby who was also Puerto Rican who lived a couple of blocks down the road from the apartments. Bobby was divorced and a retired Veteran. Eric didn't work he was on disability so you already know they had plenty of free time on all their hands. At first I welcomed the friendship that they had formed. Then I noticed that Bob started to change. He seemed to be easily influenced by others; that wasn't good. He started smoking cigarettes like they were going out of style. He started wanting to eat strange foods and only shop at certain grocery stores. Bob even started talking different; he somehow picked up a Puerto Rican accent. He wanted to drink the Tequila now with the worm. I stood by in silence and watched as Bob took on a new identity. All I could do was shake my head at what was happening in front of my eyes.

After a couple of months of hanging out with Cheech and Chon; Bob got this idea in his head to join an organization of all men that Eric and Bobby were affiliated with but I don't think he got that idea by himself. One of the rules of this organization was to address the idea of joining to the wife. So one day Eric and Bobby came over to the house and pitched me all the wonderful things about this organization. Bobby did most of the talking. He went on to say how the organization was highly respected in the community and how they take care of their own. How it would help finically if he was to join. The organization would pay rent and put food on the table, take care of Christmas and other stuff. I had that covered I didn't need help with paying my rent and feeding my family. I asked if it could help Bob get a job but all Bob heard was all the free stuff he could get out of the situation. Bob is the type to never bring anything to the table but he will pull up a chair and eat. And so as Bobby continued to talk I could see Bob's wheels turning in his brain. The less he had to be responsible for the better for him. It didn't impress me one way or the other what Bobby was saying because as I know God will supply all my needs. But I listened and afterwards I gave my blessing. I didn't want to be the one to break up their little play date. It was for Bob to decide whether he wanted to join or not.

Weeks of Bob coming home late and drunk followed. I saw nothing positive developing from his decision to join this organization. To me it just seemed like some type of college frat party. I reminded Bob that he also had a responsibility to his family and for him to also make time for that. Bob did find a job but I don't recall where. At this point, as long as he was able to take care of his responsibilities I didn't worry about the details. Well let's just say I didn't worry until one day there was a knock at the door. There stood two men from the company from which I had purchased my furniture and held an account with for years. I had been a good customer of theirs for so long that whenever I wanted something and it was over my credit limit they would allow me to purchase it with no problem. So image the shock on my face when the two men proceeded to say that they were there to pick up my furniture. I just knew that this was a mistake them being at my front door. If I would have been behind on a payment I would have thought that they would have given me a call. I've worked too hard and I wasn't about to let nothing leave out of my house.

With my mouth hanging open wide enough to catch frogs; I left the two men standing at the door while I proceeded to look for the phone so I could call the furniture store and speak to someone so these men could go on their merry way and get from in front of my door. I called and talked to the store manager. He pulled up my account information up on the computer. According to his records, my account hadn't been paid on since two months ago. He also mentioned that he did call Bob about the account. So why didn't Bob tell me so that I could pay the bill. I walked back to the front door to let the gentlemen know that I was on the phone with the furniture store manager. After about two minutes of making arrangements to double my next two payments to catch my account up; I told the gentlemen that their manager was waiting for them back at the store. As the gentlemen were getting in their van to leave Bob drove up in the car with Eric and Bobby which was strange to me because Bob was supposed to be at work. I was so beside myself with anger. When Bob finally did come in the house, I told him that recess was over.

A couple of months had gone by since the rat pack had taken a break. The temp service that Bob was working through had finished the job that he was on and so he was yet again out of work and sitting home.

Weeks of Bob having another pity party for himself had passed. Bob came to me and said that he wanted his own detailing business. Not to the level as his old pal Smitty who I hadn't seen since we moved; but his own one man show. He knew from working with Smitty that to have any type of decent van was going to cost at least twenty-five hundred dollars. Bob knew he didn't have that type of money. He went to his dad and mom but they turned him down. He went to other family members but he only got the same response. The only one that was left to ask was me. Bob followed me around for two weeks like a lost puppy begging and pleading with me to loan him the money. He just kept going on and on how it would benefit the family if he had his own business. I didn't say yes right away but after seeing everyone turn him down flat and not even bother to offer him anything, I felt sorry for Bob because I could tell that he wanted this real bad. When I saw that his own family didn't want to support him because they didn't believe in him; I wanted so badly for him to prove them wrong. To show them that he could be dependable and responsible. So I stepped up and supported my husband. I had him promise that he would run it like a business and not as a hustle.

When I got my income tax back that year; I loaned Bob two thousand dollars to get his business started. He was so grateful and in such, He promised me that he would pay me back the money. But to make sure thing got off to the right start; I went and bought a van, generator, hoses, a custom water tank and all the supplies he needed. I even got his name put on the side of the van; finally Bob was his own boss. I wanted to support Bob, but I knew putting that large amount of money in the wrong hands would a recipe for disaster. And yes, I held my breath waiting and thinking that Bob would do the right thing and pay me back. After a while I couldn't breathe so I let it go.

Bob worked hard to get his business up and running. For the next six months he had secured a couple of car dealerships and a couple of repeat customers. I was proud of Bob; he made his dream come true. There was just one set back; as quick as the money was made it was spent. We lived a fast pace life. We were both working and there was no time to be stuck in the kitchen. We ate out a lot and we were always on the go. Some times on the weekend Bob would take the boys with him and they would hang out while he worked. Bob became really close with one of the owners of one of the car dealerships where he worked. Bob's two door Cutlass had took its last breath so Sam let us borrow a car from the lot until I was able to save up five hundred dollars to put down on a 89 ford tarus.

Things were going good until one day Bob would turn my world upside down. It just so happen to be a short day at work for me. So I decided to get home straighten up the house and cook dinner. As I went outside to throw out the garbage, Bob drove up in his van and by this time across the way Eric was coming out his apartment. I called out to Bob in my sexy wifey voice and smiled at him. He didn't have time to respond before Eric called out to Bob again and motioned for him to come here. Bob got out the van and I asked him how his day was but he didn't answer me because Eric had called for him again and I guess it drowned me out. Eric waved for Bob to come to him. Did Eric not see that I was talking to my husband who had just gotten home and hadn't had the chance to greet me with a kiss yet? Ignoring me, Bob started to walk in the direction of Eric who had now come down the stairs. I called out to Bob and asked him was he not going to greet me first, his wife before he run off to his friend. Never even looking in my direction; Bob just told me to hold on that he would be right back. I thought that was so rude of him. Eric called for Bob again. I looked over at Eric wishing that he would stop calling Bob; he heard him the first time. Time stood still as I watched my husband who never came to me; walk across the yard and greet his friend with a hand shake and man hug. My heart cracked in half, I felt that I wasn't important to Bob and my world came crumbling down. How could Bob just ignore me like that? I was the one who stood by him when no one else would. I was the one who held us down when he wasn't able. I had made a beautiful home for him and took care of our children. And he just disses me like that. Where was his loyalty to me? Apparently he didn't have any for me but only to his friends.

After that, things just weren't the same between me and Bob. Well at least we had two happy years of marriage. I put all my attention on my boys; they became my first and only priority. But I did notice one thing; Bob wasn't working as much as he use to and things started getting very weird with him. One day while I was at work I had called home to check on the kids. Bob had answered the phone and said that a naked white lady had come to our door asking for help. Now mind you there are two other apartment buildings before you get to our building and there is one other apartment before ours in our building. So why this lady would walk so far and naked to our apartment, I didn't understand. Bob was sounding crazy. I asked some more question because what he was describing to me wasn't making any sense. But the more questions I asked the crazier the whole situation sounded. So I thought Bob had just made up the story joking around with me. So when I got home he was still talking about the naked white lady. I asked what happened to her. Bob said she just walked away. I asked if he tried to go and get our neighbor or call the police, Bob said no.So I asked the kids did they see anything strange that day and they told me no. I asked what was daddy doing all day, they said that he stayed locked up in our bedroom all day. I began walking through my house and started praying, something wasn't right.

Work became a good distraction for the foolishness that was going on at home. Me and Bob are starting to argue a lot. I find myself hanging out a lot with my friends from work to avoid home. Having friends at work and having friends while you're in school is totally different. You're grown now and grown folks are allowed to do what grown folks want to do. I found myself looking for the attention that Bob wasn't giving me but was so willing to give to his friends. At first I would ignore the advices from men at work. The crazier and crazier things were getting at home the more I began to think that maybe me and Bob had run our course and that maybe it was time for me to be with someone else. Bob's drinking and smoking a lot and working even less became very evident. It seemed he was taking and getting more pleasure out of that then me. He spent his days locked up in our bedroom. Our marriage was on the rocks and I didn't know if it was worth fixing or if it could be fixed.

Months had gone by and things had only gotten worst between Bob and I. We had stopped practicing making babies about six months ago. But it was the night that me and Bob were having a huge argument and a girl called the housing asking for Bob; that the shit hit the fan. I was so beside myself I think I even turned into the Tasmanian Devil that night. I told Bob to get his shit and get the hell out of my house. I was so devastated that I didn't know or understand what to do or what was happening. It took me a couple of days to stop crying. My babies just kept asking me if I was okay. I lay in the bed for days wondering what I was supposed to do next. It didn't help that Bob came to my job and scared the crap out of me early one morning coming up behind me with some flowers. He looked dead, like he hadn't slept in days. I told Bob to go away that I didn't want to talk to him. But he insisted that I take the flowers and he became very apologetic. When I would try to walk away he would only block my path. After a couple of tries and not wanting to be late for work; I took the flowers and told Bob to leave. Bob called the house at least a hundred times a day but I wouldn't answer. I don't care how many times he would call; I still wouldn't forgive him for the one call that was made. All I could think of was that he gave another girl his phone number and that she had the balls to call my house. Everyone knew Bob was married so there was no excuse. Then I would think of all the times that he stayed locked up in our bedroom; was he talking to her on the phone.

After quite some time I had really made up in my mind that I didn't want Bob back and he finally got the message. And to show Bob that I was moving on with my life; I got a new friend. And that's when things started to get a little messy. When I went to get in my car one day after work, my car wasn't where I parked it or even anywhere in the parking lot. I called Sam to see if he had come to pick up my car and he told me no, but that the car was there at his lot. I asked him why was it there and who came and got it. Sam told me that he didn't know but for me to come and get the car. At that moment I knew it could have only been Bob who took my car; that low down dirty dog. What thief in their right mind; steals a car and takes it back to the dealership; no car thief that I know. I called Bob and told him that he had better come and pick me up from work and take me so that I could get my car. Bob did just that. I cursed him out all the way there. But the other thing was who was the other dirty dog who brought him up here to get my car and how did Bob get a set of keys to my car. I know Bob took my car because the whole ride to the dealership he never asked me any questions. He didn't ask me if I was behind on a payment and maybe Sam came and got the car. He didn't ask me if I wanted to ride through the parking lot to make sure that I didn't park somewhere else since it was three o'clock in the morning when I got to work; that I could have been half sleep and parked somewhere else. Nothing; he just drove me to the dealership.

The year 2000 was very messy. I had been out of the dating game for some time now. It was obvious that the rules had changed. Everyone was making up their own rules. I wasn't prepared at all. Some situations I made the best of and other situations got the best of me. Some left me broken hearted and some left me cold hearted. I found myself in situations that I was so ashamed of. I found myself not caring about other people's feeling just my own. It was as if I was trying to collect and get whatever I thought that I had missed or given up in my twenties. There was the partying, drinking, and sex; I wanted it all.

I was going on with my life enjoying my new friends and Bob was always showing up at my front door causing a scene. Police were being called, windows were getting busted out of my apartment, tires were getting slashed and my phone was ringing off the hook. Bob was acting like me and him were still together; I guess so in his mind. He always found out who my new friends were and Bob would always chase away my friends. And the crazy thing was they would leave and not stay and stand their ground or even protect my honor. I was so puzzled with that. But I think men have their code of honor to each other that they always respect regardless of the woman. With my experience of having new friends I learned the difference between lust and love. And that every man that kisses will eventually lie to you with those same lips.

I learned that when I get in my head that it can be a very dangerous place to be. I seem to create my own world and whatever I want to happen will happen. I have to talk myself down from wanting to do those things in the real world. Sometimes I'm able to and other times I am not. Yes I know it sounds crazy because I'm saying it out loud but it is the truth. This is why people don't like telling their truth because others will think that it is crazy. I haven't learned how to disregard the pain that others inflect on me and I probably never will.

I found myself in a dark place after my friend Nathaniel had passed a week ago. Nathaniel had come to see me a couple of weeks earlier and I could tell that life had been rough on him. We talked about old times and I pleaded with him to try and get himself together. He said he knew that he needed to do better but that it was very hard. That life wasn't fair. This I knew, but I told him he couldn't give up that he had children who loved him and a woman who needed him. That would be the last time I would see or talk to Nathaniel in this lifetime. It wouldn't be much longer after that, that my mother would call me to tell me that my Aunt Earline had passed away; the one that we lived with for a short period of time when I was a little girl. Death started to be all around me. And I couldn't understand why God was taking all the good people; leaving behind the bad people like Bob to live and continue to suck up the air. I felt that Bob wasn't appreciating his life because if he was then he would have done right by me and my children. If God was taking all the good people I wanted to go too. I didn't want to live anymore if I couldn't live and be happy. I stood in the middle of my living room and wished that I was dead. For a moment I left my body and I looked down on myself as I stood there in my living room. I was willing to end my life, but it was the sound of my little boys' laughter as they played in the front yard that changed my mind. They still needed me. I had to be strong for them.

I have become two now, this is the only way that I will be able to survive this life. I understand that people will take my kindness as a sign of me being weak and unaware. Oh but I am so far from weak.

My anger and rage are very strong and can be very dangerous and too much for me to bare. It has become my protector when life mistreats me. At times I can control her and at other times I care not to. This is the cross that I carry.

Months went by and the bond between me and my boys will have to be strong. I told them that we were a team and that we had to take care of each other. And so for a while I put away foolish things. Sometime during the quietness of my life, Bob pleaded with me to give him another chance. Since he had chased all my new friends away I figured why not. Maybe a fresh start was what we needed. Bob had sold his van so what he planned on doing for income; I didn't know but I guess we would figure it all out. So the beginning of 2001 we agreed to put everything in storage and move in with his dad again so we could save some money. I knew that it was a bad idea to move back in with his dad but knowing that we would only be there for a short period of time; I agreed.

We moved in about a week or two later back into Bob's dad. Everything was quiet for the first couple of months. But then Mr. Joe was starting to have something to say about the things we did. One night I got in from work late and so I ordered a pizza for dinner for the kids. The pizza came so me and the kids sat down to eat, Bob hadn't made it in yet. Mr. Joe came in the kitchen to get something to drink and saw that we were eating pizza. He made the comment, "it's hard to save money when you're ordering pizza." I told him, "a sixteen dollar pizza ain't never hurt nobody's bank." Then he went on to say, "well it can get expensive if you order one every Friday." Well no one was planning on doing that so what the hell was he talking about. I had saved plenty of money while I was there and was paying him his rent so what was he worrying about. Then another time I was in the kitchen eating some ice cream and he came in the kitchen and said the same thing. "It's kinda hard to save money if you're spending it on ice cream," Mr. Joe remarked. I just rolled my eyes at Mr. Joe and kept eating my Rocky Road ice cream. After that day I just stopped eating in the kitchen and only eat when Mr. Joe wasn't home.

It was getting close to the time for Mr. Joe to retire so he was always looking for a way to keep his money in his pocket and make more money. He had an idea to start a business and so he was looking into the idea of buying a cement pump since cement was something that he knew. But in order to get any money from his retirement without being penalized; he had to withdraw the money only as a hardship. Mr. Joe knew that none of his kids would understand the details so when he called them all over to sign some papers; they thought that they were going to get five thousand dollars a piece. Mr. Joe told them that he would get the money, buy the pump, get the business started, name the business after them and split the rest of the money amongst the four kids. You should have seen Bob that day; he really thought his dad was going to give him the money. But I knew better all along. Bob was just dancing around the kitchen table. Bob told me that I could take the kids and leave; that he didn't want me anymore and that he didn't want anything to do with the kids. Mr. Joe just sat there laughing. I told Bob that he ought to be ashamed of himself. It was sad to think he thought that his kids were for sale and that it was so easy to sell them to who he thought was the highest bidder. I told him when this deal fell through that he wouldn't be able to buy his kids back.

Mr. Joe told Bob that he had to choose between the new family business or me and the kids. Bob happily signed on the dotted line. Nathaniel was there that day too and told Bob that he was wrong for that. I grabbed my babies up and ran out of the room crying. I will never forget that day and what Mr. Joe did to my family.

Bob looked under cooked with egg on his face when he realized his dad had got the money and didn't give him any. Bob got more egg on his face when his dad didn't put his name in the company logo. The only two names on the business were his dad's and younger brother. Bob's older brother had made it very clear that he didn't want anything to do with the business that he only signed the papers to help his dad out; so he didn't care what they did. And Bob's oldest sister wasn't about to work on a cement pump so she didn't care either. But Bob's little brother was going to college and he was the type not to get dirty so I know he wasn't going to be working on the cement pump. So that only left poor Bob to work the family business that his name was not on.

At first everyone pitched in and helped on the couple of jobs that they contracted. But then suddenly no one was available to work but Bob. Bob worked hard hoping that one day his dad would put his name on the business. Every now and then when the brothers would need some change in their pocket they would come and help Bob with a job, but that was only when they needed money not when the business needed them. But nothing like Bob who worked every day. As long as the business was running good, Mr. Joe never let Bob forget whose business it was and whose name was on it. When the business wasn't doing so good Mr. Joe would tell Bob that he didn't want anything to do with the business and would give him the responsibility. This was a hard thing for me to watch my husband go through. But then soon as Mr. Joe got a whiff of Bob doing well with the business; he would take the business back from Bob.

Of course this hurt Bob and caused many arguments between us because along with not putting Bob's name on the business; he wasn't paying him fairly either when it was Bob doing all the hard work. I use to tell Bob to just stop working for his dad and get a real job. But Bob held on to the hope that one day his father would give him full control of the business. Eventually after the business was ran down and there weren't hardly any contracts left; Mr. Joe let Bob run the cement pump but he never gave him the business or changed the name.

The cement pump sat on bricks hooked up to an old truck. When business started picking up again, Bob went to his dad and told him the truck was on its last leg and that they needed a new one for the cement pump. His dad agreed and they went looking for another truck. They found something that they both liked and Bob was excited. The idea of driving around in a new truck made him feel like a new man. Mr. Joe went back and bought the truck that they both said would be good for the business but instead of giving Bob the truck for the cement pump, Mr. Joe kept the truck for himself. Bob was so hurt, disappointed, and betrayed. As much as I wanted to; I wouldn't be able to lift Bob's head up with a crane after what his father had done to him.

Two weeks before our new apartment would be ready, me and Bob's dad got into a big argument. I refuse to let any man talk down to me or put his hands on me and Mr. Joe made the mistake of doing both. And as usual Bob stood there not saying a word. As I was walking in and out of the house from the car after packing my things me and Mr. Joe were having words. It was on one of my trips coming back into the house when I was approaching the door that Mr. Joe ran to the door pushed me out of the doorway back outside and slammed the door in my face. He tried to lock it but I line-backed the door that he was still standing behind and I injured his foot making it bleed. I told Mr. Joe for as long as he lived for him not to ever put his hands on me again. I asked him how he was going to lock me out the house, was he crazy. My two babies were in there; I would have turned into the big bad mama wolf so fast and blew that damn house down. And so of course Bob being hypmatized by the thought of his daddy giving him the family business went to his father's side and had the nerve to ask his dad if he wanted him to call the police. Really, are you serious? This man puts his hands on me and you want to call the police on me.

The police came and everyone was consoling Mr. Joe and no one was concerned with me. Two police officers, Bob and Mr. Joe; it just felt like four against one gang up on the woman. As Bob was standing by his father's side holding his hand while Mr. Joe sat in his recliner I really wanted to slap the both of them. The officer asked Mr. Joe did he want to press charges, Mr. Joe said no. the officer didn't ask me if I wanted to press charges, he just asked me if I had somewhere I could go for the night. I told the officer yes I had somewhere to go but it wouldn't be for the night; because I had no plans of ever stepping in that house again.

I finished packing up the car with me and my boy's things and left. For some reason when people think that you are down and out they like to jump on you just to put you down even further. But what people don't understand is the more they push you down, the further they go down too. And so I went and stayed with my sister and slept on my sister's couch for two weeks until our new apartment was ready. I found myself putting myself to sleep so the days could go by faster. I could hear the kids running around the house but I had no will to get up and interact with them. I felt homeless and for the first time in a long time I felt misplaced. My sister's couch became my casket for two weeks. In July of 2001 we moved into our new townhouse; Bob moved in too.

# Chapter 29

**A MARRIAGE, TWO** kids, and twelve years later my life definitely had been a rollercoaster ride with all its ups and downs. My ups were I had a good job, we lived in a nice neighborhood and my boys were young and growing. The downs were my marriage to Bob was rocky and my existence in church was not what it should have been. It had come to a halt. Despite my shortcomings and transgression; I knew God had never left me nor forsake me. As I looked back over my life; I knew that to be true. It would only be the time when I realized that it wasn't my attendance at church or my religion that was important but it was the one on one relationship that I had with God that would sustain me and I would never let go of his hand.

I thank God for my two boys. They keep me out of trouble; well lets me say they kept me from killing people who had crossed me. But the thought did cross my mind once or twice. They kept me from giving up and throwing in the towel and calling it quits. God knew what he was doing when he blessed me with them. I had to stay strong for them because one thing I learned was aint nobody going to take care of my babies or treat them right but mama. Who ever said Mama's babies and daddy's maybes knew exactly what they were talking about. Though they didn't ask to be here, they still shouldn't have to suffer just because their father and I couldn't see eye to eye or even come to a medium on life's many principles. I always thought that the man was the head of the household and that the woman stood by his side to help him, support him, raise their children and hold down the household; boy have times changed.

We had a new place, but we still had the same old problems. I would come home from work and I could see the dent in the couch where Bob had been sleeping all day. Bob was still working the cement pump but things were slow. I hated driving up to our new nice apartment and see that old pick-up truck parked in the parking lot. It was such an eye sore amongst all the nice cars that were parked around it. It stuck out like a sore thumb. I would be so embarrassed when I would come around the corner and see it. I told Bob on the days that he didn't use the truck to leave it parked in Haines City with the pump at his dad's house.

Bob had it embedded in his mind that he could just hustle his way through life. But I didn't understand that because Bob came from a family where his father drove a cement truck for a very good company. Maybe because his father wasn't home a lot because he was working could have taken a toll on Bob. But his father did financially support his family, so I can't let Bob off the hook that easy. But I continued to work ten hours a day, and while the kids were in school Bob kept his head in the clouds.

One thing I can say; he would cook because after working ten hours, I know that I wasn't about to. Some days I would come home and things just didn't look right. Sometimes I would get the feeling as if someone had been in my house that wasn't supposed to be. I would ignore the feeling at first. I would try to redecorate the house as if that would make this eerie feeling that I had go away but it never would. I ended up getting rid of all my black and gold furniture. I gave all the furniture to my mama who hadn't come to see in years but she came that day. I redecorate in a lighter pallet which did help change the mood of the house. I guess the dark colors were making my house have a dark vibe.

I could only assume that Bob's philosophy of not wanting to work probably came from seeing his mom doing cash transactions all day and making phone calls while conducting business and running a household of four kids, maybe his thoughts were that the woman of the house should do and pay everything. His mama ran and owned her own beauty shop out of their home and they even had a small mom and pops store that they operated from their house also. So when he would sit around the house days on end which turned into months; I didn't understand. I thought that maybe he had gotten the idea that if he waited long enough that someone would come by and drop something in his lap for free. I object to the notion that opportunity comes knocking at your door. It doesn't know where you live so why would it come to your door. Like everything else you have to get up and find it, tap it on the shoulder and tell it what your plans are. If opportunity or luck wants to be part of your plan fine; if not, keep it moving. I feel that you have to work to get what you want and sometimes deserve. But also remember that everything comes at a price.

The Lord blessed me with many things, but patience was not one of them. If Bob was out of a job one week, I expected him to be working within the next two weeks at least. But it's damn near impossible to find a job if you never leave the house looking for one. But when Bob did work; I still couldn't tell the difference because my load was still the same. Lately at the end of every week we arguing over money and I'm tired of it. If I paid a bill last week because you didn't have the money (so he said), why do I have to pay a bill this week when you do have the money. Fair is fair. I didn't feel like sitting in the dark or arguing anymore with Bob, so I paid the light bill. But Bob still held on to the idea that he didn't have to help pay any bills just because I made more money. So he kept his money in his pocket while I paid all the bills and took care of the kids. Our arguments became more frequent and even sometimes violent; I hate to admit. I hated when the 1st came and it was time to pay rent; Bob would just act like he had amnesia. I didn't want us living in the street; so I paid that too. Hell, even the boys knew that rent was due on the 1st. After we would have a big blowout, Bob would do the right thing for a couple of weeks by paying a bill here and there. And then he would go back to not paying anything for months at a time. His financial support wasn't constant and very hard to depend on. This went on for months until I finally got tired and I had had enough and a thought came to me. If I'm going to be paying all the bills by myself then I should be living by myself.

I couldn't get wrapped up in Bob's way of thinking. I had two boys I wanted them to know and understand their responsibilities in life. Having them see their dad act like he had no clue or just refusing to do right was not a good example for them to learn from. I promised myself that my kids would have a better childhood than I did and planned on keeping that promise even if I had to do it alone. I thought that since Bob had two boys that he would take pride in fatherhood but it was only the opposite. I think he saw it more as a hindrance. Not wanting my boys to see me and their father arguing anymore; I put Bob out. I figure if he got some fresh air and got his head out of that cloud of smoke long enough that he could think of his family enough to do the right thing by them. The jury is still out on that. People say that you can do bad by yourself but I say if you give yourself a chance you can do good too.

Me and Bob had been together for such a long time and it just literally killed my spirit to know that someone who claims to love you and you grow to trust because they are all you have; can hurt you, lie to you and disregard you so easily. Over time the hurt and pain that this causes can change a person and I could feel myself starting to change. I started to trust no one and only depend on myself.

It had been just me and the boys for a couple of months now and we were doing okay. As I was watching television one evening the news reporter called out our town saying what was once a tropical storm was now turning into something much worst and that we were a direct hit. I watched as the sky turned gray. It wasn't your normal like on a cloudy day; something else was in the air. I heard what sounded like voices as my wind chimes danced in the wind. It was as if the wind was made of spirits and they were talking. Their presence was so obvious as they stirred up and danced through the trees. I found myself just looking at my wind chimes and listening as they spoke a language that only I could understand. As I stood there and listened I said welcome. The spirits danced strong and hard. It amazed me that none of my patio furniture moved an inch. Nothing was disturbed, not even a plant was knocked over; this is how I knew that it wasn't the wind but gentle spirits with a strong voice. My patio doors began to shake wildly as if they were going to come off their tracks. My front door rattled as if the spirits were knocking for me to let them in. I didn't fear them, I only acknowledged their presence. As the night fell, I was filled with peace as I could only hear them. I once was told that a hurricane takes the same route that the slave ships took when they were on their way back from Africa. I heard the voices of the slaves that night.

I woke the next morning calm. I walked outside and saw so much destruction. Power lines had been split in half; some of their tops were on the ground. Cars and the roads were covered with debris which caused some roads to be blocked off. Trees that had been standing for decades that had stood tall and wide as if you could climb them and touch the sky; were no longer there. Some trees were split right down the middle. Some trees looked like someone had just come up and pushed them over as they rested on their side. Even though it looked like a war zone, the sun was shining and it was quiet and peaceful. Instead of the calm before the storm, it was the calm after the storm.

I walked back to my apartment where there was no electricity or running water. I woke my boys. They woke with calm in their eyes as if it were just another day that they were looking forward to so that they could go to the pool; not realizing what the night had brought. I told them to pack their back packs with some clothes. They asked me where were they going and before I could answer them the phone rang. It was Bob calling to check on us. Bob had moved back in with his dad. Bob lived in the back part of the house that had been set up like an apartment by the previous owners. Bob asked if I had any gas in the car and asked if everyone was okay. Yes, I had gas in the car and yes everyone was okay. Bob told me to pack up the car and come his way. Oh please don't mistake his concern and kindness for as doing a good deed. Bob would use any opportunity he could to get back on my good side. The only reason why he hadn't been showing up at my front door for the past couple of months was because he knew that I wasn't entertaining or having any new friends around that he could chase away. After the last incident when he broke my apartment window with the neighbor's daughter bike; I put my boys' safety first and said that I wouldn't have any new friends at my house.

The ten minute drive that it would have normally taken to get to Haines City turned into an hour drive because of all the slow moving traffic. Everyone was trying to make sense of all the damage that had occurred during the night. A row of at least ten power lines were just leaning over like knights bowing down to their king. There were no traffic lights so everyone was being polite and aware of each other on the road. It was the shock of everything that was making everyone so humble. It's when people panic that everything goes to hell.

This looked like a scene out of a movie. I stayed calm so the boys wouldn't think that anything bad had happened. I just explained to them that we had a very strong storm. When things are crazy and I'm the only one around, I seem not to panic. I quickly step into survivor mode. We made it to Haines City which didn't have as much damage as Winter Haven. There was only one place in town to get gas and something to eat and that was the local truck stop. That was the only place that had electricity because they were running off their generator. So I filled up the car with more gas and got me and the boys something to eat. After a couple of hours hanging out at the truck stop, we made it to Bob's. The boys were very excited to see their dad and right now that was all that mattered. I had to put any ill feelings that I had for Bob on the back burner so I could get the boys through what would be a difficult time.

We drove around town from store to store to buy whatever we could. There was hardly anything on the shelves. Food was scarce and overpriced, but we got what we needed in order to survive. There was no electricity or running water for the next four days in Winter Haven so we made camp in Haines City. And it did seem more like a camping trip than a natural disaster. We kept up with what was going on by listening to the radio in Bob's truck. Bob dug a deep hole in the ground and made a fire which we smoked ham, cooked hot dogs, sausages and even baked potatoes. That night I rewarded Bob for his efforts as the fire would burn under the many stars in the midnight sky. The stars were the only light at night and they shined so bright you could actually see from one street corner to the next. There was a curfew in affect so that made the nights quiet and peaceful.

As the days went on our living space seemed to get smaller and I was ready to go back home to Winter Haven electricity or not. There were four people and a dog cramped up in a space that was the size of as single wide trailer. The boys were sleeping on the two couches that we would push together at night so they would have more room and be next to each other so the y wouldn't be scared at night. While me and Bob slept on the floor. With his unwanted advances and poking; Bob was quickly getting on my nerves. Some nights when it got to be too much I would climb up on the couches with the boys and go to sleep. I was ready for this all to be over. At least if we went back home they could at least sleep in their own bed by candle light. We could open up the windows so some fresh air could flow and everyone wouldn't be on top of each other. I was ready to go home to my clean apartment and sleep in my queen size bed.

The next morning on day five we packed up the car and I was headed back to Winter Haven. Bob asked if he could come to and before weighing the pros and cons or reviewing my past experiences and not remembering the reason he was at his dads in the first place and not living with us, I said yes. I will admit Pieces as you know are emotional creatures by fault; so yes I have a big heart. I figured he could stay at least until things got back to normal.

As we made it back to my side of town the devastation looked the same as it did four days ago. Home sweet home, it never looked so good. Bob and the boys got settled in as I checked the apartment to make sure no one had broken in and that everything was still in place and working. The water was back on but still no electricity. Two days have now passed since we've got back to the apartment and we're being civil towards each other; Bob and I. we are all playing board games and cards by candle light at night and reading books during the day. I just so happen to have a twelve inch television that runs by batteries, so we sit that on the living room table and watch it some nights. We were settled in our room when the electricity came back on late one night; back to reality. Now that the lights were back on and everyone was okay, it was time for Bob to go back home; so I thought.

Bob is a very good actor and I should know. I've had front row tickets to some of his Oscar winning performances. Bob knows that my boys are my first priority and all that I want for them is a good home; so those are the buttons he pushes and the emotions he plays on. Bob begged and pleaded to come back home and at first I stood my ground and told him no. After a while he wore me down. Bob went on and on about how he wanted his family back, how he didn't want to be out in the streets because things had changed and aint nothing out there for him. The hustle game had changed; it wasn't like it was years ago when he was out there hustling. Bob tried to make it seem like he had been such an innocent soul. As if he hadn't been seeing anyone and just at his dad's all this long time just sitting in that back room all by himself. That he had been doing nothing but his little odd jobs and coming straight home. But Bob knew that I knew that not to be true. Because I learned that I can't trust people, I also learned that I can't trust what they say. So I have learned how to find out things for myself and that's when I found out the truth. I have no problem confronting anyone or asking them questions. I was always told; you don't know if you don't ask.

I listened to Bob but all I could remember was the night that I went over to see him to pick up something for the boys and he wasn't home. It was about nine o'clock and I wondered to myself where could he have been. I knew that he had to go to work in the morning so I figured he wouldn't be out too late. I just figured he was out with the fellas, so I left. I came back around five the next morning to see him before he left for work but he still wasn't home. At that point and time my brain went into overdrive. I parked along the side of the house away from the road so if he came in that direction he wouldn't be able to see my car until he came all the way up to the house. Oh it was around six o'clock in the early morning when all the fun began.

A blue car drove up and stopped in front of the house as if someone was getting dropped off. When the passenger spotted my car, they motioned for the driver to keep going. I followed the car knowing that Bob was in there but then I began to second guess myself when I caught up with the car and drove pass it not seeing anyone in the passenger seat. There was a young lady driving the car so maybe she dropped him off somewhere. She couldn't have. I was only five seconds behind them. Soon as doubt was about to set in, I saw someone's head slowly coming up in the passenger seat. They didn't sit all the way up but just enough so they could see over the dashboard to see what direction the car was headed in; that's when I saw that the passenger was Bob. He had laid the seat back and slid so far down in the car; no wonder I didn't see him at first. When I saw his face they took off and things quickly turned into a scene from the *Fast and the Furious*. I was driving like a maniac trying not to lose them. I was running stop signs, flying by other cars, cutting in front of people, driving in reverse, driving on the wrong side of the road. Thank God there were no police around; where are they when you need one. When I finally came to my senses after realizing I could have killed myself or someone else, I started to back off. I saw that the blue car was headed back in the direction of Bob's house. I calmed myself down and headed in the same direction.

When I met up with them at the house, I pulled up in front of them and parked. The driver let Bob out the car and she drove off. My business was not with her so I didn't care who she was. After all the high speed chasing and Bob trying to hide in the car; when I got out the car all Bob could say was, "shouldn't I be at home watching television"? Bob never said where he was and who the girl was in the car. Bob just basically blew the whole thing off. After saying some choice words to Bob, which I care not to repeat; Bob went to work and I went home.

Still listening as Bob pleads his case on why I should let him come back home after the hurricane; I told him that the only way he could come home was that he had to get a real job. A real job mind you.

Bob's definition of a real job was he did whatever to get money. I called that hustling. At the time of the hurricane, Bob had been working for a company installing swimming pools. The company only had four other guys working for them and if they were to lose a contract; they were sure to go under. A job to me is when you have a schedule, wages, and benefits, punch a time clock and bring home a pay check on a regular basis. But despite our differences, I wanted my boys to grow up with their daddy in their lives because I didn't. So I told Bob yes that he could come home. After telling Bob that he could come home, I guess he got cold feet because he went back home to Haines City for a couple of days and then after a while he called to have me come and pick him up. Bob didn't bring all his clothes at once. A couple of pants, some shirts, socks and underwear was all he brought at first and then finally when he knew that he would be staying he brought the rest of his things. But it was when I was folding and putting away his clothes that I got the feeling that I made the mistake of letting him come back home.

Bob was still working with the pool company. He didn't have a license so that meant I had to get up early and take him to work all the way in Davenport because I didn't trust him with my car. So already the car is using more gas and more miles are going on my car.

A couple of weeks after Bob moved home, another hurricane struck but this was not as bad as the first one named Charlie. Dominique my youngest was very fascinated with the storm and its effects and Bob encouraged it. If he could, he would take a chair and sit right in the middle of one. DJ my oldest son didn't want anything to do with the storm; he was looking for shelter. I gave Bob and Dominique the nickname the *Storm Chasers*. They would run in and out the house every time the wind would blow hard or they heard some big bag which meant another transformer was blowing out giving off a pretty blue light lighting up the night sky. It was so funny watching them running around with the excitement in their eyes as they escaped the danger of the storm. Again there wouldn't be any electricity for just a day or two but this time the water stayed on so we stayed put this time. During the night the electricity came back on but the next morning Bob doing what he does; convinced his boss at the time that we had no food or money; which was a total lie. I don't know why Bob feels he always has to do that. Sometimes I'm embarrassed so by his hustler ways. But Bob could care less as long as he gets whatever it is that he's trying to get and get away with it.

So of course being the nice guy that he is; Bob's boss told us to come over to his house. We traveled at least forty-five miles to get there. The ride down there was quiet because I really didn't feel like wasting my energy arguing with Bob trying to make him see the wrong in what he was doing or the bad luck that he was putting on our family. I guess his boss told Bob that he would take care of him as far as giving him money for gas. I just felt so embarrassed the whole ride over. Bob had money and so did I; there was no need for this. I didn't want Bob's boss looking down on us as another family living in the hood struggling because we were so far from that. My God was very good to me and mine. But yet again; Bob was trying to get over on somebody like he always tries to do. Can't he understand that it aint getting him anywhere thinking like that. When you do wrong, wrong will always come back and do you.

We arrive at this huge house and I'm thinking this can't be the right house. The house sat on a lake and had a huge diesel truck parked in the pebble stoned driveway along with two other sports cars. There was even a small camper parked on the side of the house. This couldn't have been the same man that Bob was working for and he was only paying them eight dollars an hours to install pools. But then again I thought, that's why he can live in this big huge nice house because he's only paying them eight dollars an hour. Me and the boys got out the car; I was just looking around in amazement.

As we approached the house with its well landscaped yard, I noticed a pregnant woman sitting on the porch as if she was would be ready to deliver any day now. To her right sat a pretty young lady who looked every bit of fifteen and she was smoking. Then there was an older lady holding a baby who I later found out was the mother-in-law and the youngest child. I could tell already that this was a very dysfunctional family. Not trying to be real obvious on the reason why we were there, we all made small talk. Bob's boss gives him some money and brings out a six foot white cooler full of meat from a cow that he butchered himself. I felt even more embarrassed but not Bob; he just had this big smirk painted on his face that I had seen so many times before. We stayed for a minute or two longer making more small talk. We loaded up the car and Bob's boss told us to follow him. We ended up following him to the gas station. When we got to the gas station and I had had enough of this mascaraed; I insisted that I pay for the gas. And all the while the boys were looking at me with a confused look on their face of why were we driving around in circles. After getting gas; Bob's boss told us to follow him again. This time we ended up at the supercenter. We got out the car again but this time I just lingered behind with the boys as we entered the store while Bob walked with his boss pushing a cart and filling it up. Bob and his boss went one way while me and the boys went on another. I just shook my head.

After a while they made their way back up front to the check-out register with two carts full of items. Me and the boys had already been sitting on one of the benches twenty minutes ago. After checking out we all walked to the car. I was hesitant to grab any bags because I knew that we didn't need the stuff. The ride home was just as quiet. Bob's boss insisted that he follow us home to help unload things because afterwards him and Bob could stop by the office to see how much damage was done; if any because of the hurricane.

We got home and everyone walked into the apartment at the same time. The house was cool because the air conditioner had been running. Dare I remind you that Bob told his boss that we didn't have any electricity? I think I shrunk to an inch due to embarrassment. After we were settled in, Bob and his boss left but not before I sincerely thanked his boss. Please don't get me wrong I don't mind help when I need it. But what I do mind is taking advantage of people's kindness. I couldn't say anything in front of Bob's boss but thank you because if I would have said anything else I would have put the spot light on my husband and he could have lost his job behind his foolishness. So I did as a wife does and watched quietly and tended to my children.

There was so much meat that the refrigerator couldn't hold it all. I went to my next door neighbor and took the family a couple packs of roast, chicken, and other meats. They were so appreciative. Then I thought maybe that was the reason for us to get the meat, so we could help another family who was less fortunate than we were. So after giving them the meat and other things; my heart didn't feel so heavy anymore.

# Chapter 30

**THINGS HAD SETTLED** down for a minute and we were the family that we needed to be. Bob never like the idea of working for another man and so yet again he wanted to open his own business. Bob came home one day after work and said that he and his other two co-workers were going to open up their own pool installing business and call it the Three Amigos. Here we go again. I thought something was wrong with this picture, something was up. So I asked him what was going on at work to make him want to go and open up his own business. I never really got an answer. I just think that they finally figured out how much money their boss was making installing pools and they wanted a bigger piece of the pie and not the crumbs that their boss was paying them. Anyway, it just felt like another one of his get rich quick schemes. Mind you, Bob didn't have any money so how was he going to start his own business. I would stand by my man but I wasn't going to finance my man; not this time. I did it once and he has nothing to show for it. I later found out that after that last hurricane, the pool installing business wasn't doing so good and that Bob's boss had to move out of his big house and he sold all the equipment from the business and let them go. So I didn't understand why Bob wanted to go into a business where it wasn't doing any good.

Being the supportive wife that I am; I went through the motions with the Three Amigos. Bob's part of the business was to lay out the piping for the pools. Bob's partner Marcus would dig the holes for the pool because he had the equipment for that and Jose would form the pool. I acted as secretary and bookkeeper. But before the ink could dry on the paperwork, one of the Amigos dropped out because his citizens' papers weren't legit so we could put his name on the business license or claim him on the business insurance. No one seemed to be coming up with any money to pay for supplies or any of the business expenses; I found myself acting as an investor in the company looking to be paid back. I'm still looking.

Not knowing how the company was going to get off the ground; I asked Bob did he have any new clients or was he taking over some of the clients from his boss. Well Bob had no clients and all the deals he had set up were only conversations that went nowhere. But yet all around town people were getting pools installed so I never understood why Bob wasn't getting a piece of the action. The big boys in the pool business were making big money and if you weren't already a member of their *big boys* club then they weren't accepting applications. The rich help keep the rich get even richer.

Finally, after all the red tape of forming a corporation; Bob and his remaining Amigo got a contract to install a pool. Of course Bob asked me to come along that way I could hear the terms and put together a proposal for the job. I tried to keep Bob looking as professional as possible so that clients wouldn't think that he was some dude off the street corner that they hire for the day because they were trying to find cheap labor. I wanted them to know that he was running a business and I wanted them to pay him like such. So I put my accounting hat on and went along for the ride. We drove to what seemed like a hundred miles out of the way to meet this man. When we got there everything seemed promising; then we started talking business. You could tell that the Amigos hadn't worked together for long. They were talking over each other. One would say the opposite of what the other was saying. You could tell who knew what they were talking about and it wasn't Bob. Then when Marcus would speak up, you couldn't understand a word that he was sayin.. I was so embarrassed because we tried to look as if we were all on one accord but I could tell that the client knew that we weren't. Bob was saying yes to everything that the client was saying before consulting with Marcus or asking any questions. This was making him look desperate and that wasn't a good look. Bob was underbidding and not sticking to set conditions that were put in place for all jobs. At one point no one could agree on anything and it just seemed like they were going around in circles and about to lose the client. At times the client would look over at me for some type of clarification and I would have to use what I learned in school about business to put us back in the game. In the middle of the meeting, Bob pulls out a cigarette; this was a sure sign that he was nervous. It wasn't until I reminded him that we were inside a store, that I thought it best that he go outside to smoke. He and Marcus were outside talking but it looked more like arguing to me from what I could hear. I was left behind in the store to make small talk and to convince the client that the Amigos were the ones for the job. After having a twenty minute sidebar, the Amigos came back into the store, everyone shook hands and the fun began.

The plan went as followed; Marcus would dig the hole for the pool with the dollies that they would rent and Bob would lay down the pipes and form the deck. So for their first job Marcus did just that. He would dig the hole for the pool the day before Bob was to show up to the job site. Bob asked me to come along and keep him company. Somehow I ended up digging ditches, helping Bob lay out water pipes and helping him form the deck. I had sweat running down my face so bad that I thought it was raining. Bob tried to make the experience fun for me. He knew that this wasn't woman's work but there was no one else that he could depend on for help. I could look at his face and see the disappointment and shame in his eyes. But I knew that he needed me, so I was there. I didn't complain but after the second job I told Bob that he needed to hire someone to help him. The week went good and everyone was showing up on time and work was getting done.

With me not having to be out on the job sites I concentrated more on the office work of the Amigos. I had written up work orders detailing all the duties that were to be done and the cost of it all. When it came time for the clients to pay for the work that was done, there was a problem. The clients never wanted to pay by the job but by the hour. That I never understood because that wasn't part of the contract. The Amigos didn't work by the hour, they worked by the job. Some clients wouldn't pay their bill in full and so it made it hard for us to depend on the business to pay bills. The business revenue didn't cover much. At the end of every week there was enough to cover payroll and very little left over to put up for business expenses. This went on for a couple of weeks. After a while work started to become scarce. Marcus couldn't take it anymore because he said that he had a family to support so he needed something solid. You would have thought that Bob would have had the same thought but his thought was more so that he didn't want to work for anyone. As long as Bob had enough money for beer, cigarettes, and weed; he was just fine. The hell with what bills had to be paid and putting food on the table. Bob wasn't trying to support a family he was just trying to support his habits and not to have to work on another man's job. Marcus found himself a job and that was the end of the Three Amigos.

Days go by and Bob is sitting around the house feeling bad for himself. He should be used to it by now, I am. He wouldn't keep finding himself in this situation if he would just go and find a real job. But as they say, a hard head makes a soft ass. But unlike Bob, I can't sit around and have a pity-party with him because I have to be at work four o'clock in the morning. I don't mind supporting my husband but I'm not going to take care of him or give him money for his habits. Days turn into weeks and Bob hasn't found a job yet. I wasn't getting on his back about it; I was giving Bob time to recover from his disappointment of yet another business going down the drain. But after a while it seemed like he wasn't trying to find a job; he never left the house. A month had gone by and Bob mentioned something about getting the cement pump up and running again. I told him if that's what he wanted to do since he didn't want to get a job; for him to go right ahead but I wanted nothing to do with it. I think Bob sensed that I was starting to get aggravated because he started leaving every morning like he was going to look for clients who needed a porch poured and anything involving the cement pump. But I later found out that he was just hanging out with his friends. There would be times when I got off of work and Bob wouldn't be home that I had to go looking for him for some reason or another. I use to hate driving up and down the streets looking for him. But he would always be in that same spot hanging out at the corner store. I can only assume that Bob use to call someone to come and get him after I would leave for work and the boys were off to school because I know he didn't use to walk all the way back to Haines City.

And there I would find him hanging out with drug dealers, scrubs, old men and drunks instead of working. The old men who had already figured out that their life was over and their best years were behind them, were giving out advice to the young guys who would listen. I would always tell Bob if he kept listening to them that he was going to end up like them; old, alone and talking jive that only drunk ears wanted to hear.

Things were really starting to try my patience; the very little that I had left. The lights, water, phone, car payment, rent, food were all falling on me and I was getting the same silent treatment from Bob when I would ask him for some money to help pay bills. Sometimes he would even act like he had caught amnesia. I knew Bob had money because he had cigarettes and beer that I knew I hadn't been buying. But when I would ask Bob for money he would just tell me that he didn't have any. And for the first couple of times I would except that answer and just go and pay the bills myself because regardless of what Bob didn't do; didn't mean that the bills still didn't have to be paid.

With him not helping me pay the bills was getting on my nerves but it only kicked started off that everything Bob did; was getting on my nerves. Bob had started smoking a few years ago which affected our sex life. I'm a kisser, I like to kiss and I missed kissing Bob but cigarettes don't taste good. I feel that a lot of passion is in kissing. I bet that's why prostitutes always say no kissing because that's where the feelings get involved. I got that from watching *Pretty Woman*. But what she said made a lot of sense. Bob had a nasty habit of leaving the ashes in the bathroom and kitchen sink after he smoke that drove me crazy. I never bought any ashtrays because I figured if I didn't then he wouldn't smoke in the house and have the house smelling like smoke. It started to seem like Bob couldn't see past himself enough to think about others and realize that his second hand smoke could be harming others. He just refused to go outside and smoke.

Then he had this thing of lying in the bed all day with the door closed watching television. He would get mad at me because I wouldn't join him. I hated lying in the bed all day with the door closed. Its two o'clock in the afternoon; why are we lying in the bed anyway. When I closed my bedroom door, it felt like I was closing my kids off from me. My mother use to stay in her room all day with my step-father all day and I couldn't stand that. We hardly saw her unless she was coming out of the room to get something for him. And if we needed to ask her something we would have to talk through the door because though we would knock on the door, she would rarely open it. I made a promise to myself to never do that to my children. That my door would always be open to them and that I would always be available to them.

Bob's idea of helping to clean up was a joke. I figured if he couldn't help me financially then he could have helped me in other ways around the house like cooking and cleaning up. That way I wouldn't have to feel so overwhelmed after coming home from work and helping the kids with their homework. But I guess that wasn't a thought for him either. Bob had more clothes on the floor than he had in the closet or his dresser drawers. One day out of the week; Bob would cook and that was usually on Sunday; lucky me. What else could a woman ask for? Was asking her husband to get a job be too much out of the question. Oh and sex was so much out of the question for me by this time. Not so much because of the smoking; I can have sex without kissing but I just couldn't get in the mood or stomach the fact that a man expects you to allow him to climb on top of you and you have to look up at him taking care of his business, taking his time and loving every minute of it like he earned the right to have dessert when he didn't eat all his vegetables. He wants me to perform my wifely duties regardless of whether or not he carries out his duties as a husband. My thing is if you can't act like a husband outside of the bedroom then you don't get to act like a husband inside the bedroom.

Things have become very tense between me and Bob. It has become a game of tug of war. Through and through Bob expresses his love for me with his words but it is not enough for me because his actions only expresses that he doesn't love me or his family. I have no doubt that he loves me but love can't pay the bills. Can you picture me going down to the electric company with the final notice in my hand and asking them please not to turn off my lights because my husband won't get a job but he told me that he loved me. I'm standing there telling this to the receptionist and she's giving me this dumb look like that's nice but we don't except love as a payment. Now how are you paying your bill today? What does she mean love don't pay the bills. That's all Bob seems to figure that's how they get paid. Bob thinks that if he just says that he loves me then everything is going to be okay. You mean to tell me that we can't buy a house, a car, and clothes or even put food on the table with his love for me. I know that but someone needs to tell Bob. Reality sucks.

Bob coming home every day after playing in the streets and leaving me to work and pay all the bills is starting to take its toll on me. Bob won't even give me money to buy a gallon of milk. Weeks go by and enough is enough. I can't sleep because I'm upset because this is not what I bargained for as my life. He won't help me pay the light bill, put gas in the car; he won't even give the boys lunch money. Helping me pay the rent is out of the question and him buying groceries; well let's just say we'll get full off of wish sandwiches before that happens. What gets under my skin the most is that this man knows what it takes to live and he knows what he is supposed to be doing as far as being head of the household. He is responsible for three other people besides himself. If he knew that he wasn't going to be able to handle the responsibility then why did he ask me to marry him if he wasn't going to do right by me? My marriage to Bob had damaged me.

I've always said, don't do what I want you to do, just do what you are supposed to do. That is what will make me happy because I have no right to make you do anything.

I don't want Bob to touch me. I dread the nights and having to share a bed with him. I'm fighting with him the whole night because he's poking, rubbing and groping on me all night when all I want to do is sleep so I can go to work in the morning. Just let me hold you so I can go to sleep; is his excuse for cuddling up to me. At first it starts off as just a hug then I'll drift off to sleep and then I'm awaken by him trying to force himself inside of me. After about the third time of being woken up this way; I don't feel like fighting so I throw him out of the bedroom and make him sleep on the couch and I lock him out the room. Other nights I just go and get in the bed with one of the boys. Then there are nights when because I'm so frustrated with all that's going on and I want him to feel my frustration, I'll just grab the lamp off the nightstand and knock him over the head with it and he'll finally get the point that I want him to leave me alone and we all get sleep that night. I'm now down to one lamp, I broke the other one.

When I would come home from work, the boys would tell me how he stayed in the room all day with the door locked. I already knew what he had been doing; getting high. This was another thing that Bob did that got under my skin. He had been getting high very since I knew him but he was more discreet and would never do it around me or the kids. I thought that once we had our first son that he would stop but that didn't happen. At times it slowed down but it never came to a complete stop. I think that's part of why he would never get a real job; the fear of having to give up his true love.

---

As soon as I would get home, lie down and fall asleep; Bob would sneak off with my car. Bob knew that would be the only way that he would get my car. One because he didn't have a license, two because I wasn't paying the car payment and insurance just for him to go around joy riding. If he would have been going on somebody's job so he could work, then that would have been a different story. I'm at my wits end and I can't take anymore. Life is overwhelming me with all these problems and I am trying to keep a happy face for my boys. But I'm not feeling like myself anymore. I find myself many times crying out to God in the midnight hour asking him why won't he make Bob do right by me. God answers me; because he gave us free will. He lets me know that's why our love is so special to him because we choose to love him; that he doesn't make us. What reward is there in making someone do something that they don't want to do? When you make someone do something it means nothing. It's only when they choose to do something that you know they care. I understood God's words and he understands my cries. God comforts me and he rocks me so softly until I fall off to sleep.

Things are starting to get tight. There's not enough food, money, or gas to last from one week to the next. I just can't believe that Bob is just standing by watching our life fall apart. I'm doing the best I can with what I have. I feel like I'm in a house with three kids instead of only two. There are two adults here and both of us should be working. I don't feel like I'm living day to day, just surviving and it shouldn't be like that. The world was made for animals to survive and for people to live. What was going on in Bob's head? The same way his parents feed, clothed and put a roof over his head, he had to do the same. It's his turn now, he's the parent.

When Bob came home from where ever he was at, I told him to go and get a newspaper because tomorrow he was going to go and look for a job. Bob went and brought a newspaper and told me to look through the paper for a job for him. My jaw fell to the floor. Was he serious? Yes, he was. I turned to Bob in disbelieve. I told him that I couldn't look for a job for him, that he had to do that himself.

The next couple of days would be nerve wrecking for Bob and irritating for me. I go to work and listen to the women as they sing their husband's praise. They talked about how their husbands pay the mortgage or are adding on to the house in some type of weekend project. And I sit and listen as they recall the details of a cruise they just came back from over the weekend. I look at their large diamond rings and the nice cars that they were driving; and I wished that was me. Then I listen to the guys who talk in pride about their children, the little league game they went to or the trip to Disney that they're going to take over the weekend or how they're taking the car to the shop for a tune up or going shopping for a new one. They talked with pride about all the yard work and how good it looks; and I wish that was Bob. You could tell that they are the head of their household, protector and provider and that their wives are their partner. I envy both of them.

Where did I go wrong? What did I do that was so wrong that I'm so miserable now? Bob doesn't understand my pain or frustration at all. He's got it made. He knows that the boys, the house nor I will go without if I have anything to do with it. But I'm tired now. I am literally burned out physically and emotionally. My youngest son once asked me why woman cry when they get married. I told him it was because we are happy that we met this person that we love but we are trusting and putting our lives in someone else's hand who had promised us that they will respect, cherish and love us, protect us, and provide and we have to trust that this person will do all the things that they promised. There is no guarantee that this man is going to do those things but we believe him and so we are both weary and scared. We are leaving our parents who did those things without a second thought or hesitation. They were I security net and now we are going out into the real world.

For a couple of days Bob went looking for a job. He leaves the house about three o'clock in the afternoon to go looking. Who do you know goes looking for a job three o'clock in the afternoon? How about somebody who really aint looking for a job. He would come home around six and say that he didn't find a job; no duh. This went on for a couple more days until one morning I told him that I was going to ride with him. He looked like the cat the swallowed the canary. We drove to one place, some type of resort. There was a position open for a landscaper. Bob went in the office and I stayed in the car, after a while Bob came out accompanied by a gentlemen. I let down my window and Bob asked me how much he should ask for an hour wage. I told him not to ask for anything less than eight but no higher than ten. I mean I don't think they're going to pay you fifteen dollars an hour to cut grass. They agreed to the pay and Bob got the job. Bob got a job at the first place we stopped. If it was that quick and easy, it made me wonder if he had been really going to look for a job all this time. I didn't think he needed me to come along, or did he?

I just knew that Bob getting a job was the beginning of something good for all of us. My stress level would drop and I would stop hating the sight of him when I walked in a room. I couldn't have been more further from the truth if I had gotten on a boat and went to China. Bob got paid on the week that I didn't so that meant that a check was coming in the house every week. The signs were there early that that wouldn't be the case. The first week that he got a full paycheck I didn't ask him for much at all because I wanted him to enjoy his first check. Bob didn't believe in splitting all the bills down the middle. He didn't believe that whoever got paid when a bill was due then that's the person who paid the bill. He didn't believe in bringing all his money home. There was no plan with our finances that he liked.

I gave Bob the responsibility of paying the car payment because he used the car five days a week and I only used it for three. His job was further from home then mine was, so he was putting all the miles on the car. After a while Bob started skipping car payments. I would pay them after I found out about it because I didn't want the people to come and reposes my car; I needed to get to work.

Bob would never deposit his money in the bank; mine was direct deposit arranged through my job. I never saw a check stub from Bob so I never really knew how much he made. And please don't ask me what he did with his money because I couldn't tell you. Did he feel as if he was being less of a man if he brought his money home to his wife? I always brought my whole check home; that way my family and I could benefit off my hard work. I never knew any other way to do it. I didn't mind so much because when you looked around my house you could see my money. I was paying rent so that my family could live in a very nice place which was a gated community with a pool, basketball court, tennis court, gym, conference room, green grass and trees and sidewalks. I was paying for a decent car and my home was furnished very nicely. The kids were clothed and I had a closet full of clothes and shoes. I got a manicure and pedicure every two weeks. So I really didn't see the problem in bringing your money home; I only saw its benefits.

All this fighting, cursing and throwing things wasn't good for the boys to be seeing. It had gotten to the point where the only time Bob would pay a bill is after I turned into a she-devil. Me having to turn into a she-devil every week just so he would pay a bill was making my pressure go up and that wasn't good. There were times when I would pay the rent of seven hundred and fifty-five dollars and the remaining bills due totaled around three hundred fifty-three dollars. Bob would only give me two hundred dollars for the bills. I would tell him that it wasn't enough. He would just look at me and tell me to put the rest with it. I didn't have the energy to argue so there I was picking up his slack

There would be times when I wouldn't ask Bob for money but just tell him to go and pay the electric bill and at first he would do okay with that. Then every other month our electricity started getting cut off and it never failed that it always got cut off around the time that I got paid. I found out that Bob wasn't paying the whole bill or he wasn't paying it on time. It's okay when you know what's going on in your household but when someone else gets a whiff of it; it really stinks. One day when I got off of work and I went to go and pay my rent. I walked into the office and the landlord asked me if I knew that my electricity was turned off that day. I told her no; that I had just gotten off of work and came straight to the office. After paying my rent I left the office. I was so embarrassed that the landlord knew that my lights were off and I didn't know.

I drove to my apartment and went inside. And sure enough, there sat Bob, DJ, and Dominique with no lights on. I just looked at Bob with sheer amazement. How could he let this happen? I looked at my two little boys and I knew that they didn't deserve this. I was too tired to argue at the moment and they didn't need to see me angry, so I just told everyone to get in the car.

The electric company's office was closed by the time we got downtown, so of course we or should I say that I had to use the special black phone that hangs on the outside of the building in one of those metal boxes. I called and talked to an operator so I could get our electricity turned back on. She told me that it would be a couple of hours before anyone would be out to the apartment to turn the lights back on. To make the best of a situation, I decided just to take the family out to dinner while we waited. I was mad and embarrassed because my boys were out here in the streets with no electricity on at home and they have two working parents. I was mad because I depended on Bob to do what he was supposed to do and I trusted that he would do what he said he was going to do. But he didn't which caused me to have to take care of things. There he was standing in front of me looking down at the ground like a thirteen year old boy who just got caught smoking in the bathroom. I just looked at him as he was telling me how sorry he was and that it wouldn't happen again. Haven't I heard that one before?

Bob use to always say that I wanted to be the head of the house and that everything had to go my way. But that wasn't true. Bob puts me in that position every time he doesn't do what he is supposed to and I have to clean up his mess. Yes, I can be strong minded when I need to be for my family but I never wanted to be the head of the household. When I leave things up to Bob they either get half done or don't get done at all. The things that don't affect my boys; I don't worry about. But if it's going to affects my boys then I'm going to try to fix it before they get hurt by it.

After dinner and sometime wasted in the store, we finally made it home. The electricity was back on and so I got everyone settled down and ready for bed. Me and Bob would talk but not much would change. Where we would fix one problem then another problem would just as quickly take its place.

Bob never puts more than five dollars at a time in the gas tank. This meant that we had to stop at the gas station everyday which wasn't cost efficient at all. I suggest to Bob just to fill the car up with gas when he got paid and that way the gas would last a whole week until I got paid then I would fill the car up. Bob wanted nothing to do with that plan. So instead there was many times that we were scrapping up pennies for gas because I hadn't got paid yet and Bob swore that he didn't have any money.

Groceries were just the basics adding up to no more than eighty dollars when Bob went shopping because he never wanted to spend more than that. He bought groceries like we were cave people; just meat and bread. We hardly ever went shopping together or as a family because there was always an argument. Bob would never buy snack for the kids or kid friendly foods so when they would come home from school they could just throw something in the microwave if they were hungry. Bob never bought anything extra; that was all left up to me. I truly think that Bob cared more about making sure he had money to last him through the week for his little habits. Great example, my youngest son came to me and said that he needed a pack of crayons for school which cost only two dollars and some change. Bob had just gotten paid that week so I told my son to go and ask his dad. I think it good for a son to receive things from his father sometimes. That way his son can look up to him as a man; even if it is just over a small box of crayons. It's just the principal of the matter for his son to see his father as a provider. Well I could tell just when my son had asked his dad because you could hear Bob yelling from one end of the house to the other. "Where are the crayons your mom bought"? My mission failed. I didn't send my son to him for him to remind my son of the things that I do for him. My son already knows that he can depend on me; that's why they come to me first so that don't have to hear no from their father all the time. Bob obviously didn't get the point and was referring to the crayons that I had bought at the beginning of the school year. "You don't need any crayons, borrow some from your friends"; is what I hear him yelling to my son. You could hear Bob pulling open drawers in the attempt to find a box of crayons. My son came back to me with the look of disappointment on his little face. I told him not to worry that I would buy him some crayons. I took my son and we left to go to the store and when we came back, Bob suddenly left. After being gone for maybe fifteen minutes, Bob came back home with a new pack of cigarettes and a beer. You figure it out.

Incidents like this continued for weeks. Bob had no problem putting his selfish needs before his family's needs. One fall my oldest son needed a jacket. He had gone without one for the past two years because Bob had convinced me that he didn't need one because the weather wasn't that bad. And I felt bad because I listened to him. He just didn't want me to spend the money. I'd rather for my baby to have had the jacket and let him determined if it was cold enough or not for him to wear his jacket. But this year was different and I was determined to get my baby a jacket regardless of what Bob said. I asked Bob for half of the cost of the jacket, he said that he didn't have any money which I knew was a lie. I told him that I was going to the store to buy DJ a jacket. Bob didn't offer to make this a family affair and come along with us to the store. He just laid on the couch watching television requesting that I bring him back a pair of work boots. Huh, how is it when I ask you for something, you don't have it. But when you ask me for something I'm supposed to have it. My son needed a jacket and all Bob was worried about was getting him some work boots but didn't want to give me any money for either. Needless to say like a good mother and wife that I am; I bought my son his jacket and I bought my husband his work boots.

# Chapter 31

**WELL, THE DUKE** has done put me down. You know how men call their cars Betsy; well I called my 89 four door burgundy Ford Tarus the Duke. I got the Duke back in 99 from one of the car dealerships that Bob use to work at when he had his car detailing business. The Duke was good to me for a good couple of years. I even put in a new stereo system with some bass in the trunk for him. The Duke started getting from point A to point B just a little bit slower than usual. The Duke had blown a hole in his radiator which Bob tried to close up with some radiator paste but it wouldn't hold. Then the Duke's transmission was starting to slip so I decided that it was time to put the Duke to rest.

I looked in the papers for a couple of days and did my research until I came across what I was looking for. I wanted another Ford Tarus that way I could keep it in the family. Finally I came across the car that I was looking. I called the dealership and we haggled back and forth for a while until we both were comfortable with a deal. The next day; Bob, the boys and I all piled into the Duke for one last ride.

Bob had gotten frustrated and aggravated with the Duke a couple of weeks ago so he suggested that I drive. He was so aggravated with the Duke that he had took out the new cd player and speaker box that I paid for and he pawned them without my permission. He told me after he did it and he kept the money. There were no words in the dictionary that could describe the betrayal that I felt. But that wouldn't be the last time Bob would do something so low like that.

I didn't mind driving the Duke, it was only right for me to see the

Duke off; he had been good to me. A trip to the other side of town that would normally take thirty minutes, was taking the Duke an hour and a half. The Duke was doing the best he could but when it came to going over the bridge, Duke had me a little worried. I thought that I was going to have to get out and push him over the bridge. After a lot of praying and pacing ourselves we made it to the dealership. I gave the Duke one last look over and thanked him. I have learned to appreciate everything that God has blessed me with whether it is big or small, new or old. I handed the keys over to the car salesman. I watched as he parked the Duke in a grassy field along with some other cars who too had seen better days.

The car salesman walked us to the front office as we were doing some paper work he told me that the car that we discussed over the phone wasn't ready yet and wouldn't be for a while that it hadn't come from his other car lot just yet. But he went on to say if I was in a rush and didn't want to wait that I could choose from other cars on the lot. He left me and Bob alone so we could decide. I walked the lot but saw nothing that interested me. I knew that I wouldn't becausee I had already had my heart set on the Tarus. But Bob on the other hand was just eager to get a new car and told me to pick something. We had a few words between each other because I didn't appreciate him putting his two cent in when I was putting my fifteen hundred dollars down. So instead of continuing my argument with Bob, I told the salesman that I would just stick with my first choice.

Since the car wouldn't be ready for hours the salesman told me that I could have a loaner car to go to the mall or run any errands that I needed to until my car was ready. When the car salesman handed me the keys to the nice loaner car; Bob insisted that he drive. Mind you he doesn't have a license nor did he have any insurance and the salesman sign the car over to me so I'm responsible to get this car back the same way it left. None of that matter to Bob even after I informed him. And so not wanting to argue with Bob in public anymore, I gave him the keys. This was supposed to be a happy day for me; I was getting a new car. I've slowly learned to choose my battles with Bob because he can really send me into a frenzy sometimes with this temper of mine and my boys don't need to see their mama like that all the time. The ride home was nice I must say hell; we were driving in a new car. Bob had that stupid smirk on his face like he was the king driving a Royals Royce.

It just made me sick because he was enjoying himself off of someone else's expense.

It took us longer to get back home because Bob took the scenic route. I think he was enjoying the new car just a little too much. When we finally got home and parked, everyone go out of the car except for Bob. Me and the boys started to walk up the sidewalk to the front door and Bob was still sitting in the car. I looked back at him and asked him what he was doing. He said that he had to go to the store. This puzzled me because we had just passed fifty stores on the way home, so why didn't he stop at one of them. Why did he wait until we got all the way home and everybody out the car before he said that he needed to go to the store? I just had that *you've got to be kidding* look on my face. "Why didn't you stop on the way", I asked him as if I didn't already know the answer. I just wanted to hear it come out of his mouth. I didn't wait around for the answer because I knew he was going to make up a lie and not just say that he wanted to ride around town so his friends could see him in a new car. So they could think that his pockets were big and that he could afford a new car. The boys looked at me and asked me where their daddy was going. Instead of answering them right away I turned to Bob and suggested that he take the boys with him since he was only going to the store. That was out of the question. Bob said no and pulled out of the parking lot. I just shook my head and took the boys in the house. What I really wanted to do was yank his ass out that car through the driver-side window. But I didn't have the energy anymore mentally to deal with Bob and his crap.

Not to my surprise, Bob came back home three hours later from going to the store. Mind you the store is only two blocks away from the house on the corner. I know Bob didn't need anything from the store. So I asked Bob which store did he go to; the one in Alabama. I waited for the answer this time because I knew something stupid was going to come out of his mouth. He said that he was just riding around and stopped by his dad's. So Bob drove all the way to the City just to ride around in a new car and show-boating around in a car that wasn't his but he wanted people to think that it was. I could just imagine how he was acting; all slid down in the driver seat like he was on the Jamaican bobsledding team, acting like he was cool, with his arm hanging all out the window and all the while; doing his little head node to the fellows who are standing on the corner as he rides by them doing three miles an hour. I just wonder how fast he's going to be driving tomorrow when he pass by them same fellows in his that old pick-up truck with no bed. In any event, I was ready to go and get my new car.

I let Bob drive us back to the dealership so he could enjoy that new car smell. When we got there it was dark and the car was there but it was being detailed so we went in the office and finished up the paperwork "we"; meaning me and the salesman. Bob sat there and just watched as I signed all the papers and handed over fifteen hundred dollars. He didn't even bother to reach in his pocket to hand me a dollar. When the salesman handed me the keys to my new car I thanked him. But, when he suggested a second set for Bob I corrected him very quickly with a dirty look and told him that I only recalled one person handing him any money for the car and that's the only person who needed keys.

After a while the car was ready and it was time to go home; it had been a long day and everyone was tired. Bob looked at me with his hand out as if to tell me that he was going to drive. I don't like driving a long way at night, or at night when it's raining and tonight it was doing both. But before he could get a word out of his mouth, I pushed his hand away and told him that I was driving my new car home. If he was mad, I didn't care at that moment. He had done enough joy riding for the day. Excuse me for being selfish, but I didn't recall him holding his hand out with any money in it when it was time to buy insurance or give the dealer the down payment for the car. I wasn't in the mood to let Bob reap the fruit of my labor again.

The ride home was nice. Powered windows and locks, an air conditioner that worked, the dash board lit up, the gas meter worked; there was even a cd player. It took me only a couple of days to get use to going out and getting into my new car. But the thrill was short lived because it wasn't too long before Bob would start with his little games with me about the car.

There had been many times when I would come home from working a twelve hour shift, talk and play with the kids for about an hour than lay down for a nap. After a couple of hours of a nap; I would wake up to Bob and my car gone. I would ask the boys how long their dad had been gone. They would tell me that just as soon as I would fall asleep, he would leave; ain't that a…. something. You already know what I really wanted to say. Soon as my head hit the pillow and he knew that I was sleep; he would get my keys and leave the house and sometimes he wouldn't come home until it was time for me to go to work the next morning around two a.m. he wouldn't even have called when he thought that I might have woken up from my nap to see if I needed anything, had to go to the store or even to tell me that he was hanging out with the fellows and that he would be home after a while. You know, respect goes a long way. Disrespect will get you popped. What if there had been an emergency or something. There had been a couple of times that I didn't even make it to work because by the time Bob got home with my car I would be pass my boiling point. I would be out of control with so much anger. When he would finally get home with the car, I was ready to fight. Not only because he had my car and was making me late for work, but also for having me sitting up here worrying about his stupid ass thinking that something done happened to him because that should have been the only reason for him not calling home to check on us since he had the damn car.

But no, he just out there joy riding and show-boating with my car like he had anything to do with it getting it. I didn't trust Bob with my car. By Bob not having a license my worst fear would be that he would get into a car accident, jump out the car running from the scene leaving my car on the side of the road. I know what I'm talking about. He's done it before; not with my car of course but with the old pick-up truck. That's why it doesn't have a bed on it.

We had just moved into the new apartment home and Bob was still working for his dad running the cement pump. It was the end of the summer and time to get the kids ready to get back to school. It was a normal day and I had planned on taking the kids shopping when I had gotten off of work. After a smooth day at work, I got home where I and the kids were sitting in the middle of the living room floor planning out our shopping trip. Out of nowhere like a mad man; Bob came busting through the front door scaring the crap out of everybody as he was covered with mud from head to toe and his clothes were torn. He was out of breathe looking like a runaway slave who just escaped from his masters' plantation. Bob made a b-line straight to the bathroom in the mastering bedroom passing by me and the boys with our eyes as big as fifty cent pieces; looking at each other wondering what the heck was going on.

I called for Bob to ask him what happened to him and what in the world was he doing. He ran back to the living room as if his pants were on fire. Hysterically he told me to call his daddy and tell him that his truck was stolen and then he ran back into the bedroom. I've learned not to take what Bob says as the gospel; he is a very good actor. I was very hesitant and suspicious of what he was saying as I remained sitting on the floor. Mind you, it was payday and it was a big one because they had been working well all week. So my first thought was that he was trying to get out of having to give me any money for the boys' school stuff.

So I began to think; who would want to steal that old pick-up truck? It was on its last leg, it was an eye soar and everyone in town knew who that truck belonged to so it wouldn't make any sense to steal it. I had to shake the state of shock off of me so I could get some answers for Bob. I told Bob that I wasn't going to call his dad. I told Bob if the truck got stolen then we needed to call the police. I finally got off the floor and went into the bedroom. I watched Bob walk pass me to his dresser drawer to get clean clothes while still insisting that I call his dad and tell him the truck was stolen. I still didn't believe him so I started asking questions. "Bob, you mean to tell me that someone came on the construction site while you were working and stole the truck". That was the million dollar question and that's all it took for me to get the truth from him.

Bob told me, "no" as he dropped his head and looked down at the floor; there go that thirteen year old boy again. "The road was wet", he said and that he took a sharp turn around a curve and that he hit another car that was coming around the curve on the other side of the road. Bob said that he jumped out of the truck, ran through another construction site, and hid in the woods, waited for a while then ran home. That sounded like something he would do. I asked Bob why was his pants all torn. He said they must have gotten torn when he jumped the fence. He felt his back pocket where he always puts his wallet and after realizing that there was a hole in it he came to the conclusion that he had lost his wallet.

Bob insisted that he go back and look for his wallet. It seemed kind of funny that that was the only place where his pants were torn. Not wanting to have anything to do with the situation, I told Bob that he wouldn't be able to find his wallet in all those woods, that his wallet was long gone. I was still stuck on the part where he jumped out the truck and ran after he hit the other car. But Bob insisted we go and look anyway and for me to take him to his dad's. Bob quickly cleaned up and changed clothes and we all got in the car.

He showed me the construction site where he had jumped the fence, the woods where he had been hiding, and as we slowly drove by the scene of the accident; Bob slid down in his seat. The state troopers were there now doing their investigation. As we passed, I spotted the truck on the side of the road. The cement pump was still hooked up to it and it the truck had a huge dent on the side of it right where the truck bed starts. There was no other car or an ambulance on site. I told Bob that I couldn't believe that he left the scene of an accident. I asked him did he even bother to see if anyone was hurt before he decided to run off like a chicken. He told me no that he just jumped out the truck and ran. I gave Bob a strong look of discuss. He got mad at me because I was mad at him because yet again he only thought of his own life when he had inflicted the life of others. I just prayed that everyone was okay. We argued all the way to his dad's.

We got to his dad's and Bob gave his dad some story of how someone stole the truck. I didn't say one word, it wasn't my place. The only way the insurance company would pay for any damages done to the truck was that the truck had to be reported as stolen. Bob didn't have a license so he wouldn't be covered on the policy. Like father like son but in this case like son like father; Bob's dad went along with the stolen truck story. Mr. Joe called the police to say that the truck had been stolen out of the driveway. Fifteen minutes later a state trooper's car pulls up in front of the house. Low and behold, guess who steps out the car? Yup, the same state trooper that was at the scene of the accident. He had brought along another trooper with him. Unlike Twinkies; police never come alone.

The trooper questioned everyone. He asked Bob where was he when the truck got stolen. He told the state trooper that he was in the back room sleep. So the trooper asked where was the truck parked and they showed him that the truck was parked next to the room where Bob had said he was sleeping. And so the trooper looked surprised when Bob said that he didn't hear anything. I couldn't believe my eyes but here he go again about to wiggle his way out of trouble. I think the second trooper had a feeling that Bob was lying, so out of the blue he turns to Bob and says that the eyewitness at the accident said that driver of the truck who jumped out of the truck had on a red or burgundy shirt. Really, he couldn't have come up with a better lie than that. Well we knew that the state trooper wasn't telling the truth because Bob had come home and changed his clothes. Bob knew then that he had the upper hand and he started yelling at the state troopers that whoever said that was lying; as if he was trying to justify himself. The trooper came over to me and asked where I was. I told him that I was at work and he could check my time card. That was the end of the questioning for me from the state trooper; he walked back over to his car.

After a while the trooper told Bob and his dad where they had towed the truck. When the troopers got the information they needed and felt that they had done their part, they left. You could tell that they were disappointed. Sometimes I really do hate that saying, you know the one; *stand by your man*.

Mr. Joe wanted to go and see the truck so we headed over to the yard where the trooper said the truck was. I don't remember much of the conversation over there because the whole time Bob and his dad were trying to get the details of their story straight as I sat in the back seat looking at both of them being up to no good. I really was still in amazement of everything that was going on. I was supposed to be taking my boys school shopping but instead I'm dealing with foolishness. When we finally got to the yard, there was a police officer already there. Mr. Joe had said a couple of words to the officer but nothing detailed like he had with the state trooper.

I actually got to see the truck up close. If the truck looked like that, I could just imagine what the other car looked like. In my mind I was thinking about the other driver. Who was going to pay for the damages to their car and I hoped no one was seriously hurt. Who did the trooper put at fault for the accident? I don't think Bob or his dad was even concerned with the other driver's well-being. I never heard them ask about them.

Bob and his dad walked over to the truck and looked in. the officer said someone had gone shopping. He noticed that there were plastic grocery bags in the front floor board. Bob opened the door and started taking the bags of meat out of the truck. Mr. Joe told Bob to leave the meat in the truck. My thought's exactly because if he took the groceries then to me that was a dead giveaway that they belonged to him. Why would you care about some meat that was in a wrecked truck unless you had just spent the money on it? But Bob being the person that he is grabbed the bags out of the truck. Needless to say, when I was finally done with his little masquerade, I took the boys shopping without any financial support from Bob. Till this day, I don't think he lost his wallet because he never acted like he was devastated about losing his wallet but the one time he mentioned it at the house and he never asked me for any money in the two weeks that followed. You figure it out.

A week or two later the truck was parked back on the side of the house with only a sheet of wood where its truck bed once was. And that's why I don't want Bob driving my car.

# Chapter 32

**WELL FOR A** couple of months Bob had been working at his real job where he has to clock in and out. Thanks to my younger son, Bob got the job at the resort. You see, in order for him to get the job he had to go and take a drug test. In the past when he needed to take a drug test and pass he would just walk around the house with a gallon of some special tea and drink it the day before his drug test to flush out any impurities. But now doctors have come out with a new drug test and the tea doesn't work anymore because the test was able to read pass the tea and detect anything that wasn't real collard greens. So Bob had me to ask my youngest son to pee in a cup. I told him that I wouldn't and for him to be man enough to ask him and be man enough if my son said no. I wasn't going to ask or force my son to do anything that he didn't feel comfortable doing. I just think that it's ironic that when his children ask or need him to do something he can't but he expects his kids to do something for him when he needs it. I recall those crayons were only two dollars and some change, while DJ jacket cost thirty-five and I was only asking for half of that.

Despite his short comings towards his boys; they never thought any less of him. My son was willing to help his father. I felt that it was degrading and I told Bob that it would be the last time that he would ever put his boys in that type of situation. As I handed him the cup he took it as if we were obligated to do this for him. I looked at my husband with shame and discuss. I had to suggest that he at least tell his son thank you. And he did as he all while not making eye contact with his son. He headed to the bathroom to prep himself for the drug test. I just looked and wondered when was all the foolishness with him going to stop.

As we sat in the clinic we all knew that he would pass the test. While waiting in the lobby for their father to return from behind the doctor's door; I gave my boys another reason why not to do drugs.

Even though Bob is working nothing has changed or gotten better. Sex between us has stopped completely. He hides his pay stubs and just refuses to pay an electric bill that is due this Friday. But it is because of your son that you have a job in the first damn place and you can't see fit to keep the lights on for him. I reminded Bob Monday and he just looked at me like I was talking French. As usual I knew that it would be left up to me to pay the bill. I started to hold hatred in my heart for him. I truly think if Bob and I would have been able to get past our money problems that we would have had a chance of being happy; when you ask someone to marry you; that comes with a lot of responsibilities. So my thing is if you can't live up to those basic responsibilities than don't ask anyone to marry you and don't promise that you can give them the world when you can't because the other person is going to be expecting it.

I don't know but something was stopping him from realizing that he was the parent now. Maybe he never got use to the idea that he was a father or maybe no one taught him how to be one. But I thought that once you bring that baby home the parent thing just automatically kicks in; it did for me.

You would think that as a parent you would sacrifice any and everything for your children under reasonable circumstances. I thought that during Christmas time that Bob would have a different frame of mind; but he didn't. For the past couple of years, the boys would make a Christmas list of things that they wanted. They were never greedy about what they asked for so I always made sure that I got everything on their list. Bob would ask me what the boys wanted for Christmas and that would be the farthest that would go with him. I guess he figured he did his part by acting concerned. I think one year he did help me buy a bike and a cd that they wanted. It use to just get so under my skin Christmas morning as I watched the boys unwrapping all their gifts and Bob would still be in bed. He later told me why he stayed in bed. He told me it was because he was shame that he wasn't the reason why the boys were going wild as they ripped off the wrapping paper on their remote control cars, game units, toys, new clothes and shoes. But I didn't feel bad for him because he made the choice not to buy the kids' presents. His choice was to spend his money on his habits and not on his boys. I wasn't going to let my boys go without because of what their father wasn't willing to do for them. It brought me so much joy to see them happy. I can recall my first Christmas with Bob before the boys was born. I had bought him a couple of presents; he didn't buy me anything. I still have the robe that I bought him those many years ago. I still haven't gotten over the emptiness that I felt that Christmas morning.

I've gotten use to a lot of Bob's not doings and I've learned to make the best of it but it comes a time when everyone reaches their breaking point and one day I came to mine. He normally takes me to work on Fridays since I have to be to work at four in the morning and he doesn't have to be to work until eight. We both get off at two- thirty so I would have to wait for him but on Saturday and Sunday he was off so I would leave him the car because he was home with the kids. There were a lot of Saturdays and Sundays when I would have waited for more than an hour after I gotten off of work before Bob would arrive to pick me up. One time when I had gotten off of work early; I could have sworn I saw Bob pass by my job on his way to the City. My coworkers would be walking to their cars shocked that I was stilling waiting on a ride. I was just as shocked as they were. I had to catch a ride home that day. When I got home, he was home and I asked him why didn't he come and pick me up. He said that he had forgotten. So I asked him when he had seen that I hadn't made it home by a certain time, didn't it dawn on him to come and get me or that he forgot to do something. Bob told me that he knew that I had probably caught a ride. But it wasn't for me to have to catch a ride when I have a car. I politely explained to him. Since I was kind enough to let you have the car so you wouldn't have to find a way to work, I figure it only fair that he come and pick me up from work so I wouldn't have to find a way home. He just looked at me like I was talking in French again.

I hated all the miles that were being put on my car but it was the only arrangement that would work for both of our work schedules. It was a long stressful day at work and I was ready to get home this particular day. Of course when I got off Bob wasn't there and that puzzled me because he was off on Saturday so there was no reason for him not to be able to pick me up on time. I had sat and waited for a very long time. Everyone was leaving and asking me if I needed a ride. Most of them lived in the opposite direction and I didn't want them to go out of their way, so I would just wave to them that I was okay and I would wait for my ride. But after a while it started getting real late and I was starting to worry. I went back into the building to use the phone to call home to see if Bob was still home or had he left by any chance.

When I called home Dominique answered the phone. I asked if his dad was home and he told me yes. All I could think of was why was he home and why wasn't he here waiting for me in the parking lot when I got off of work. I asked Dominique if his dad was sleep. He told me no but that he was in the bedroom. I told Dominique to take his dad the phone and let me talk to him. I could hear Dominique on the other end of the phone calling to his dad to get his attention. I could hear Bob mumbling and Dominique telling him that I was on the phone. Eventually Dominique handed him the phone. When I knew that he was on the phone because I could hear him breathing, I asked him what was he doing and why he wasn't at my job to pick me up from work. He replied to me that he was there. I was stunned at his response and I knew something was wrong because his words were slurred and he wasn't making any sense.

He was saying something but I couldn't understand exactly what he was going on about. It sounded like he was having a conversation with himself and forgot that I was even on the phone. I interrupted and asked him what he was talking about. I couldn't hardly understand him, it sounded like he said he was on a UFO. Then he finally starting speaking so I could understand him; he said he was in the parking lot. Even though I could understand him now; he still isn't making any sense. I brought to Bob's attention; if he was in the parking lot at my job then how was I able to talk to him on the phone while he was at the house. Bob just kept insisting that he was at my job waiting for me in the parking lot. And then he would start talking in another language and it wasn't French. He really did sound like he was an alien. Then he would go back to speaking English. And for half a second I started to think that I was going crazy and maybe he was in the parking lot. So for the next ten minutes I spent convincing myself that I wasn't crazy and convincing Bob that he was not outside in the parking lot at my job. But when I finally decided there was no use and he didn't realize that he was still at home talking to me on the phone; I told him okay and hung up the phone.

I stood there stunned and playing back in my mind what had just happened. Did Bob even know that he was even talking to me? Then I realized I had to get home to my babies and make sure that they were safe. The look on my face must have said it all because my friend Lynn stopped to ask me if I'm okay. I explained to her the conversation that I just had and she asked me if I needed a ride home. She lived in the same complex so I took her up on the offer. All the way home, I tried to make sense of it all but I couldn't so I laughed to keep from crying in front of my friend.

As we approached the gate at our complex to go in, guess who was coming out. You guessed it, Bob. He had the dumbest look on his face. I asked him where he was going. He said that he was on his way to pick me up from work. I paused to make sure that I heard what I thought I heard him say. And I just looked at Bob because I wanted him to hear what he had just said. There was no use of him going to pick me up from work. I had gotten off of work two hours ago and as he could see; I was home now after having to find a ride. Bob just sat in the car looking at me like he was in a daze. I got no response from him so Lynn just drove off and dropped me off at home. I wished someone would have warned me of the twilight zone that I was about to walk into when I opened the door to my apartment.

When I got in the house, I got a strange vibe like something was really wrong. I went to sit my keys and purse on the counter and there on the breakfast bar sat a half of a sandwich which looked like someone took a bite out of it and then balled it up like it was a piece of paper. The wrapper sat next to it and the other half of the sandwich nearly completely eaten except for one or two bites was on the floor and stuff had been knocked off the wall. This was all so strange to me because the boys know how I am about a clean house when I came home from work. The dog was running around like he was crazy. DJ was sitting on the arm of the couch holding the handle to my bedroom door. I asked him why was there mess on the counter; he said that he didn't know. That puzzled me. Where is Dominique I asked him? DJ said that his little brother was locked up in my bedroom. That puzzled me even more.

"Why was Dominique locked up in my bedroom", I asked DJ? But before he could answer me Bob walked into the house. "They've been fighting", DJ had finally answered. "Who had been fighting"; I asked still puzzled as I looked around the room. DJ said that Dominique and his daddy had been fighting. I was shocked at what I just heard and I was about to turn into she-devil when I turned to Bob and asked what were they fighting for. He didn't answer he just focused his attention on the half eaten sandwich that lay on the counter. DJ went on to tell me that they wouldn't stop fighting so he told Dominique to just go in my bedroom and lock the door until I had gotten home.

What the hell is going on, am I in the right house? I called for Dominique to come out of the room. When he came out of my bedroom; he was just beside himself huffing and puffing as if he had been in the fight of his life. This was not a condition that I wanted to see my child in. My baby was nine years old and weighted no more than cucumber. I asked Dominique what was going on. He said that his daddy kept yelling at him after I hung up the phone with him earlier. That didn't make any sense to me so I turned to Bob and asked him what Dominique did for him to yell at him. I was trying to be patient and give Bob a chance to make all of this makes sense to me because I was seconds away from just ripping his throat out with my bare hands. Bob just said that Dominique is always trying to get him in trouble. What the hell was Bob talking about? Right now he was sounding like a five year old or something that I would expect for DJ to say. "What was he supposed to be getting you in trouble about"? I asked Bob because I was totally confused. If he was referring to him not coming and picking me up from work; that was his fault and had nothing to do with Dominique. I was losing my patience with this whole situation and I wasn't getting any answers from Bob so I just went ahead and asked Dominique to tell me everything that happened after I got off the phone with his dad.

Dominique began to explain that when I got off the phone with his father that his daddy came in the living room where he and DJ were playing the video game and he started stepping on the game and saying that Dominique was always getting him in trouble. Dominique then said that he asked his daddy not to step on the game because he was going to mess it up. Bob replied that he had bought the game and that he could mess it up if he wanted to. Correction; I bought the game. So Dominique went on to say that after he asked his daddy not to step on the game that his daddy then picked up the game unit, opened it up and snatched the game disk out and threw it across the room. Dominique told his daddy that the game disk wasn't his and that he was going to break it. He said that his daddy got mad and said that he didn't care whose disk it was and then threw the game unit down on the floor. Dominique said that he got mad and told his daddy that he didn't have to do that, started crying and ran out of the house. He said that his daddy ran after him and caught up with him in the breeze way, picked him up and threw him against the wall. Dominique said that he got lose and started running back to the house. He said that his daddy was chasing after him and fell. By that time DJ had come outside after them and his daddy was getting up off the ground. He caught up with Dominique again and jacked him up. Dominique said that his daddy was really upset now. Dominique went on to say that's when DJ started yelling at their daddy to put him down. Bob let him go like DJ said and that's when Dominique ran in the house. DJ followed his little brother to keep his father away and told him to go in my room and lock the door. Dominique said that he could hear his daddy yelling at DJ when he finally made it into the house. "Daddy came to the bedroom door and was beating on it telling me to unlock the door and to let him in. But I didn't, I shouted for him to leave me alone. Daddy kicked the door and I kicked it back and then he kicked the door even harder". DJ said that's when all the stuff on the wall fell. Dominique said he could hear DJ telling his daddy to get out and for him to just leave. Dominique said that when he knew that his daddy was gone, that he unlocked the door and came out the room. But he said that his daddy came back in the house and DJ told him to go back in the room and lock the door. Again DJ told his daddy to leave. His daddy finally left and he said that's when I came home. Give me a minute ya'll; my head is spinning.

I just stood there in shock, it all sounded like a movie to me. I can't believe this hell is being raised in my house. I couldn't say anything. I was just looking around making sure that I was in the right house because right now I felt disrespected and I felt that my boys are not safe in their own home. But most of all, I felt that my children were not safe around their father. How dare he put his hands on my baby as if my son was not his son but like some nigga in the street that double crossed him in a card or dice game?

Bob finally spoke, "I'm grown, I'm his daddy and ain't no punk like him going to disrespect me". Bob stood there with his fist balled up and was biting his bottom lip as he was looking a Dominique. I don't know what Bob thought he was going to do with that balled up fist, but

I knew what he wasn't going to do. Today would be the day that I caught a mother-fuckin charge and gladly.

My question to Bob was how Dominique was being disrespectful by asking you not to step on his game unit and not destroy the game disk that wasn't his to begin with. Bob didn't answer he just continued to stare down at Dominique.

Bob has always had a chip on his shoulder about Dominique from day one. I don't know if it is his own conscience that bothers him for not being there for his birth. Then there was the issue of Dominique's very light skin color when he was born and way pass his first year. Bob is dark so he questioned whether Dominique was even his or not. My mother and Bob's mother are both red women because of their Indian heritage. So I put Bob's doubts to rest; Dominique is definitely his son. Dominique is the baby boy and not into physical sports like his older brother and Bob are. But Dominique is more outspoken then his older brother who is very quiet and don't like fuss. When Dominique was a baby I use to take him with me when I would go somewhere so Bob wouldn't feel overwhelmed by having both of the boys while I was out running errands or whatever. So it just became a habit to bring him along with me as he got older. I guess Bob might have taken it as me spending more time with the baby of the house then him.

Knowing all of this I looked at Bob and told him that just because Dominique speaks up for himself not to pick on him. Still starring down at him, Bob stepped up to my son. Before I would stand there and watch Bob hit my son, I didn't have a problem being the reason that he would draw back a numb. I walked into the kitchen and stood next to the knife block set that was sitting on the counter.

Bob started yelling in Dominique's face saying that Dominique walks around like he's white and reminded him that he wasn't white. If Bob was referring to Dominique talking and acting like he was educated, stayed neat and clean, and not outside flipping on a pile of dirty mattresses, ate at the dinner table, and did his chores; then I guess he's white. I remember when I was in high school and I got teased because of my accent and I talked proper. My friend use to call me cracker. At first I took offense to it but he told me that he thought my accent was cute and that cracker was just his way of acknowledging that he knew that I was educated. But what Bob would say next about his own son was neither a compliment nor acknowledgement in any way.

Those white boys don't like you. You're a nigga, nothing but a bastard; you're nothing but a coward. You are walking around here looking like a crack-head. You look like a monster with all those teeth in your mouth. As the words came out of Bob's mouth, it was like someone was cutting my skin with a knife. I couldn't believe that he was talking to his own son like that. At that moment I lost all respect for Bob. I knew that my son's feelings were hurt. I wouldn't have blamed Dominique if he would have cussed his daddy out. I looked at Dominique and the look on my son's face would pierce a mother's heart. I told Dominique to tell his father if he thought that he was a bastard then he must be a son of a bitch. I know I was wrong for telling my son to say that to his father but at the moment I was mad. And of course Dominique did not repeat what I said even though I gave him permission; he knew that I was speaking out of anger. One thing I did teach my boys was to never be disrespectful to any adult. And though their daddy would never win the father of the year award they would still respect him and love him the same.

I stepped between the two of them and tried to justify my son. Yes Dominique needed some braces and yes weeks would go by before Bob would cut Dominique's hair so he would just comb his hair to the back until Bob would decide when he wanted to or not to cut their hair that weekend. Which I didn't understand that because Bob made sure that he kept his own hair cut. So why he couldn't cut the boys hair when he cut his hair is a mystery to me. And about the braces I would have had money to get him some braces if Bob would help pay a bill or two which would free up some money to get my baby some braces. And we lived in a very nice neighborhood where there were no black kids so all their neighborhood friends were white. But DJ and Dominique knew who they were; they were two little black boys. How dare he talk to my baby that way? I was really ready to kill Bob that day. I had to really talk myself down from doing just that.

I had finally had enough. I just walked away to go to my room. While in my room I heard Dominique yelling for someone to let him go. I ran back out to the living room and asked DJ what happened. DJ said that his daddy was choking Dominique. That's when I lost it; I felt myself leave my body. I watched as I went in the kitchen and grabbed a knife and I was ready to deal with the situation. I was beside myself. I began to beat on my chest with my fist like I was Xena the warrior because at this time I could take on the world. I went back in the living room. I told Bob to step to me because I was going to put him down. Bob saw in my eyes that my soul was black and he knew that I was talking the truth. But he didn't move, so I stepped to him and I placed the blade of the knife against his throat and looked him dead in his eyes. I told him if he ever touched my son again that I would drop him where he stood. I said the words but it was not my voice that I heard. At that point I no longer saw Bob as my husband or the father of my children but only as a stranger in my house. Bob knew I was serious and so he backed away and started that mad cry you do when you're mad but can't do anything about it. I had made up in my mind that Bob had to go, it was over between us. No harm was to come to my children by the hands of another; not even their own father's. I knew that I needed to leave this house before something really bad happened. I returned to the kitchen to put the knife back in its place and went to my room to change my shoes.

Bob came in the room after me just grabbing my arm trying to pull me close to him to hug me but it only turned into a wrestling match between us. I just started throwing punches at him and they landed everywhere on his body. I was picking up anything that my hands came in contact with and was throwing it at him. At one point I just turned to Bob and firmly told him so that there would be no misunderstand; that I didn't want him anymore, that I didn't love him anymore, and I didn't care whether he lived or died. Bob left the room and yet again went towards Dominique who along with DJ was still standing in the living room. I could hear him tell my son that he had caused all this madness and he was the reason why I was kicking him out. DJ grabbed Dominique by the arm to keep his father from getting any closer to him and told him to come with him and they left the house for a minute. They didn't stay gone for too long. They came back in the house and sat down in the living room.

Bob started to tell me how much he loved me. I didn't want to hear that. I told him to get out of my face but he didn't move. How could you love me and not love what is a part of you. I heard DJ tell Bob that he had better get out of his mama's face. I was surprised that he spoke up because he usually is very quiet and no matter what his dad usually does, he never would say a word against him. "You heard what your son said", I reminded Bob with pride. Bob turned to DJ who at this time was sitting on the arm of the couch. Bob now challenged his older son; "oh you think that you can climb this mountain then come on". DJ didn't move but he looked his daddy right in the eye and told him that he wasn't scared of him. I finally was able to walk out of my bedroom with my shoes. I just walked over to the chair that was empty and sat down so I could collect my thoughts. "I've got to get out of here", I kept telling myself. "This can't be happening". I could feel all the evil that was in my house.

I told the boys to get ready so we could go. When I got ready to walk out the door I turned to Bob and told him that I was leaving now, not that I was running away from anything. I told him that he had better remember this day because this was the day that our marriage ended for good. He just laughed in my face. I told him that he can laugh now but that he will cry later and that I would see to that. I walked out leaving him standing in the middle of the living room. I was outside in the fresh air breathing oh so deeply. I couldn't believe that Bob just stood there and laughed in my face like I had just told a joke at some comedy club. I could feel it; something was really wrong.

I went to go and get in the car and as I was going to unlock the door on the passenger side for the kids; who were just standing by the car, I noticed a lot of grass and dirt stuck on the front bumper. What the hell? I went over to wipe off the debris. When I wiped everything away I noticed that my car had gotten all scratched up. This only made matters worse; as if it could. I told DJ to go and get his daddy. When Bob came outside I asked him what happened to my car as I pointed to the bumper where the damage was. He said nothing happened to my car. So I asked him what he hit. Looking at the bumper he said nothing. I knew that I wouldn't get a straight answer out of him so I just went and got in the car leaving Bob standing in the parking lot.

I drove to my sister's house but I don't remember the ride over there because I was so numb. I got to her house and I just cried. I sat there just shaking my head in disbelieve of what I had just left. And even though I told my sister what happened; it still seemed like I was describing some movie that I had seen at the theatre. And by the look on her face; she couldn't believe it either. Me and the boys stayed at my sister's for a few hours. There was no rush to get home but I knew eventually I had to mustard up the strength to get back home because the boys had to go to school the next morning.

When we got back home, it was very late. It was probably more like early morning than late night. I walked in the house and it was dark. The only light was the light from the television in my bedroom and that peeked through the cracked door. Bob was asleep so I put the boys to bed and I slept in their room for the night. I locked the bedroom door so all the hell raising that had happened earlier that day wouldn't have a chance to rise up again.

Morning came and not too many words were spoken. The boys were gone off to school and Bob had gone to work. I had the house to myself. I just looked around from room to room and recalled all that had accord the day before. What happened yesterday, I could never let happen again and the only way that was going to be possible was the problem had to go.

Bob got home from work that night and so we had a talk. I told Bob that he had to leave because I didn't think that my children; his own sons, were safe around him. His children should not be afraid of him but respect him. I told Bob that he had put DJ in a bad situation when he feels that he has to defend his mother and younger brother from his father. He is only a child himself. Bob looked me dead in my face and asked me what I was talking about. I told him the way that he carried on yesterday in this house. You know that jackleg had the balls to sit there and say that he didn't know what I was talking about. Oh he got jokes now.

I looked at Bob; who was looking at me waiting for me to enlighten him on what I was talking about. So I asked him if he remembered what he called his younger son and how he was acting like a mad man around here. He calmly told me no. I looked at him knowing that he was lying. He continued to say that when he had gotten off of work yesterday that he had meet up with some friends and they had gave him some *sweetwater* and that it had him so hot that he came home and passed out. Oh so that explains all the craziness that took place yesterday. I knew something had to have been wrong with him because Bob doesn't act like that. So that's what was wrong with this fool. He was half out of his mind. He probably did think that he was on the planet Mars because he was talking like he was. But I am a mother first and I am supposed to protect my children. If I let Bob stay and he get a hold of some *sweetwater* again, who is to say that the next time the situation won't be worst. How will my children feel knowing that I'm not protecting them from harm when I have the chance? With that in mind, I told Bob that he had two weeks to find himself somewhere to stay.

In my mind I was counting down the days because I couldn't wait until he was gone. I had been in this position before. No, I wasn't going to throw him out on the street. I knew from the past experience that in many ways this separation was going to be the best thing for me and the boys. And this would be the last time because Bob wasn't coming back. I can't take anymore. The Father, The Son, and The Holy Ghost would have to come down from the heavens themselves and tell me to take Bob back before I would let him back in my house again. I knew by him leaving that I wouldn't have a chance to stress or wonder whether or not he was going to do what he was supposed to and whether or not I had to hold back from what me and the boys needed just in case I had to pick up his slack. And most of all my boys would be safe in their own home.

I use to say that I would stay with Bob for the boy's sake so they would have their father. But if it's not in his heart to be their father, then he won't be and there's nothing that I can say or do to make him do right by his children. I didn't want them to experience the pain that I did because I didn't have a father. I never knew that they could experience pain because they have one.

My mind has to be right so that I can raise my boys or I'm no good to them as a mother. Even though me and their father would separate the boys would still have their father in their life, he just wouldn't be living in the same house with them. I would never attempt to stop them from seeing him or him seeing them. They could call him whenever they were ready. Their father would still be in their lives just no longer in mine.

# Chapter 33

**TWO WEEKS HAVE** passed and Bob hasn't said a word about whether or not he has found a place to stay. I bet he thinks that I'm playing or that I forgot. I couldn't wait to get off work. After Bob had the little incident with my car that he couldn't explain, I don't let him drive my car anymore so I have to go and pick him up from work. All day I was contemplating whether to go home and pack his stuff, drop it off at his dad's or mama's then go pick him up or go pick him up first and let him pack his stuff himself and just drop him off wherever. I decided to go home and pack his things up then go and pick him up. As I was packing his things, I felt so as ease because finally I was going to have peace in my house and so I became anxious to get it all over with. I knew that I could handle the household because I had been doing so anyway for the past couple of weeks.

I went through every dresser drawer until they were empty to make sure that I got all his clothes. I discovered a few check stubs and some pawn slips. A couple of the pawn slips said that Bob had pawned some video games. Oh so that's where they disappeared to. Before Bob had gotten a job at the resort, things in the house kept coming up missing. My boys kept coming to me saying that they couldn't find their video games and that puzzled me because when I would suggest that maybe they lent it out to a friend they would say that they hadn't. Then I would suggest that they misplaced it but again they would tell me that they hadn't and would show me where they kept all their video games. We would search the whole house and turn up nothing so I would end up buying another game. After the boys games kept coming up missing they decided to hide their games. It never dawned on me that Bob would steal from his kids. But from me I wouldn't put it pass him. I recall my baby brother giving me a huge 14 karat gold two-headed lion ring. The ring was so big it stood out like one of those jeweled candy rings. I wore it with pride and sometimes I wore it around my neck on my gold necklace. The ring was so huge it would get admired at work by my co-workers who would make the remark that it was the size of a high school lock. I loved that ring; I loved it more because my baby brother gave it to me. Bob would admire it too. I took it off one day to clean it and the next day when I went to look for it; it was gone. The ring was so big it would be very hard to miss and you really didn't have to look that hard for it. It would really find you. At the time I asked Bob several times had he seen my ring but he insisted that he hadn't. But there amongst his things was the pawn shop slip that he had indeed seen my ring. The slip was dated so long ago that I knew it was too late to buy my ring back. Bob had taken something from me; it wasn't so much about the ring as it was about the loss of trust and the feeling of betrayal yet again coming from him.

There sat four large black lawn garbage bags of Bob's worldly possessions; everything that he owns and had accumulated over the last thirty four years by the front door. I looked around the house to make sure I got everything so Bob wouldn't have to come pass the front door. After being satisfied that I had packed everything, it was time to go and pick him up from work. I knew that the boys would be home from school by the time I got back and I really didn't want for Bob to put on a show like he had done the last time I put him out. On the way to his job, I was just wondering how he would react when he got back home seeing that all his things had been packed.

When I arrived at his job, Bob was waiting in his normal spot. I don't know whether he was happy to see me or just happy that another work day was over. The conversation on the way home was normal. I had to stay calm and not let on that I had been busy at the house already packing his things. It seemed like it took forever for me to get home, but finally we arrived. The boys, who had already made it home from school was in the house playing their video games.

"What is this"? Bob asked when he walked in the door looking down at the garbage bags by the front door. As I walked in behind him and closed the door, I told him that it was his stuff. I reminded him that his two weeks were up and that it was time for him to leave. Bob looked at me as if this was his first time hearing of such a thing and that he didn't get the memo. Throwing my hands up in the air, I asked Bob not to drag this situation out by trying to buy time or make a scene for the boys. He started telling me to hold up as if to stop time. Bob wanted to know if this was the way that I was going to handle the situation by just throwing all his stuff in a garbage bag and kicking him out. But what he doesn't understand was if I had handled it any other way he wouldn't have been there talking to me but he would have been six feet under and I would have been in cell block 3. So to me this was the best way to handle things so we could both live to see our golden years. I nodded my head yes to his question. Bob went on to say that whatever he did that day, that he was sorry and that he wanted his family. When he saw that I wasn't about to change my mind, he only insisted that I wasn't being fair. Was he being fair drinking *sweetwater* and being half out his mind when I left my kids in his care. Was he being fair treating my son like he had stolen something? Was he being fair by not helping me with the household or the boys? Let's really talk about who's not being fair.

Bob started rambling through the bags to make sure all his stuff was there. He had everything but time. He started walking around the house looking for anything to grab. First he went to grab the WD40 from up under the kitchen sink. Then he went to the boy's bathroom opening up all the cabinets' doors just searching for anything; he only grabbed some Band-Aids. He walked to the master bedroom opening up the dresser drawers and the closet doors. But as he could see; his things were no longer there. Once he saw that all his things had been packed, he started going to the nightstands and checking them along with looking on the dresser. He strapped up some toe nail clippers and some spare change. After having enough of watching Bob do his treasure hunt; I spoke up. I told him that he could stop looking for stuff because I had packed all of his things; even his dirty clothes.

I walked out of the room and stood by the front door. I asked Bob where he wanted me to take him. Ignoring my question at first, he asked me for the ten dollars that I had owed him. Bob said that I would be wrong for putting him out knowing that he didn't have any money. I reached it my pocket and gave him the ten dollars. I asked him again where he wanted me to take him because no matter how much he stalled; he was getting out of here today. He just stood there in the living room and his crocodile tear act that we had seen so many times before began.

He grabbed Dominique and pulled him closer to him; hugging him and telling him that he loved him and how sorry he was for calling him all those mean things. By the look on Dominique's face, I think he took his father's apology with a grain of salt. But it was not my place to sway him one way or another to accept his father's apology; that was totally up to him. Still holding on to Dominique; Bob reached out for DJ and pulled him close and told him the same as he hung his head down in shame. His father asked him if he knew that he loved him and DJ just nodded his head. To my surprise the boys weren't crying for their father or begging him not to go. I guess they had had enough too.

It wasn't so much that he didn't love us, we knew that but Bob was just making our everyday life a little harder to cope with. Life was already hard enough with its normal everyday struggles. We all know that life isn't an easy ride and that it's going to have it bumps. But don't make the ride harder by taking a wheel off the wagon your damn self.

Yes, I was touched by the little father and son scene, but I still wasn't changing my mind about putting Bob out. The only thing that kept running through my head was how Bob called my baby a crack-head, a monster, and at some point throwing him up against the wall. I felt bad that I wasn't there to protect my son because from the first day that I held my babies in my arms I promised them that I would do just that.

Bob kept repeating that he didn't want to go. I told him that this time he had no choice. I wasn't going to stand by and watch him mentally destroy my boys. We as parents are to encourage our children and equip them with thoughts of strength and wisdom. Not tare them down to nothing. The more I thought about what Bob had done the more I knew that I was making the right decision. I grabbed one of his bags and headed to the car. Bob finally told me to take him to his mother's house as he grabbed the remainder of the bags and put them in the car. On the way to his mom's house Bob just kept placing blame on me for putting him out and saying that I didn't want a family. But I did want a family; I just didn't want a dysfunctional one.

I couldn't deal with the arguing every week because he wouldn't help pay bills or clean up and take time with the boys, continuously asking him to stop smoking in the house so to not kill us all with his second hand smoke. The routine of never having any money to do any family activities was disappointing. All work and no play can make for a boring life. I had so much pinned up anger in me that our arguing had gotten totally out of control. I would just go into total rages when we argued. It seemed as if my anger wouldn't subside unless I had thrown something and broke it.

I remember one time there wasn't anything in the house to eat and I only had ten dollars left until payday which was two days away and Bob had some money in his pocket. I had asked him to go to the store and buy two cans of chili which were two dollars a can and to buy some crackers so that I could feed the boys. Bob told me that he didn't have any money and I knew for a fact that he did so I knew that he was lying. But instead of me arguing with him about it I just went to the store and bought the chili and crackers myself. When I got back from the store I prepared the food so that my babies would have something to eat. I had gone in the bedroom for something and when I came back to the kitchen; guess who was standing over the stove with a bowl in his hand getting some chili. Oh no, he ain't; my babies haven't even eaten yet. Bob couldn't give me any money to help buy the food but he could help eat the food. I just stood there looking at him as he filled his bowl up with chili. I think at this point; I was hotter than the chili. Bob sat his bowl on the counter while he was getting something to drink out of the refrigerator. I looked down at the bowl of chili and thought to myself that I had rather see it on the floor than one spoon full in his mouth. When Bob turned around from the refrigerator, the bowl took flight and went flying across the kitchen. Shocked; Bob looked at me and said that I was crazy. I wasn't crazy, I was just tired of him standing by and making me take care of everything and then him come around and benefitting from it. I told him that he wouldn't be eating chili tonight. Since he couldn't buy the food then he couldn't eat it either. DJ walked in the kitchen and looked down at the mess on the floor. "I'm not cleaning that up", he said and he walked back out. I wasn't going to clean it up either and I too walked out the kitchen after making my boys their chili so they could sit down to the table and eat. Eventually it did get cleaned up by somebody.

I had gotten tired of the fact that two working adults lived in this house and we couldn't make it from week to week because only one adult was being responsible. I was tired of scrapping up pennies to put gas in the car or for buying a loaf of bread. I was tired of the fact that

Bob was acting like it didn't bother him and it was normal to struggle. He was the reason we were struggling and it was bothering me. I knew that when I would be by myself with just me and the boys that I could make ends meet. I could get another job and replace the income that Bob never brought home in the first place. I was tired and I had had enough. I reminded Bob that he was the reason that he was getting put out but as long as I had my boys; I had a family.

We finally made it to his mother's house. We all got out the car without taking the bags out the trunk. Bob went into his mother's house first while me and the boys hung around the car. After some time when he didn't come back out we headed in. We walked in the middle of Bob telling his mom that I was putting him out yet again. She asked him why but I didn't hear him answer her but it really didn't matter because I knew that he wasn't going to tell her the truth anyway. Nine out of ten he would make it look like my fault so he could remain the apple of her eye. But I didn't care anymore; let her deal with him. Bob always had to seem like he was the victim and that he didn't do anything wrong. I told Bob that he could tell her whatever lie he wanted to in order to make himself look good. If only they could have been a fly on the wall for the past fifteen years to really see all the stress and heartache the Bob had put me through. If they only knew that it was me pulling us through while he only stood by on the sidelines and watched. Bob wanted everyone to believe that he was the glue holding this family together and that he was the one for our progress. But little did they know that he couldn't even provide for us majority of the time because he wouldn't either keep or get a job. But as a good wife; in the past I have tried to hold his imagine to his family so it could be a positive one. I never called his mother with our problems and never put her in our business. But his mother was fair. She never took sides just the truth.

As we stood in her living room she told me that if I was putting him out so that I could be with someone else that my new relationship wasn't going to work. But that was so far in left field for the reason why I was putting him out. So then she turned to Bob and told him the same thing. She was so far in left field yet again. I quickly assured her that a man was the furthest thing from my mind. Bob didn't say a word. I was waiting for him to tell her why I was putting him out but he just stood there.

The truth needed to be told so I went on to tell her what Bob had done to Dominique a couple of weeks back. She told Bob that he was wrong for what he had done and told me that if he apologized to the boys that it was up to them to accept the apology. I totally agreed with her on that. Then she went on to say for me not to hold a grudge against him. I totally disagreed with her on that. One thing that I have learned about me is that I can be your best friend but I can also be your worst enemy. And holding grudges against someone was my way of working through the pain that they have caused me. All because someone apologizes to me doesn't mean that the pain that they have caused instantly goes away at the last symbol of the word sorry. I have to work through my pain and understand why you have caused me pain. And until I can understand why; I hold on to it.

But the advice coming from his mother was a little bitter sweet. I really didn't want to hear any more from her because here was a woman who stood by and let a man put a gun to her own son's head and didn't say a word or do anything to protect her son and to make matters worse; she stayed with this man after the incident.

Whatever; the lights would have gone out in Georgia that night. If you want to stand by and let someone deface your child and be okay with it, than that's you but it's not going to fly with me and mine. Dominique and DJ are a part of me; when they hurt, I hurt. Bob better be glad that a grudge is all that I'm holding against him.

I had said all that I was going to say. I headed back to the car and popped the trunk. Bob came out and started helping me remove the bags from the car and take them in his mom's house. After two trips; I made sure that he had everything. After him and the boys said their goodbyes for the day; I got them settled in the car and we left. I didn't feel empty but more relieved that all the arguing and fighting would be finally over. I drove off not looking back to see what if anything that I may have left behind.

On the ride back home I had a talk with boys; nothing that they hadn't heard before. I just wanted them to know that they could call their father whenever they wanted to and go and see him whenever. That no matter what happened between me and their father; that he will always be their daddy and no one could change that but that he wasn't always going to be my husband.

I realized at that moment that it is amazing what goes on in your house behind closed doors. No one would ever know anything was wrong because we are so good at putting on that *"everything is wonderful"* face when we go out into the world knowing all the while that the walls are literally crumbling down and landing to your feet as only a cloud of dust. But with the strength of God; we rebuild the walls and they go back up stronger than before.

The ride home was quick. Walking into my house and feeling the presence of peace was well anticipated and very much welcomed. The boys went to their room and I just went and sat down on the couch listening and starring outside. The view outside was different; it seemed clearer. The sky seemed bluer and the trees were greener. I felt so at ease now. I realized that the home that I had worked so hard to be beautiful and safe for my children had turned into a war zone for me and their father. I have to make sure that the boys know that I did this for all of us. This battle was no longer mine. I couldn't fight anymore. As the sound of the boy's laughter came from their room, it filled the air and I knew that God had me and that he would fight this battle for me.

As I lay in my bed that night looking at the stars reassuring myself that I did make the right decision. That night I prayed to my heavenly Father; I asked the Lord to help me to maintain my mind, body, soul and to mend my broken heart. He wanted me to know that I was covered in his Grace and protected by his Mercy.

The phone rung and I hesitated to answer after checking the number and seeing that it was Bob. I knew how nasty his mouth could get when he was mad. Bob knew me very well and he knew what buttons to push to get under my skin. I picked up the phone only to say hello. He started off saying how much he loved me and how sorry he was about everything that had happened. I only listened in silence. He then went on to say how he never thought that he would be out of the house again. But what Bob didn't understand was that a person can only take so much. I continued to listen in silence.

After a moment Bob began to say how his mom didn't want him there and that he had nowhere to go. He said that his mom started fussing at him after we had left. She told him that could only stay a week or two but no longer. I always thought if you couldn't depend on anybody else, you could always depend on mama. But I guess not; I think he burned that bridge a long time ago or they tore it down together. Another long pause followed after Bob told me his situation. I just know he wasn't waiting for me to tell him okay that he could come back home. That wasn't going to happen in this lifetime. I knew that the only way Bob would learn how to grow up and be a man was to make him stand on his own two feet. I just hung up the phone and went to sleep.

For the next couple of days the phone calls kept coming. Three or five times a day Bob would call me but never asking to speak to the boys; which should have been his only concern now and not me. But he continued to use his energy blaming me because he was out the house. And I used my energy standing firm by my decision. Yes, I put him out because he wasn't doing what he was supposed to be doing at home as a husband or as a father. Bob would never man-up to his mistakes and always try to throw side-bar in our conversations that I was seeing someone else. But that was the farthest thing from my mind. I didn't want us to be enemies I would tell Bob when he would start with the blame game. I tried to get him to understand that we needed to stay civilized for the boy's sake. Because if we couldn't talk to each other without yelling; how were we going to raise our boys. I expressed to Bob that our broken relationship had nothing to do with his relationship with his sons. Bob expressed to me that if he wasn't with me than he didn't want anything to do with his sons. How immature can a person get? I hoped that it was only his anger talking. But it would be his actions that would speak volume.

I needed to do something to keep busy getting my mind off Bob and to start paving the path for my boys and my future. I took a new position at work that paid more money but only had me working three days a week so I decided to enroll in college and attend class the other four days of the week. In the coming weeks me and the boys would become closer. We worked together to make this transaction as smooth as possible for all of us. I enjoyed getting up in the morning with the boys seeing them off to school. Friday would be the only day that I wouldn't get to see them off. But when I would walk out the door in the morning while they were still in the bed sleep, I would say a small prayer as I turned the key to lock the door that the Lord would keep us safe until we would meet together again that day. It would be about six o'clock when I would call back home to make sure that they were up and getting ready for school. Dominique would get ready for school and before he left the house he would call me to let me know that he was leaving. I would tell him that I loved him and for him to have a good day at school and that I would see him when I got home that afternoon. When it was DJ turn to leave he would do the same and I would tell him that I loved him, have a good day at school and that I would see him when I got home that afternoon. Their voices were like the voices of angels speaking to my heart and putting my soul at ease. My boys never gave me any major trouble, they had their growing pains but I allowed them to be boys.

Bills were paid, gas was in the car, and food is in the refrigerator. The boys were healthy with clothes on their back and new shoes on their feet. Things were a little tight but nothing was getting cut off. The phone calls from Bob continued for weeks but he still hasn't made arrangements to spend time with the boys. Through his begging and crying , along with his pleading to come home and his sometimes degrading and black mailing me for sexual favors in order for him to do for his boys; which only happened twice before I put a stop to that. I knew to stay strong and not let him come back home because I already knew what he had to offer me and that was nothing but uncertainty and stress. I was out of that situation, so why would I want to go back I would sometimes ask myself. The only answer I could come up with was the fear of being alone.

# Chapter 34

**IT'S BEEN A** month since Bob has been gone and all is well; out of sight out of mine as they say. That is until one day at work while at lunch; Carmen and I were sitting at the same table together. Carmen made small talk with me only to mention that she had seen my mother-in-law and that my mother-in-law told her that I had put Bob out and that he had stayed with her for two weeks but that she didn't want him there so he ended up moving in with Debra. My jaw dropped and literally hit the table. I guess Carmen saw the look on my face because then she went on to say how she had heard that but never came to ask me because she didn't want to get in my business. I can only wonder what made her change her mind. She really picked a fine time to get in someone's business.

Of course I was stunned at what Carmen had told me. In all the phone calls that I had received from Bob; he had me under the impression that he was still living with his mother. Debra is a very familiar name to me. Debra is the lady Bob got with during our second separation. It wouldn't surprise me if she was the one who had called the house that night that me and Bob got into our big argument and I kicked him out. The news of him living with Debra took me by surprise. I had mix emotions. Not mad; more like frustrated because I wanted him to suffer. I wanted Bob to learn a lesson on life. Instead he went and found someone else to lay up under and while they pay the bills. Had he been seeing her for these last couple of months? My woman's intuition tells me; yes. I knew someone who knew Debra so my plan was after lunch to find Kelly and ask if it was true or not. I lost my appetite just thinking about it, so I just sat there.

On my way back to the office I walked in silence and was feeling very numb. After finding Kelly I asked if Bob was staying with Debra. At first she kind of hesitated to answer me I could understand her loyalty to her friend. But Kelly did confirm the story of Bob living with Debra. After Kelly let the cat out the bag, I guess she felt relieved as if she had been waiting for me to come and ask her. Even though she use to smile and speak to me every day; the past couple of weeks it had been the way she smiled and spoke to me that had me a little puzzled but I never gave it too much thought. She was standing in front of me now as if she had a secret to tell. But you know that the one who needs to know is always the last to know. Kelly went on to say that she was late for work that morning because she had gone to Debra's birthday cookout that she had last night and that Bob was there. That just added more fuel to the fire.

I got back to my desk; I couldn't even concentrate on my work anymore. I was so ready to go home. My head felt like it was on spin cycle. How dare he go and live with another woman. We were separated not divorced. I couldn't wait to get home. All that crying and begging he had been doing on the phone like he really wanted to come back home and be with his family. I feel like he was doing that because his mama was kicking him out and he needed somewhere to go.

I finally calmed myself down enough to call Bob at his job when I got home. I just wanted to hear from the horse's mouth if the rumor was true. I left a message with his boss to have him call his wife. I didn't want his boss to get confused thinking that I was Debra calling for Bob. I guess after a while I drifted off to sleep because the next thing I knew I was waking up to the phone ringing. I heard someone on the other end say hello and I recognized the voice on the other end was Bob. I didn't beat around the bush; I asked him when he was going to tell me that he was living with Debra. He told me that he wasn't living with Debra. But I already knew that was a lie. So I went on to ask him how was the birthday party. You could hear a pin drop. Bob told me that yes he was there at the party but not with Debra. But in my mind that translated to; yes I got time to go to a party but I don't have time to spend with my boys. Bob went on to say that he was hanging with some friends at the party. I really didn't want to hear anymore lies. I called him a liar and told him that his mother was telling people all his business and saying that he was living with Debra. I wanted to know the truth and I learned what's good for the goose is good for the gander. I have picked up some bad habits hanging around Bob. Lying and manipulating had become a daily lesson in which I had a good teacher. I turned the tables around and told a little white lie myself. Is a lie better or purer because it's white? How come we never say a little black lie? Anyway I told Bob that I saw him at the party and that I had seen him from a parked car. Bob asked me whose car was I in. I told him not to worry about that, just for him to know that I was there. Whose car I was in should have been the least of his concerns.

Bob insisted that he was not staying with Debra; that was his story and he was sticking to it. He went on to say that he was sleeping on some dude's couch named Jerome after his mama had put him out and that Debra lived a couple of apartments over. He said that him and Jerome was just hanging out and walked over to the cookout and was playing cards. But from what I was told he was cooking on the grill. That was not hard for me to believe because Bob likes cooking on the grill and any chance he can get to show off his cooking skills he was game for it. But knowing that the truth was in there somewhere and that Bob was going all around it; I hung up the phone.

I'll see for myself what's going on. They say believe none of what you hear and half of what you see. I'm still trying to figure out whom the hell are *they*? Anyway, I had to come up with a plan. There was some detective work to do. I don't know where I picked up that habit but it's a good one to have. Oh, I know where I picked that up from; me. I trust no one but myself at this point and one thing I do know; I'm not going to lie to me.

First thing first; I had to find out where exactly Bob was living. I asked around and I found out what I needed to know. When I found out that Debra lived in the same complex that Bob's brother lived; it made me think back when Bob use to hang out at his brother's a lot all of a sudden and wouldn't come home until late. At first he use to take me but then after a while he stopped taking me over there. I guess he figured that I wasn't comfortable around his brother's girlfriend's friends. They were a bit colorful for me. Was he really hanging with his brother those times that I wasn't with him? When he stopped taking me over there I thought it was because he was trying to holler at one of them colorful chics.

I didn't seek out to go over to Debra's apartment right away; my problem wasn't with her. I had no interest in going to cause any drama for people to look at. My problem was with Bob. You may ask why I had a problem with Bob when I was the one who put him out. Maybe for me, it was just the principal of it all. Bob's always figured or should I say wiggled his way out of a situation of having to face responsibility and he always found someone else to cover for him; including me.

I knew that Bob was living a ways from his job so I wondered how was he getting to work. One morning I left my place early so that I could get to his job and see for myself. When I arrived, he hadn't got there yet. I decided to park in the parking lot and wait. I backed up next to some trees that hid me from the road on one side and by a white truck that hid me from the front entrance so when he drove up I could see him but, he couldn't see me. One after one, cars pulled up, but Bob got out of none of them. After some time a small white car passed by and parked two cars up from me. Bob got out the car only to leave the driver side door open as if he was just going to run in and back out. He went in the office; I assume just to clock in. Since he was in the office, I took the opportunity to get out my car and stand by the front of it. Bob came back out and headed back to the small white car. He didn't even know that I was standing there. As he went to go get back in the car, I called out to him from the shadows of the early morning. I could tell from his sudden jump that I had startled him. When he realized who I was from the shadows, the look of total surprise was all over his face. He walked over to me and said hello as if I was an old friend that he hadn't seen in years. I asked me if he was surprised to see me. He said yes as he stood there looking like the cat that swallowed the canary or my husband who was driving the car of the woman who he claims that he's not living with. Either way he was just standing there.

I looked at the little white car and then back at him. I knew it was Debra's car without him even saying a word. That woman's gut feeling was at work again. After realizing he had been standing in the same spot and the car was still running; Bob suggested that he go and park the car and come back to talk to me. When he came back I asked him whose car he was driving. I already knew the answer I just wanted to see if he was going to tell me the truth or tell me a bold face lie. He admitted that it was Debra's. Bob said it had started getting hard for him to find a ride to work and so Debra had let him use her car to get to work. He said that he took her up on her offer because he wanted to keep his job. Pointing the blame at me was one of Bob's favorite pass times. He went on to say that it wasn't like I was going to come and get him to take him to work if he would have called me. And for once I had to admit; he was right. I wouldn't have come and got him; I let that be clearly known. For what for him to put all those miles on my car and put two dollars' worth of gas in my car; no thanks, I'll pass. I changed the subject and asked him with a very short tongue and little concern how he was doing. He just looked me up and down admiring my new white tennis shoes and said that he missed me and the boys.

Bob never looked me straight in the eye while he was talking to me. That was a sign of guilt of some kind. He was good for always lying or bending the truth about something. I had a feeling that Debra wasn't just letting him drive her car for nothing without him promising her something. Like maybe he told her that he would pay her car payment. Nawh, it couldn't be that because I'm his wife and he didn't pay my car payment when he was living with me and driving the car putting all those miles on it. I looked at Bob and told him that I just stopped by to see how he was doing since I hadn't heard from him to make arrangements so that he could see his boys. I told him that I didn't know where he was living since he left his mother's house. I didn't want to hold him up any longer so I told him that it was time for me to go. Anyway I had seen what I had come to see. Bob told me to come back later on around lunch time so me and him could talk. I told him okay that I would come back not really knowing if I would or not. But before I left I wanted to see how sincere Bob was about missing his boys. I asked him if he had anything for the kids for groceries. Not that I needed anything, I just wanted to see his reaction. To my surprise, Bob reached in his pocket and gave me a twenty dollar bill. Now that wasn't a surprise. This was all that he had to give to his boys after being gone for over a month. Nothing had changed it was the same old, tired Bob. He told me that was all he had. I'm quite sure it was after he had spent up all his money on Debra's birthday cookout. Please tell me what the hell I'm supposed to do with twenty dollars for two boys. I just looked at the twenty dollars as he proudly put in my hand. I knew not to ask him for more or I would have been out there all day. As I went to get in back in my car, Bob asked for a hug. Hesitatingly I did and as I went to go walk away he tried to kiss me. As I pulled away from him I reminded him that his privileges and benefits had been revoked. I got in my car and drove away but not before I told him that he needed to call his kids.

I got back home and got the boys ready for school. All the while the thought of Bob driving Debra's car stuck in my head making me think that more was going on between the two of them. That afternoon on my way back to his job; I was confused on even why I had agreed to come back. Was I wanting him to come back home now that someone else might want him and I was afraid that he wouldn't learn his lesson and to reap the benefits of my long suffering. They say it's better to have a piece of a man than no man at all. Or was I afraid that if I did leave him out too long that he would never want to come back home. Or was it just to prove to Debra that she meant nothing to him and that I still had my wifey powers of putting him out and being able to call him back home whenever I wanted to. Or maybe I wanted just to hear what he had to say. To see if he was singing that same old tired tune or if he had learned a new song. No I think right now I just wanted Bob to remember even though me and him were no longer together that he still had an obligation to his boys and with every breath in me; I was going to make sure he stood up to it. I'll be damn if he puts another woman before my boys.

I pulled up at his job and parked. I didn't see Debra's car so I assumed she came and got it. Bob must have seen me come in because I was only there for two minutes before he came driving up on a golf cart. He sat there smiling as he told me that he was glad that I had come back. I asked him what was going on and what did he have to talk to me about. Bob began to say how he didn't like being out of the house and how he never thought that he would be out on the streets again. He began to stare off into the trees. I explained to him that a person can only take so much before they can't take anymore. Just Bob began to make small talk so I could be in his company; I saw Debra drove by the parking lot in her car. It seemed like time had slowed down for that very moment. She looked over in our direction and I could quickly feel my other half look her dead in the eye from a distance to let her know that yes we were there and not trying to hide the fact. There was almost a dare for her to come and say something to us. My other half was eagerly waiting. I think that she should know that she was not a threat to us. I hope she didn't think that she took Bob from me because she didn't; I put him out. I hope she didn't think that I was there to ask him to come back home because I wasn't. I had to calm my other half down because there was no need of fighting over him because you only fight when something is worth the punch. But Debra kept going. I guess she wanted to have lunch with him too. I told Bob that Debra had just passed by. He looked over to the direction of the road. He told me that she comes by later and picks up the car so she can do her running around for the day. I don't know why he felt the need to explain to me about what she does with her car; we could care less.

I bet Bob just thinks that he landed on his feet. He gets put out of one bed only to land in another a few weeks later. I know his co-workers knew that Debra was coming to the job so now he has his new girlfriend and wife coming to see him. Bob shook his head and said that it wasn't like that at all. That he didn't have a choice after I put him out and that he had to survive and the only way to survive was to keep his job. I just found it awful peculiar that of the friends that Bob calms that he so call has; like he knows all of central Florida that he couldn't find a homeboy to take him to work or his brother even. I didn't feel sorry for Bob and whatever he was saying was going in one ear and coming out the other. It was time for the boys to get out of school and I needed to be there. They are my first priority now. Nothing else matters to me at this point. I told Bob that I had to go and for him to take care of himself. As I started my car I heard Bob tell me to come back tomorrow and have lunch with him. He wanted to spend time with me. I just looked at him with that; are you serious face. I couldn't believe that he was still in denial about me and him and thinking that he still had a chance with me. I told him I didn't think that I would be back for lunch. So he suggested that when he got a chance that he should call me instead. I agreed to that because I was just going to hand the boys the phone anyway. I knew that we needed to stay civilized for the boy's sake. I reminded Bob that he needed to stay in contact with the boys to let them know that he hadn't forgotten about them. I just drove off heading back to the house wondering if Bob and I could see past ourselves and really stay civilized towards each other for the sake of our boys. It wasn't their fault that me and their father couldn't make it work.

A week had passed by and everyday like clockwork my phone would ring: 6am, 9am and at 12pm. I would just let the phone ring. On the caller ID box it would read Autumn Leaf Resort; it was Bob calling me from his job. After a couple of mornings of this I got tired of being woken up so early because I didn't have to go to work and I wanted to sleep in. When I finally decided that I had avoided Bob long enough and seeing that he wasn't going to stop calling; I picked up the phone and told him to stop calling me so early in the morning. That didn't stop the phone calls. Bob was determined to continue to declare his love for me but he never said one word regarding his kids. What Bob couldn't comprehend was that I would have respected him more if he would have stood up to his responsibility to his children. He would have had my full attention. He never got the hint.

One day while at work; my other side got the best of me; I call her Nette. I know Bob had told me that he wasn't living with Debra just using her car and still living with Jerome, but something about that didn't sit well with me. I never believed him anyway. It was a slow day at work and I saw a window of opportunity open. My gut just wouldn't let me rest so I asked my friend Tamekia; if I could borrow her car to make a trip just to look at the scenery on the other side of town. I also asked Tamekia if she knew of the apartment where Debra was supposedly staying. I knew that she knew. One thing about growing up in the country; everybody knows everybody. The directions she gave me were much different than I remember Bob going when he would go to his brother's house. But I really wasn't surprised. Bob was always taking the back roads to somewhere knowing that I didn't pay attention to where we were going whenever he drove and that I was easily to get lost. I learned that the way he drove to his brother's place was totally out of the way of how Tamekia told me how to get there. The directions Tamekia gave me only took me ten minutes to get there. When Bob would drive over there it took us thirty minutes. This made me think even more that Bob was hiding something. Maybe he was scared that on one of his late night creeps while over his brother's place that I just might show up.

All the way over to Debra's apartment I just kept reminding Nette to stay cool and not to go over there acting like an ass; good luck with that. Because I knew her and the littlest thing will set her off when she already at a certain point. Just the fact that Bob had lied about staying with Debra was enough to earn him a beat down by Nette. I wasn't trying to buy myself a ticket to jail. Been there, done that and I wasn't trying to visit anytime soon.

Arriving at the complex; I just started riding up and down each street of apartments because I didn't know exactly which apartment

Debra lived in. I just knew that she drove a white car. The place looked all run down. Where the grass once grew, there is now only dirt. No blinds were up to the windows, just sheet for curtains. I remember those days. You can tell the air conditions aren't working or that there's no central air in the apartments because as I drive by many front doors are wide open. Young guys were hanging out under the shade tree; kids are running in and out the house not bothering to close the door behind them, mothers are yelling for the other kids to come in the house. Twenty minutes of riding up and down the rows of endless brown and tan apartments and there was no sign of the little white car.

I pulled over to one of the shade trees where the guys were hanging out at and I asked if they knew anyone by the name of Debra and if they knew which apartment she lived in. They looked at me as if I was an undercover cop or something. The answer no came out their mouths but the look on their face was that they knew but they weren't going to tell me. Oh yeah, I forgot what side of town I was on. There is true loyalty in the neighborhood I must say. Getting the hint I drove off and drove around for another ten minutes or so before I came across an apartment where the door was open and kids were in the yard. I walked up to the door and knocked. Two ladies were sitting on the couch talking. They were so into their conversation that they didn't even see me come up to the door. After noticing that someone was standing in their doorway; they stop talking. I told them that I was looking for a lady by the name of Debra and that she drove a white car. I asked them if by any chance they knew her. They said no and I believed them.

Where does Debra live?, I asked myself. As I headed back to my car, I looked to see if I could spot a white car. Today was Saturday so I knew Bob was off. Seeing this whole idea as a lost cause; I gave up looking and decided that I would come back another day. But instead of me leaving; Nette had me make sure that I had covered the whole apartment complex. Maybe it wasn't meant for me or Nette to see Bob today. I just sat there in the middle of the road not turning left or right because I really didn't want to have come all this way and then leave without my mission complete.

Don't leave, go back and try again, I heard a voice say and it wasn't Nette. For what; I was asking the voice. I had been there for almost forty-five minutes with no luck. Just as the thought cleared my mind; a little white car passed by me leaving out of the complex. Oh my God, that's the car; I told myself. I drove up behind the car and looked at the license plate to look at the sticker for the month of her birthday which ironically is the same as mine. I know you're asking how I knew her birthday month; like I said earlier, I've come across the dealings of Debra before. When I saw the plate I knew for a fact that it was the car. I honked my horn to get the driver's attention. It was a young girl driving; maybe it was one of Debra's daughters. The young girl stopped the car before she entered the main road. I got out the car surprised that she even stopped. I walked up to the driver and asked her if she was Debra's daughter. She answered yes without questioning who I was. While smiling, I then asked her where exactly Debra lived; as if I was a friend of hers and hadn't seen her in a long time. Again without any hesitation her daughter gave me directions to Debra's apartment. She told me to go back up the hill all the way back until I see another white car parked in the yard and that would be the apartment. I thanked her and she left. I followed her directions and found the apartment. I realized the reason why I couldn't find her apartment earlier because her apartments were a different color and design from what I was told where she lived. She did live in the same area as Bob's brother's place but not in the same complex. There were two complexes that shared the same entrance road and I had been looking in only one area. I guess it was meant for me to talk to Bob today after all. I drove up to the apartment where a white car was parked in the yard like the daughter had told me.

Four small children played in the doorway that doubled for the apartment parking spot. A broken air conditioner unit sat on a pile of trash on the curb at the driveway. There was more dirt than grass for a lawn. The door stood wide open like so many others that I had seen. I got out of my car and just looked around and noticed that there were a couple of young ladies sitting in the white car. I was just thinking of how hot it was and how I hope that the young ladies sitting in the car wasn't part of Debra's crew because I wasn't concealing. But then again I didn't need to be because I had Nette who was always ready at the thought of a bitch thinking that she might want to swing.

I walked up the driveway singing out hello, hello as I approached the door to knock on it. Debra came to the door and I looked her dead in the face and asked for Bob. She looked at me as if she was expecting me to have shown up at her front door sooner than now. But I wasn't chasing after Bob so now was fine with me. Debra and I never had words with each other and for my sake I never planned to unless she got out of face with me first. I use to wonder why a woman would always get mad at the other woman that her man was seeing. What we as women need to understand is that we should never get mad at the other woman because she only believes the lie that he told her just like you believed the lie that he told you. Another point is she's not the one who lied to you, took those wedding vows, made a commitment with, looked you in the face and said he would love you and never hurt you; he did. The other woman wasn't the one that you were putting your trust in; he was. The other woman was being just as naïve as you were.

From the doorway Debra turned and called for Bob. When she stepped to the side there he stood in this small kitchen that was no bigger than a broom closet preparing something on the kitchen table and all I could think of was how when he was at home I could only get him to cook on Sunday. But here he stood in the kitchen of this matchbox apartment like he was right at home. Bob quickly looked up and saw me standing in the doorway. I thought that he would try to show off or react in some crazy way because he was in front of Debra so to make her feel good or feel like she was the number one woman in his life now; but he didn't.

As he stood there in that kitchen and I saw him; he didn't look like my Bob anymore. At first glance he looked so dark and worn out like he hadn't slept in days. Maybe it was just the fact that the apartment was dark due to the fact that there was limited sunlight coming in. I'm use to a lot of sunlight in the house only because my place had large windows and patio doors; okay enough about me. This place only had a very small window in the kitchen and that was for ventilation. Bob walked to the door looking a little confused but not surprised that I was there because he knew how I was. I wasn't threatened by anything and I was afraid of no one. Life has taught me to speak up for myself because a closed mouth can't be heard.

At first I thought he wasn't going to speak to me and tell me to go home. But I knew that he knew better than to do that and I could feel Nette tapping on my shoulder the closer and closer Bob got to me. Bob stepped outside and turned to pull the door closed behind him. I asked him sarcastically as I looked around at the run down place if this was where he was staying now. Bob knew exactly what I was getting at because compared to this place, I felt like all the years he lived with me;

we lived at the Buckingham Palace and that includes when we lived in the government housing or the projects if that's what you want to call it. Again Bob said that he didn't have any choice. His mama told him that he had to leave that he couldn't stay with her, he couldn't go back to his dad's because now he was married and moved into his new wife's house and rented out his house. He said his friend Jerome; who's couch he was sleeping on for a couple of nights out the week girlfriend got mad and had a couple of words to say about him being there and so he thought if he slept on the floor that she wouldn't mind him being there as much but it didn't matter; she didn't want him there anymore. He expressed how tired he had gotten of sleeping on the hard floor anyway. Bob said that he had saw Debra one day (yeah, right I saw a pink zebra yesterday too.) and she asked him what he was doing on that side of town. He said that's when he told her what was going on between me and him. Bob said that she told him that he was welcomed to stay with her until he got on his feet and that she would take him to work. I bet she did.

To some degree I did believe what Bob had told me. His mouth usually curls up on the end when he's lying and his mouth didn't do that so I had to believe he was telling me the truth. I asked him did he think that I would find out that he was living with another woman after he told me that he wasn't. He just shook his head and asked me what he was supposed to do when he had nowhere else to go. I didn't have an answer for him. I reminded him how he would call me nearly every day but not once did he mention that he was living with Debra. He washed over that and told me not to think that by him living with Debra it was permanent, that he was just there to get on his feet. I don't know who he was trying to convince me or himself. I'll believe it when I see it.

Nothing that Bob was saying to me held any weight with me anymore so I changed the subject. "When are you going to come and spend some time with your kids", I asked him. I wasn't expecting him to have a place or time for me to meet him and drop them off to him because he hadn't in the past couple of weeks. Take them to the park, a football game, the arcade room or something I didn't care but he had needed to do something with them instead of spending time doing nothing with them. Bob told me that he didn't know but that he had something for them. He went back into the apartment and in a minute or so came back out with some money in hand. Money was nice but him sending time with them is more valuable. Just as he was handing me the money, he noticed that I wasn't driving my car. With a small chuckle in the back of his throat; Bob asked me whose car was that that I was driving. Being careful not to give him too much information, I told him that it was just a friend's. I looked down in my hand and counted the money that he had given me. He had given me fifty dollars. I didn't complain seeing that I had just got paid and the boys really didn't need much.

There for a split second was an awkward moment between us as we stood outside. Bob looked at me and I at him and I think we both knew what each other was thinking. We thought that we would be to-gether forever. But that wasn't going to happen. I came, I saw and now I can leave. I told Bob to take care of himself and that I would see him around. He said that he would call me soon. I got in the car and I almost felt sorry for leaving him there in all that mess. But then I became upset and confused because I couldn't understand why he didn't work at or do the right thing by his family when he saw that there was nothing like home out here in these streets. Why couldn't he just have done right by his wife and children? Home is always where the heart is. The drive back to my job was long and quiet because there was no one there to help me to understand the cycle of this life.

While arriving home with my two boys in the back seat and pulling up into my gated community, it was sweet as I took in its beautiful scen-ery and its sense of tranquility but I knew that if I wanted to understand the cycle of this life that I would have to keep living and see it to the end. And I didn't know whether I was willing to do that or not.

For the next couple of months Bob did keep in touch by phone. He gave me money when he could but he never came to pick up the boys which was something that I would have preferred over money and I'm sure the boys would have too. Then after a while things got quiet; a little too quiet. There were no phone calls from Bob at my work or at home. I didn't hear from him anymore. I don't know if I was relieved, shocked, or even appalled by his actions. With him not calling me anymore, I just assumed that he and Debra were trying to make their arrangement into a thing for them. More power to them is what I say. There would be no need for me to act like a bitter woman and call Debra to bad mouth Bob to her because the things that he didn't do for me that made me kick him out, he would definitely do for her so that he wouldn't find himself out on the street again. That's what I think a wise man would do but let me not forget that I'm talking about Bob who was not wise enough to know what he had until he lost it. And on the other hand I didn't want to look like a woman scorned trying to get her man back; which I was definitely not. So I let dogs lay where they may and I let the quietness carry on.

# Chapter 35

**MUCH TIME HAS** passed; almost a year has gone by. College, the boys and their sports activities, and work have consumed my time. I'm content with my present situation as my life goes on day by day. After being in my new position at work for over a year I'm starting to notice that I'm having back problems from sitting in a chair all day. I thought problems only occurred when you stood on your feet all day and not when you sat on your butt. I know the problem was coming from me being so top heavy. I've always been top heavy but after the birth of my boys I just exploded A couple of years ago before I started having back problems and was just feeling mushy about myself; I did look into having a breast reduction. I made an appointment with some doctor who came recommended. He walked me through the woods, hills, valleys and grandma house; only to be rude and tell me that he wouldn't give me a breast reduction and for me to lose weight; that would help my breast go down. I had told him that when I had lost thirty pounds once before that my breast didn't move so him telling me to lose weight went in one ear and out the other. Do you know that he had the nerve to spend me a bill for one hundred and ninety dollars? So I went back to work just as mushy as before.

College was done now but I still needed something to occupy my mind and time. I didn't want to let my training go to waste so I decided to go and look for a job in the field I went to college for this second time. What a disappointment; they only want to pay you seven dollars an hour for a medical administration position. Are they serious; do they know how much I had to pay for them classes and all the medical billing and coding that I had to learn and all they want to pay me is seven dollars an hour. No thanks, I'll pass. I'll just stick with my first degree in Accounting and try to find a job.

There was an aid in the newspaper for a hotel needing a night auditor. I faxed in my resume and then I called to see if they had received it. Whoever I was talking to seemed like they couldn't understand English and I definitely couldn't understand whatever they were speaking so I decided I would call back at a later time. The second time I called and spoke to someone I asked if in fact were they hiring, if the position was still available and had they received my resume. The second call wasn't any better than the first time I had called. Whoever I was talking to this time acted like they didn't know what I was talking about. So with all the confusion I just got frustrated and hung up the phone. I took all of this as a sign from God telling me that it wasn't time for me to have another job but it was time for me to take care of myself.

My back pain was my main problem, but let me tell you that gravity was not my best friend. When I took my bra off it looked like I had four arms and that aint cute unless you are a Hindu goddess named Kali who has six arms and is blue. When taking a shower, I would throw my breast over each shoulder so I could wash my stomach. I'm exaggerating a little bit about having to throw them over my shoulder but they were in the way. I use to have to pin together my bra straps in the back for more support. I never knew what size I really wore. The store size bras only went up to forty-four double D so that's where I stopped.

My bra cup runneth over with breast. The deeps in my shoulder from where my bra strap would dip into because of the weight of my breast would remind you of the ditches that we see on the side of the road that you try to avoid ending in on a bad rainy day. I hadn't seen my nipples in thirteen years because they were always looking down at the floor. I could never just look straight down to see my feet; I always had to lean forward a little. At night when I would go to bed without a bra on and lay down on my back, my breast would either fall back and into my face or throat or fall to the side into my arm pits. When I wanted to roll over I would first have to scoop them up out of the way. With clothes on they were packed in to look perky but there was no denying that they were huge. With clothes off it was more like a day on the farm milking the cows; a hot mess.

But it had been a couple of years since I had seen that rude male doctor or any doctor for that matter. So I thought this time since I was getting older that it would be best for me to get a primary doctor and stop going to the clinic. I remember once I had an eight o'clock appointment at the clinic and the doctor didn't see me until two-thirty that afternoon. I knew I would have to wait because I was at the clinic but damn, I didn't want to spend my whole day there. I spent forty-five minutes in the patient room and only seen the doctor fifteen minutes of that. Needless to say; that was my last visit to the clinic. I had good insurance; why not use it.

When it was time for me to choose a doctor, I chose a female doctor. I never felt comfortable with a male doctor when it came to examinations. Even though they are professional I still believe that when a male doctor sees a vagina his dick gets hard. His dick doesn't know that he is a doctor's dick and is supposed to act professional. All he knows is that there is a vagina in front of his face and his instinct is to want to go in. And anyway I assumed that a female doctor would share my concerns since we both have the same parts. So after much debating with myself; I gave my new ob/gyn a call.

I went in for my annual which you know how much we all look forward to that like we do the plague. After the big event was over; you know those lovely five minutes that seem like forever when they say relax and instead we're holding our breath. I told my doctor about my neck, my back and shoulder pain that I was having due to my heavy breast and asked if she recommended that I have a breast reduction. I think before I even finished my sentence she told me to start looking for a plastic surgeon and she would gladly write a letter of approval for the procedure. So I went on the search for someone who could relieve my pain and change me.

I found my surgeon. During the initial examination, I was so embarrassed because the doctor had to actual lift each breast to exam them and they were way more than his hands could handle. He was lifting my breast as if they were the biggest pumpkin that you could find at one of those pumpkin patches you go to around the holidays. It's cute when you see the little toddlers trying to pick up a pumpkin twice their size that they are and struggling to put it in their little wagon. This was not like that; this was not cute at all. Thank God he had a nurse in their to assist him. She made me feel a little at ease too by her being there. The surgeon took the necessary pictures that he needed to make his case to the insurance company. I felt like I was in a lineup. I had to turn left, then right and face front again. He told me that I was definitely a good candidate for the procedure and not to worry.

Well after four weeks; I received a follow-up letter in the mail from my doctor's office just to let me know that she also sent in a letter to my insurance company recommending that I have the surgery. My surgeon sent me a copy of his letter that he also sent in to the insurance company. But two things in his letter didn't sit well with me. First the letter said that I was a white woman and second they had put a copy of the snap shots of my breast. Why did I have to see that; it ruined the rest of my day. You know how people say; take a picture it will last longer. Well they weren't lying because the image of me is still stuck in my head. You know how we always put ourselves in denial about things but I couldn't deny what the photos were telling me. I knew that my breast was big but I always bought pretty lace bras and enhanced my cleavage with nice shirts. I could no longer deny what was in front of me in black and white. Not matter how much I dressed them up; it wasn't pretty. My jaw just dropped to the floor. I was having second thoughts about having the surgery before I got the letter and the photos, but not anymore. What was I thinking about? That maybe they would disappear by themselves. My bills don't disappear as much as I wish that they would; so why did I think that my breast would. Maybe I should have breast feed more.

It's Wednesday and it's a week before my surgery. I'm scared and glued to my bed with fear. The boys are tip-toeing around the house because they don't know what's going on. I'm scared, I have no appetite and all I want to do is sleep because that is the closest thing to death right now. I'm scared that I'm going to look funny. I'm wondering how everyone is going to react to me when I return back to work without my assets. I know that they will notice. Then again maybe they won't. Maybe I won't look funny but marvelous. If that's the case then I know the other ladies are going to hate because we hate to give each other compliments; I don't follow that rule. Why do woman do that to each other? Maybe if we complimented each other more we wouldn't listen to the crap and sweet lies that men tell just because they want to get in our panties. Or believe that we should look like the airbrushed pictures in a magazine that tell us that we should look a certain way so that they can sell their products. Our self-esteem is low because we are always putting each other down.

To be honest I was fine with my big breast until they started causing me to have back problems then I really took notice of them. As I said they were my assets but now they have become a liability; that's some of that accounting terminology that I learned. I will admit; I use to get a lot of attention because of the size of my breast. And at first yes I was flattered by it, but there was a person behind those breasts and I rather she got the attention for the person that she was. I wondered if I would feel different about myself after my surgery. How would I look I also wondered? The days approaching my surgery; I began to stand in front of the mirror with my bra off and push my breast up to where they were supposed to be just to see how it would look with upright smaller breast. Needless to say, my hands weren't big enough to handle all of that so I never could get a good example of it so I just had to use my imagination. It's weird how you watch television and look in the magazines just to see all these women who are peeling out the big bucks to get breast implants to get bigger boobs. They don't realize that in about twenty years from now they'll be peeling out the big pucks to get them removed.

The day of my surgery had finally arrived. I was getting dressed and so far everything was going good. I didn't have any butterflies fluttering around in my stomach; I was okay. I kiss my boys on the forehead as they passed by running through the house doing whatever they do in the early mornings of their summer days. I had explained to them a couple of days ago that I would be going to the hospital today and what I was going for and that I would need their help around the house because I would be very sleepy and in pain for many weeks. My boys are twelve and thirteen now; I have raised them to understand responsibility as well as nurtured them to be understanding. The surgeon explained to me that the surgery would only take a couple of hours and since it was an outpatient procedure that there was no need for me to have to stay overnight at the hospital as long as I had someone checking on me every couple of hours.

I walked through the house giving it a once over making sure that everything was in its place. My ride is running late but I'm okay. I walked outside to get some fresh air and my ride drives up. Sis and my good friend Tamekia had arrived to accompany me to the surgical center. I had packed an extra set of clothes, my Strawberry Shortcake fleece throw and so I would feel safe; I took my cute bright yellow stuffed animal ducky that my oldest son DJ gave me that he won at the game room at the mall. It was time to go. I kissed my boys on the forehead once more to assure them and myself that I would return home safe.

We drove over to the surgical center with no one saying a word. I think we were all silently praying. Gospel music from the car radio filled the air. My sister knows how emotional I can get; she knew the music would keep me calm. Pieces are emotional creatures and I live up to my sign. At this point though I don't think that I was feeling anything but unbelief that I was actually and finally going to get rid of something that had become my trademark or something people identified me by. You know how people say; hey, you know that girl named Antoinette; the one with the big chest. I wondered whether or not my breasts were really that big that people could identify me by them. Every time I would go somewhere I would always try to catch the reflection of myself to see if my breast were really that big of a deal.

We finally arrived at the surgical center; there was no turning back now. I took a deep breath as I got out of the car and looked up at the blue sky. Well Lord here I am and it's all in your hands now. I walked through the double glass doors and into the lobby. Cherry wood cabinets, wingback chairs, there was a coffee area, flower arrangements sat upon tables, nice wallpaper and the air conditioner had to be set on sixty degrees; it was quiet yet peaceful. I checked in at the front desk and then we all had a seat in the lobby. We sat in the lobby only for a minute before a nurse came up and acknowledged me and ushered me to the back to prep me for surgery. I hadn't seen the doctor just yet, so Sis and Tamekia were allowed to come back to my area. We made small talk and laughed and prayed to ease the mood; I could feel the butterflies starting to flutter.

It came time for Sis and Tamekia to leave when the nurse came in to announce that the doctor was ready to see me so that he could make his measurements and marks. Sis being the loving big sister that she was and in my mother's absence; assured me that everything would be okay and that she would be right there waiting for me when I got out of surgery. She squeezed my hand and left out of the room.

My surgeon entered the room and he had a serious face. He didn't say good morning so I said it to him. He says good morning back to me and asks me to stand; he gently helps me off the bed. He proceeds to open my gown as he stands directly in front of me. He studies his canvas in silence. Then he asked me what size I wanted my breast to become. In my panic not wanting to look like a freak; I spoke. I told him not to make my breast the size of apples but to make them more like the size of a cantaloupe and rid them of the watermelon image that they presently were. he pulls out his measuring tape, a black permanent marker and something that looked like a cookie cutter all the while not taking his off the work that he was about to do. He drew on my skin with his black marker. Making his marks and taking his measurement with a steady hand. I didn't get freaked out until he drew a line right down the center of my chest as if he was drawing that line to cut me wide open like they do when an autopsy is about to be performed on a dead body. Now the butterflies in my stomach have taken full flight; forget the fluttering. All I could say was, "yes Lord". A tear ran down my check. The doctor finished up his markings and left without saying a word. I guess he was in his zone. The nurse helped me back into my bed and I just laid there thinking whether or not I would see my boys again.

Well Sis and Tamekia returned to my room along with my anesthesiologist. He assures me that he is going to take real good care of me and give me a good cocktail so that I won't feel a thing during my surgery; I hope the hell not. I have low tolerance for pain. He seems to be a man of his word. I hate needles so to distract my attention of being stuck with one; I make more small talk with Sis and Tamekia while I'm holding my breath and praying the whole time. I really have a lot going on right now with myself. The nurse comes in and says that it's time.

Nothing feels real right now and I'm filled with concerns as I am being wheeled down the hall into the operating room. The last time that I can remember being in an operating room was twelve years ago when I was giving birth to my baby boy Dominique.

As I was rolled into the operating room the first thing I noticed was those huge operating lights that hung over the operating table. They looked as big as the satellite dishes in outer space. I had seen the operating lights all the time on those hospital shows on television. I was amazed how they really do look like they do on television. I remember the nurses in the operating room; they were black to my surprise. I don't remember seeing that on television. Any way they said good morning to me as they were getting things ready for the doctor to perform my surgery. I thought that was very nice of them. I looked back up at the ceiling and noticed six extension cords hanging from the ceiling. I thought that that was weird to have extension cords hanging from the ceiling. But as I thought more about it, it did make sense. It wouldn't be a good idea to have a whole bunch of extension cords on the floor; God forbid that someone would trip over one and bump into the doctor as he is trying to clamp a blood vessel; oops their goes a bleeder. Or the doctor is operating using one of those power tools they use to cut bone and someone trips and bumps the operating table; oops there goes an arm.

I guess the drugs are kicking in because now when I look up at the ceiling the extension cords are now swinging back and forth. No one had touched them; I thought to myself, so why are they moving. That's when I knew it was time for real. I said one more little pray to God while I was still in half a right mind. The last thing I remember was the anesthesiologist say that they were going to move me over to the operating table. He grabbed one corner of my sheet and the other two nurses grabbed the other corners. Before my head could hit the table; I was out.

I can only guess that I made it to the operating table because when I woke up, I was back in the recovery room. I just remember thinking how I didn't recall dreaming about anything like you normal do when you go to sleep. How when I looked at the clock, it was a quarter till two. Thank God; I made it through.

Oh my God, when I woke up I was so cold and in pain. Not really pain but I was just uncomfortable. The nurse came over because she heard me moaning. I told her that I was very cold so she went and got me a warm blanket. She asked me if I was in any pain. I told her that I wasn't so much in pain just that I felt like I had been run over by a truck. She pushes the button so to give me more pain killer through my IV; it couldn't work fast enough. After about five minutes; despite her efforts I was still cold and uncomfortable. She ran to get me another blanket and medicine but this time instead of putting the medicine in my IV, she gave me a shot right in my thigh. Whatever gets to the ache faster is alright with me. I asked the nurse for my sister and she went to find her. As I laid there, I recalled the time when I woke up; a quarter till two. I was in surgery for almost six hours and I don't remember anything. Six hours of my life were gone. I looked down in the direction of my chest. Through the height of the bandages; I could tell that some of my breast was gone too.

I tear rolled down the side of my face; a tear of relief. I was relieved because I wouldn't have any more back pain. I was relieved because I no longer had to safety pin my bra straps together for extra support. I was relieved that the ditches in my shoulder would fill in and become smooth again. I was relieved that I would finally know my bra size and buy the right one and not just take what was available to me and make it work. I was relieved that the stigmatism that came along with big breast would no longer be mine. I was relieved.

The nurse came back in with Sis who came in and began to fix my hair; like the mother she is too me. I didn't know if my eyes were deceiving me or if the cocktail had worn off; so I asked Sis if she could tell a difference and were they gone. She peeked under my cover and looked at my bandages; she assured me that they were indeed gone. The nurse had informed me that my surgeon had removed what totaled to be five pounds from my chest. She assured me that the difference was already noticeable; I had to agree with her on that. She went on to tell me about how I was going to love my new breast; my smaller boobies that is. She was so excited for me. She went on to tell me that I wouldn't have to wear a bra and that I would be able to wear little halter-tops. I didn't even wear those even when I didn't have boobies at the age of eight. She told me that my boobies would sit up and stay up by themselves. I was listening and I appreciated her support but all I knew was that I was uncomfortable and ready to go home. I guess the nurse could tell so she cleared the room so that I could get a little more rest.

After some time I started to feel okay enough to get dressed with Sis's help of course. I sat up in amazement because when I didn't have a bra on; I was use to my breast falling to my waist or sticking out past my nose when I looked down. But then again I was bandaged up so nothing was moving anyway; forgive me I think I still have some of the cocktail still in my system. I just kept asking my sister how I looked; with a smile she told me that I looked good. I had two tubes running out of each side of my breast with a small balloon sack attached at the end. The nurse had explained earlier what needed to be done and the care that I would need; Tamekia had already volunteered to take first watch. I immediately noticed that I couldn't move my arms or sit up by myself. Sis finally got me all dressed and now it was time to get in the wheelchair so I could go home. It was just Sis and me in the room and I was scared to move. I didn't think that Sis could handle my limp body and the weight of it because I was in no condition to bare the weight of myself alone. Just then a tall, fine, and very handsome black male nurse walked by with a wheelchair and asked if it was okay if he could help me. I looked over at Sis and we mustard up a sisterly giggle and I quickly answered yes. I might have had a cocktail but fine is still fine. He gently held my hand and told me to lean on him. He didn't have to tell me twice. He told me to take my time that it was okay; that he had me. I know, I know but I don't care what ya'll say; God is good. Oh my goodness can I take him home please; was all I was thinking as I leaned on this handsome young man. He placed me in the wheelchair and rolled me out to the car and helped me in being careful not to startle me in any way. Get in the car, get in the car please; is what I wanted to say to him. But I knew I couldn't take him home, it was the cocktail in me talking. When he saw that I was settled in and okay; he smiled at me and told me to take care.

Tamekia was in the back seat and in my drugged state of mind, I called out her name to acknowledge her and thank her for coming with me. The drive home was just as quiet as it was on the way there, but a little bumpier. Every bump and dip in the road; I felt. I think we may have gotten home quicker or maybe I was just too drugged up to notice the distance and plus I slept most of the way home. Still in the mist of feeling like I had been run over by a truck; it reminded me that those big old things were really gone.

I was mostly scared because of my limited ability to move. We finally made it back to my place and to my boys. It was a very slow process for me to get from the car to the front door. Where was my handsome nurse when I needed him? With much effort I finally made it to my white fluffy bed and got settled in.As my boys looked at me with much concern; I assured them that I was okay. They never really wanted me to have the surgery in the first place. They thought I was perfect just the way that I was.

My pain killers weren't wearing off anytime soon because the nurse had gave me plenty to carry me through the night; so all I could do was sleep. Sis was very supportive in my time of need; she went and filled my prescription, bought me sprite and orange juice because she knew that I wasn't going to have an appetite whenever I did wake up from my nap but that I would be thirsty. Tamekia stayed by my bedside until Sis returned and well into the night. I knew Tamekia hadn't seen her own family all day and I wasn't in any condition to do anything other than sleep; I told Tamekia that I would be okay in the hopes that she would excuse herself, but she didn't she sat there and for the next six hours I slept. After she knew that I was settled in; she assured my boys that she would be back to check on me. And there she stood by my bedside in the mid-night hour emptying my drains when I awoke. I was so out of it. Tamekia left for the night and said that she would return in the morning. You never know who your true friends are until you go through something. I can honestly say that Tamekia was a true friend and I will always love her for that. DJ and Dominique slept at my bedside on the floor that night; one on each side of me. My angels would watch over me through the rest of night. Every couple of hours DJ would gently tap me on the shoulders throughout the night to make sure that I was still alive and to give me something to drink through a straw. I would greet him with a smile to let him know that I was okay and to thank him. The medication that the doctor gave me was so strong; a smile was all I had the strength to give. I know if a plain old aspirin can knock me out; I knew I didn't have a fighting chance trying to function with this medication. Tamekia would call the next morning to make sure that I had made it through the night. Day two after my surgery Tamekia came by again to check on me and all I could think of was that I must look like a chicken head. Oh well, what did it matter I wasn't going anywhere anytime soon anyway. I stayed conscience long enough to see Tamekia empty my drains, and then I was out like a light. The next time I awoke; it was the next day. I had to go to the bathroom so bad and my throat was dry. I called for DJ who didn't hesitate to come and see what I needed. DJ helped me to the edge of the bed. Barely above a whisper; I told him that I was thirsty. He helped me to the bathroom very slowly. After I sat on the throne he left me to get me something to drink. As I sat there I started to feel strange. I remember saying, "Lord catch me", then everything went black. My head hit the wall so hard that it brought me to. I heard the Lord say "stand up and walk to the bed; I will help you". I stood up and walked back to my bed without a stumble or fall. When DJ came back to the bathroom I was gone. He searched for me and found me lying in my bed. He asked me why I didn't wait for him to come back and get me. I told him that it was okay, that God had helped me back. For the next couple of days I would only sleep.

Four days after my operation; it was time to go and see the doctor so he could check his handy work. Dominique would brush my hair which he took pride in because he wanted his mama to look pretty. When Tamekia arrived she would help me to get dressed and put finishing touches to my hair. I felt like a little baby. The moment of reality came when I was able to button all six buttons up on my shirt where before the surgery I could only button four.

When I got to the doctor's office, the nurse greeted me and asked how I felt. I told her that I was very soar. She promised and assured me that I would look great in a couple of weeks. I was doubtful because I couldn't think pass the pain that I was feeling. I sat up on the examination table and took my shirt off with Tamekia's help and placed on a robe. My surgeon came in; ironically he was smiling this time. He asked if I was doing okay and since I was breathing I told him for the most part yes. And if he didn't pull out any black magic maker I would be doing even better. The doctor opened my robe like he had done once before and started peeling back the bandages that he had so carefully wrapped me in only a couple of days earlier. As he peeled away the bandages; I became stiff as a board with fright of feeling any more pain than I already had. Seeing this, my doctor tried to talk me through everything that he was doing. But it didn't help; it only made me cringe even more. I never looked down at my chest but only noticed the blood stained bandages that covered them. Seeing all the blood; I wondered if I ever would heal.

It was time to remove the tubes and drains from the sides of my breast. The doctor warned me that I would feel a little tug; that's what I was afraid of. The nurse grabbed my hand and held it to comfort me. I looked at Tamekia's face and by the look on her face I really didn't want to see what was going on. So I stared out the window instead into the blue sky. I can honestly say that when someone is pulling something out of your body; it is the weirdest feeling that you will ever know. By me being a big baby when it comes to pain; didn't help the situation at all. It felt like he was taking out one of my ribs so he could give it back to Adam.

When the tubes were finally removed; I got brave and took a peek at my chest. All I could see was the blue thread that circled my nipples that the doctor used to stitch them back into place. The other thousand stitches that connect my breast back to my torso were threaded inside my body and they would dissolve as my body healed. But I had at least a hundred pieces of white stitch tape going across my chest to cover up where the doctor cut me. I felt like the Bride of Frankenstein. I regretted peeking and only wondered what had I done to myself. My doctor put new bandages on me and wrapped me back up and told me that I was healing well. I'm glad he could see that by it only being four days since my surgery. Tamekia helped me get dress and we headed home. I had to make a quick stop by my job to pick up my check. There was a clerical error on my check and when personnel tried to explain it to me it made no sense to me at all. I think it was all the medication that I was on. With all this walking around that I was doing, it was making me tired and all I wanted to do was go home and get in the bed.

For the next couple of weeks I could not dress, feed, walk, or bath myself; I would have to depend on others for that. Apple juice, sprite, along with pain killers would be my breakfast, lunch and dinner. Well because of all the apple juice that I had been drinking; I had to go to the bathroom a lot. I couldn't sit up by myself so DJ had to get on one side of me while Dominique was on the other side and they would gently push me up, then swing my legs around to the side of the bed and sit my feet on the floor. Scared of the pain, I would slowly stand to my feet with them on either side of me like crutches and then we would slowly assemble into a train formation and make our way to the bathroom. One would be in front of me so that I wouldn't fall forward and one would be behind me so that I wouldn't fall back. Every muscle in my body hurt. Instead of walking like a train; I felt like I was hit by one.

I was very discreet as I placed myself upon the throne. I started to feel funny. I didn't know what was going on. I felt sick and dizzy. I went to lean on the wall but it was too far away. I called for DJ to come and stand on the side of me. While I was sitting on the throne; I placed my spinning head on his stomach and suddenly everything went black. When I came to my boys were just standing there looking at me and I was still sitting on the throne. I was confused about what had happened so I asked them both if I had passed out and they said yes. My forehead was covered with sweat. I looked at DJ and noticed that his shirt was soaking wet also. Dominique wiped my forehead off with a towel. After a minute or two I managed to get myself together. DJ and Dominique slowly walked me back to my bed. They propped my pillows and laid me back down. I could only lie in one position and that was on my back. DJ came every four hours with a little white pill to ease my pain. I never knew that I would hate lying on my back. I guess when you're not doing anything then it's pointless.

Sometimes when I would go to the bathroom I would take a quick look at my profile reflection in the mirror. I still hadn't got brave enough to remove my bandages and really take a look at myself. But through the bandages that were still wrapped around my torso; I looked flat chested. I hadn't been that small and flat chested since I was thirteen and I wasn't that small than; I don't think.

Three weeks after my surgery; I'm able to move about on my own but very slowly. My wrapping around my torso is now replaced with a sports bra but my padding and stitches remain in place. I was finally able to sit up on my own but only if I had a lot of pillows piled up behind me. I can't go to sleep comfortably because I can't lay on my stomach or side. I long for the day that I can. Some nights I carefully force myself to lay half way on my side but then the next day my ribs hurt. That's a funny thought because before my surgery when I would lye on my stomach my breast would cover my ribs so I couldn't feel then anyway. Being able to barely move around; made it impossible to run errands because I couldn't drive. Tamekia would come be every Friday and pick me up to take me to pick up my check, go grocery shopping along with paying any bills. One Friday when Tamekia came by, she surprised me with a get well card and some flowers that my friends from the office had gotten together and got for me; that was so sweet of them.

I'm still in some pain but it's a different kind of pain. It's more like electric shocks shooting through my body. I know that the nerves are trying to heal but I'm trying to wing myself off the prescription. I don't want to become addicted to pain killers. At first when I saw the prescription it was for thirty pills with no refills. At first I thought that it wouldn't be enough for all the pain that I was in, but on the contrary it was enough. I have to overcome the pain.

I woke up early one morning and I wanted to take a shower. I cautiously and very slowly made it to the bathroom on my own. I stood in front of the mirror with my clothes on. First my front view, now my side view; my chest looked extremely small. But now it was time for the big reveal. I slowly peeled off my clothes from my body. "Okay girl, you can do this", I told myself as I was standing in front of the mirror now with only my sports bra remaining. I took a moment to brace myself and then I removed my bra and then all my bandages. I just stood there looking at the reflection that starred back at me. "The Lord heals me", I said to this reflection as a single tear left my eye. I looked at what I assumed to be or are supposed to be my breast. I can't really picture them as breast because they look more like two square beef patties glued to my chest with black olives sewed in the middle of each one with blue thread. Across the bottom of the two squares look like they're being secured by at least one hundred pieces of tape that runs down to the top of my rib cage. Well the tape is not exactly white anymore; they're covered with blood along with green and yellow gook. I just stared in amazement because I hadn't seen my nipples in thirteen years and even though they were now attached to my body by blue thread; I was still glad to see them. "So that's what they look like", I said to myself. I was frozen there for what I know was a very long time. "Everything is going to be okay", I heard the Lord say. I slowly turned away from my reflection in the mirror and stepped in the shower. I turned on the shower and watched as the water fell like rain. I stepped into its stream as the water fell upon my tender skin it hurt so I grabbed my sponge and slowly took a shower praying that I had made the right decision by having the surgery. I know there were tears mixed in with water as it all went down the drain but I just couldn't stop crying.

After a long shower, I got dressed and went to lye in my bed. I thought to myself; that they don't show this part in the documentaries. The doctors should offer some type of counseling after surgery so patients can deal with the physical as well as the mental changes that occur. For the next couple of days I would have my good days and my bad days. On my good days; I couldn't wait to go bra shopping and for my friends at work to see me. And on my bad days; I longed for the comfort of my mother. I wondered if I was the same person because a part of me was gone now. Would I even be noticed anymore? I had gotten so much attention because of my breast that they had become a type of tool for me in a sense.

At my next doctor's appointment; my blue stitches were removed. As my body would heal any blue stitching that the doctor wasn't able to remove would just poke through my skin and I would gently pull it out. As time went on the white stitch tape was no longer white but blood stained and it was no longer sticking to my body. As they began to loosen; I would peel them off one by one. One day I think that I must have gotten impatient and I sat in my room and removed the remaining stitched tap that lingered behind. Time had passed and as God had promised: my body was healed.

Finally I'm able to go bra shopping which I would find out would not be an easy task. Nothing felt right anymore. Before my surgery; I had too much to put in a bra and now it feels like I don't have enough. But through much trial and error I found what I needed. Now my stomach, butt, and thighs need to fall in behind my chest and get smaller. I know what I'm about to say might sound crazy but my craziness is my truth. I like dreaming about myself because in my dreams I am never fat. So that leads me to believe that there is a slimmer me inside that wants to come out. I've always had a pretty face and I had a great body before I had kids; like all woman do. I think a fifty pound weight loss would be good enough. I just want to slim down and have that muffin top go away. I guess that I will be on that weight loss quest until I reach it. But for right now I'm going to dress, press and be the Diva that I am.

Not able to return to work just yet, I was relaxing at home when suddenly my phone rung. I didn't check the caller id box before I answered it; I would soon regret doing that. I noticed the voice; it was Bob on the other end. I hadn't heard from him in such a long time. Bob told me that someone had seen me and came back and told him. Bob's tongue can be very hurtful when he wants it to be. I'm shame to say that I picked up that bad habit from him. Bob conversation with me started off very nice. But the longer I stayed on the phone with him; I knew his tongue was getting hot. Bob went on to tell me that this person who had seen me told him that there was something different about me. And so I told Bob that I had had surgery to reduce my breast size because I was having back problems; I would soon regret that too. Bob expressed his concern for my health and wished me a speedy recovery. Then I heard a chuckle in the back of his throat; I knew then that something fowl was about to come out of his mouth. Bob went on to say that I probably looked like Big Bird from Sesame Street. Bob really knew how to say hurtful things and push my buttons. Bob knew that I was very sensitive about my weight. It hurt me to my heart that he called me Big Bird but not surprising that he would say something to try and hurt me. My jaw just dropped and I just slammed the phone down. I was too mad to cry. But I knew that he was lying about someone seeing me because I hadn't been anywhere. But that was another thing about Bob; he always knew what was going on in my world. I really did believe that he had people watching me. But I'm going to see if I can get those checks like Big Bird. Let them run back and tell that.

# Chapter 36

**I RETURNED TO** work six weeks after my surgery and no one said a word. I guess everyone figured that it was too much of a touchy subject to talk about and that it really wasn't office conversation. Plus I figured that Tamekia had filled them in on my progress as the weeks went on. For the most part things were going okay until a tragedy hit our nation on 9/11. I will admit; things got tight. Gas prices seemed to be going through the roof over night. Financially some weeks were better than others. I found myself trying to decide whether or not to pay the cable bill or skim off the top of another bill and catch it up the next time I got paid. I was avoiding any bills collector's call if they were calling because my bill was a week late. Really people, really. I found myself watching the caller ID box because they would call all time of night. Your phone rings ten o'clock at night and you answer not looking at the ID box because you think it's your special friend calling and instead it's the bill collector asking a dumb question like; "why are you late and when do you expect to pay your bill". I would tell them the reason why I'm late was because I decided to feed my kids this week and if I don't decide to feed them next week, well then I'll send them a payment. Normally that just got me silence from the other end of the phone and I would just hang up. I learned that your struggles come to make you stronger and wiser. I don't mind that but could they come with a warning first, so that I can be ready.

The worst feeling that a mother can have besides the death of her child is not being able to feed her child. I fed mine; I could do without MTV for a month or two. Many days I had nothing in my freezer but ice;

and God still put food on my table. And even though Bob was not living with me and the boys, I still did expect him to help out financially. I don't know why I did. If he wasn't helping while he was living with us; what on earth would make me think that he would help when he wasn't living with us. I thought that maybe the fresh air had done some good by now; not.

But I don't blame Bob totally; I blame our lawmakers. For some strange reason they think that a family of four should be able to live off of both working parents making six dollars an hour. That is our minimum wage rate at the time and most employers are sticking to just that. After all these years you mean to tell me that's the summit that our minimum wage had reached. Society was so far behind. That's why the rich are able to stay rich and the poor will always be poor and us lucky ones will fall somewhere in the middle. And politician's wonder why we have so much crime. I take that back, they don't wonder why; it's just the fact that they don't care why. They need to come down off their high chair and sit on the bench with the people who elected them into office. I would like for them to work on a job for a year paying six dollars an hour with no health insurance or any paid benefits and see how they like it or even live off it. I bet they'll run back to the capital and change minimum wage. But I don't see them coming down off their high chair anytime soon; we're just left with doing the best with what we got. I know it's hard for the politicians to look pass everything that they have and look down on the people and say that we don't need anything; whatever.

I just want to show you just how far six dollars an hour can go. You're doing it big if a job offers you seven dollars an hour and you've hit the jackpot if they pay you eight. Now mind you; you have your basic every month bills like rent, water, lights, car payment and telephone bill, car insurance and let's just throw in cable to even it out. Now I'm not in the six dollar an hour category, I'm more in the jackpot stage at this time of my life but still; bills are bills. Rent would be seven hundred and up if you live in a nice neighborhood or own your own home. The electric bill may run you eighty dollars or more and that depends on if you spend all day yelling at the kids to keep the front door closed because they're letting out all the cold air. Water will run you may fifty or sixty dollars depending on how long you want to take a bath. Phone bill can be eighty or less if you don't make any long distance phone calls. Your car payment won't be too high if you got good credit; so that means the majority of *us* is paying three hundred a month or more. Your car insurance if you have to, you can get by with just PIP and Liability which will run you a hundred a month and that's only if it's not being financed. And nine out of ten if it's not being financed it's on its last wheel anyway. And if you're getting full coverage; be prepared to pay close to two hundred a month. Now there's cable, which is if you want to watch more than the eight channels that your antenna will pick up you're going to cough up fifty dollars. Now you do the math and we haven't even talked about food, gas, personal needs or entertainment. Groceries are going to run you at least one hundred and fifty a week. I know it does me and I only have me and my two boys. They have to have their breakfast pastries in the morning for breakfast or their cereal. And that two different boxes because neither one of them like the same kind. Oh yes, their hot pockets for their after school snack and whatever we decide for dinner, because you know that I'm still not cooking. Gas is crazy at almost three dollars a gallon. Public transportation is starting to look very inviting,

Oh my God, did I mention clothes and shoes. Where I come from we got new clothes only twice a year; at the beginning of school and at Christmas and a pair of shoes had to last the whole year. Now a day these kids expect something new every month or every time you go to the store. Who got money like that? And still let's not mention their toys, CDs, DVDs along with the latest gadgets that society says that you just have to have. You have to have lunch money to put in the kids account at school. They want to join the little league football team. When they get older they need money because they want to hang out at the mall with their friends. Go to the high football game and dances. And don't forget senior year; that's a bill all on its own, but I still have some time before I have to deal with that. Thank God for small favors. Totaling all these things up make you need to have two or three jobs. But we get by with what little we have; we always do.

But I can't blame the politicians' either because they're only doing what we let them get away with. We elect them to represent us in front of a congress group of many who are supposed to have our best interest at hand. We elect them and put them in office due to the big promises that they shoot to us that they're going to do for us once they're chosen. But once they're in office, they only do two of out the ten things that they promised us and it takes them forever to do that. And we just stand there and smiling, waving and shaking hands, and hold

up their signs only to put them back in office the following election year hoping that they will finish what they started, but they don't. And yet we just keep smiling and waving instead of putting a fire under their butt to do what we elected them to do or get someone in there that will. Enough about politics; my brain hurts

My boys are as different as night and day, so that keeps me on my toes. DJ my oldest son loves sports. Football and basketball have his interest. He wants to go pro. And Dominique; well let's just say he ain't getting dirty for nobody, so track is his thing to do. He's wants to be on the Olympic track team. Little boys and their dreams but yet life has its own plans for you. You just hope it likes your dream. DJ wants to buy me a big house and Dominique wants to buy me a pink Lamborghini; picture me in that. I think it's cute that they think so much of me and want for me what they think I want for myself or what they think I deserve. But I want none of those things because just the sound of their laughter brings me the most joy. But what little boy doesn't want the finer things for their mother. I just think God made all little boys that way. I never put any pressure on my boys but I did teach them that if they put good into whatever they do then they will get good out of it.

I found myself having a pity-party one day after taking Dominique to the dentist and found out that he was going to need braces. The braces, pulling out four of his baby teeth, and getting two cavities filled is going to cost well over five thousand dollars and my insurance is only going to cover seven hundred of that. I just walked out of the dentist office and looked up to the sky and said Lord, how am I going to pay for this. I've come to learn that when God speaks to you; He speaks very clearly.

I got home and after pacing the floor for some time; the Lord said go and get the newspaper. So I told Dominique to go and get me a newspaper; I just wanted to see what my horoscope had to say about my day. A lot of times it makes a lot of sense that it's scary. Dominique returned with the newspaper and I went straight to the horoscope section. I read it and I kid you not it said; today you can talk anyone into anything and sell them your idea. And I'm saying to myself; if I can sell anyone on giving me a job, then I'll be happy. So I looked in the classified; low and behold there was the exact aid in the paper for the hotel night auditor position that was there two months earlier. Right then I knew that God had held that position for me until I was ready for it. I called to make sure that the position hadn't been filled; it hadn't. I asked to speak with the manager and after only five minutes of being on the phone with him; he asked me to come in for an interview; God is good.

Well, there I was a week after being on my second job which is part-time and I find myself in a daze. My feet are killing me and they feel like they are on fire because I have been standing on my feet for six and a half hours straight in heels with no break; I'm not use to this. I'm use to done had a break, ate lunch, smoked a cigarette; even though I don't smoke, read the paper, done washed the car, ran a mile and took a nap. To make matters worse; I'm standing here listening to my new boss talk me to death or so close to it that I want to pull out my eyeballs and shove them down his throat so he can shut up. He seems very arrogant and cocky in that fact that he owns his own hotel. He's standing here going on and on about a survey that the guest have to fill out after their stay at the hotel. Now mind you; this is not your typical survey that's ten questions on that little index card that the housekeepers place on the nightstand by the phone. This man had about twelve pages with about twenty different categories and he wanted to explain each and everyone one of them to me. He just kept talking. He loves to give scenarios about every little thing. He talks to you as if you are a child or from another country and don't fully understand American culture. And even though he is not from American and makes it very clear that he is only here for one thing and that's to make money off of us, he comes across as if he has mastered the American culture and he alone knows our weaknesses and he has figured out how to capitalize on them. What a slap in the face. I found myself kept having to remind myself why I was there. Gas and food is what I kept saying to myself over and over again in my head.

One of his scenarios went like this; when you go to BK and order a burger do you notice the people cooking. Ten years from now when you go back to that same BK and order a burger; they'll still be back there flipping burgers. Is that all that they inspire to be; my people don't think on such a small level. I just couldn't believe that he let that come out of his mouth. I thought that he was so rude for saying that. I was taught that whatever you do; do your best. If they like flipping burgers; let them. Everybody can't afford or are aspired to own a BK but that doesn't make them lazy or less intelligent. Someone has to flip the burgers that keep the people coming in to buy the burgers in order to keep the BK running. They could become flipper of the month.

As I'm listening to all of this belittlement; I keep asking myself what the hell was I thinking this morning when I put these shoes on. I keep shifting my weight from side to side thinking that it would give me some type of relieve; but none came. I know in the last three days I have heard or should I say; listen to my new boss brag at least a dozen times on how he bought this place and turned it upscale. Don't get me wrong; I'm proud of him for his accomplishments. But what I'm trying to figure out is how in the hell this man come here from across the water with nothing and in ten months time of being here buy a six million dollar establishment. Oh I forgot; that's politics for you. I've been here for thirty-four years and can't get my forty acres and a mule; they can keep the mule.

Besides listening to the relentless reminder of how lazy and unambitious we Americans are there's a double punch with my second job; there's a four foot, buck-o-five, New York accent talking bobble-head looking chick walking around here training people because she's leaving in a couple of weeks. I just want to walk up to her and pull one small string of hair off the top of her mushroom shaped head and say; poof be gone. She acting like she's the head chick in charge. I guess her badass attitude is supposed to make up for what she lacks in height; even with heels on. Chick, sit down somewhere.

As I was training on the computer after only my second day; she gone to come and flop her butt down in a chair next to me with her note pad and said "okay tell me what you know". I'm looking at her and thinking to myself; you really don't want me to tell you what I have learned because you just might get your feelings hurt. And plus I'm still working on making sure that I get here on time and making sure that I remember to clock in. But instead I just looked at her and smiled while saying in my nice but you are irritating me voice; that I was just still familiarizing myself with their system. I guess she read all through that because she quickly snatched her note pad and herself from the chair leaving it the same way she found it; empty. What made her come to me after only two days of just going through the steps to be set up for training; I couldn't tell you. Why did she act like I was supposed to know just as much as she did and she had been there for four years? I barely remembered her name. I don't know why she tried me like that, but she never made that mistake again.

Three weeks have passed and its payday. So I get to work and those who were off today came to the job to pick up their check. So I asked bobble-head if I were to get a check also and she told me no. I think I stopped breathing for a second or the earth stop spinning; I really don't know which one. I couldn't make since of the fact that I had worked three weeks and couldn't get paid for the two weeks that fell in that pay period. I was ready to clock out and do a fifty yard dash to the front door and break a personal record. Bobble-head reminded me of a paper that I had signed on my first day of work agreeing not to get paid until after my six weeks training. I know that I was new here at this job but I wasn't new here on this earth. No one in their right mind would agree to something like that. She turned around to the computer and printed out this so-called paper and handed it to me with a smirk on her face. I read over the paper again and politely pointed out to her that nowhere on that piece of paper did it say that I would not receive a paycheck until after my six week training was complete. But what it did say was that I would be paid minimum wage until my six week training was complete and upon my completion that I would receive the difference from my hired hourly rate for those six weeks. I handed her back the paper with the same smirk on my face and she disappeared to the back office. Minutes later she returned with my manager who I learned liked to hide in his office and made bobble-head handle his dirty work but she knew that she would need reinforcements for this one. He asked if we could step outside and talk; I didn't have a problem with that. He went into some dragged out speech about his past employees and how he would spend a lot of money training them and they would quit shortly after. But what did that have to do with me? Well needless to say I set them straight about my position. I hadn't been wasting gas and time, changing my sleep schedule, and leaving my boys at home just so I could come to work and not get paid. My manager wrote me a personal check. It's sad that people will try and under mind you if you don't speak up for yourself.

There are times when I looked around and couldn't believe I was maintaining and believe me I know that it wasn't without God's help. The responsibility of working two jobs was heavy at times. Some days I looked forward to working because I knew a bill had to be paid that week and that I would be able to pay it because I got paid that week.

I have days when I feel content with it just being me and my boys. Yes there's a different type of stress that comes from my situation but I do welcome it; because it's life. So at the end of the day when everything is said and done; my soul praises the Lord in those moments because I know he is with me. The responsibilities of life I will carry but my burdens God will bare. Then there are days when I feel so overwhelmed and think that life isn't fair. My soul praises the Lord and he comforts me.

With working two jobs, I guess my brains got a little scrambled because against my better judgment, I called Bob one day out of the blue. I could tell that he was in front of a group of people because when he is, he always does his big macho manly voice. You know how guys talk around other guys so that they know that they still the man and have their balls. Knowing that I was in for a show and that he was ready to put one on; I asked Bob how he had been doing and that I hadn't heard from him in a while. I could hear his audience in the background and they sounded like they had already put a couple of rounds down. Bob told me that he had been doing okay and that he was just hanging out playing cards. Bob was careful not to give a clue to the guys around him exactly who he was talking to on the phone. I found it very interesting that he could find time to play cards with the fellows but he could find time in the past six months to spend some time with his sons. I asked Bob if he wanted to speak to his boys. He acted as if he didn't understand the question by never saying yes. Instead of repeating myself because I know he heard me the first time, I just asked another question since he couldn't find it in his pride to acknowledge his boys in front of his *boys*. Already knowing his answer; I asked Bob when did he planning on coming and seeing his sons. He told me that he didn't know but asked me how they were doing. I could only image if he would spend some time with them that he would know. But that's just a mother's way of thinking or is that just common sense. I told Bob for the most part that they were doing okay.

Truth be told; DJ was missing his dad because they watched sports together. I would occasionally sit down and watch a basketball or football game with DJ and he would be patient with me by telling me all the players' names, what they did and how good they were at the position that they played. At first I would be all interested in what was going on but then after a while watching men run back and forth on a court just to see who could put a ball in a net that hung twelve feet above the ground; became a little boring. Despite however boring I thought it was, I would watch the whole game. I could tell that he really enjoyed my company being there in absence of his father but that he would have enjoyed the game even more so with him. DJ had his good days and he had his bad days. He would wake up sometimes with an attitude before his feet would even touch the floor in the morning. I thought maybe he just had a bad dream. Some days he would just walk around all day mad at the world. On the days when I wasn't having a bad day; I would try to do the understanding mother approach and tell him that things were going to get better. But on those days when I wasn't feeling so sunny; DJ really would try my patience. At times I had to remind myself that he was my son because my first instinct was to go upside his head and tell him to snap out of it. But I knew that this situation was hard for him. On the other hand on his good days he was the perfect, caring, loving and adorable son any mother would love to have. So I learned how to take the good with the bad and keep my hands to myself. Dominique on the other hand didn't mind so much the absence of his dad; he was just fine with how things were.

Bob hadn't given me any money in a long while, so I tested the shark infested waters and I asked. I never asked Bob for any money for myself because I could handle me and mine, but he still had a financial responsibility towards his sons; it was the principal of the matter. Not hearing anything in the background, that gave me a clue that Bob had moved away from his audience so that he could answer me. He told me that he had something for them and that he would bring it by later. I heard what he said but took it with a grain of salt; I didn't have a mustard seed. I felt like he was just saying anything to get me off the phone. But I told him okay very hesitantly and hung up the phone. I'm glad I didn't get the boys all excited by telling them that their father was coming by because later came and went and there was no Bob. Two days had passed and there was still no Bob. I called his cell phone but there was no answer. Was he trying to avoid me? It was time for a little ride.

I grabbed the boys and a little hand bat that I carried around in the car for protection and we headed to Bob's so called temporary residence. As we drove up to the apartment complex, DJ looked around the area seeming puzzled and asked me with his disapproval if this was where his daddy was staying. I told my son yes and then Dominique looking just as puzzled asked me why his daddy was living in this dump of a place. I could tell that they were not pleased or comfortable in this environment. "This is where Debra lives and he lives with Debra now", I tried to explain to them. But the more I talked the more they looked just as puzzled.

As we drove up to the apartment; the scene looked familiar to me. There was a car parked in the driveway-doorway and there sat a young pregnant girl on the hood of the car. The front door was open and there were four kids running in and out the apartment looking like they hadn't taken a bath all week. On the ground next to the front car wheel sat a baby car seat with a baby sitting in it. Two other girls and a guy where standing by the trunk of the car talking. I parked on the curb and got out. As I approached the front door Debra was on her way out. I asked her if Bob was there. With a crazy smile on her face; she told me no, that he had just left with one of his friends in the truck. She acted as if she was glad that I had just missed him. I told her okay and that I would just wait for him. I walked back to the car. Looking like he was ready to go; DJ asked me was his father there. I told him no, that Debra told me that he wasn't there. DJ asked if we were going to wait on his daddy to come back. It seemed like he would have been relieved if I would have said no because I saw his disappointment when I told him yes. I told him that we would wait for only a little while. I got in the car looking for a place to park so that I would be out of the way. So I just parked in front of the adjoining apartment's parking space; no one was living there anyway. I pulled my car in backwards just in case some mess kicked off and I would have to get away fast. Within the next five minutes it seemed like the whole neighborhood came out of their apartments to see who that woman was that came looking for Bob at Debra's house.

From my car I could see Debra talking on her cell phone. I could only assume that she was calling Bob to let him know that I was there. Everyone just kept walking around the car that the pregnant girl was sitting on just talking all loud trying to make like there was something about to jump off. But I had my bat ready just in case anyone felt a little froggy. Me and the kids just sat in the car and waited. I just looked in amusement at this circus act that was being performed in honor of me. The guys were dressed in plain white t-shirts that were ten times too big. Their shorts were following the same guide lines. The shorts that they wore were so big that they came down to their ankles. And for those who did have on pants; the waist band came down midway to their butts because no one wore a belt anymore. But they wore tank tops so that you could see their colorful boxers. An hour had passed and there was no sign of Bob. The kids were ready to go and I was too for the most part.

I think another hour or two had passed and it was getting dark. By this time I was really ready to go home but maybe that is what Bob was hoping for so he wouldn't have to see me. The circus crowd had thinned out by this time but another crowd quietly took its place. On this side of town you could tell what time it was by just looking around at the people that were out. Woman and children went in while the gangsters and gals came out. Some began to standing behind my car which made me a little uneasy but I think they were just checking to make sure that I wasn't *the man*. I was just hoping that they're were trying to stash anything back there so just in case *the man* did ride up on them, they won't have anything on them but on my car. The scene throughout the night would be them running and hiding when they didn't recognize a car and then five minutes later they would see police on foot patrol in the neighborhood. Dominique would ask me why the guys were hiding. I would just tell him that they were doing something that they knew that they weren't supposed to be doing but that they weren't as brave and badass as they pretend to be. DJ just kept saying for us to go and I told him in a minute that we would. The guys just kept walking so close to my car that I was keeping an eye on them through my rearview mirror. I knew that Bob knew that I was here and I was going to wait him out. Ten minutes later a large black truck pulls up next to me. The driver rolled down the windows and all you heard was the music blasting. It took me a minute to realize that it was Bob driving.

I thought that when Bob opened the door to the truck, that he was going to get out and hug his boys; but he didn't. He just sat there in the driver's seat jamming whatever song that he had playing. Acting like he was new money because he was driving this nice truck; bobbing his head with a drink in one hand holding it up high. He still hasn't changed; he loves show boating with someone's stuff. By his body language he was giving the impression that the truck was his, but I knew better. I knew he recognized my car when he drove up. It was almost like he got enjoyment from knowing the boys are seeing him in the nice truck. Then I thought that maybe he didn't make any sudden gestures towards the boys was because he didn't want to put himself in an awkward position with Debra. But what she and any other woman that he chose to be with needed to understand that as long as he had breath that those were his children and as long as I had breath I wasn't going to let him forget it. When Bob didn't react to the boys the way that I thought a father should who hadn't seen his sons in over six months should react; my first thought was to curse him out. But then my second thought was to not embarrass myself in front of my boys. Needless to say; I went with my second thought.

I got out of my car and I walked over to the driver side of the truck where Bob was still sitting and jamming. I must of had the look of my first thought on my face because I could read Bob's facial expression of pleading with me not to curse him out; he knows me very well because he has helped to make me this way. Bob started the conversation between the two of us in high party voice by asking how I was doing. Quietly trying not to awake Nett, I told Bob that maybe we had been missing each other the past couple of days because of our work schedule. He agreed that he had been a little busy. But I knew better than that. I knew Bob had been avoiding me just like he was trying to avoid me tonight by staying away for so long knowing that I was there. I'm not dumb, I know that was him that Debra was talking to on the phone letting him know that I was there waiting on him. But just like Bob knows me; I know Bob.

Bob finally turned the music down and I watched as his eyes glanced over in the direction of the apartment where Debra was now standing in its doorway. She was none of my concern and never would be. I got Bob's attention back on the matter at hand and told him that he boys were in the car and did he want to say hello to them. I was puzzled because Bob still hadn't got out of the truck yet. I really wasn't puzzled; me and Bob both knew why he hadn't stepped foot out of that truck yet. He told me yes that he wanted to hug his boys and told me to tell them to come to him. I turned to the car and motioned for the boys to come to the truck. They both got out with the littlest approaching first. Bob hugged Dominique and introduced his son to the guy that was sitting in the passenger seat of the truck who by the sound of his ancient must have been Jamaican. DJ was next but he didn't receive a hug from his daddy; only a man to man handshake which I don't think DJ appreciated or wanted. He needed to feel his daddy and hear his heartbeat.

Bob being the proud papa for a moment looking at his two offspring's stand before him asked the boys how they were doing. They both said only okay. After some small talk between the three of them fell silent; I stepped in and asked them if they were ready to go. I already knew the answer but I didn't want Bob to think that I was trying to rush them but I knew that there was a better place to have father and son time besides out here on the street.

Bob reached down and placed some money in my hand as if he was giving me a peace offering. I looked down at the palm of my hand and the usual fifty dollars laid rest there. The word *thanks* was all I could come up with at that moment because any other words that would have come out of my mouth would have been a cuss word or two, three, or ten. Bob finally got out the truck assuming that the coast was clear since he had gave me some money. As if giving me the money had earned him a safe pass. But that wasn't the case at all. I just realized at that moment that you can't make someone do something that they don't want to do. If Bob didn't want to spend time with his kids; then I couldn't make him.

I watched as Bob walked over to where Debra and the little crowd had gathered; leaving us standing there alone as if we meant nothing to him. I think at that moment, I was no longer his wife but just the mother of his children so I got my babies back in the car. I looked around at everything that was going on around me. It seemed like I was watching a movie on the big screen. My life was playing out right before my eyes and I didn't like this part of the movie. On the way home that night I vowed never to come back to this apartment again to ask Bob for anything. I refused to rip and run the streets or act like I'm on some type off stake out looking for him to take care of his kids. If he didn't care enough for his kids to do right by them then that was his problem; not mine. Or was it?

# Chapter 37

**I'VE GOT TO** find something to get involved in. I've got to get my mind off the fact that I am alone. I believe that's why I stayed with Bob for as long as I did; the fear of being alone. I know that I have kids and I'm deeply involved in their schooling and sports activities along with working two jobs but it's not filling the void. The boys don't need my around the clock attention anymore. When they go outside to play or at the friend's house for sleepovers; that's when I'm let alone with my thoughts and reality hits me hard.

Everyone has hobbies that they get involved in that sometimes it takes over their whole life or at least a lot of their time. I need to find a hobby before I go slap crazy. But I have to find something that I like; I like getting lost in fantasy. Not the fantasy when you're lying to yourself but more like the fantasy of making things what you want it to be like or better than what it is. So I started buying books and novels; my new hobby was reading. But after completing my four books; I lost interest in my hobby. Nothing could fulfill this feeling of emptiness of being alone that I was feeling and it wasn't fair. The walls seemed to be closing in on me. There is no one around to talk to. There is not one to turn to on my lonely nights. There is nothing there but the radio and all it does is play love songs and that wasn't helping because all I was doing was wishing for the life that they were singing about and crying because I didn't have it. It's funny how when I was with Bob and everyone knew it; how guys were always whistling at me and wanting to tell me something. Now that we're separated and he's not living with me; no one is whistling.

There is no one here to laugh with. There is no one here to hug and snuggle up with after making love. Hell, there's no one here to make love with. There is no one here when I wake up from one of my nightmares to remind me that I'm okay and that it was only a dream. There are too many demons from my childhood that I have to deal with while I am asleep and now I have another one while I am awake. I can't do this by myself and why should I have to. I can feel myself falling into a deep dark hole. I've been here so many times before and I don't want to stay.

The phone rings and I recognize the number. I didn't want to deal with him right now, but I answered the phone anyway. I said, "hello" wondering what in the world could Bob have wanted. He started his conversation off by asking how I was doing in his cheerful voice as if he was talking to a friend that he hadn't seen in a while. I told him that I was doing fine and I asked him what was going on. I know Bob wasn't just calling for the heck of it so I was just preparing for and anticipating the big bang. "I got my own apartment out here where I work at", I heard him say on the other end of the phone. I was just surprised that he even had the balls to get up and get something on his own. I asked him what his address was so that I could bring the boys over to see him. He quickly mumbled out an address which made me very suspicious on whether it was the correct address or not. I could tell that he really didn't want to tell me the address. He went on to tell me or should I say warn me that Debra and her sick mother moved in with him because they had got kicked out of their apartment. Boom, did you hear that; that was the big bang.

I asked Bob why did Debra and her mother get kicked out and what the deal was with them staying with him. I really wanted to hear this lie loud and clear, so I sat up in my bed. He told me that they got evicted for not paying rent. Bob said that they moved in with him because when he didn't have a place to stay, they let him stay with them. I wasn't that mean and stewing in my own pot that I couldn't understand him wanting to return the favor. How nice of him to be so considerate of others. With my lips pressed tightly together so a peep wouldn't come out; I continued to try and listen and get pass the fact that him and Debra are now living together despite that fact that me and Bob are not divorced but only separated. What the hell was going on? Has this mother-sucker lost his mind? He must have because he thinks it's okay to call and tell me like it ain't nothing. Bob couldn't even pay rent when he was with me and his kids and now he's gotten an apartment and done moved some chic and her mama in. When I checked the calendar this morning; it was not April the first. I will be a fool but just not today. I am truly feeling sick to my stomach. This is not fair. I'm not living with anyone and if I was he would be calling me everything but the child of God. And he wouldn't just leave it at that. Bob likes to stab you with his words and then pour salt in so it really hurts. He would always tell me that any man that comes around that he wasn't looking to come and make my place his home that he would be like the rabbit in Alice in Wonderland and only be looking for a hole to fall into.

I listened as Bob tried to explain to me his new living arrangement which now didn't seem temporary at all now that she has moved them in with him. What are the boys going to think when they find out that a woman other than their mother is living with their dad? It was different when he was living with her because he wasn't on his feet and he said that it was temporary. This is totally different; aint nobody put them out, they put their self out by not paying the rent. Oh so you mean to tell me that Debra and her mother couldn't go and stay with any of her family. I can only assume that Bob told Debra that he was moving off her couch because he had gotten his own apartment. She probably saw the nice place that he was about to move to and saw an opportunity to move out of the match box she was in. but Bob had only gotten a one bedroom apartment. Where was everyone going to sleep? More important where were the boys going to sleep when they stayed over for the weekend? I just continued pressing my lips together forbidding a twerp to come out. I didn't want him to hear the anger in my voice. He probably would have mistaken it for me being jealous and it wasn't even that type of party.

Bob went on to say that he didn't know that they weren't paying the rent. He even went on to say that it wasn't until the repo-man came for the car that he knew that they hadn't been paying the car payment. Bob said that since that was his only way to work; he went on ahead and paid the car payment for Debra so that they wouldn't take the car. At this point I know I saw steam coming out of my ears but could someone please hand me a towel so I can wipe the egg off my face. And before I knew it my lips parted and I heard myself say, "You did what"?

The idea of me trying to control my anger just went out the window

I had been playing Betty the peace keeper for long enough. I needed Bob to know exactly how I felt. For the past couple of months Bob had been calling me nearly every day ensuring me of his true love for me and assuring me that no matter what he was sure that we were going to get back together and grow old together. And that his living situation was only temporary despite what others may have believed and yes by this time people in the streets were starting to talk. But I made very crystal clear to Bob that I didn't see what he saw in his crystal ball just yet. Maybe I should give him some time to get himself together and prove to me that he could change and be the man that he saying that he wants to be for me. It was only a thought. So I understood him getting his own place. So him telling me that he had let Debra move in was very confusing and didn't sit well on my stomach and to tell me that he had paid her car payment was a bit much to swallow. That was just too much icing on the cake.

When Bob told me that he had paid her car payment; it reminded me of one of me and Bob's many arguments that we use to have. Our car payment was due; me and Bob had both got paid. I asked Bob for the money and he told me that he would go and get a money order. But I knew that he was just making any excuse not to put the money in my hand. I knew if Bob would have walked out that house that he wasn't going to go and get a money order. Hell, I might not see him again until 2:30 in the a.m. He knew that I never got a money order to pay the car payment; I always used Western Union. He assured me that he would make the car payment but at this point I didn't trust him. And why he wanted to change the way I had been making the car payment made no sense. I looked at him with the side eye and made another sugges-tion. I suggested that since he didn't want to give me the money that I would go with him to Western Union and help him fill out the paper work since he didn't know how to. What I said that for? Bob snapped at me saying; "girl I'm going to pay that car payment, damn". Right then and there I knew that he wasn't. I asked him who the hell was he yell-ing at and that yelling at me wasn't going to stop me from asking him to take care of his responsibilities. I shouldn't have to ask you anyway. Needless to say we never made it to the Western Union.

As always he kept his money in his pocket while I went and paid the car payment the next day. He knew that I had money, so he knew the car payment was going to get paid whether he paid it or not. He didn't offer to give me half or to pay me back for covering his bill. He just acted like we never even had that conversation. So when it was time for him to get off of work and I was supposed to pick him up; I acted like he didn't need a ride and that he could walk home. Two can play this game. I sat in front of the television enjoying a home improvement show admiring the wonderful work they had done with remodeling the kitchen. Not feeling one ounce of guilt; I went on with my day. I greeted both my kids when they came home from school, helped them with their homework and prepared dinner. I guess it was around seven or seven thirty when Bob finally walked in the door. I thought that he had made good time because he made it home before dark. A twenty mile walk aint no walk in the park.

"Why didn't you come and pick me up", was the question of the hour that Bob asked me. "The same reason you didn't pay the car payment; because you didn't want to", was my answer. Like I said, two can play this game. "Oh, my bad I thought since you didn't want to help pay for the car that you didn't need to help use the car. I thought that people pay for what they need", is what I told Bob all the while I sported a little smirk on my face and continued to stir up the mashed potatoes. Don't nobody want no lumpy mashed potatoes. I could see in Bob's eyes that he wanted to do more than just walk away.

So excuse me if I lost my cool points; I'll get some more. I just lost it when he told me that he paid Debra's car payment. How you going to take care of someone else's, when you wouldn't even take care of your own? I called Bob everything but the child of God over the phone. I didn't even give him time to respond. I just hung up the phone. I needed to give myself time to cool off before I took him a house warming present. For the next couple of weeks I just kept going over and over in my head how was it that he could afford an apartment that was two hundred dollars less than mine but when he was here he couldn't or should I say he wouldn't give me one red cent for rent. I decided that it was time for me to pay Bob a visit that weekend. Anyway the boys needed a haircut.

When I got off of work and got home that afternoon, I told the boys we were going to their dad's to get them a haircut. I thought that I would get there a few minutes early to his job before he got off so I could follow him to his apartment because in my gut; I knew that he hadn't told me his correct address. When you know somebody, you just know them. When I had got to his job he had already left for the day. But an old friend of mine who Bob and I used to work with a long time ago; was still sitting in her office. I walked in her office and we caught ourselves up with small talk of what the past couple of years had dealt us. She remembered DJ from when he was a baby and couldn't believe how fast he had grown. I hadn't had Dominique yet before she left the company. She was surprised to see that I only had two sons and enquired if they were both from Bob and I told her of course. Changing the subject; she asked if I was looking for him and I told her that I was. That I was trying to catch up with him before he had got off of work. Hoping that my friend would lead me in the right direction; I hinted that he told me that he lived somewhere on property. Friends, how many of us have them. Friends, the ones we can depend on. My friend couldn't tell me exactly where Bob lived because of policy but she did suggest an area where if he was living out there on property his apartment would probably be in. There's always more than one way to skin a cat. We made a little more small talk before me and the boys said our goodbyes and we were on our way.

Somehow the direction that my friend gave me never lead to the street that Bob told me that he lived on. I got totally confused and lost. Me and the boys drove and drove all around that property. I was changing streets, going in opposite directions, looking for street signs and I still came up with nothing. At one point I just started looking for a little white car. I didn't realize how long I had been driving around lost until DJ asked me what I was doing. I told him that I was looking for his dad's new place but I think he may have given me the wrong address. After an addition twenty minutes of riding and not finding the apartment or the white car; it was obvious that Bob had lied to me about exactly where he lived. I went up front to the front desk where the guest check in knowing that by now my friend had probably went home for the day so there was no use in driving way back there back to her office.

I went up to the clerk and asked if she knew of a Bob and that he worked at the resort and that I was his wife looking for him; that he had given me an address but that I couldn't find it. It wasn't like I was lying. She went in her office and pulled up a file and called the phone number that was on file to try and get in contact with him. But the telephone number was my house number so that didn't help. Then she stated the address that was on file. But the address was my home address so that didn't help. By the puzzled look on my face I guess the clerk knew that those weren't the answers that I was looking for. She closed his file folder and told me that she couldn't give out any more information. It seems he never updated his file with his new address. Maybe because he really thought our separation was going to be temporary so he didn't feel the need to waste time and update his address.

I had just bought a cell phone last week, so I stepped outside and tried to call Bob but I couldn't remember his number. I tried the numbers that I could remember in a couple of different combinations but they were all wrong. So I went back into the lobby and asked the front desk clerk of the resort if she could direct me to the apartment's office. At that moment a gentlemen walked up who also worked at the front desk. The lady clerk told him that I was looking for an employee who worked there and also lived on property, the gentleman asked her if she had called the number that was on file. She told him yes but that it wasn't a good number. Flipping through the papers of the file folder; she looked for another number. The gentlemen suggested that he would look on property for him and send him up to the lobby. He asked me what Bob's name was and he left. Me and the boys sat in the lobby for a very long time. It seemed like thirty minutes had passed. The gentleman and neither did Bob ever come to the lobby. I continued to wait but by this time now an hour had passed. I went back up to the desk clerk and asked her to give me direction to the office of the apartments. She did and again I was on my way.

I found the apartment office with no problem and for that very moment I was proud of myself for not getting frustrated with the whole situation and didn't just say never mind while turning around and going back home. I walked into the office that you could tell use to be an apartment once upon its life. There was a young lady sitting behind the desk. On the back patio sat the golf cart the gentlemen from the front desk had driven off on. By then I could only assume that he had no intensions of coming back up front. I told the young lady behind the desk that I was looking for Bob and he had given me an address but that I couldn't find that street on property. She quickly replied to me that Bob stayed in apartment 1804. I don't know whether I was surprised that she told me so easily where he lived or that she referred to him by his first name. I asked her if she could please show me exactly where to go. I had wasted so much time already that I didn't feel like wasting anymore.

We stepped outside the office and she pointed me in the right direction. I got back in the car and had a little giggle with myself. Bob actually thought that he could lie to me about where he lived and I wouldn't find out the truth. He knows me better than that. Hell he taught me the hard way how not to trust anyone because I couldn't trust him. I don't know why he even tried me like that.

I found the apartment and there was the little white car parked in its parking space; I came to a stop. Dominique asked if this was the apartment. I didn't answer him. He and DJ both agreed that this place was much better than the other place that he was living at. I too had to agree with them on that. Looking around at the green grass, palm trees and well manicure landscape; you could say that Bob had done well for himself. Yes it was nice maybe a little too nice if you ask me. We all got out of the car and slowly walked up to the door that said 1804.

I knocked on the door and covered the peep hole so whoever answered the door couldn't see that I was there and warn Bob or see that it was me and pretend not to be home. I didn't hear a peep but you could feel the presence of someone on the other side of the door. I didn't know how Debra would act with me showing up on Bob's door step but I hoped that she didn't start no mess because I wasn't dressed to kick no ass but I would in a skirt if I had to. This was Bob's apartment anyway; she was just *the help* as far as I was concerned. After some time, the door opened and there stood Bob. He looked like a deer caught in headlights. Knowing that he had given me the wrong address made my arrival there that much sweeter. Someone please hand him a towel so that he can wipe the egg off his face; it's starting to run. But the look on my face was priceless.

"Hey, how ya'll doing?", Bob greeted us with his nervous fake laugh. He grabbed Dominique first like he always does, but he's not impressing me by showing Dominique any special attention. But I knew that it was his way of apologizing and showing that he really does love him. Bob knows that he was wrong for what he did to Dominique and his conscience shouldn't be at rest until he does right by him. DJ gets the usual high five and half a hug from his dad. I guess Bob still doesn't know how to react to DJ since that day that he stood up to him. Still standing at the front door; Bob expressed how glad he was to see everyone and thanked me for bringing his boys over to see him. But he said it in a way as if I was the yellow cab driver who was dropping them off from picking them up from the airport. I just stood there looking at Bob in disbelieve of his acting scene because my thing was this; I never told you that you couldn't see your boys, so why you haven't made arrangements to come and see them; I haven't the slightest clue. But I realized sometimes you just have to bite your tongue and not say what you really want to say for the sake of others. I let Bob have the stage for his scene because I knew that he was just trying to make a good impression on the boys.

Holding on to the little smirk that had implanted itself on my face; I looked at Bob and asked him if he thought that I wasn't going to find him. He started to speak and the corner of his mouth started to curl up. I interrupted him because I didn't want to hear the lie that was about to come out of his mouth. I told him that the lady at the office showed me where he lived. I told Bob that this was a far cry from the address that he had given me. Looking like he had gotten caught with his hand in the cookie jar; Bob finally invited us in.

"So what's been going on?", Bob asked as he made sure not to go any further than the kitchen which was located immediately on your left as soon as you walked in the door. I let the boys talk to him and I stood there in its foyer looking around at his new place. Woven wooden baskets with fake plants were placed on a stands and winery pictures hung on the wall. There was a big nice plush chair and couch with tables in the living room. On the back patio; there sat a couch and loveseat. Looking at their design; I think they came with the apartment. Pastel colors were the thing back in the eighties. There was a nice dinette table that Bob would mention later that he got from a yard sale. The place had low ceilings which made it feel a little cavey. I guess I had gotten use to the twelve foot ceilings in my place and all the large windows. But here there was only one place where the sun came in and that was through the sliding glass patio door. But overall it was still a good fit for Bob. I guess Bob noticed that I was checking out the place and called himself giving me a compliment by saying that he tried to decorate like me and how he was trying to make it look like home. You could tell that he tried to decorate but it was nothing like home. But why would you try to make this place like home when you could have still been at home if you would have showed how much you appreciated home. Don't worry; I wasn't waiting for him to give me an answer.

From the corner of my eye, something in the kitchen caught my attention. It was the sink full of dishes. Someone needs to keep up and get on their housekeeping duties. As I looked around more, I noticed a mini bar stand. It seemed as if no one had a problem of getting their drink on because the mini bar had at least twenty bottles of liquor covering its top and bottom shelf. This was right down Bob's alley. Two of Bob's favorite pass times was drinking and going over someone's house to play cards. That wasn't my thing. Spades was the big card game down here in the south. I use to play Spades too when I was a little girl with my brother and sister. I must say that over the years the game has changed or should I say the people who play the game have changed. These fools down here in the south take this game too serious. They'll be ready to put their mama out her own house over a game of Spades. If they had a bad partner; oh Lord watch out. They calling each other out their name one second and be laughing about it the next. I don't see anything funny about someone calling me a bitch just because I didn't lay out the right card. But play me a game of Maid or Go Fish; then it's on and popping.

Bob finally gave us a tour of the place. Debra and her daughter were sitting in the living room. I held no grudges; I spoke by saying hello. Even a stray dog deserves a pat on the head. Plus I had to show my boys that I could be a woman and not act a fool in difficult situations. And to be honest Debra never came out of left field on me and so there was no need to treat her with anything but respect.

I thought that when I saw the mini bar that it was the icing on the cake; but it was just fueling the fire inside of me. It was what I saw next that made the volcano erupt. There on the wall as big as day was three large portraits of Debra's grandson. She was hanging shit up on the wall like this was here place. Oh hell no; Bob didn't even have pictures of his boys on the wall. There was only one bedroom and Debra's mother was sleeping in it. She was old and needed help taking care of herself. Bob said that she had suffered from a stroke which made things ten times worst. What made me ask the next question I don't know, I just know that I did? "If her mom sleeps in here then where do you and Debra sleep"? I really didn't care but after the words came out of my mouth; it was too late to put them back. Bob directed me to a utility closet that sat on the other side of the apartment off of the kitchen. When he opened the door; there laid on the floor a twin size mattress with sheets on it. I looked at him like; damn. You're paying rent for a place and you're sleeping in the utility closet. I just looked at Bob like he was the dumbest person that I had ever met in my whole entire life. I think I let out a little chuckle; a jail cell is bigger than that. Oops, my bad. I'm sorry but if I'm paying rent than I get a room.

After getting over the shock of Bob's sleeping quarters I told Bob that the reason why I was really there was because the boys needed a haircut. I sent DJ back to the car to get the clippers just in case Bob didn't have any. Bob told me that it was fine that he would cut their hair. Bob grabbed a chair and a small table setting up shop right there in the foyer. When DJ returned with the clippers Bob asked who wanted to go first. This was always a debate between the boys. I would always have to push one of them forward and it was always the one closest to me; this time was no different. I felt a little insulted that we were right there by the front door. It was like the closer to the front door we were, the quicker Bob could rush us out.

As Bob cut the boys hair he made small talk with them asking them about school and the girls. The boys kept their answers short. I could tell that they were uncomfortable with all that was going on. Here was their dad, their mom and their dad's friend who happened to be another woman who was living with him; all sitting here in this apartment trying to act like everything was okay and normal. I tried to make things easier for them by not acting ugly towards Debra who was still sitting in the living room with her daughter not saying too much. I got the feeling that Debra was probably trying to hear what me and the boys were talking about with Bob. But he only said a couple of words to me trying to keep me in the conversation. He didn't let anything slip out that might give Debra a clue that he had been talking to me on the phone or at any time before now.

For the next twenty minutes Bob was in a cold sweat walking that very fine line trying not to disrespect me as his wife and Debra as the one who he was living with. But it was too late, I already felt disrespected just by them being there. After finishing the boys haircut; Bob cleaned up, gave the boys a big hug and told them bye all while standing in the foyer of his apartment. I was shocked with his meet and greet. Puzzled that he didn't offer himself; I asked if he wasn't going to walk us to the car. I could tell that this whole situation had made Bob nervous not sure what moves to make because he didn't want to offend anyone. But like I said, for me it was already too late. He turned to Debra and told her that he would be right back as if he needed permission from her to do what I asked him to do; not.

Slowly Bob walked me and the boys to the car but was always looking out and keeping a view of the front door as if he anticipated for Debra to suddenly come out. If she knew what was best she would stay where she was; she did. It was taking a whole hell of a lot of discipline for me to remain acting like a lady under these circumstances. My city roots wanted to show themselves and Nett had her kick ass boots on. But I knew this was not the time or place for that; my boys were here. They ran over in the grass and played catch with the football that they had brought along with them. As I was watching them play Bob spoke freely and asked me to please not make a scene that this was only temporary until Debra and her mother could find a place to stay. I looked at Bob whose eyes were filled with regret and guilt. I told Bob that I wouldn't say anything or make a scene as long as he remember that he had two sons who lived on the other side of town that he was responsible for and as long as he did that then me and him wouldn't have a problem. When you start putting other people before them then you will hear my mouth, until then I'll be cool. Because to be frankly honest I for some reason at that moment I didn't care about Bob living arrangement that he had going on. I didn't want Bob back; he had put me through way too much for the last twelve years that we had been together. What I wanted and what were important to me I already had and that was those two boys playing catch with each other; that's all that mattered to me. But in Bob's mind for whatever reason he thought that we still had a chance of making it; like I said in his mind.

Me and Bob stood outside and watched our sons play for a while. It was starting to get dark and the mosquitos were coming out. These things looked more like dragonflies they were so big. Me and the boys got in the car and the strangest thing happened; Bob handed me fifty dollars for the kids without me even asking. It just seemed more like another peace offering to me. If he thought that all he had to do was give me fifty dollars every two weeks for our boys when on the other hand he was paying five hundred and something to put a roof over someone else's head then he had better think again. Debra wasn't working so that only left Bob to cover all the bills. I knew for a fact that he was paying seventy-five dollars every weeks for the big screen television he had sitting in his living room. He has a cell phone so I know he has to put minutes on it and I know that aint cheap because he talks too much. So if he thinks that I'm going to stand by and watch him give his kids crumbs after he had done feed everybody; he is sadly mistaken. This would be the first of many visits to come.

# Chapter 38

**FOR THE NEXT** couple of months; I made it my business to be at Bob's place every Friday that he got paid. The same fifty dollars kept coming into my hands until one day I decide to speak up. I asked Bob if that's all he thought his kids were worth to him was fifty dollars. I told him that fifty dollars wasn't even enough to buy groceries for them for the week. I wanted to throw the money back in Bob's face. Bob told me that it was all he had but I knew that he was lying as usual. I told Bob that he had just kept giving me the fifty dollars because I hadn't been making a big scene about it but that he knew that it wasn't enough. I told him that he was sitting over there paying rent to put a roof over someone else' s head and paying a car payment that wasn't his, buying groceries, paying the phone bill, electric bill and a cell phone bill. I tried to point out to Bob that he was doing more for someone else who wasn't his responsibility more than he was taking care of his sons that were his responsibility. His response to me was he had to live too, and by all means; I totally understood that but he was missing the point that he still had kids to take care of too. I had to let Bob know that I was paying the same bills he was and more. I'm paying for shoes and clothes, school lunches, field trips, school dances, them going to the movies, trips to the mall and birthday presents which he didn't get nothing for his son. Showing me no sympathy; he just stuck to his excuse that he didn't have any money. I bet if he would let *the help* pay her own car payment like he did me; he would have some money.

Instead of continuing to let Bob think that he was just going to give me what he wanted me to have for the boys and knowing that they deserved more than them same ass pitiful fifty dollars that he kept giving me for them; I thought long and hard about my next step. Bob must have read my mind because he asked me if I was going to put him on child support. I just stood there looking at him refusing to answer. Seeing that I didn't answer right away he knew that it was my next step. Why wouldn't he want me to put him on child support when I have given him plenty of time to do right by his sons. It wasn't like I was asking for his whole paycheck, I was just asking him to be fair in sharing the responsibility of raising his kids and he acted like he couldn't figure out how to do that. I would have been satisfied with just a hundred dollars every two weeks, I told Bob. If that was all I wanted then I should have told him; is what Bob came back at me with? But I felt like I shouldn't have had to tell him how much because he lived with us; he knows what it takes to maintain my household. I left with no more being said thinking that we had a mutual understanding. The following pay period Bob stuck to his word and gave me a hundred dollars.

Finally Bob was stepping up to the plate but it wasn't long before he stepped back down again. And me knowing Bob; I should have known that it was too good to be true. The following pay period and then thereafter; Bob started back giving me only fifty dollars. It was getting cold and the boys were going to need pants but that was no concern of his. That Friday after sending a couple of hundred dollars on the boys for their winter gear and not wanting to waist any more words on Bob; I went home and called the local child support office and made an appointment. Because it was obvious that Bob didn't understand the words that were coming out of my mouth.

The following week I was sitting in the child support office. I had been here before a few years back before me and Bob had got married and I put him on child support. Back then he only had to pay twenty five dollars a week because he had quit his job so he wouldn't have to pay child support. Those were his exact words that he let come out of his mouth. But when we got married I dropped the child support because I thought that it was the right thing to do and at the time it was. For some reason I was under the impression that if you were married that you couldn't file for child support. But that wasn't true. My caseworker asked me if the father was still in the home and I informed him that the father had been absent from the home for over a year now. In that case; I had all rights to put him on child support. One thing I know; you don't learn nothing until you go through something. But it wasn't until I left the office whether I questioned myself if I was doing the right thing. The word child support left a nasty taste in a lot of people's mouth for some reason. But my thing was this; if Bob would be a man and handle his responsibility on his own I wouldn't even be in this building. But he won't. So what am I to do just stand by and let him off the hook? In so many ways I have already done that. I'm working two jobs and taking care of my boys. Maybe Bob didn't understand the full concept of parenthood. So I figured that I would get someone to explain it to him better; the law.

Some child support papers came in the mail a couple of weeks later. I filled out the paperwork and got a money order for the processing fee and contently mailed it off. I know Bob is going to hit the roof amongst other things when he gets the papers saying that he has to go to court. Knowing Bob like I do; he might even quit his job so he doesn't have to pay. It's not like he hadn't done it before.

A couple of weeks had passed and I hadn't heard from Bob. I no longer felt the need to waste my gas to go and pick up a messily fifty dollars from him so I hadn't seen him either. Not hearing from him I guess him and Debra must be having fun. Another week had gone by before one day he did call. Bob said that he was just calling to check on everybody to see how we were doing. I could hear this tone in his voice about him as if to say that he was doing just great out there partying, drinking, and carrying on. As if he wanted me to know that he was living it up. That was just the vibe that I got from the conversation because he really wasn't talking about much. He just called so that I could hear all the noise in the background. I think that he mentioned that he was riding around with one of his friends. It probably was the guy with the black truck. But then again I thought that since I hadn't heard from him in a while that he was just trying to be noisy to see if I had gotten me a new *friend*. But I had made up in my mind the day that I put Bob out that no other man would come in my home and be over my boys. They had a father, even though he wasn't acting right; they still had one and they didn't need any man to come in and think that he would be taking their father's place. That much I owed my boys and their father.

I told Bob that we were doing okay because we were. I reminded him that Christmas was coming up. He replied that he knew and asked me how much I would need from him. He sounded sincere so I told him that I would need two hundred dollars because the boys were into all those video games and stuff. I asked him was that asking for too much. He told me no that I wasn't asking for too much and that he could handle it. He mentioned something about not wanting to use up all his minutes on his phone and said that he would call me again later. That was fine with me because then again I thought that he was calling because he had got those child support papers.

I think Bob knew something was up with me because when I started back going to pick up the fifty dollars from him I wasn't fussing about it anymore. He asked me if I had put him on child support. For him to ask me that, I figured that he had gotten the papers in the mail. But I didn't answer his question on whether I did or not just in case he hadn't got them yet; I didn't want to let the cat out the bag. Not really waiting on me to answer him; Bob simply stated that he didn't care if I had of put him on child support because they were only going to make him pay me the same fifty dollars that he was already giving me because he was going to tell them that it was all that he could afford. And that he was going to tell them that I was working two jobs. As if to say the more money I made the less he had to pay. Aint that a bitch; nope it's just Bob. I was shocked by what he said but then again I wasn't. I should have known he would try to find a way to avoid his responsibility yet again.

I told Bob that I was sorry to burst his bubble, but the system didn't work that way. In the past the judges use to listen and buy into those lame ass excuses that these guys use to come up with for the reason why they didn't help take care of their children financially. Twenty five dollars a week, he would order them to pay. I use to listen to them in court; the whole while they stood there in front of God and everybody with their Timberland boots on, Tommy jeans and a Polo shirt, gold watch and big chain, ear pierced, cell phone clip on the hip. They didn't tell the judge they weren't staying with their mama and driving around in a candy painted sitting on twenties car. But the first thing out their mouth is they weren't working and don't have any money. The judge finally got hip to the game and starting making the guys pay what they weigh.

It is a shame to think that you have to make a man take care of his kids but that you didn't have to make him lay down with you to make them. I guess the man sees more fun in making them then he does taking care of them. But the same pride and pleasure they took making babies he should sustain in raising them. I feel if a man does not take care of his child willingly then he is denying that child to his face. That kills a child's self-esteem and it makes the child think that his father doesn't love him enough to want to take care of him. His father; the same person responsible for that child being there in the first place.

I hope Bob did tell the judge that I was working two jobs; that way I can tell her I had to get a second job because he wasn't helping me with the kids. Oh and for him not to worry that I would tell the judge that he gave me fifty dollars every two weeks; that is when I decided to go and pick it up. A pair of shoes alone is costing a hundred and up. So yes, go run and tell that. He was just hurting himself and helping me to prove my case. I had to break it down to Bob of how the system works now. It's not like the judge is taking his whole check; hell it wasn't like I'm asking for his whole check. The system is only taking a percentage of what you make. Bob's stupid response to that was he don't make nothing. What he said that for I don't know; it just threw me into overdrive. I went from zero to one hundred in two point zero; I think the earth stop spinning for that second. I looked Bob dead in his eyes and told him if he can put a roof over another female's head then he can help with the roof that's over his kid's head. If he really thought that I was going to stand by while my boys just watch him go and do for somebody else and not do for them; then he had better think again. Because as long as I was mama and I was breathing; he was going to do for those boys. I was going to make sure they got their money off the top just like Uncle Sam does. They were going to get their money before he even seen his check. I think I felt my horns poking out.

Bob made the comment that that was all I wanted to do anyway was put him on child support and have him in the system. He made it very clear how he didn't want to be wrapped up in that mess; is how he referred to it. I wasn't feeling sorry for Bob at all. This was not what I wanted. What I wanted was a hundred dollars every two weeks. I never asked him for nothing for myself. All I asked him to do was to help take care of his boys and he acted like I was asking for too much. But since he wanted to take my kindness for a weakness and just do half of what he was supposed to do because you felt like it and because I wasn't out there in the streets making a scene. Don't get me wrong; there were times when I wanted to. But since I was being calm and collective about the whole situation Bob figured that he could just give me what he wanted me to have and I wouldn't say or do anything about it. I learned that there are other places to fight besides the streets. I just left because I got tired of talking about the situation and standing there listening to Bob who was trying to talk his way out of his only responsibility was making me volcano ready.

For the next couple of weeks Bob would call and talk to me about whatever. We never let the conversation get serious because there was still tension between us. I could always tell when Debra wasn't around because when she wasn't Bob would talk about sex and how much he missed "me." like Dorothy said in the Wizard of Oz, "there's no place like home." Late one night Bob had the nerve to call me. I was surprised when the phone rang so late. I thought it was the sheriff or something calling me to tell me that someone had been in an accident involving drinking while driving and that they needed for me to come and identify the body. Ever since I put Bob out; I've been fearfully waiting for that call. But this time it wasn't the sheriff department but it was Bob and he had been drinking.

"Hey baby, what's up, what are you doing", were the words that came out of his mouth when I answered the phone? I was lying in bed watching television and that was what I told him. I asked him why he was calling me so late. I didn't want to be bothered with him, so I asked him where was Debra. I knew she wasn't around because he was calling me. His exact words were; "that bitch gone somewhere. Where ever she at, she can stay. Baby come and get me." I was stunned yet again by the words that were coming out of his mouth. I figured him and Debra must be having a bad night. But I know this nigga didn't just ask me to come and get him just because he and Debra are arguing. I explained to Bob that I was not his rebound chic, his go to girl, or his ass on the side. That he had lost all benefits and privileges when he moved her in. Now if he would have just gotten an apartment by himself we could have made some arrangements and appointments for some special sessions because don't get me wrong; I got needs too and he still is my husband so it would have been all good. But because of his stupid decision to move Debra in with him and not just her; her mama too that canceled out any special attention from me. I'm sorry but I couldn't help him. I told Bob to go to bed and sleep that shit off and that Debra should be back in the morning if not later that night and maybe they could make-up then. But for me and "mine"; we were in the bed and I had no plans of getting up. Not wanting to hear any of that; Bob started begging and pleading for me to come and get him. I told Bob yet again that I wasn't coming to get him. Trying to be the bigger person in this situation and not do anything that I would regret in the morning because let's face it; it had been a very, very, very long time since "my girl" got to exhale. I could tell that Bob was drunk and upset that Debra had left him home alone. How does that saying go; you can't turn a hoe into a house wife. Sometime men just have to learn the hard way. I knew that I could get him to lie down and go to sleep once I calmed him down after getting him to talk about what was bothering him.

I told Bob to tell me what happened tonight that made Debra leave and him turn around and go to the store and buy some liquor. I felt like Dr. Phil. Bob asked me if I knew how people would avoid other people when they don't want them to see something. I replied yes, but I had no idea what the hell he was talking about so I just kept listening hoping that he would give me a clue. He said that Debra had been avoiding him all day. She didn't want him to touch her, kiss her or even let him get close to her. I continued to listen to Bob while reminding myself that I had put myself in the friend zone for him so to not take anything he said personal. He went on to say that she was in the kitchen cleaning up and she was holding her head in a funny way. At first when he saw her holding her neck that way he said he didn't say anything because he thought she had caught a crook in her neck from sleeping on the couch. Bob said he went to clean off the breakfast counter and Debra was holding her head up straight, he had noticed that she had a passion mark on her neck and that he didn't put it there. Bob said that he got mad and asked her what that was on her neck. Debra acted like she didn't know what he was talking about so he pointed at it and then pushed her upside her head with his finger. It sounded like there was trouble in paradise to me.

After trying not to let out a chuckle which I managed to do, I asked Bob what Debra told him about the mark. Bob just said that she yanked away from him and she pushed his hand away still acting like she didn't know what he was talking about. She was saying like "what, what, that aint nothing". Then she proceeded to hold her head back down to hide the mark. Bob said he told Debra that it wasn't any use of her hiding it because he had already seen it. Trying again to hold my composer by not saying I told you so or laughing at him because I told him to watch out for her since he already knew her history and not remind him that from what he told me that they weren't a couple that she was just staying there until she found a place for her and her mom. Which I don't know why he kept telling me that lie when I knew better; I just sat there in silence and continued to let him talk because for one; he was getting exactly what he deserved. Lay down with dogs and you get up with fleas.

Bob just went on, saying that he knew some shit was up since yesterday because her daughters had come by and picked her up and they all had that smug look on their faces and they were being secretive about where they were going. Bob said that he could only figure that Debra's husband Will was back in town. From my understanding of it all, Will was Debra's husband who left her after she cheated on him with another man. Or should I say boy. Will was a truck driver who eventually got tired of Debra's hoeing ways and eventually moved to Georgia and met another woman who he had twins by. It was never really clear to me if whether or not they had gotten a divorce or not. But when he's in town he does come and sees his daughters and so I guess Debra uses that opportunity to slide up next to Will and get on his good side while he's in town. You know a man don't turn down nothing but his collar.

Poor Bob, he was still going on and on. He hadn't really calmed down yet so I was still listening. Bob said that he told Debra that he knew that she had been with Will and that two could play that game. He said that he told her whoever she was with yesterday that she could go back there. Bob said that he told her to get the hell out of his apartment. He said that he had locked her out and that she hadn't been back. The first thought that came to my head was; if she's not there than who's watching after her mama.

Laughing only in the inside, I asked Bob did he really lock Debra out the apartment. He said yes the hell he did. He said he figured if she could be with her husband then he could be with his wife. "If Debra can call him and ask for stuff and he gives it to her, why can't I do the same with my wife"? I told Bob that I was sorry for his luck but two wasn't playing that game over here and on that other part he figured wrong. He had better go back and recalculate some things. Did he really want to know why he couldn't do the same with his wife; just for the simple fact that I wasn't that dumb? I knew that he had called me just to get back at Debra. Just to see if I would be weak enough to tell him that yes, I would come and pick him up so she could think that he was lying up with me. But he wasn't about to use me. I told Bob to go to bed. I guess that wasn't what he wanted to hear because the next thing I heard was the click of the phone which meant he hung up mad. I really didn't care. He had a lot of nerve in the first place calling me; his wife with that bull. Come calling me like I'm a safety kit. I don't think that I have *open in case of emergency* stamped across my forehead. He done lost his mind.

For the next couple of weeks it would be the same old same old between me and Bob. He could call and I would listen. Sometimes I would put my two cents in and other times I wouldn't. When the conversation would eventually turn into an argument because I would get tired of him calling me telling me about him and Debra's problems I would just hang up the phone. Bob would tell me that I was the only one he could talk to and that I was his best friend. I didn't mind being Bob's friend because we needed to be at least that for the boy's sake. It was good that Bob saw me as a friend and someone that he trusted to confide in. But what Bob didn't seem to understand was that I was still his wife and I didn't want to hear about him and another woman.

Halloween came around and it was an eye opener for me. Normally I took the boys trick or treating, but this year would be different. DJ was invited to a Halloween party and Dominique still wanted to go trick or treating by himself with his friends. I was proud of the fact that my boys were popular and they had friends who really wanted to be around them. I never wanted for my boys to be the one's having to grow up throughout their life trying to make themselves fit in or trying to be accepted. After dropping everyone off I went back home and I was just sitting there by myself. No; this was not happening I told myself. I was all alone. The kids were out with their friends and Bob was over there with his girlfriend/roommate; whatever he wanted to call her and I think that depended on what day of the week it was. And I was here alone just sitting here and looking around realizing that I didn't have a life; that my whole being had nothing to do with me what so ever. The trick was on me. I knew that I had to make some changes. I needed to get a life; maybe tomorrow because there was nothing that I could do about it tonight. I just starred at the phone waiting for the kids to call me so I could come and pick them up.

Life went on as normal; kids going to school along with their sports activities and me going to work at both my jobs. For a moment there was peace and quiet. When things were too quiet I filled my house with music so my mind didn't wonder off into a world of its own. If my soul needed to be feed; it was r&b. if my spirit needed to be fulfilled it was gospel. If my mind didn't want to remember; it was classical. Music became my way to escape my reality of being alone.

Thanksgiving came and so of course I cooked a big dinner and invited over family. No Bob, he didn't even call. The day after Thanksgiving was Bob's birthday. I asked the boys if they wanted to get their father a birthday card and the y both said no. I wasn't really surprised by their answer. What else would they say? Bob had been in his place for over six months and he hadn't once come and got the boys for the weekend to spend the night over there. But I knew for a fact that Debra's crumb snatching grandchildren had been over there several times because I could hear them in the background while Bob was on the phone calling me complaining about them. So why hadn't DJ and Dominique been over there yet, I couldn't tell you.

I think it was a week after Bob's birthday when I got a phone call from him. I thought he was calling to fuse because I didn't call him for his birthday, but that wasn't the case. Bob started his phone call like normal with his hey what's going on and how's everybody doing. And I responded with my normal reply; okay. "I was in a car accident last night and Debra is in the hospital with a broken hip. She can't walk". Those were those words that came out of Bob's mouth. But I thought Bob was lying because he will make up a story in a minute just to get my attention. I remember one time before when we were separated and we were not on speaking terms; at least I wasn't. Bob had called the house and left a message on my answering machine. He knew that I was home and that I didn't want to talk to him. Bob said, "Babe, daddy had a heart attack and I'm rushing him to the hospital", he rung up the phone. He said it so fast trying to sound like he was in a panic. So I turned right around and called him back. As if I didn't understand the message he left; I asked him what he had said and what was wrong with his dad. I knew his dad was in good health so him having a heart attack was questionable. Bob said, 'Oh nothing, I was just playing so you would call me back because you won't talk to me." I still wasn't talking to him; I just rolled my eyes and hung up the damn phone on

Bob without saying another word to his dumb ass.

So by him telling me that he had gotten into an accident I handled like a wooden nickel. I repeated what he told me to make sure I heard him correctly and then I asked him what happened because I still didn't believe him. Bob said that he and Debra were having a night on the town riding around with another couple. Already I don't feel sorry for him so I rudely interrupted and said, "Oh you all riding around like couples now?" Bob tried to clear himself by saying that at first it was just him and Peter riding out then Debra's daughter asked them to take her home since they were on their way out. Debra's daughter then asked Debra to come along with her because she didn't feel right riding alone in the truck with two guys. Knowing how much Bob likes to showboat with other people's stuff; my gut feeling said that he was driving. I asked Bob was he driving. My gut was right. Bob said yes that he was driving but that the accident was not his fault.

Bob said that it had been raining and that the road was wet. He said that he was just driving like normal in a two lane. A car came up flying pass them trying to change lanes. Bob said he thinks that the driver in the car had thought that he had passed them enough to that he could get in front of them but that he hadn't. When the driver got ready to cross over into their lane, the back bumper of the car hit the front fender of the truck which caused Bob to swirl hard causing the truck to flip three times and ended up in the ditch upside down. After Bob told me all of this, I came to the conclusion that he was telling the truth.

I asked Bob if he was okay now that I believed him. Bob said that he got fifteen stitches on his forearm where it went through the windshield of the truck and that he was scratched up pretty bad. I asked him how Debra was doing. I do have a compassionate side of me and anyway Debra has never done anything to me for me to be mad or upset with her. When it comes to life and death we have to put all foolishness to the side. Bob repeat that Debra's hip was broke and that she couldn't walk. He said that at the accident; when he went around to Debra's side of the truck she couldn't get out because she was lying on the door where the truck had landed. So he said that he went back on his side of the truck and tried to reach through the open driver's side door to pull her out. He had got her to that side but when she went to try and stand up; she couldn't so he had to leave her there. When the paramedics had arrived they had to get her out of the truck. Bob said that he felt so bad about wrecking the truck and about Debra not being able to walk. He stated the she was going to need physical therapy in order to learn how to walk again. Well this is one thing I do know; if it walks like a duck and sounds like a duck; then it is a duck.

The whole time I was listening to Bob tell me what happened; all that kept going through my head was *God don't like ugly*. I fault both of them and that they got what they both deserved. Debra thought that she was doing something big by playing house with someone else's husband. I figure she thought that since someone was with her husband that she would return the favor and be with someone else's husband. Like I stated before; Debra is no stranger to me. Debra has been around since me and Bob's first separation and at the time she was messing with another young man and Bob. And from word on the street; the young man was looking for Bob to fight him after he found out that her and Bob had been messing around. I never looked for Debra to confront her about Bob because she was never my concern. From watching other females; I learned a long time ago to never fight over a man.

And as far as Bob; did he really think that he wasn't going to be punished in all of this for lying to me. He had told me many times that the only reason why Debra and her mother was there was to pay the rent. I knew that he was lying. But if that was the lie he wanted to believe; who am I to stop him. Just know that I didn't believe it. If the situation between them was the way that Bob said it was then why was he worried about what passion marks that Debra had on her neck. Bob shouldn't have cared if she walked around looking like a cheetah with all them marks on her. Just as long as she had her half of the rent and when her mama's social security check came he got the other half of the rent. Why were they sleeping in the same twin bed together in the broom closet? Bob could have slept on the couch while Debra and her mama became bunk bed buddies. Why did he get so upset when she would leave him home alone to go and see Will if all she was; was the *help*. Hell, when she left to go see someone, he should have been getting dress to go out and see someone. And that someone did not include me.

I really didn't know how Bob was expecting me to react to the whole situation that he had just laid out for me. Silence came from the side of my phone for quite some time. Bob finally broke it by saying that he was going to go now and get some sleep because he had to go to work in the morning. I could only come up with the words, "alright then, I'll talk to you tomorrow".

Karma is such a lady. I had told Bob a long time ago; nothing good would come to him until he did right by me. It's funny how when Bob was with me; his wife and two sons that he didn't want to handle his responsibilities. I wasn't asking Bob to do no more than what he was already supposed to do as a husband and a father. Bob thinks that he can just keep getting away with not doing his part. But one thing that Bob had to learn; you must pay where you lay. Well now that Debra can't walk; she can't work or look after her mother. So now with Debra without a job and her mother going to a nursing home; that leaves Bob to pay all the bills. Like I said; Karma is such a lady.

I was glad to hear that everyone was alive and everything; I really was. No, I take that back. I must confess that a small part of me wished that Bob would have died in that car accident. Only for the simple fact that what was the use of him being around if he wasn't going to do right by his sons. I wasn't worried about me; I'm over Bob. I've had many years to get to know him and to know that he makes a better friend than a husband. So it was my mistake for marrying him. But his sons didn't know him and that's what he should have been focusing on and not parading around town with someone who was less than lady like. In my many angry moments, I have told Bob that he is worth more to me dead then he is alive. He doesn't mean me or the boys any good. Bob won't do right by us and he probably never will. I know one time or another we have felt that way about someone in our lives whether we care to admit it or not. Or is it just me. I'm just being real. All is far in love and war. I think that God may have fought that battle just a little bit for me because he knew that I was tired.

It may be sad to hear but my craziness is my truth. I was satisfied for a moment knowing that they were hurt and in pain even though it was a different kind of hurt and pain that I was carrying around. It was still some form of suffering and discomfort and that's what I needed the both of them to feel. Because I was hurt and in pain due to the fact that I just wanted Bob to do right by his sons and he wouldn't. It was as if Bob had chosen another family to do for and not his own. I heard the word in the streets about Bob and Debra. About all the parties that they had been hosting at Bob's apartment as if they were the new couple. Bob was too busy drinking and partying with her that he had no time to spend with his sons. That hurt me to the core to know this and to look into my sons faces only to be reminded of the last name that they carried.

I guess I had been feeling venerable in the next weeks that had passed. I found myself feeling sorry for Bob that he had gotten hurt in the accident. I started to wonder what if he had really died. The man that I had trusted and consumed myself with for the past fifteen years would have been gone. I found myself calling to check on Bob and inviting him over to the house. And of course he accepted my invitation; I had no doubt that he would.

Bob hadn't been back in my house for so long that him being there felt very strange. I knew it would look different from what he remembered because I had bought new furniture since he had been gone; everything was new. I remember the first time I had done that, I gave all my furniture to my mother. Two years had passed and I got bit by the bug again.

One day I walked in my front door after work and my house just didn't feel or look right. The next day I called a local charity organization to donate the furniture to them and to see if they would come by and pick it up. The furniture looked too new to sit outside by the dumpster. They said that they would come the next day. When the two men arrived to pick up the furniture I knew that there was going to be a problem. One gentleman; he had to be in his sixty weighing four hundred pounds easy. He was breathing heavy and sweating and all he did was knock on the door. The other man looked like he was seventy years old and he just volunteered for the day to get out of the nursing home. I brought them in the house to show them the furniture that they would be picking up. The overweight gentleman came in the house and just leaned over on the arm of the couch. I guess he was just glad to feel some air condition. He acted like he needed an oxygen tank. The older gentleman just stood at the door hoping that no one would ask him to do anything. While still leaning over the arm of the couch; Mr. Hefty turned and said that they couldn't take the furniture because the couch had a small rip on the arm of it and they don't do any repair work on furniture. Really, the rip was only three inches long and it came from me repeatedly cleaning that spot off. So the other gentleman who was with him finally made his way in and looked at the furniture. He asked his partner was he sure that they couldn't take the furniture. So I asked Mr. Hefty if he could still take the other two pieces of furniture;

the loveseat and the chair. He told me no that it had to be a complete set. The look on the other gentleman face said otherwise. I just shock my head and kept my words to myself. I knew they would look for any excuse not to take the furniture. I knew that when I saw them getting out of the truck. The furniture was big and I just think that Mr. Hefty was being lazy and didn't want to lift the furniture. So I told them that was fine and I thanked them for both their time and showed them to door so they could stop sucking up my cool air. I was always told that it is better to give than receive. I would never give anyone anything that I wouldn't receive myself.

I called a friend and asked if she knew of anyone who was in need of some furniture. She said yes that she knew of a young couple who had just gotten their first apartment and didn't have anything. A couple of days later the couple arrived at my house in a van with a new born baby in their arms. They were overcome and shocked that I was giving away my furniture. The y kept asking me if I was sure that I wanted to give it away because it still looked brand new. I assured them that I did. One thing about me; I'm not attached to material things. I enjoy them and then I move on from them. It all had to go all my furniture, end tables, television stand, curio stands that lite up, pictures off my wall; all of it. I even gave them a dvd player. The young man was so happy that he just starting dancing in the street while his wife gladly understood his display of appreciation and this blessing from God. I felt good that I could help bless someone else. I don't know how they did it but that packed that little van so that everything fitted. God is good.

When Bob had arrived, he looked around like he had never been there before. I know it probably felt strange to him but it felt even stranger to me as well. Knowing that he had been with another woman; caused me to be a little hesitant with my movements toward him. When he gave me a hung I was careful to not let my body get too close to his. I made sure I kissed him on his cheek and not in his mouth when he reached in for a kiss from me. I would sit down on the couch next to him but not too close that I might give him the impression that I might want to cuddle with him. I made sure that my bedroom door was closed so that there wouldn't be any question or not that that's where we would end of before the night was over.

Even after Bob sat down on the couch; he looked uncomfortable be-ing there. But he knows me and he knows my ways. I haven't changed my ways since he had been gone. They might have enhanced themselves a little but they hadn't changed. The tension was there and yes we both felt it but we tried to ignore it the best that we could. We sat in silence for a while waiting for one or the other to say something. Then we managed to make small talk. After some time Bob took his shoes off and that's when I knew he was comfortable. I asked Bob how was he doing. He answered looking back over his shoulder as if someone was going to jump out and grab him. It kind of puzzled me that he just sat down and didn't ask where the boys were. But seeing that the boys didn't come out of their room at first either; I called the boys out of their room to let them know that their father was there. I'm surprised that they didn't hear his voice. They obviously didn't even know that the man had come into the house. They came in the living room; said their hellos to their father which was short and sweet then they went back into their room and shut the door. I could understand that because the last time that their dad was in the house it was like we were in the Twilight Zone.

For a couple of minutes I just observed Bob's behavior. I asked Bob what was the matter. That he wasn't talking too much and brought to his attention that when he is on the phone with me that he has so much to say. For one when Bob is on the phone he tends to talk a lot of shit but when he is in my face he tries to act all calm, cool, and collective because he knows that I will go toe to toe with him and even go on top of his head. But I already knew what his problem was; it wasn't easy playing house with everybody. His girlfriend Debra; at least that's what I'm going to call her, is on one side of town and Bob's wife and kids are on the other side of town. His dilemma is not to let the girlfriend find out that he is over his wife's house so that the girlfriend can keep her unemployment and her mama's social security check's coming in so that they can continue paying the rent. Me on the other hand; I could have cared less. I have had my fill of Bob over the past fifteen years and I was done with all of that. You're probably asking how I know all of Bob's household business; because despite of what you may think, Bob tells me everything. Even the stuff I don't want to know about.

Bob replied that nothing was wrong. But I couldn't tell by the beads of sweat that was popping up on his forehead and it was seventy-three degrees in that house.

Bob then said that he was hot and he took off his shirt. I saw the scar on his forearm which was all of twelve inches long. It hadn't completely healed and I could tell that he had just put some medicine on it. When he told me about the cut; I didn't think it was that massive. Scarred for life, he was. I told Bob, that he had to put his shirt back on. He was getting a little bit too comfortable. Get out the kitchen if your ass can't stand the heat; is what ran through my mind but I didn't tell Bob that.

I began just staring at his wounds as he began again telling me how that was the arm that went through the window and that the other arm had all the cuts on it from all the broken glass. Bob turned his other arm over to show me all his cuts and bruises that he had sustained in the accident. Just then Bob's cell phone rung and he answered it. The person on the other end of the phone asked Bob where he was at. Bob answered by saying that he was over a friend's house and that he would call him back later. I just looked at Bob and rolled my eyes. He acted like I didn't know that it was Debra calling him. Now every woman knows when a guy is talking to another guy on the phone; he calls him by name. And if he's over a friend's house; he names that friend. And a guy doesn't tell another guy that he will call him back later; he always says I'll hit you up later.

Bob's conversation just proved that I was no longer important to him. Instead of him trying to keep his girlfriend a secret from his wife, he was now trying to keep his wife a secret from his girlfriend. Now he was making it feel like he was cheating on Debra with me; like I was the other woman. His phone rang again but this time he went outside to answer it. I knew for a fact then that it was Debra calling him. When Bob came back in the house he smelled of smoke. Bob only smoked when he was nervous about something. I asked him if he wanted a glass of water. He told me no and that he had to go. Bob hadn't even been there an hour. It wasn't like he was in a rush to go or anything like that; I just think that he felt like he should have never came in the first place. Deep down I had to be honest with myself; I could tell where his loyalty now laid. I didn't mix words with Bob or try to make him stay. I showed him the door. He turned to me but never looking up at me. He held his head down and looked at the floor as he told me that he would bring me two hundred dollars for the boys to help me with their Christmas gifts. He gave me a hug and told me that he would call me later. The whole time that Bob was there; he never gave me full eye contact or had a full conversation with me for that matter.

---

The boys must have heard the front door close because they came out of their room. They asked if their daddy was gone and DJ had a confused look upon his face. I told them yes that their daddy had gone. I stood there as I realized that he didn't even tell his boys goodbye. I walked over to the patio door and watched through the blinds as Bob pulled off in Debra's car.

# Chapter 39

**IT WAS THE** beginning of December and Bob's birthday was last week. I did call him to wish him a happy birthday but he didn't answer his phone all weekend. Maybe he was too busy celebrating to answer his phone. I got kind of stressed out about Christmas. But that's nothing new I always do. Bills still had to be paid and now Christmas had to happen. I found myself robbing Peter to pay Paul and borrowing from Pat to make it all come together. My boy's happiness is my first agenda. Some bills will get paid and others will just have to wait until next month. I guess because of all the stress, my hormones were out of whack or I was out of my mind because I found myself calling Bob.

I started the conversation by informing him that I had called him last week for his birthday and that he didn't answer. He acknowledged that fact that I tried to call him and told me that I wouldn't believe where he was; the reason why he couldn't answer his phone. So I jokingly implied that he was probably somewhere drunk from all that partying that he was doing for his birthday. He agreed that it would have been nice if that was what he was doing but quickly corrected me and told me that he was in jail. My jaw just hit the floor. This man can't stay out of trouble to save his soul. Every time I turn around Bob is in trouble with the law about something. After picking my jaw up off the floor; I asked Bob what he had went to jail for. "Because of them damn kids", was his reply and I'm thinking to myself what kids were he talking about. He couldn't have been talking about DJ and Dominique because he doesn't even spend time with them. So I asked him what kids he was talking about. "Debra's grandkids", he told me.

Bob said that he had gone to pick them up from her daughter's house since Debra couldn't drive and the other daughter didn't have a car. He went on to explain that on the way back to the house he got stopped by the police because the kids were standing up in the back seat and no one was in a car seat and to make matters worse; he was drinking. And last time I checked; Bob did not have a license. Bob went on to say that they got him for a DUI and took him to jail. I hope that he wasn't expecting anything less but knowing Bob, he probably did. Bob said that he had a friend in the car with him so the friend ended up taking the kids home. I was so furious with Bob but on the other hand I looked at it like another punishment for his stupid decision not to honor his vows to be a husband to me and except his responsibility of being a father to his children. When will he learn? He just running around like he wild and don't have any sense. If he keeps it up, he's going to end up in a 12x12 or a 6x3. Both of them are boxes it's just that one is above ground and the other is six feet under. But now he's out now. It seems like he never gets punished for long.

No matter how much I looked at Bob's dilemmas as punishments and no matter how much satisfaction I was getting from it; I knew that the only thing that would make me feel better was having my day in court with Bob. Watch out for a woman scorned. Right now I'll give it to him; he's having his cake and eating it too. He's acting like life is just a big party. But I'm ready for his party to be over. I know that I have given him some rope to hang himself when I sit around and not make a big deal that though we are separated, we didn't agree to see other people and yet he is living with another woman and even though he tries to deny it and half way hide it; he is in a relationship with another woman and he is still married. But now I'm ready for the rope to tighten around his neck and watch his feet dangle in the wind. It seems to me that Bob had gotten too comfortable in his position and forgotten the rules of the game.

It wouldn't be long until I got the date of execution. I checked the mailbox every day for the next week. The following week I received my letter of validation. Court papers came in the mail saying that our court date for child support was February 20. I would like to see how much of this cake I can shove into his mouth. But until then I got to get these kids ready for Christmas.

When it came to Christmas, I enjoyed it just as much as my own kids did. I loved my Christmas tree which I spend and arm and a leg for decorations. This year we will be doing all silver. Every couple of years I'll change the theme on the tree. For a long time it was gold with all white lights.

December the first which is my mother's birthday; the Christmas tree goes up and I never turn off the lights. And a candy cane will never have the pleasure of touching my tree. I tell the kids to make a list of three things that they might want. A lot of times both of them want the same thing like the latest game unit that's out and the latest game for it. They don't ask for the most expensive things. They're really good boys who do help me around the house and the y do good in school so Christmas morning instead of them just waking up to their three gifts that they ask for, they both have at least ten or more presents waiting for them. Those are the types of Christmas' that I wished I had when I was their age.

Dominique is into cartooned stuff and my DJ is definitely into sports. But this year Dominique wanted the hottest toy that was on the market this year; a remote control HUMMER2 Jeep and he wanted a black one. Last year car makers made this army vehicle domestic and it was all you saw on the streets. It did look nice and every male big or small wanted to have one. I went to four different cities and went in every store looking for this thing and I still came out empty handed. I didn't want to let my son down; I had to find this thing. So I got a little smart and asked the store when their next store truck would come in and how many HUMMER2 trucks did they have on order. When the store truck was due to come in I was there. You would have thought I was there standing in the food stamp line, I got there so early. I got what I came for and went and put it on lay-a-way. All the other gifts were easy to find so there was no need for me to go on a massive treasure hunt; I could re-lax. Even though bills were still coming in, I was doing the best I could with what I had with no help from Bob. He hadn't given me the two hundred dollars yet like he had promised me. And knowing his track record; I wasn't about to hold my breath or have my boys Christmas de-pend on it. I went and bought all the boys gifts myself. I didn't want to take the chance of budgeting for the two hundred dollars and then him changing the amount or him not giving me the money at all.

Now we single mother's all know; when it comes to Christmas time, a bill or two won't get paid because the money for the gifts have got to come from somewhere. The *other* people have the luxury of charging everything to their credit cards and spend the following year trying to pay it off. But mamas know how to make Christmas miracles every year. We just don't pay the bill and get an extension and let the balance roll over to next month. I am not good on a budget; that is out of the question. Budget is such a bad word to me. But one week I guess I went overboard but it was for the boys so I really didn't care but I found myself having to go back and take the HUMMER2 off of lay-a-way and use that money to put gas in my car so I could make it through the rest of the week. That was the last thing that I wanted to do but it was also the only thing I could do. I felt so bad when I saw them take the HUMMER2 and put it on the piles of items there were to be returned to the shelves. But I just knew that I shouldn't have any problem getting another HUMMER2 next week when I got paid; so I thought.

There was still no word from Bob, so when I got my check the following week, I ran out to the store to get back the HUMMER2. I ended up going to three stores and there wasn't a HUMMER2 in sight. My heart just fell to my feet. All I could do as I walked aimlessly around the store was think how could I have possibly let this happen. I didn't want to disappoint my son. At that very moment I felt so desperate. I felt like a crack head looking for the next hit and was willing to do anything to get it. My baby had his heart set on that HUMMER2 and I always made sure that they got what they wanted and this time there could be no exception because this time it would be my fault if he didn't get it. With no HUMMER2 in sight I had prepared myself for his disappointment. But nothing can really prepare you for that. I was even saying a little prayer as I was walking to the front of the store to leave. *Lord you know my baby had his heart set on that HUMMER2. And it's not his fault that I had to take it off of lay-a-way.* Don't get me wrong I know that you're not supposed to pray about material things but I think I was just looking for comfort for this situation that I had gotten myself into.

I guess God was answering all prayers that day because on my way out of the store, I walked by the cosmetic counter and something caught my eye. It wasn't the perfume in the glass case because I wasn't looking to buy any perfume. But it was what I saw through the glass case that my eyes could not believe. There under a pile of other toys was a HUMMER2. I had to take a second look because I didn't want to seem delusional because of my wishful thinking. But there it was, the HUMMER2. Chills ran through my body and my heartbeat made a triple rhythm. There was no one behind the counter so that I could acquire about the HUMMER2. I looked around franticly to see if there was anyone near so that I could try and find out about the HUMMER2 and its current status. There was no one around. I began to panic. Just like a cop; where is a cashier when you need one. Oh my God, all of a sudden a cashier appeared out of nowhere.

"Excuse me", I said to the cashier who stood in front of me and appeared to be at least to me at the moment; a Christmas angel at this point; I asked if that HUMMER2 belonged to anyone. I asked hoping that she wasn't going to say that it was hers and that she just had it back there until she got off of work to take it to her car. I pointed to the pile of toys that were behind her. Because by the look on her face she was more concentrated on the display case and had no idea what a HUMMER2 was. She looked over her shoulder and told me no that it was just sitting back there because she had been so busy and hadn't had a chance to take it back to the toy isle just yet. My heart started to make its way from my feet back to its proper place back in my chest. Her words were music to my ears and I started to do a little dance in the inside. I asked her if I could have the HUMMER2. I stood there holding out my hands out like a baby who was being asked to be picked up. "Sure", she said as she recovered the fifty inch box from the bottom of the pile and handed it to me. Don't judge me but anything is possible with God. I thanked her and if I could have spoken ten different languages, I would have thanked her in every one of them. I walked to the front of the store with a grin that was plastered on my face; that if I went to hell right now it wouldn't have melted off. Being a mother is the best job that a woman could have. I loaded up my car and sat there for a moment before driving off. I don't care how it may come across to you but to me God's favor is something that I've come to appreciate.

But with Bob on the other hand, I have some unfinished business. The two hundred dollars that Bob said that he was going to give me only would cover DJ's bike and Dominique's HUMMER2 that I had already bought. So now when he did give me the two hundred dollars it won't be to buy presents, it would be to put the money back in my pocket because everything was done. But I couldn't let Bob know that or he would never give me the money for the boys for Christmas. I would let the weekend pass before I called Bob that Monday morning to see when he wanted to meet up. I knew that he had gotten paid the Friday before but I didn't want to act like a vulture. I just hope that he hadn't smoked and drank it all away.

I called Bob that morning and to my surprise he said that he had the money and would bring it to me later that day. I really shouldn't say that I was surprised that he had the money because if he knew like I knew *which he did* he had better had them boys' Christmas money because he knew that I didn't mind acting like a fool if I had to come over there and get some straightening when it came to my boys and what concerned them. But our conversation was civil so there was no use for me to fly off the handle. This meant only one thing to me; he hadn't got is notice to appear in court for child support. I hung up with phone with Bob with the impression that I would see him later on that day.

Monday, Tuesday, and Wednesday had come and gone with no sign of Bob. Thursday was my last day off for the week so I thought that I should give him another call because I wanted this manner handled before I went back to work. I figured the reason why I hadn't seen Bob was because he couldn't find a ride over to my place. Why he hadn't call; I didn't know. I don't know why men do half the dumb stuff that they do. I wouldn't mind going to pick up the money if he didn't have a ride if that was the problem. Since I was off I didn't mind the long ride out to his place but if it had been a day which I worked that would be a problem because after a long day at work I just want to go straight home and not running the street trying to find Bob.

I called Bob at home, making sure that I was being on my best behavior; which at this point is damn near impossible dealing with Bob. But despite the run around feeling that I was having; I held my composure. One thing that I've learned about Bob is that if you don't say anything about the pink elephant with wings in the room; then he won't either even if the elephant is starring him right in his face. When I called Bob, a little boy answered his phone. The little boy couldn't have been no more than five years old so what the hell he was doing answering Bob's phone; red flag number one. I could hear all the other kids in the back ground. The little boy asked who this was. I explained to the little boy that was not the way to answer the phone. I said it calmly reminding myself that I was talking to someone else's child. I couldn't blame him for his ignorance; it was his parent's fault. Everyone who has kids is not a parent. They just feed the kids and send them outside to play all day until it gets dark to keep them out of their way. I corrected the little boy and told him that he was supposed to say hello and then ask who was speaking. Still being bothered by the fact that someone was answering Bob's phone other than himself; especially a little boy, I asked to speak to Bob before I lost my cool. I just shook my head as I heard the little boy calling for Bob to come to the phone. I heard Bob say, "Hello" on the phone and my first question to him was why he had a child answering his phone. Before Bob could answer my question it just made me believe that the little boy had done this more than once and had become comfortable doing it. So that also lead me to believe that the little boy had been around Bob a lot to know that it was okay for him to answer his phone.

Bob went on to say that he didn't hear the phone ring and that the little boy who answered the phone was Kenny. I wasn't surprised that Bob couldn't hear the phone ring with all those kids running around over there. Bob acted like it was okay that the little boy had answered the phone and maybe it was. Maybe I was reading too much into it. I went on to explain to the Bob that the reason why I was calling was because I hadn't seen him all week. As if he didn't notice that, but just in case he hadn't I needed to bring that to his attention. I then reminded him that he was supposed to drop something off to me on Monday.

Miraculously he remembered but said that he had been so busy. How do you get so busy that you forget about your kids? I was just wondering. Bob mentioned that he had to go back to court and meet with a lawyer involving the car accident and that he had to take Debra to therapy, get some paper from her doctor and get them sent off. He insisted that he hadn't forgotten about me and the boys, but it sure didn't feel that way to me. Bob again assured me that he would drop the money off to me Saturday since he would have to come on my side of town. I told Bob all right then, that I would see him Saturday. Me knowing how Bob is; if I didn't get the money from him soon, he wouldn't have it to give and then blame it on me because I didn't come and get it. So if I didn't see him on Saturday; he would definitely see me on Sunday when I got off of work.

Saturday came and went and no Bob. Were you surprised? Why; I wasn't. Sunday when I got off of work I already knew that I wasn't going straight home. I already knew that I wasn't going to be a lady about the whole situation when I did get to Bob's apartment. And for most I already knew that Nett would be waiting and ready for any shit to pop off. Even though Bob had told me that he was busy the reason why he hadn't dropped off the money; I just felt like it was more to it than that and I was going to find out exactly what. But first I had to go and pick up the boys and then we could get to the bottom of this as a family.

After stopping at the house to pick up the boys, we took a ride that we had taken so many times before but this time it seemed like every light in town would turn red when I got to it or that I was driving behind Ms. Daisy. It seemed like it was taking me forever to get to Bob's place. But I knew that it was God slowing me down so that I could cool down before I got there. I didn't bother to call Bob to let him know that I was coming. Why should I? He never called me to let me know that he wasn't. And anyway I didn't want to give him the heads up to give him time to leave. Because to be honest, I was feeling a little froggy. I had kept my mouth shut and my hands to myself for so long about so many things and I felt that neither I nor the boys were getting the respect from Bob that we deserved. Through this whole transaction I was honest with my boys about what was going on between me and their father. But there was nothing that I could say to them that would explain his absence towards them.

The whole ride over to Bob's I just felt like he had been avoiding me, with him making arrangements to drop by but never did. So since it seemed as if he was having a problem coming to me and bringing me what he said he would give me then I'll just come to him. This would have been the most that he would have done for the boys since he had been gone. The least Bob could do was do right by the boys for Christmas. Hell, he did nothing for them on their birthdays. I just needed a piece of mind to know that Bob loved his kids. From my understanding when you love something you protect it, love it and take care of it. It was already heartbreaking for me to see that Bob was not willing to be the man to me that he had promised or the husband that I needed him to be. But to watch and see him not be the father that my two boys deserved for him to be was devastating because now my children are hurting and as much as I want to take away this pain from them; I can't.

When we arrived in the parking lot of Bob's apartment, we all spotted Debra's little white car so we knew that someone was home. I knocked on the door and Bob answered it. The look of surprise on his face could not be put into words. He was dressed up as if he was about to go out somewhere. I didn't bother to speak; I just walked in. I could hear him hugging and greeting the boys behind me who I had left at the door with him. I walked into the living room and there was Debra and another couple who looked also to be dressed to step out on the town. Did I walk in on them about to leave going on a double date? I turned around and headed back for the front door. I wasn't planning on leaving just yet; I was just making sure that the boys were completely in. They were but Bob had left the front door open. I think he knew that something was about to hit the fan; you can call it what you want to.

Bob came in the living room and I just stared at him eye to eye. I was waiting for him to say something stupid like; he didn't have the money, just so I could go ham on his ass. Not that I really needed a reason because a good cussing out from me to him was long overdue. Oh I just wanted him to say something; anything so I could just cuss him and everybody in that apartment out the front door. But Bob saw the look on my face so he kept his words to a minimum. He asked if we all were doing okay but by his body language I could tell that he wasn't. He seemed nervous for some reason. At first I didn't answer him but only stood there wondering why he was asking such a dumb question. But then again I didn't want to look like the villain so I answered saying that we were fine. I wasn't making matters any better by still looking around as I walked over to the breakfast bar to have a seat. It may have just been me but it seemed like Bob was stalling for time. Even though I hadn't said anything; Bob knew exactly why I was there. I don't think that Debra knew that Bob was going to give me any money for the boys. But whether she knew or not had nothing to do with nothing and I didn't care whether she knew or not. But it seemed as if he didn't want to give me the money in front of her. Bob walked into the kitchen and started shuffling around some papers that lay on the counter as if he was looking for something. I knew that he was avoiding the matter at hand. I could see the big lump in his throat from a mile away. I just looked at him because I was not about to make this situation easier for him as much as I knew that he wanted me to. I had come to terms some time ago with Bob and Debra's situation. Bob wanted me to believe that nothing was going on between the two of them but I knew better and accepted it even if he didn't want me to. Because he knew as long as I thought otherwise, that my front door would be still unlock for him. But I changed the lock and even put a bolt lock on my door.

Debra and the other couple were making small talk. After finding no more papers to shuffle around; Bob came out of the kitchen and headed towards the bedroom. When he returned I had gotten up from my seat and headed towards him. Bob placed some money in my hand. I stood there and counted it to make sure it was all there and it was. I looked over at the boys who always had that look of being uncomfortable whenever we were over at their dad's. I could understand why because there they were caught in the middle as children normally are when the parents are parting ways.

Bob headed to the front door and opened it saying, "See you all later" as he was guiding the boys out the front door like they were unwanted guest. Something went through my body like lighting; I think Nett took over "See you all later", I heard myself say to Bob. I said it so loud and sharp that everyone in the apartment stopped talking and looked in my direction. That was all he had to say to his sons. He hadn't even spent ten minutes with them and when was the last time that he even saw them. I guess that didn't matter to Bob. He told me that they were fixing to leave. I reminded Bob that he hadn't seen his boys in weeks and questioned him if that was all the time that he had for them was ten minutes.

"Me and Frankie are fixing to go somewhere", were the next words that came out of Bob's mouth but I wasn't trying to even hear that. At this point I felt so bad for my boys. Bob had seemed to have forgotten all about them. He never calls to talk to them. He only calls me just to ask if we can get together so he can come and have sex with me. He never stops by to see them but yet he can caught a ride or drive Debra's car to go everywhere else. Bob never comes by and picks up his sons for the weekend but yet he always has a house full of people and all the kids running around. And no, I'm not just going to drop my boys off where it seems like they are not wanted. But it just seems funny to me how he has time to go everywhere else, pick up everybody else's kids, and do everything else with everybody else. Then again, no it wasn't funny because now I felt like by Bob shuffling them to the door that he was dismissing his sons and by saying that him and Frankie were about to go somewhere; he was putting others before is children like he had done so many times before but this time it was to their face in front of other people and I wasn't about to have that. The fire in me was already lit but now it was burning out of control.

I heard the four letter word come out of my mouth and it shook the apartment walls as I told Bob that I didn't care where he and Frankie were going and that he could spend more than ten minutes with his sons. You could hear a leaf drop on the river water; that's how quiet that apartment got. And I dared anyone to say anything to me. I went back and sat down at the breakfast bar. I think that I may have made Frankie a little uneasy because after ten minutes of silence, he got up and said that he and his girlfriend should go. I didn't mean to make him feel uncomfortable because my anger was not directed at him but if you were in the room at that time, you felt it. Bob stopped Frankie and told him that he didn't have to go so Frankie sat back down.

Bob turned to me and asked me why I had to come over to his apartment and act that way. I sat there and just looked at Bob not answering his question because I knew that he already knew the answer to that dumb question that he just asked me. I stood up and walked into the living room. I'm thinking one because I had held my peace long enough and two because obviously he forgot where his sons live that he can't come and see them. So if the father can't come to the children, the children will come to the father.

I guess I did need to answer Bob's question just in case he thought otherwise. I told him because he had just come over here and starting playing house and forgot about his two sons who were still his responsibility regardless of what. I looked over in Debra direction letting Bob know that she was the *what* that I was speaking of. Nett on the other hand was looking in Debra's direction daring her to say something so she could break her other hip. But Debra just sat there in the chair not saying anything. She just had some stupid grin on her face.

"She's here because you put me out", Bob went on to explain as if I needed an explanation from him for the reason why he couldn't spend time with his kids. And yet he's talking about some woman that is irrelevant to me and mine. Bob went on to say that he didn't know what I expected for him to do after I put him out on the street. First of all let's get one thing very clear, I didn't put him out on the street; I took him and his stuff to his mama's house. It was his mama that put him out and on the street. Bob was sitting on the couch next to Frankie while he tried to plead his case. Bob knew that sitting next to Frankie that he would be in the *safe zone*. Bob knew that I wouldn't try throwing anything at him if I didn't have a clear shot because I never want to hurt an innocent person in my stage of anger. Now if he would have been sitting next to Debra; I would have acted like I was pitching in the ninth inning at the New York Mets game.

But technically the more I think about it; Bob put his own self out when he defaced his own son by calling him a bastard, a monster, and a crack head. The last thing I thought Bob would have done when I put him out was to shack up with his lover and play house. Because mind you; we are still married. When I brought that point up the apartment got even quieter than before. Bob didn't address that issue but went on to say that he didn't know why I was complaining anyway. That I had done what I wanted to do and that was to put him on child support. I guess he finally got the papers in the mail. I didn't deny the fact that I put him on child support. I reminded Bob that the last time when we talked on the phone that I had given him a choice and I asked him did he remember. I could tell by the long pause that he was giving me that he didn't want expose the contents of our conversation that me and him had only a few days ago; in front of Debra. Or was it the fact that he didn't want Debra to know that he had been calling me in the first place. I didn't care if she did or didn't know.

Just like in our conversation; I told Bob that I wouldn't put him on child support if he didn't have anyone that was living with him but in his present situation I felt as if he was being disrespectful to our marriage and to our sons. As I sat there I could see Bob's demeanor change but I wasn't prepared for what was about to come out of his mouth. Bob said "well, you see that Debra is still here and that he wasn't going anywhere". Wow; hold up, stop the presses and hold my mule. This nigga done finally grew some balls but this was not the time. Not that he's trying to make a monkey out of me! I must give it to him though; he could always perform well in front of an audience. But he forgot that I always win the award for leading crazy bitch in a drama scene. Why he did that? Bob knows not to try and front on me because he already knows that I could care less what the people think. I already know that he's trying to make himself look manly in front of Debra; if that's possible. But don't do it at my expense. Now see, I got to shut it down.

I started off slow by repeating what Bob had told me on the phone since he was trying to save face; his. I went on to say how Bob said that the only reason why Debra was still there was because he thought that she was going to get some money from the accident. Bob told me when she got the money that she was going to give him some of it. And that the only reason why he let her mama stay there was because she was giving him money from her social security check to help him pay the rent because he couldn't afford it by himself. Bob also said that as soon as he got all the stuff straighten out with his license that he was going to put *everybody* out. And I was as lady-like as I could be when I asked Bob to stop begging me for my goodies just because he kept complaining that Debra's goodies weren't good and that hers was broke. And scene; I heard the applause in my head and I knew that I had won yet another award. Debra just sat there with the craziest look on her face. She didn't say a word.

Bob's only response was a shrug of his shoulders and a yeah-okay as he tried to wipe the egg off his face from what I had just said. Hoping that Debra didn't believe a word of it; Bob looked over in her direction with the puppy eyes. Yes, I will admit that sometime after Bob had gotten into his accident, that I had a moment of weakness. I will also admit that now that Debra knew; it was making me giggle inside like a little school girl. But why am I trying to justify the situation to myself; Bob is still after all my husband.

When oxygen returned to the room after being sucked out from everyone gasp of shock; Debra slowly got up from her chair and grabbed her walker. With Frankie's girlfriend assistance; Debra made her way to the front door. Frankie himself finally stood up from the couch and grabbed his girlfriend's purse that she left behind. He fell in line behind his girlfriend but not before putting in his two cents about the whole situation. Trying to be the person of reason as if I wanted one, cared for one or even asked for one; Frankie told us that we needed to calm down and that I shouldn't be talking like that in front of the boys. And maybe he was right but at that moment Nett didn't care and I didn't have any control of what came out of her mouth.

Personally if you ask me; it wasn't the boys that Frankie was so concerned or worried about. One thing that I have noticed in this situation and similar ones like it; the friend will always take up for their homeboy no matter how wrong he is. I must admit girlfriends do the same thing for each other. Instead of Frankie telling Bob that he was wrong for; living with another woman while he was still married and still going to his wife's bed and for using Debra's mama for the other half of the rent money, or that he should spend more time with his kids. The only thing that Frankie could come up with was; telling me that I shouldn't talk like that in front of the kids. Really, was that all he could find wrong with this whole situation. Frankie was about to feel my raft but I had to remember that he was an innocent bystander in all of this and he was just trying to help his homeboy get out of a very sticky more like malaises situation. So before I did anything that I would later regret; I went outside and sat on the steps to get some fresh air. The boys followed behind me but went off in the yard and busied themselves with hitting some golf balls with a club that they found by the front door on the porch.

I sat there on the steps and watched as Debra penguin walked her cripple self to her car and leave with Frankie's girlfriend. Not really caring where they were going, I just aimlessly watched the car as it left out of the parking lot. After taking in some fresh air and now being able to think clearly; I was just really over the whole situation with Bob with trying to get him to understand that he needs to start spending time with his boys. The whole time that we were outside; not one time did Bob come out? I let my mind rest as I watched the boys play their version of gulf. I couldn't have been sitting outside on the steps no more than twenty minutes before Debra's car returned back to the apartment. I just sat there and watched again as Debra shuffled out of the car and penguin walked her way back to the apartment. I knew that she felt like less than a woman. I know that I would have if I were in her situation. Shortly after the door closed behind her my attention went back to my boys and their golf game.

I think the boys were on the ninth hole when Frankie came outside and sat down next to me. He asked if I minded if he talked with me for a minute. His body language was funny because he didn't know whether to be ready for a hug or an elbow from me. After realizing that he was safe Frankie began to express his opinion. He began by saying that me and Bob need to sit down and work things out. After going over the past year in my mind; I told Frankie that there was nothing to work out. The problem that I had with Bob was how could he go and set up house somewhere else and play family guy when before when he had a home and a family he couldn't play that guy. But at the same time that he's over here with Debra playing house, he is calling me telling me that he wants to come home. I knew if I had told him that he could, he would have left her. But at the same time I wouldn't want him back. Bob wouldn't want to come back home because he misses his family, he would only want to come back home because I was making life easier for him. But at some point I feel like why I should have to take care of a grown ass man. When I would ask Bob for money for the kids, and he always said that he doesn't have any money or only gives me fifty dollars. But he's over here with Debra and all of a sudden he can pay a car payment. At least over here he's paying half the rent. When he lived with me he acted like he didn't know when rent was due. Over here he pays the lights, water, phone, cable, and even bought a big screen television. I had to turn into a full blown she-devil before he would give me any money for bills. Who is this new Bob that I see? Where the hell he was at when we were together trying to raise a family.

And how is Bob going to say the he loves me and wants to be with me when he's living with another woman. Men always want their cake and eat it too then have the nerve to want some ice cream. I finally took a breath so Frankie could finish his point. "Well I don't know about all of that", Frankie said disregarding everything that I had just said, "but you guys need to talk". I don't know why I even wasted my breath talking to Frankie. But then again I can understand him not wanting to be put in the middle of something that had nothing to do with him. Frankie's girlfriend finally came out of the apartment seeming a little irritated. She looked at Frankie and told him that they needed to go. That let me know that she didn't want any more to do with this whole situation. This was not something she signed up for and this was definitely not something she got dressed up for. Frankie got up without saying a word and they headed for the parking lot.

After they drove off, it didn't take me long to realize that me and the boys were outside alone. Did Bob even care that his kids and wife were outside; obviously not. I couldn't make him care so all I could do was continue to care for me and mine and move forward. I starred at the door just knowing that it would open up at any second. And when it didn't I looked at it even longer. It was time for me to realize that the door had been closed in this chapter of my life and that it was time for me to move on. I got up from the steps and headed toward the grassy field where my boys were still discovering their golf swing. I only made it to the parking lot before I called out to the boys so we could leave and go home. They had gotten so involved in their golf game that they didn't realize how late it had gotten. No more playing by the light of the sun but the street light lit their path. I stood by the car trying to clear my disappointment in Bob from my face. I wanted to spare them that much; hell I needed to spare myself.

While I was waiting, a small white four door car pulled up in the parking lot. Four adults and at least seven little kids poured out of the car. There wasn't a child older than six in the crowd. Infants were being carried in baby carriers; others were being totted on hips and the ones who could walk on their own followed behind. I watched as the herd headed to Bob's front door. No one knocked; they all just walked in as if they lived there. The car doors were left open so I stood starring at the car to see if anything else was going to crawl out. But nothing did. I just stood there in disbelieve of what I had just seen occur. I wasn't just standing outside; at this point I felt like the outsider. I was left standing alone and that's exactly how I felt; alone.

DJ and Dominique finally made their way to me at the car. I realized that I was not alone. Just then a truck drove up next to us. A man and woman got out. They were dressed as if they had attended church earlier that day. No one said a word to me so neither I to them. The man; who I later would learn was a pastor, went to the back of this truck and removed two new kids' bicycles off the back of it. The pastor rolled one bike to Bob's front door and knocked. Before anything was said, I had already figured out what was going on. You know how every year the church will ask the members to donate gifts for less fortunate children for Christmas so that the kids would have at least one gift under the tree Christmas morning. Parents would put their child's name on a list along with the one thing that they would want and then it would be delivered to their home. Now mind you that these parent (single baby mama's) who put their kids name on the list because they so-called can't afford to buy them anything for Christmas are the same parents (single baby mama's) who are walking around with hundred and two hundred dollar purses. So they want you to believe; they just got some booster to go in the store and steal it for them while they only pay forty dollars for it. These SBM can't afford their kids Christmas but they are getting their hair done, making sure that they are getting their nails done in every color of the rainbow. While buying a new outfit every Friday night so they can go out to the club. But then again maybe they can't afford to buy their kids Christmas because they got about five or six of them running around and the fifth or sixth baby daddy isn't trying to help. But that's only the case if they even know who the baby's daddy is. They can't give the mother of their children any money to help get these kids something for Christmas. That's because these MBDs (my baby daddy) are riding around in hoop-dees that they done paid a quick couple of thousand for a flip paint job so when you see it coming its purple but when it passes by you its blue, then as you watch it drive off; it's green. But then another thousand done been spent to put some tires and rims on the car. But these are the same parents that can't' afford to spend thirty dollars on a kid's bike. It's hard for the church to help the children who really need it. I'm talking about the children who are in homeless shelters and the children who have ended up in the orphanages because they had to be removed from an abusive home.

I watched as the pastor knocked on the door a couple of times before Bob came and finally answered it. It probably took him so long because he might have thought it was me. Bob greeted the pastor and he presented Bob with the bike and directed him to the truck. The next thing I know, Bob made his way to the truck and got another bike off the back of it. It really didn't bother me that the kids were getting gifts; they shouldn't be held accountable because their parents don't have their priorities in the wrong order. One of Debra's daughters has four kids; none over the age of six and she had one on the way. I was happy for the kids that they were getting new bikes but what set me off was how Bob had just walked pass me as if I wasn't even standing there. He acted like I didn't even exist. As if I was the wind that he could not see but knew that I was there.

Since he didn't say anything to me, I said something to him. I asked him if those were new bikes for his grandkids. Bob told me that the bikes were from the church as if I already hadn't figured that out for myself. Bob said that Debra had put her grandkids name on the list and it was easier to have the bikes delivered to his apartment to make sure the kids got their presents. I didn't understand why they had to be delivered to Bob's apartment and not just to the kid's house where they live. At this point it just seemed to me that in everything that Bob did, it just seemed that he had forgotten about his own kids. Here he was having bikes delivered to his place for someone else's kids to make sure they got their presents, when he hadn't even made sure his sons had what they were supposed to have to make sure they had a good Christmas.

The only reason why I got the money from Bob was because I had to come and get it. "No one delivered anything to me"; I said to Bob as he walked off from me. Bob just looked at me in a strange way as he passed by me with the bike and headed back to his apartment. By this time everyone had seemed to have come back outside.

When Bob reached the front door where everyone was standing and waiting for him; he dropped the bike and handed some keys that he had had in his hand to one of Debra's daughters. Bob then turned and rushed towards me with his fist balled up. In the blink of an eye; Bob was standing less than an inch away in my face and there was nothing between us, not even air. I didn't move; I didn't even flinch. What was going through my mind was I could not believe that Bob was going to try and show out in front of these people. What I was hoping was that Bob would think before he made his next move because what was about to happen was, Bob was going to get embarrassed in front of his new found family if he raised his fist to me. What was he trying to do, show his loyalty to them by hitting me? Was he really going to hit me in front of his children? Bob had done many stupid things in our marriage but one thing that he never done was put his hands on me. I couldn't believe that Bob was really going to try and shine on me. But then again; there was the audience that he needed. I didn't mind taken home a second award tonight; not all at. To me, at that very moment Bob was no longer my husband but a stranger. I looked at Bob right in his eye straight to his soul. I heard myself tell him that if he hit me that I would drop him where he stood. I felt myself reposition my body as I dared him to hit me. Dominique was standing next to me on my right with the golf club in his hand waiting for his daddy to even act like he was going to hit me. DJ was standing on my left. He had balled up his fist waiting for someone to even act like they wanted to move. And there we stood, once united and now divided; us against him. I looked at the man that I once trusted and loved. He saw the woman that he once protected and would always cherish. Bob relaxed his hands and backed away.

It's not worth it, I heard someone from the crowd say. Bob headed back to his apartment picked up the bike and headed in. While me and the boys were getting in the car, Bob and the pastor came back outside. Bob walked up to me and said that the pastor said that I needed to read the bible and pray. My jaw just hit the ground because in my state of mind I heard or it seemed like that the pastor was blaming me. I told the pastor that I wasn't the one who needed to pray. I felt the pastor was being blind to the whole situation. So I felt it my duty to enlighten him of what was going on. I told pastor that I wasn't the one sitting up here married living with another woman and not taking care of his kids. But you want me to pray? Then what is it that Bob needs to be doing because from what I could see, he was the one around here sinning. Pastor didn't say a word. But it would be weeks later before I would really hear and understand what the pastor was trying to tell me. God was going to fight my battles and get me through this. There was no need for me to be out here fighting with Bob. It was just that in that moment the only voice I wanted to hear was someone telling Bob that he was wrong and what he seemed to be willing to do for someone else, he should be just as willing to do for his very own. I walked away from Bob that night with a heavy heart; not feeling anything but hatred towards him. He became just like a nigga in the street to me; a total stranger.

I wouldn't hear or see Bob until January in family court. Oh wait, I take that back; Bob stopped by for Christmas. At first the visit was civil but fifteen minutes into his visit, he had to say something slick out of his mouth about how I better be taking care of his kids. Those were the exact same words that came out of his mouth back in 2000 when he left a message on my answering machine and that night I spent the night in jail. I had just got off of work. It had been a long day and I was tired. I was only in the house for five minutes when I heard this stupid message on my answering machine from Bob. He was saying in his half mac daddy and pimp voice; how I had better be working and how I had better be over there; meaning the Haven, taking care of his kids and making sure that they were feed and have a roof over their head. As I was listening to the message I figured he had been drinking again and got some liquid courage. After listening to the stupid he left; I was wondering and thinking well if I'm supposed to do all that then what the hell was he supposed to be doing? It is so easy for people to tell you what the hell you're supposed to be doing but forget what the hell they are supposed to be doing. It takes two to have a baby. Why did he waste my tape leaving this message? I got the kids in the car and went to the City to hunt Bob down.

I found him under the shade tree and that's when the fun began.

Bob walked off from me as I was giving him a piece of my mind. Bob went and got into his car. I leaned into his car to finish telling him how I didn't appreciate him leaving that message on my phone about me taking care of our kids while he spends his days drinking under the tree. It wasn't until I leaned into the car that I realized that Debra had been sitting there the whole time when I first pulled up. That's when the argument exalted. Because I couldn't believe he had her sitting in the car when just two days ago he had called me and told me that he loved me. This nigga don't know whether he wants to be hot or cold. Bob pulled off and drove around the corner to his dad's house. I pulled in behind him to block him in. He jumped out the car and ran into his dad's house. Just like his shadow; I was right behind him.

I tried to knock Bob's head off with an iron as I had him trapped in the corner in one of the bedrooms. Bob's dad was home and after he realized what was going on, he called the police. When the police arrived, I was outside busting out Bob car windows and they arrested me. I don't know where Debra had disappeared to and I didn't care. It was Bob's blood that I had a taste for. That landed me a night in jail and fussed at by Sis who came to pick me up afterwards. I can mark that off my bucket list.

I can only guess that Bob was surprised that the boys had a great Christmas despite the fact that he wasn't there. I didn't understand why he thought that this Christmas would be any different from any other. I always made sure my boys had a good Christmas regardless of what Bob did or did not do for that matter. Hell, when the boys were two and three years old; they had a television and vcr in their bedroom. That should have let him know then that it was me all along holding things down and together. But he already knew that and that's why he could say the stupid crap he was saying because it was already done. So when Bob said those words this time I didn't want to ruin the kids Christmas and I didn't want to relive my jail experience. Which wasn't bad; I just didn't want to make a habit of it. I got up off the couch with a smile on my face and my teeth locked to kept my tongue in; I showed Bob to the front door for both our sakes because I knew that he was going to try and push my buttons and I knew at this point that the police couldn't have gotten there quick enough to save him. Bob tried to use that reverse psychology crap on me by saying; in that stupid voice of his that his kids had better had a good Christmas. I slammed the door so hard in

Bob's face that the walls shook. Who the hell does he think he's talking to? Who in the hell do he thinks been taking care of them since the day they arrived on this earth? It damn sure wasn't his ass. Please excuse me for cussing but this nigga done made me mad.

# Chapter 40

ME AND THE boys have moved on and occupied our time without Bob. Bob still calls but only to invite himself over to have sex with me and every time he does I say no and ask him where Debra at then I hang up the phone. Bob has taken the position and made it very clear that if he doesn't have anything going on with me then he has nothing to do with his kids.

Me and the boys moved into a new house; renting it of course. The boys have changed schools and made new friends. The absence of their father had affected DJ very much; I'm not going to lie. He has started to keep himself isolated in his room and his grades in school are not that good. I'm keeping him involved in sports to keep him motivated and to let him know that now he has to start and form his own path to becoming a young man. I see my son struggling to find his way. Since their father doesn't come to see them I ask the boys if they want me to take them over there but they only say no. Since their father doesn't call them I ask them would they like to call their father but they only say no.

Our day in family court finally came. The whole morning I was wondering how Bob was going to make it to court because he didn't have his license and I knew that Debra wasn't stupid enough to let him drive her car and she come along. My question was quickly answered when I arrived at the court house. As I was walking through the parking lot headed toward the front steps of the court house, I spotted Bob and his dad getting out of the car. I knew then that I was in for a show. I wish he would have kept his dad out of our personal business. Somehow Bob caught up with me before I could cross the street.

At first he acted like we weren't there for the same reason. I guess he hesitated to speak first because he didn't know what type of mood I was in. I will admit I was in a civil mood that day. There was no reason to be acting crazy because all you had to do was walk across the street to get to the jail and I wasn't trying to go there this early in the morning. I was trying to be the mature one so I said good morning to Bob first. He said good morning back as he wiped the palm of his hands off on his pants as if they were sweaty. I could tell that he was nervous; he looked like he was walking that final mile on death row as we approached the court house. Dead man walking; was all I kept saying over and over in my head.

I walked into the court house lobby and through the metal detectors before they did. There were so many different courtrooms, that I didn't know exactly which one I was supposed to go to for child support. I went to the receptionist desk with court papers in hand that I had received in the mail telling me the date and time to be at court I asked the receptionist which courtroom was I to appear in. I guess Bob had the same problem because he came up and stood next to me. But instead of him asking the receptionist and before she could answer my question; Bob snatched my papers out of my hand and starting reading them. The papers had some personal information on them that I didn't want Bob to see. But then again who in the hell did he think he was snatching my papers out of my hand. Bob's dad just stood there as usual not saying a word while Bob acted stupid. My first thought was to just tackle him down to the ground and snatch my papers back but I really wasn't in the mood to go to jail this morning like I had mentioned earlier. So I reached for my papers but Bob moved them away so that I couldn't get them. One, two, three; the more I reached for my papers, the further Bob would inch away and throw up his arm to block my reach. I got tired of Bob's little game and told him to give me my papers back in a voice to let him know that I was not playing with him. I didn't want to go to jail but he was about to make me lose my temper very quickly. I asked him why he was coming up in there acting like a damn fool. And of course; he had no answer for himself or his behavior. I wanted to punch Bob square in the face. I had to remember that I had come to take care of business and I refuse to let Bob get under my skin. I finally snatched my papers back from Bob.

I composed myself before turning to the receptionist so she could finally answer my question and then I could be on my way. I looked at her and she looked at me; trying not to comment on what she just witnessed she directed me to the elevator and I walked off. While I was waiting for the elevator; Bob and his dad caught up with me again. I refuse to get on the same elevator with that fool. When both elevators hit the first floor of the lobby; I made it my business to get on the opposite one from Bob.

When I got off the elevator on the third floor; there was a line of people waiting to sign in and fill out an information sheet. I signed in, got my information sheet and went to sit on the other side of the lobby far away from Bob. Why, I don't know but Bob came and sat down next to me. Was he really trying my patience today? Was he trying to make me lose my religion? As I was filling out my information sheet I could hear Bob reading over his. "My address is 418 North 8th street", I heard him say. Now he knew good and God darn well that wasn't his address but his father's address. I didn't even bother to look in Bob's direction. I just shook my head and continued to fill out my paperwork. Here he was up to his old games again. This time he was going to try and scam the courts and hustle his way out of having to pay child support. I was just hoping that the court had gotten a little wiser to the game since the last time I had dealt with the court about child support.

At first I was holding my peace but this was my time to fight for my boy's sack. I asked Bob why he doesn't just put down his real address. I asked him at his age wasn't he tired of playing these stupid games. Last time I put him on child support somehow he talked me out of it and so I didn't show up to court and but they still ordered him to pay twenty-five dollars and week; which he didn't pay. Bob didn't say a word. I told Bob if he didn't tell the court where he lived that I would. Bob just ignored me and kept reading over his paper. "What is my income; I'm going to tell them that the resort property has been sold and we are under new owners". Bob read this aloud too so that I could hear. He was being such a jackleg today. I asked him what the property being sold had to do with his income. Even though the property sold and had new owners, he was still working the same amount of hours and getting paid the same income as if it was with the prior owners of the property. Again Bob ignored my question. I just shook my head even more. I finished my sheet and went to turn it in. There was an empty chair far away from Bob; I went and sat in it.

I guess finally Bob got finished lying on his information sheet and turned it in. Bob turned and slowly starting walking in my direction which was totally opposite from where he had been sitting. There was a not empty seat around me so I knew that he wasn't coming to sit by me. Bob asked me if I was mad at him as he came across in front of me. I ignored Bob because I knew he was trying his best to make me come out of character. He paused for a brief second as he looked me up and down. I know he was trying to find something to pick at me about. I hesitated to say anything to him but the longer I ignored him the longer he would have stood there. Taking a deep breath while being careful not to say anything out of the way; I told Bob that I didn't come here for this foolishness that he was trying to stir up. I rolled my eyes at Bob as he was just staring at me with a stupid look on his face as if he had no idea what I was talking about. But I knew any minute that something out of his mouth was going to go with that look on his face. Referring to my new found makeup and with a smirk; Bob asked me why I had that orange stuff on my face. Before I could even respond he walked away. One thing about Bob is his tongue can be very deadly and rude. I had just started wearing makeup and he made me feel like I was looking like a clown.

Ladies, you know when you first start wearing makeup how you have to experiment with it until you get it right; well I was still in my experiment stage. My last experience with makeup was when I was still living with my mama and we remember how that turned out; green. So now in my early thirties I was giving it another try. Sometimes we can put too much on and walk out the house looking like a clown. Sometimes you can put too little on and it looks like you missed a spot. I guess this morning I may have put too much on. Orange is closer to brown so I guess I'm getting there. But Bob still didn't have to be rude and say what he had said. I could feel the steaming rising on the top of my head. I better stop before I melt off my makeup.

I looked around the room as I was amazed at how many people were here for child support. I don't understand why woman have to go through all of this just to get these men to take care of what they already know is their responsibility. But the crazy thing is that this carries on from generation to generation. This is learned behavior I think, but who is teaching this to our young men. I have talked and preached to my boys so that they have a clear understanding that no matter what happens between them and a young lady; that if there is a baby involved that they are responsible for that child whether they stay in a relationship with the young lady or not. They know how it feels to have an absent father and I don't want them to put an innocent child through that.

I looked around the room at all the different cultures that made up the crowd. There were grandmothers there with their grandchildren, there were mothers there with their children, there were ex-husbands there with their new and ex-wives. They were all there just to come to court to either fight to get child support or fight to not have to pay child support. And yes there were women there who just like me came alone; looking for justice in this whole situation the only way that they knew how and that only the courts could give.

I guess we all sat in the lobby for about forty-five minutes before the bailiff came out and called everyone in the courtroom who were there for a child support case. Bob's father had to wait in the lobby. Once in the courtroom; those who brought the case to the court's attention sat on one side (majority were woman) the ones who were order to come to court (majority were men) sat on the other side. I took my seat and just stared straight ahead at the judge's bench hoping that the judge wouldn't be a man. I could hear Bob to my far left talking all cool to the other men as if he had control of the outcome of today. "She not going to get nothing out of me", I could hear him tell them. "I'm just going to tell the judge that I can only afford to give her fifty dollars a week." I heard the other men laughing. I don't know if they were laughing with him or if they were laughing at him.

Twenty minutes later the judge came in; it was a woman. The Lord had heard my prayers. Maybe today justice would be served. Forty minutes had passed and I watched as one by one each case was called to the judge's attention. She served justice to the mothers and children on a shiny silver platter; you go girl. She was throwing some of the guys in jail who were behind in paying child support. They told her of their sob story that they were not working and like a deaf man; she wasn't hearing that. She told them they would sit in jail until someone brought them the child support money that they owed because their fresh white Nike *air ones*; told her a different story. With each case I could feel Bob's cockiness disappear little by little. Two hours into it there were two couples left besides me and Bob. That was one of the disadvantages of having your last name begin with a P, when something is going in alphabetical order; you get called close to next to last. And in every case scenario I would be hoping not to be the last one and this time wasn't any different. One couple was called up and when they were done, it was me and Bob's turn.

Mostly the judge spoke to Bob. She asked him was it true that he had two children by the names of Dominique and DJ. Bob answered the judge like the day he said his wedding vows; "yes, I do". The judge then asked Bob if he had any other children that he was responsible for. I looked over at Bob who after noticing that I was looking at him and was hanging on every word that was about to come out of his mouth because I just knew that he wasn't about to claim those crumb catchers that were at his house; Bob hesitated to answer. "Yes I do", Bob answered. My jaw hit the floor. No this nigga didn't. I knew that Bob was up to his games but this was really not the time or place for it. I just pictured myself flying through the air like Wonder Woman (that's my Shero) and kicking Bob in the face with my six inch red boots and throwing my gold rope around his neck so that he would tell the truth; remember I'm in my Wonder Woman outfit. But the judge quickly took care of my light weight. She next asked Bob if the additional children that were not named on the petition in this case biologically his. I already know what Bob was thinking; the more kids he claimed the less the judge would order him to pay me. But you can't claim what isn't any of yours and that's a fact of life. I looked back over at Bob and starred up and down at this pile of….. You can add your own words because you already know what I want to say. I knew that Bob felt my heat ray vision beaming on the side of his two-faced face. He finally answered the judge and told her; "no". He better had said no because if not we would have been back to court for another whole different type of case. The judge wanted to make sure that Bob understood the question and that she understood his answer and she made it very clear to him when she said, "then, you are not responsible for them." I could feel that last tiny bit of Bob's cockiness do a Casper.

The judge then went on to ask Bob if he was paying any medical insurance on his biological children. I had to giggle inside when she added that last little part. Bob stood there and said that yes *he* had insurance. But he didn't say that he had insurance on the boys. He was trying to answer the judge's question but do it in a way that it couldn't be said that he was lying. Half-truths always seemed like a whole lie to me. Yes he had insurance but he didn't have the boys on his insurance policy. It was a wonder that Bob's teeth wasn't just falling out of his mouth from lying so much. I had had enough of this stand-up that Bob was performing. It wasn't funny anymore; it really never was. I spoke up because I just couldn't take it anymore. I told the judge that Bob didn't have any insurance on the boys that I did. I pulled out my insurance card with both their names on it and mine. I handed it to the bailiff so he could hand it to the judge so she could see for herself. She asked Bob for his insurance card. He started fumbling through his wallet as to look for such a card that he knew didn't exist. "I just made my co-pay on it." Bob said as he was digging through like he was reaching to the bottom of a barrel filled with ice trying to get the last beer. I just shook my head at Bob. As I looked at him digging through his wallet; I noticed that it was the same wallet that he claimed that he had lost so long ago. I wonder where he found it. He probably found it in his front pocket where he put it. You figure it out because I'm tired of trying.

After some time; Bob did manage to come out of his wallet with something. He handed it to the bailiff to hand to the judge. She looked at this card that she was handed and sent it back to him by the bailiff. She then looked over at me and said that she would give me the allowed credit for having the medial insurance on the boys. She then put her attention back on Bob and asked him if he was contributing with the up keep of the home. "Yes, I'm paying the rent", Bob said. There goes another one of his half-truths. Yes he was paying rent but not for where his sons lived but where he lived with his new instant family. Just add liquor and they will grow. I became the chuckler in the crowd. I just looked at Bob and laughed. I heard it this time so I knew it was out loud. Again I had to interrupt Bob's show. I explained to the judge that Bob didn't live in the home where his sons and I lived. I went on to make it clear that Bob had not lived in the same home with us for over a year. I looked at Bob to let him know that his jokes are not funny to me. Bob in return protested against my answer and told the judge that he hadn't been gone a year. "Well, how long have you been gone away from home?" the judge asked. Bob told the six months. He said it so proudly as if it was to help his case that he wasn't away from his home as long as a year. What Bob didn't realize was the bottom line was; he wasn't there. I wonder if Bob could find some common sense in the bottom of that wallet of his. I guess you can't find what you never had in the first place. When it came to me and the kids; Bob didn't show any type of common or sense.

I'm just standing at my podium just observing the atmosphere. This seems to be going well; let's continue shall we. The judge's was still on Bob when she started to speak, "on your information sheet for income you stated that your company has changed owners. What does that have to do with how many hours you work?" Bob just stood there in silence. I think he was remembering when I asked him that exact same question about three hours ago. I'm sorry; the judge made me giggle again. She better stop it or she's going to get me kicked out for disturbing the court and it's going to be all her fault. The judge went on to ask Bob if he still worked the same amount of hours which is a forty hour work week. Not being able to come up with a lie quick enough; which shouldn't have mattered because they weren't working, Bob was forced to tell the truth. "Yes, but by us changing owners..." the judge cut Bob short. She heard what she needed to hear and that was the word; yes. The judges went to tapping some numbers into a calculator that she had nearby for emergencies like this one. "Well by my calculations, you will be paying two hundred dollars every two weeks." The judge announced to Bob. I think I saw his knees buck; I'm not sure. The bailiff had better go stand next to Bob just in case he needs to catch him. Then again he can let the floor catch him.

After Bob let what the judge had just said marinate on his brain; which was only two point five seconds, he turned into a two year old boy having a temper tantrum. "I can't afford that." Bob yelled. He then insisted to see another judge. I couldn't believe that Bob was acting like that. "You can afford it; you just don't want to pay it." I said aloud to him before I knew it. The judge had calculated for Bob to give up 32% of his income every two weeks. Hell, I was giving up 98% of my income. We all know I want to use another word but shoot; he was getting off easy if you ask me. Bob was still in shock but now he was acting like he was having a seizure. You would have thought that he had ants in his pants and scratching his head while babbling on. "I can only afford to pay fifty dollars every two weeks." Bob went on to tell the judge. "Well sir, I'm sorry but that's not going to be enough for two kids." The judge said while looking Bob dead in the eye. "You may have a seat outside in the lobby and I will call you back in for your second hearing. Is that okay?" the judge asked Bob. Bob just wanted to know one thing; would he be able to speak to another judge. I guess he thought that if he spoke with another judge, preferably a male judge; that maybe he would get another chance to try and buck the system. The judge told him yes and that the bailiff would bring him back in. Bob said that would be fine and let out a sigh of relief. I was volcano hot. You could see the steam coming from the top of my head. This jackleg was really trying to get out of taking care of his kids. I just looked over at Bob looking him up and down because right now he was the one looking like a clown.

Exiting the courtroom, I went and sat on the benches in the waiting area while Bob sat across from me. He didn't stay put for long. Bob started pacing back and forth. I could tell that he wanted a cigarette real bad because his nerves were bad. "This doesn't make any sense," Bob's father began to say. "You two need to work this out together and stop putting each other through this." I just wanted to know what I was putting Bob through because from my view it was clear. Now if he wanted to see me put Bob through something I could really start letting Nett off her diamond crushed leash. But my mind was made up and this was only the first step of the process for me. Bob never replied to what his father was saying, just by looking at him I could tell that he was too busy trying to come up with a reason not to have to pay two hundred dollars of child support every two weeks. "Man that is too much money for two kids every two weeks," Bob suddenly blurted out. "That's a hundred dollars every two weeks for each of them," Bob said acting like he was just in total shock about the whole thing. I had to put my two cents in to drive it home. "Well if you break it down even further more Bob, that's only fifty dollars a week per child. So if the boys needed some shoes, they would have to wait two weeks in order to by them. And then I would have to put some more money with it in order to cover taxes or they could just wait until the end of the month for when you've made both payments. But if they save their money for shoes answer me this; what money will be used to buy them food. To even keep a roof over their head is costing me 1150 a month plus lights, water clothes and the extras that they always want. So you see; your two hundred dollars every two weeks only nips the surface of what it really takes to take care of your boys. Don't worry; you'll still have enough money left over for your beer, cigarettes, and liquor." Instead of acknowledging anything that I had just said, Bob told me that I should move then.

"Find a cheaper place to live", he told me. I think he misunderstood me. I wasn't complaining about what I had to do for my boys; I was just letting him know what needs to be done for my boys that I do. I told Bob that maybe if he stopped taking care of someone else's kids that maybe he could afford to take care of his own.

I could feel myself getting loud and Nett was about ready to take over the conversation. The lobby was nearly empty except for one or two couples that were in the courtroom with us as they also wanted to see a second judge. Bob became so distraught over the whole situation of what the judge had sad that he walked over to some guy that was sitting with his wife and started talking to him. "Man, I can't afford this; they want me to pay two hundred dollars every two weeks. Where am I going to get that type of money from? I have to pay rent." The man didn't say a word; he just shrugged his shoulders at Bob and looked at his wife. The man had his own problems to deal with; he was here with his new wife by his side while his ex-wife was in the courtroom putting him on child support. After not getting a response from the gentleman; Bob just walked away.

After about twenty minutes the bailiff came out to the lobby where we were waiting and called everyone back into the courtroom that wanted to see a second judge. There was a new judge seated on the bench and we were the second case that was called. "Mr. Bob," the new judge started off, "can you give me any reason why you can't pay this amount?" All Bob could come up with was, "I can't afford this amount." The judge, who is now a male; proceeded on with his questions for Bob, "Mr. Bob", the judge said to Bob as to make sure he addressed and recognized him as a man, " are you still working the hours that you reported to the court?". Bob was searching for some type of leverage, "yes but I have bills too." Bob said. "Yes the court recognizes that and this is why the government came up with a formula for the court to use to calculate child support. So by our calculation of using the hours that you reported that you work; you are to pay two hundred dollars every two weeks. Is there anything else?" the judge asked. Bob had no response. The judge's decision was final.

I left the courtroom feeling like I had won this round but I also felt like it didn't even have to come to this point. Bob on the other hand walked out of the courtroom like he had been sentenced to death row.

When the checks started coming, I let the boys know and I divided the money amongst them and put it towards anything that they may have needed at the time. If they didn't need anything the money went towards groceries and gas which was the case most of the time because by the time Bob's child support checks came; rent was paid, light bill was paid, clothes were bought, all their needs and even many of their wants had already had been met. I will admit Bob did obey the court order for the first two years but then Bob wasn't working anymore and I truly think it was by choice and not by circumstance. If he didn't work, he didn't have to pay child support was his thought and if they couldn't prove that he was working then the court wouldn't make him pay; so he thought. So Bob found a job where they paid him two hundred dollars in cash a month and he lived rent free because he would manage the apartment complex where he would be the handy man. But what Bob forgot was; all because he didn't pay child support didn't mean that child support would go away. All because he had put it out of his sight and out of his mind didn't mean that the court did. So for the next year and a half it was touch and go with Bob paying child support. He would go four months without paying it and I would report him. Bob would scrape up the money that the court would ask him to pay just to keep himself out of jail then he wouldn't pay again for another four months. After this song and dance with Bob my feet started to hurt and the melody became old. So when the checks finally stop coming; I let the boys know that too. But the only thing with that was they couldn't tell the difference because I was still working two jobs and making sure my boys were well taken care of regardless. Lord; you are my provider.

Many moons, eclipses, and thunderstorms later; Bob and I finally got a divorce. I paid for it of course and it was worth every penny. I was free and able to start to begin to heal from much heartache and pain that Bob had caused me over the years. I was left with so much anger which had nested inside of me. My concern is no longer with what Bob does or doesn't do for his boys. My only concern is my boys.

# Love, Life and Liberty

**IT WASN'T EASY** being a single parent and working two jobs. There were times when emergencies would come up and I would either have to pay a bill late or not pay it at all. There was no help from Bob just a cheer from the crowd as he sat on the sidelines and watched with a beer in his hand. It was a struggle at times but God always made a way. As I raised my boys I constantly would tell them to stay focus and get their education because we have things to do. We have business to take care of. When I said this to them; there was an understanding that I wanted them to become positive additions to our society and not just the statistic that someone else had proclaimed for them to be because of the color of their skin.

I look around and I see how our young men are just walking around having babies by several different young ladies. I can't say women because they are so young. But if I call them girls they may get offended. But the truth be told; that's all that they are; girls. They're having so many kids; these young men honestly can't take care of them financially let alone emotionally. Then we have the young ladies-girls raising all these babies alone. And with every new man she meets she tries to bring him into her home hoping that she had found a father for her children. But he's only there for a couple of months leaving behind a new mouth for her to feed. Now what is she to do? This young lady-girl finds herself doing any and everything it takes to take care of her kids and some of its not pretty. Eventually she will find herself on the EBT system just so she can afford to put food on the table for her four kids. She swallows her pride because she knows that someone else is depending on her. She is all that they know. She is all that they have. I know because I've been there too. Meanwhile daddy is somewhere making more babies that he can't take care of. But I guess I do have to give them their props for that thirty minute every six months quality time visit that they utilize to see the kids. I think the kids wouldn't know what to do with themselves if they would see their father more than that. I think that the fathers deserve a golden star for their efforts; not. I'm not saying that all our young men are like that but they are running a tight race to be.

I, like so many other single women who were raising their children alone, found myself trying to keep the balance of being a mother to my children and not losing the woman inside of me. And sometimes the urge to be a woman tipped the scale. I never bought another man into my house to live. Not that I didn't want to but it was out of respect for my boys to never have another man over them other than their father. Deep down I knew that I owed Bob that much. And so for years at a time I would have no social life. For me it was home, work, to the store, the boy's school, the boy's activities and back home. I would watch as other woman would change men every couple of months and to me that was just too much traffic coming in and out of the house. And what they don't understand is that their children are watching them. The children have figured out that every man that you bring into the house is not *uncle*. We sometimes get so caught up in trying to keep a man's attention on us that we don't pay attention to our children who are looking up to us for guidance. Now I must say, I take my hat off to the women who are working, going to school, keeping a home, and raising their children; they're doing the damn thing. Don't get me wrong; when I wanted curiosity to kill the *cat* I found myself in some short term situations and the only evidence of that was a broken heart. But then you have more than a few young girls who want to use up their *cat's* nine lives all in one week with every Omar, Keith, and Jahiem, Stephan, Curtis and Bobby in town. That's not a good look and that doesn't make them a woman. We have to start having more respect for ourselves and our children than that. Our men have confused real woman with what they see in the music videos. No, we are not the stripers that you see swinging off of poles. We are the mother of your children. But then again who can get mad at them when we are walking around like a bulletin board advertising ourselves in the most un-lady like way. Our clothes are four sizes too small so that everything is hanging out below the neck and out the back. But then again who can get mad at them if they think that we are clowns either because we walk around with this loud color hair; red, green, orange and yes let me not forget the blonde that we put in our head. Whose job are we working on looking like BoZo the clown? You know I love me some BoZo, but not on the job. We have to respect ourselves before we can ask for others to respect us.

People's values have changed. It's no longer about the well-being of your family and the nurturing of your children. Our children can quote a rap song but they can't read a book. What ever happened to making a safe home? The pride of having a strong family is no more. Instead it's about materialistic things. We tend to walk around with our fake designer bags that were bought from a flea market or stolen from a warehouse. We have the nerve to walk around acting like we have spent a monthly mortgage on them when it only cost the same as it would have to fill up our gas tank. Who has more than whom? Why does that even matter. It seems society has its priorities all mixed up. Things have changed and gotten so far from the truth that it is easier for someone to listen to a lie when they know the truth for themselves. The titles that we carry have become more important than the respect we have for one another. It amazes me how fake we can be towards each other and it is so sad how living this life will change us.

I am left with a hole in my soul that won't heal and there is much pain in my heart that I constantly feel. Why do we have to have pain in our lives is what I have always wondered. What is its purpose? To have heartache is the worst pain. To lose a loved one is unspeakable pain. To be disappointed is unwanted pain. Pain hurts and there is nothing that keeps it from happening. People kill other people and sometimes even themselves because of pain. Being in pain helps nothing; so why does it exist. There are times when I just look around at the people and I can see pain and discouragement on their faces. They look so hopeless. I feel so sad. My own pain at times has left me questioning my own existence. My own pain at times has left me wondering aimlessly in this life. I pray to God that He will heal the weary and that one day he will relieve us from our pain.

Many years have passed and I still have a void in my life that I cannot fulfill. If I take my life; I go to hell. If I continue to live my life; I am in hell. I'm so tired of trying to find the pieces to complete my life. The pieces that make me feel whole. The biggest piece missing for me are love and happiness. I lost the love of my father when he died. I lost the love of my mother when she buried him. She wonders around in this life lost without him. She carries with her the hope that she will one day live again with him in the next.

I don't think that I will ever really know happiness. Or at least have it hang around long enough so that I can get used to it. I didn't grow up with it much as a child. And throughout the years when it did enter my life it came only for a very brief moment as if it knew it couldn't stay.

The golden rule was to treat others in the way in which you would want to be treated. I followed that rule, but it didn't follow me. I thought that if I stayed true to myself and love without expectations', judgments, or trickery that it would be returned to me as well. But I've learned along the way that people will take your kindness and mistake it for your weakness.

I did know love once and I want to find it again. But I am afraid that I never will. I have so much love to give but no one to give it to. What good is having such a big heart filled with so much love only to keep to yourself. At times I am confused why God made me the way that I am and then put people in my life that he knew would hurt me, leave me and betray me. This world and the people in it have taught me many lessons, some that I care never to repeat again in this life or any other for that matter. How am I to continue on with this journey of life when I have seen so much and it has taken so much from me? I have no guarantee that I will ever find the pieces that I need to make me whole again. They say good things happen to good people. Well here I am good, but where are you?

My mind stays confused, my heart broken, and my spirit weary. I don't know how to fix it. My father is dead and I will never get the pleasure of knowing how great of a man he was. I don't have that relationship with my mother that every mother and daughter should have. I'm afraid that maybe our time has passed. But I pray that it has not. Now that I am a mother; I empathize with my own. It's hard to dwell and continue living when you're barely alive inside. Trying to find a reason to live on when the person whom you thought you would share this world with has gone on before you. Having to explain this loss to your two little girls when you can't even make sense of it yourself couldn't have been easy. I hope peace will find my mother while she still dwells here on earth; this is a daughter's prayer.

Being abused by two step fathers both physically and mentally has left me sad for the little girl in me who never got to be happy. She lives within me where she is safe and I will never let her die. Affairs of the heart with men over the years have brought me to my knees. I was left behind alone to pick up the pieces of my broken heart and of myself. So I still sit and wonder where is the good; for me. Where is my happiness? I feel that I am left to wonder this life alone. This is not good enough for me. I deserve better than what has been given to me but instead I fight only with myself. I want to just go; let me go. But I cannot. I can't go; I can't leave behind my sons to face this cruel world alone. They were there when I needed a reason for living. Without them I had no will to go on. They were there for me; I have to be there for them. I have to warn them about this place. I must stay and teach them how to be better than the man who came before them. I must teach them to keep God first in their life and that everything else they should ever need will follow.

Meanwhile, I cry endlessly in the shadows of the night of the thought that I will never find love and that love will never find me. I try to stay distracted with little things while I wait for the pain to pass. My heart aches so from its emptiness. I have given so much and received nothing in its return. I look to my Heavenly Father for understanding but he says nothing; He comforts me. My tears are pure and full of pain; He so gently wipes them away. Many nights I cannot sleep; only cry. And though he doesn't say a word; he rocks me in his arms, he comforts me. He hears my cry and he pities my every groan and moan. Throughout my life I learned to surround myself with beautiful things because in beauty there is love. But nothing can take the place of receiving pure, untainted love from someone. But I still continue to surround myself with beautiful things so that I can see love. I have been such a fool to think that I would find love as pure as my own. Instead I find pain, lies, trickery, and selfishness. There is so much pain that has nested in me that it has taken away from me any hope of finding happiness. I have taught my sons how to love, respect, and treat a woman. I never want another woman to feel the hurt, pain and emptiness that I have throughout my life because of a man at the hand s of my sons. My boys have seen me fall into a dark place. My boys have wiped away my tears that have been cause not by them but of another. By my bedside they sit and watched over me in the middle of the night to ensure that I would gain the courage to want to live another day.

But it is in my darkest hour when I sit and wonder if I die tomorrow would I really care; no because I am tired. My search for love has turned up nothing. It has only left behind me a path of broken pieces of what was once my heart. The path reveals where I had given it unconditionally. It has been dropped to the waist side by others who had no concern of where it landed. The gesture of returning it to me in the same condition that it was given seemed not to be an option for them. So here I am poisoned with not caring or wondering what tomorrow may bring because I know that love does not wait for me there. I desire my dreams in the place of the warmth of the sun on my face. God made me the creature that I am, but I am afraid that he created no one for me to dwell with. So why should I stay. There is nothing for me here. Do I dare say goodbye now in the hopes that my dreams will never end. I am still here because I have no right to place this burden on my children. I watch as my oldest son tries to walk into manhood the best way he knows how without the help of his father and my youngest son tries to prepare himself for the corporate world because he is afraid that it will be the only family that he has after I'm gone. Thou through no fault of their own but only of this world; they have taken on the role of Cain and Able. What is the strength of my life; has yet to find their own.

Sometimes I seem to be drowning in this sea of life. What makes it worse is that everyone seems to be standing along on the land just watching you never once throwing you a rope to help you ashore. It's not until God whispers for the waters to stand still that I get my footing and stand up so that I can walk upon the shore. It is then that I am reminded of Job. I should be oh so honored that God choose me to test the waters. I am still here because if I give up the enemy wins. The enemy didn't give me life and he has no right to take it. I refuse to just lay down and give it to him. The enemy doesn't have control over my life; he doesn't even have control over hell; God does. God says who goes to heaven or hell; not the enemy. God did not create me as a quieter. He gave me the life that he knew that only I could handle. I have to stay and see what the end is going to be; who I am but a mere vessel. My kindness is not my weakness but my search for love is. Someone once said that the most precious thing in life is to know that you were loved.

Love is a crazy thing. There are so many different types of love. You can never put them all in the same basket. You love your brother and sister because no matter how many times you wish they would go away; you know that you would miss them if they go. You love your mother and father because no matter what; you know they only want the best for you when they tell you no like their parent's did them but for some reason they don't remember all the dumb stuff they did when they were teenagers. You love your best friend because no matter how many times you ask to borrow her little black shirt, she always says yes and she will tell you if your butt looks big in them jeans. You love your favorite television show because no matter how many times they show the reruns; you'll sit there and watch it like it was your first time. You love your favorite pair of heels because when you walk into a room they announce you. You have that special blanket that you love; you've had it since you can remember. You love your dog like it was a child because no matter how many times he makes a mess; those big brown eyes get you every time. You love your favorite ice cream that always makes you go back for seconds even though you know you shouldn't. You love that lip stick color that makes you poke your lips out just a little bit further. There is one love that will make you lose all your sense; the love of a man. Loving a man will make you look like a fool and make a fool out of you. You don't even see it but everyone else does. And though your best friend tries to warn you; you'll ignore her thinking that she's only saying something against your new found love because she either jealous or mad because she doesn't have a man. But it will be that same friend who will be there for you to cry on her shoulder and you will never hear the words, "I tried to warn you or I told you so", come from her lips.

I sometimes wonder if men are capable of loving anyone but themselves. The fact of the matter is the only thing that means anything to them is the thing that they carry with them every day of their life and is never out of their reach; and I'm not talking about their wallet. Yes they tell us that they love us but what is it that they really are in love with. It seems that men really don't see us for the loving, caring, devoted, supportive individuals that we are and that's so sad. They have this concept that we want to own them if we identify them as the person that we chose to be loyal and devoted to. I wish they would just allow themselves to let go of that slavery mentality. We only want to love them because that's what God made us for.

It seems the fact that you entrust them with your heart means nothing to them. The fact that you are and have rearranged your life for them means nothing. The fact that you believed in them when no other would means nothing to them. The fact that you share a part of yourself with them that you can never get back means nothing. The fact that they are willing to cause you pain means nothing to them.

I once asked a man how he saw me as a woman. He told me that I was damaged, hurt, but that I had good intentions and that I meant well. I'm not saying that the truth didn't sting a little but it stung the most. I knew then that me being a giving person, seeing how when I do love; I love deep, that I wasn't selfish, and how I showed my affection would never over shadow the hurt and pain that I continued to carry. We all have our different levels of ourselves. My thing is; the other person can only see the things that they bring out of you. If something has been done to me that damages me but I don't allow it to destroy me that means there would be evidence of it still there. Just as if a person shoots someone but doesn't kill them; the wound is still there. It's not bleeding and the wound has healed but there remains the scar.

If you see my intentions and that they are good then why won't he acknowledge them. But when I see that you don't acknowledge them then I don't have the desire to fulfill them. If I mean well it's because I know no matter how much I put forth an effort my actions won't change the situation. I feel that I have to suppress anything that I may want to do because sometimes it is seen as doing too much too soon and the favor is never returned. I've been told that I love too hard and too deep. It seems a man only wants what he needs out of a relationship. He's only going to give you twenty percent of himself and the rest is for you to find on your own. So now I am frustrated because I see that his intentions are truly; none. So I'll hold my tongue and my heart because I feel that yet again it is about to be broken by the hands of another. But what good does it do me? I am filled with sorrow so I cry and hold my peace instead. My concerns are not his and he lets me know. There seems to be no compromise in this situation. He feels that if he does he would be made a fool of because of what others before me have done. I feel that I am already a fool for believing that if I could love him enough that he would only see the person in his presence; me and not the person in his past; them. So, is he not too damaged as he once told me that I was and he just doesn't realize his own condition? I knowing this of him, I want to stay and help him to heal so that he too can see that there is still life to live and someone worth loving. I need him to let me love him so that I too can believe the same. But as I lay beside him my cry becomes mute to his ear, his mind and to his heart. But God will heal my heart so that I will love once more.

I've had so many disappointments in this lifetime and at times I've felt so defeated. As I look back over my years, I know that My Heavenly Father watched over me and would never give me more than I could bare. And I know that I never would have made it without Him. In my darkest hour and in my deepest despair; my God was there. Yeah, it would have been easy for Him just to have stepped in and fix my problems but what would have been the lesson in that for me or glory in that for Him. God didn't leave me as I went through my trials or my tribulations; instead he walked with me so that I could understand my purpose and His being. In the mist of my troubles I did learn to trust God and I gave him the glory even before I knew the problem was worked out because I had faith and I believed Him to do so. There were many; though they may have bent me, I refuse to let them break me. At times I did stop and cry out to My Heavenly Father and ask why me? My Heavenly Father told me; my child that He needed me to be a witness to and proof of God's grace and mercy so that I could tell it to those who would come along after me because as I saw Him, they would see Him in me. I Am... My Father's Child. Oh by far, I am not perfect but God doesn't want us to be. He only ask that you be open to Him and believe in Him; and this I do. No one knows my pain and anguish like my Heavenly Father. But it is because of my faith and His love for me that I am able to go forward in this life. It is because of Him that I have the strength to endure. It is because of Him that I stand. My faith and trust doesn't belong to this world neither does it deserve it. I've come to learn not to expect anything from this world for it owes me nothing. But that I owe God everything. Yes the road was rough but despite my own ways and short comings; He kept me and saw me for what I am. Someone once said; if you can look up then you can get up. I made up in my mind that every morning when God wakes me up; I shall get up. This life has taught me many things. Some things I understand and other things I never will. I don't think that I'll ever get used to being alone. But why should I have to. I was born alone, I will die alone, but I don't want to live and love alone. Some say; how can you miss something that you never had. But you can when you know that it should have been there all along. I am only left with my thoughts now of walking down the aisle in my beautiful white wedding dress at the wedding of my dreams as I marry the love of my life. I carry with me my thoughts of having a little girl so I could have spoiled her and mended the wounds of the little girl who lives inside of me. Barden me while I sit here and wait for my life to begin because for the first forty years of my life I survived; but for the next forty years I want to live.

My dreams have a way at times of never letting me forget my past. They latch on to remind me what I fear the most. With every scar that I carry with me, I am reminded of a terrible time. From the crown of my head to the sole of my feet my scars tell their story and they hold secrets of their own. And in my prayers I am reminded that I Am... My Father's Child. That if I seek My Heavenly Father that He will hear me and deliver me from *All* my fears. I hold on to the thought; what once I lost I will one day find again.

The security that a little girl feels when she looks up into her father's eyes was taken from me when my father died. Loyalty was misplaced by my mother with every new man she brought into her life to replace him. To allow another to bring harm and hurt to your own is unthinkable. To participate is imaginable. As long as my abuser lived, I lived in fear. Not until his death, did I fear no more.

My innocence was as a flower in the morning dew and was not meant to be forcefully broken from its stem leaving it bruised only to wither away in the shadows. At times my humbleness is of no use to me because it cannot protect me. My bitterness has become too hard to hide. If I give into my bitterness, then my transgressors have won and it makes me no better than them. But I am better so, I choose to take what was meant for evil and use it for good. I am not here by chance but by My Heavenly Father's favor. If I don't speak out then all the pain and tears meant nothing. So hear my voice when I say that I Am.... My Father's Child and that the weapon that was formed against me far from prospered. I rejoice for the day when I will see my Lord's face. For even as I live here on earth; in His presence I am free.

I take authority in knowing that my children shall be free to laugh and play. To develop their mind, build their body and protect their soul. My healing shall come by the sound of their laughter. I am the protector now. My arms shall extend for their comfort when this world becomes cold to them. My mind will be open for understanding when this world won't give them a chance. My soul will mourn for their sorrows that this world will share with them. My heart will always beat with love for them when this world shows them none.

Fathers; raise your sons to become men and love your daughters so that they know just how precious they are. Mothers; raise your daughters to become women and love your sons so that they will know just how important they are.

I may not have had control over my circumstance but I did not let my circumstances have control over me. I am not my past I am my purpose. I Am... My Father's Child.

# <u>You Knew</u>

*You knew you had to have me to yourself the moment you meet me.*

*You wrote my name down in your book adding to the list of so many that came before me.*

*You knew that there was something special about me when you saw me for the first time.*

*You would watch me from a distance meaning not to stare.*

*You knew that you wanted me to know you better.*

*You knew that you were the love of my life.*

*You had already declared your love for me.*

*You knew that once we met that I would feel the same about you.*

*You knew that I could never truly live without you and that you were the only one who could fulfill the desires of my heart.*

*You knew that there would come a time that I would feel alone and you would be there.*

*You knew that you would tell me things that only my heart could hear and no words from my lips could express.*

*You knew that it was not going to be easy, but you never gave up on me.*

*You knew that one day we would meet face to face And that I would humbly take my place by your side.*

*You knew from that moment we would never part.*

*You knew that my eternity with you would mean more than a lifetime with anyone else.*

*O' Heavenly Father...I'm so glad You Knew.*

*~Antoinette*

www.ingramcontent.com/pod-product-compliance
Lightning Source LLC
Chambersburg PA
CBHW060423100426
42812CB00030B/3291/J